Pro iOS Table Views for iPhone, iPad, and iPod Touch

Tim Duckett

Apress®

Pro iOS Table Views for iPhone, iPad, and iPod Touch

ISBN-13 (pbk): 978-1-4302-3348-0

ISBN-13 (electronic): 978-1-4302-3349-7

President and Publisher: Paul Manning
Lead Editor: Tom Welsh
Technical Reviewer: Brent Simmons
Editorial Board: Steve Anglin, Ewan Buckingham, Gary Cornell, Louise Corrigan, Morgan Ertel, Jonathan Gennick, Jonathan Hassell, Robert Hutchinson, Michelle Lowman, James Markham, Matthew Moodie, Jeff Olson, Jeffrey Pepper, Douglas Pundick, Ben Renow-Clarke, Dominic Shakeshaft, Gwenan Spearing, Matt Wade, Tom Welsh
Coordinating Editor: Tracy Brown
Copy Editors: Valerie Greco, Sharon Wilkey
Compositor: MacPS, LLC
Indexer: SPi Global
Artist: SPi Global
Cover Designer: Anna Ishchenko

Distributed to the book trade worldwide by Springer Science+Business Media New York, 233 Spring Street, 6th Floor, New York, NY 10013. Phone 1-800-SPRINGER, fax (201) 348-4505, e-mail `orders-ny@springer-sbm.com`, or visit `www.springeronline.com`.

For information on translations, please e-mail `rights@apress.com`, or visit `www.apress.com`.

Apress and friends of ED books may be purchased in bulk for academic, corporate, or promotional use. eBook versions and licenses are also available for most titles. For more information, reference our Special Bulk Sales–eBook Licensing web page at `www.apress.com/bulk-sales`.

Any source code or other supplementary materials referenced by the author in this text is available to readers at `www.apress.com`. For detailed information about how to locate your book's source code, go to `www.apress.com/source-code/`.

For Lucy, Kath, and Isaac

Contents at a Glance

Contents

About the Author

Tim Duckett designs and builds software with tools such as Objective-C and Ruby on Rails. Having been online since the early 1990s, he's worked with all kinds of clients in all kinds of sectors. Along the way he picked up an MBA and is a certified project manager, but asks that you don't hold those against him.

He lives in Sheffield in the UK with his family and far too many pets. In his spare time, he walks the dog, enjoys single malts, takes photos, and dismantles gadgets.

You can find him online at `http://adoptioncurve.net`, and on places including Twitter and GitHub as `timd`.

About the Technical Reviewer

Brent Simmons has been programming since his first Apple II Plus back in 1980. More recently he created TapLynx, a framework for creating iOS apps without programming. He also created the RSS reader NetNewsWire and the weblog editor MarsEdit. He's a cofounder of Sepia Labs, where he writes Glassboard for iOS. He blogs at `inessential.com`.

Acknowledgments

It's my name on the cover, but there's a whole host of people without whom this book would never have happened.

At Apress, Tracy Brown, Michelle Lowman, and Tom Welsh cracked the whip that got me from one end of the project plan to the other, and were very gracious about my procrastination and constant content changes. Sharon Wilkey and Valerie Greco unsplit all my infinitives. Brent Simmons was both kind and constructive as the technical reviewer, and if he laughed at my mistakes, he didn't tell me.

Aral Balkan and Sam Easterby-Smith were my metaphorical training wheels as I wobbled off to start my career as an Objective-C developer. And there are other people, too numerous to mention individually, who over the years who have provided support, inspiration, ideas, and source code. Tom Armitage is responsible for taking the only decent picture of me in existence.

Finally, none of this would have happened without the unconditional love and support of my family, who put up with all my grumbling and grumping while I wrote this book. I'm very lucky to have them.

Introduction

If you're an iOS app developer, chances are you'll be using table views somewhere in your development projects. Table views are the bread and butter of iOS apps. With them, you can create everything from the simplest of lists to fully tricked-out user interfaces.

Table views are one of the more complex components found in UIKit. Using them for (potentially boring!) standard user interfaces is quite simple, but customizing them can become much more challenging.

This book has a task-oriented focus to assist you when implementing customized table views. Although it delves deeply into the table view API, you can always choose the level of detail you want to dive into. This book aims to be a reference and customization cookbook at the same time, useful for beginners as well as intermediate developers.

What This Book Covers

Chapter 1, "Creating a Simple Table-View App," introduces the table view with some examples of the current state of the art. After showing you something of what's possible, we'll start out with a very simple table view–based app for the iPhone, which will introduce you to the `UITableView` and its main elements. The app will also act as a starting point for later versions, and it'll be a working prototype that you can use as the basis for your own experiments.

In **Chapter 2, "How The Table Fits Together,"** you'll look at how the parts of the table view work together. You'll see the main types of `UITableViews` and their anatomy. You'll learn how to create them both with Interface Builder and in code, and how to use the `UITableViewController` class as a template.

Chapter 3, "Feeding Your Tables With Data,"is about where the table gets its data and how you get it there. It shows how the table keeps track of sections and rows, and covers some of the software design patterns that the `UITableView` classes exploit.

Chapter 4 "How The Cell Fits Together," focuses on the cells that make up tables. You'll see how cells are structured internally, and how they're created and reused. It also covers the standard cells types that come for free with the `UITableView` classes.

Chapter 5, "Using Tables for Navigation," covers an almost-ubiquitous feature of the iOS user interface, and shows how tables can be used to navigate through a hierarchy of data in a simple and consistent way.

The constrained size of the iOS user interface presents some challenges when it comes to presenting large amounts of data. **Chapter 6, "Indexing, Grouping, and Sorting,"** presents some ways of arranging the data in tables, to help users find their way.

Chapter 7, "Selecting and Editing Table Content," shows how you can use tables to manage data. It covers how to add, delete, and rearrange the information, and some of the interface aspects that this entails.

In **Chapter 8, "Improving the Look of Cells,"** you will start to look at the process of going beyond standard cell types to customize the look and feel of your table views. This chapter covers two of the quickest ways to make the cells look the way you need them to.

Chapter 9, "Creating Custom Cells with Subclasses," takes customizing cells to the next level. You'll learn how to use custom `UITableViewCell` subclasses to gain detailed control over cells' appearance.

In addition to changing the look and feel of cells, you can make them truly interactive by embedding controls such as buttons and sliders. **Chapter 10, "Improving the Cell's Interaction,"** presents how to do this, as well as building cool table features such as slide-to-reveal, pull-to-refresh, and search.

Finally, in **Chapter 11, "Table Views on the iPad,"** you'll look at the iPad's split-view controller, which provides a flexible two-pane interface familiar from apps such as Mail.

The Style of This Book

I've tried to bridge the gap between two styles of book—the in-depth treatment of every last little detail, and the cookbook of specific point solutions. Both have their place, but sometimes I find that descriptions of very detailed, elegant solutions with lots of features can obscure the detail of the problem I'm trying to solve. Equally, sometimes cookbook solutions are too specific and don't easily lend themselves to adapting to my specific situation.

In the code examples that follow, I've tried to balance the two styles. The visual polish and extraneous functions are kept to a minimum, which hopefully results in examples that illustrate how to build a solution while also acting as a building block for your own code.

The Book's Source Code

You can download the source code for each chapter's examples from the Apress site or from GitHub at `http://github.com/timd/Pro-iOS-TableViews`.

Although that's the quickest way to get up and running, I encourage you to take the extra time to key in the code yourself as you go along. With Xcode's code completion, it doesn't take that long, and code that has flowed through your eyes and brain, and then out to your fingers, is much more likely to sink in and make sense.

Where to Find Out More

Beyond the pages of this book, there's a wealth of other information available online (not to mention the great range of other Apress titles):

- For a general overview, Apple's **"Table View Programming Guide for iOS"** is a detailed guide that covers most of the topics in this book. This is available online at `http://developer.apple.com/library/ios/#documentation/userexperience/conceptual/TableView_iPhone/AboutTableViewsiPhone/AboutTableViewsiPhone.html`, or in Xcode's documentation.
- Apple's **iOS Developer Library** has full documentation for all Cocoa Touch libraries. It tends not to include examples in the documentation itself, but the Library is the one-stop shop for a detailed reference for each class, protocol, and library. Again, this is available online, at `http://developer.apple.com/library/ios/navigation/` or in Xcode's documentation library.
- **Online forums** are a fantastic resource. Sites such as Stack Overflow (`www.stackoverflow.com`) are the place to go for practical advice. Chances are, a number of people will have met and overcome the same problem that you're experiencing, and the answer will be there. Stack Overflow's customs and practices can be a little daunting at first, but it's worth persevering. There are no stupid questions, after all, just questions that haven't been answered yet.

- A general **Google search** will often throw up answers from blogs. There are some extremely talented individuals out there who regularly post about how to do this or that with iOS and Objective-C, and many of them also point to source code on their sites or GitHub and the like.
- Apple also provides some fairly detailed **source code examples**. Your mileage may vary with these. I sometimes find that they can be a bit overcomplicated and can obscure the core technique that I'm trying to grasp. But they shouldn't be overlooked, if only because they've been written by engineers with an intimate understanding of the frameworks.
- **Universities such as Stanford and MIT** place entire semesters' worth of lecture modules online, both on their sites and on iTunes U. Their technical education is some of the best on the planet, and some of the online lectures are taught by Apple engineers. These are definitely worth checking out.
- **Local user groups**, including CocoaDev, CocoaHeads, and NS$city$ (where *$city$* is a location near you), are groups that meet regularly around the world. It's an iron law of software that there's always someone who knows more than you do about a topic, and problems are always less daunting when discussed with them over a beer or two.
- **Mailing lists** such as cocoa-dev don't perhaps have the profile of sites such as Stack Overflow these days, but can still be a useful resource. An excellent example (which covers not just coding topics, but design and business issues as well) is `http://iosdevweekly.com`.

Finally, if you've battled with—and resolved—some gnarly issue, then *post about it yourself*, whether that's on your own blog or a site like Stack Overflow. Even if the topic has been covered numerous times before, there's always room for another take on a problem. Your unique point of view could be just what someone else needs.

Contacting the Author

Tim Duckett can be found online at `http://adoptioncurve.net` and on Twitter as `@timd`.

Chapter 1

Table Views from the Ground Up

In this chapter, you'll start your exploration of table views. It begins with an overview of what table views are and some examples of how they're used in practice. Then in the second section, you'll build a simple "Hello, world"-style table view app to introduce you to the components behind the user interface and help you to contextualize the detail that's going to come in later chapters.

If you're just starting to use table views, it's worth taking some time to build a very simple one from scratch before diving into the gnarly details. However, if you've reached the stage where you feel more confident about how the components of the table view jigsaw fit together and want to get straight into the code, feel free to skip the rest of this chapter completely. I'll cover the elements in detail later, so you won't miss out.

What Are Table Views?

Examples of table views are to be found everywhere in iOS apps. You are already familiar with simple tables, implemented as standard controls such as the iPhone's Contacts app or the iPad's Mail app, shown in Figure 1–1.

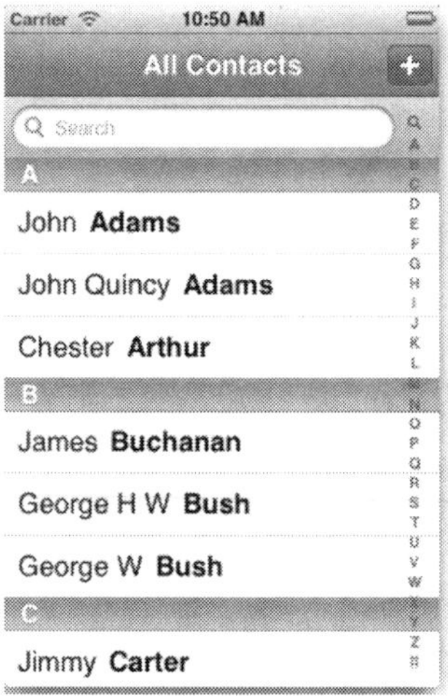

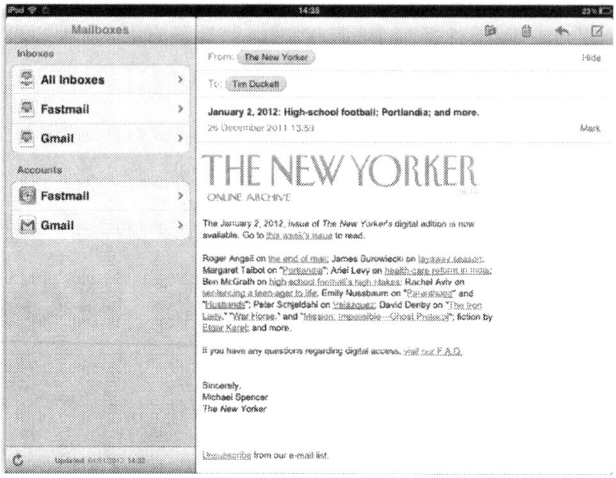

The iPhone's Contacts app

Mail on the iPad

Figure 1–1. *Some basic table-based applications*

At the other end of the scale, the default look, feel, and behavior of the table view and cells can be customized to the point where they are hardly recognizable as table views at all. Figure 1–2 shows some examples.

Figure 1–2. *Examples of table views in action on the iPhone*

On the iPad, table views are often used as components of a larger user interface. Figure 1–3 shows an example from the wildly successful (and addictive!) Carcassonne game.

Figure 1–3. *Two table views in action on the iPad*

The Anatomy of a Table View

The table view displays a list of elements—or cells—that can be scrolled up and down vertically. They are instances of the `UITableView` class and come in two physical parts:

- The container part—the `tableView` itself—is a subclass of `UIScrollView` and contains a vertically scrollable list of table cells.
- Table cells, which can either be instances of one of four standard `UITableViewCell` types or custom subclasses of `UITableViewCell` that can be customized as required.

Figure 1–4 illustrates the parts of a table view.

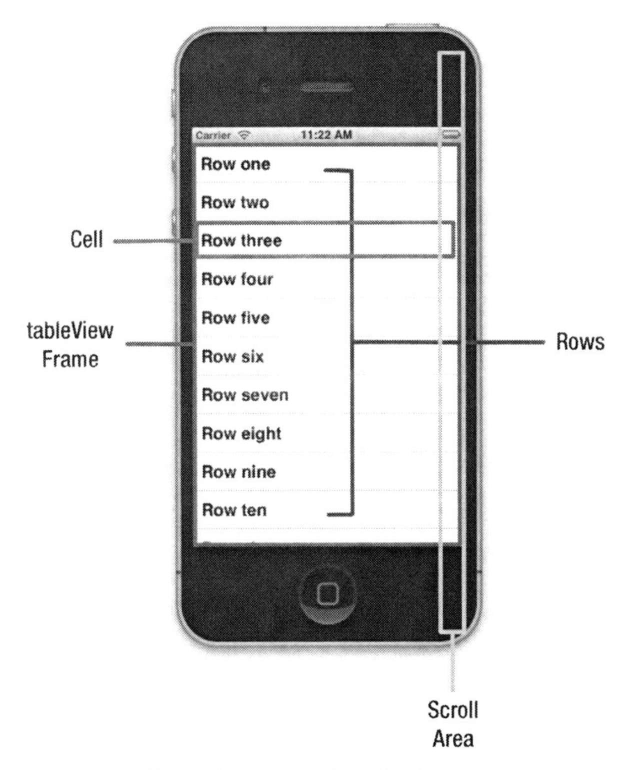

Figure 1–4. *The basic anatomy of a table view*

Table view operations are supported by two `UITableView` protocols:

- `UITableViewDatasource` provides the table view with the data that it needs to construct and configure itself, as well as providing the cells that the table view displays.
- `UITableViewDelegate` handles most of the methods concerned with user interaction, such as selection and editing.

Creating a Simple Table View App

In the rest of this chapter, you'll build a simple "Hello, world"-style table view app from scratch. It will show you how the container, cells, data source, and delegate all fit together and give you an app that you can use as the basis for your own experiments.

I'm going to take it deliberately slowly and cover all the steps. If you're a confident Xcode driver, you won't need this hand-holding—just concentrate on the code instead.

Still with me? Okay—you're going to do the following:

- Create a simple, window-based application skeleton
- Generate some data for feeding the table

- Create a simple table view
- Wire up the table view's data source and delegate
- Implement some very simple interactivity

It's all very straightforward but useful practice. Onward!

Creating the Application Skeleton

For this application, you're going to use a simple structure: a single view managed by a view controller, and a NIB file to provide the content for the view. Fire up Xcode and select the Single View Application template, as shown in Figure 1–1.

> **NOTE:** With each new release of Xcode, Apple frequently (and pointlessly) changes the templates that are included. You may see a set that is different from those shown in Figure 1–5. Check the description of the templates to find the one that will provide a single-view application.

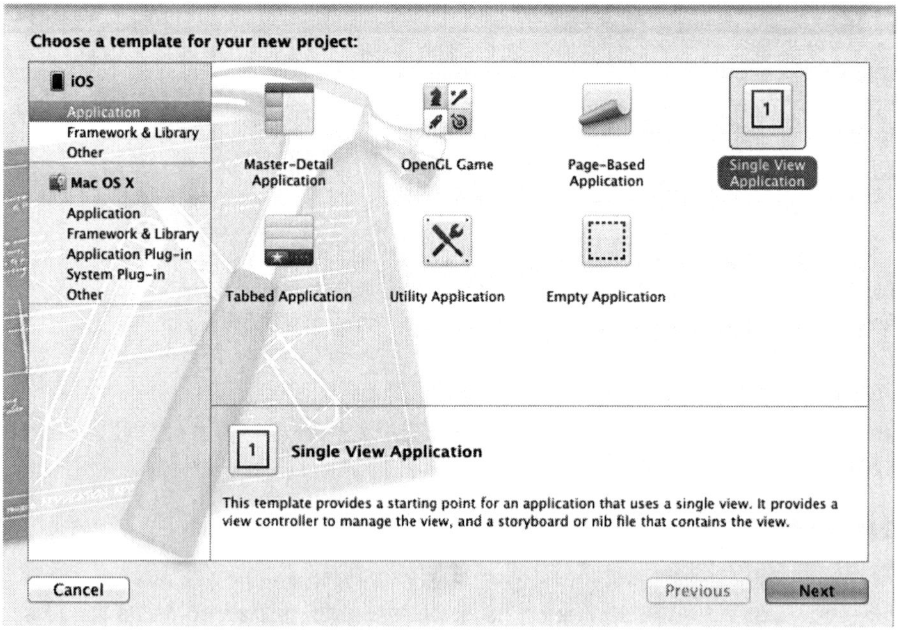

Figure 1–5. *Xcode's template selection pane*

Call the application **SimpleTable**. You're going to build an iPhone version. You don't need the storyboard or unit tests, but you do want automatic reference counting. Make sure those options are selected as needed, as shown in Figure 1–6.

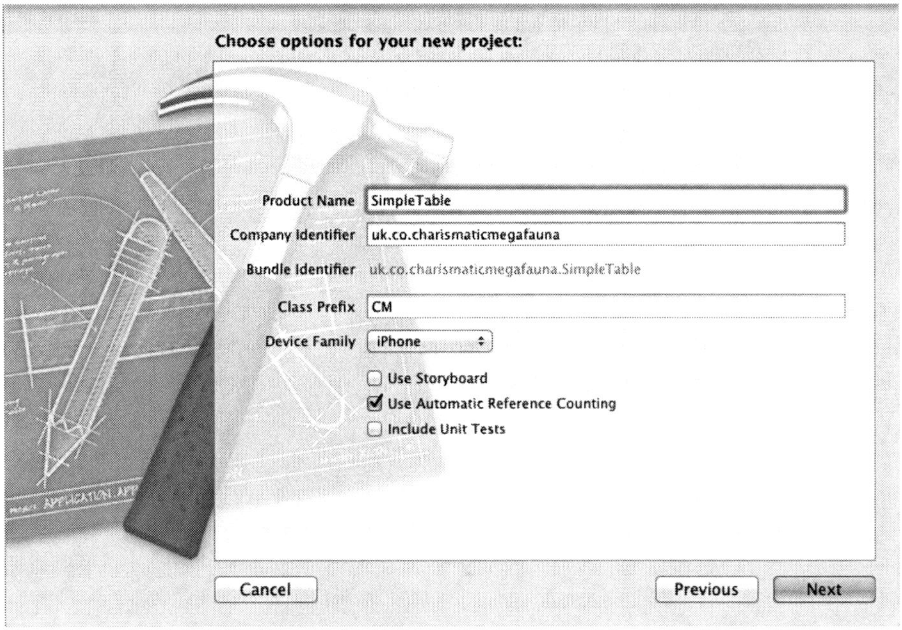

Figure 1–6. *Name the application.*

The Class Prefix setting will be prefixed to the names of any classes that you create within the application—so in this case, the `AppDelegate` class would be named `CMAppDelegate`. This prevents any chance of you inadvertently creating classes that clash with existing ones, either in the iOS SDK or any libraries that you might be using.

The choice of the class prefix is entirely up to you. I tend to use CM for Charismatic Megafauna, but you could use something along the lines of ST for Simple Table instead.

Finally, you'll need to select a location to save the project to. You don't need to worry about creating a local Git repository for this project unless you particularly want to.

When you've reached this point, you'll see the project view of Xcode, with the initial skeleton of your application. It'll look something like Figure 1–7, assuming that you've stuck with the SimpleTable application name.

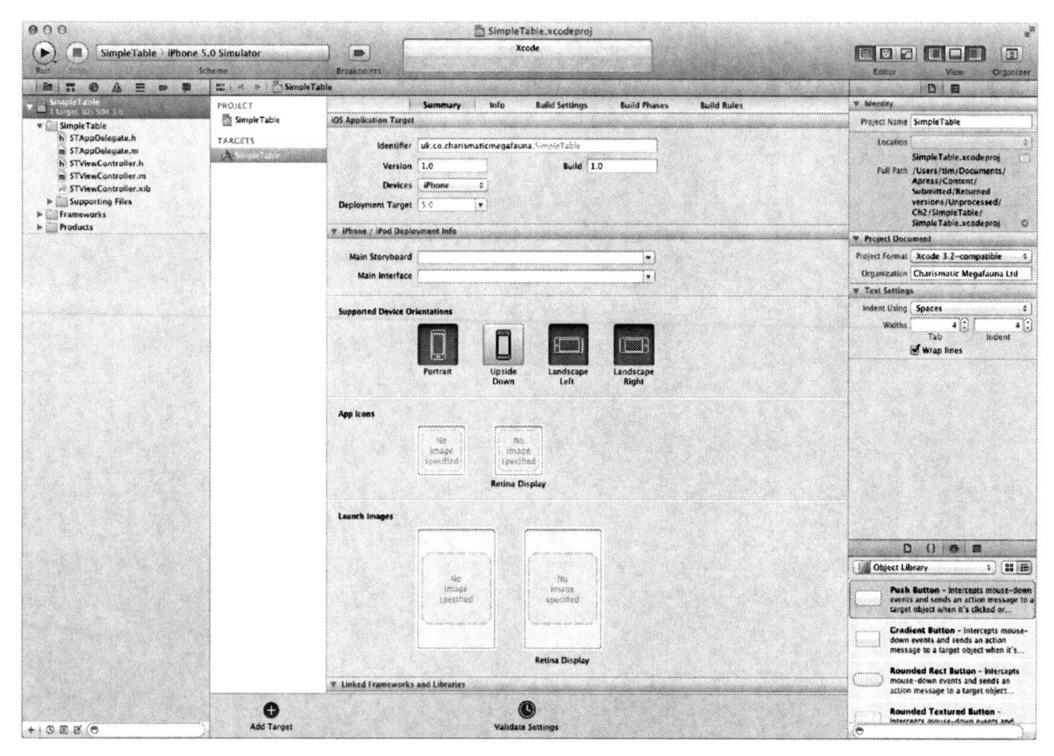

Figure 1–7. *The initial Xcode view showing our new skeleton application*

You'll see that you have the following:

- An app delegate (`STAppDelegate.h` and `.m`)
- A table-view controller (`STViewController.h` and `.m`)
- A NIB file containing the view (`STViewController.xib`)

At the end of this chapter, you'll look again at how these fit together. For the moment, you'll be working with the table view controller and its NIB file.

Generating Some Data

Before you start with the table view itself, you need to create some data to feed it. Because this is a simple table example, the data is going to be simple too. You'll create an `NSMutableArray` of `NSStrings` that contains some information to go into each cell.

The data array will need to be ready by the time the data source is called by the table view—so where to create it? There are several options, but one obvious place is in the view controller's `viewDidLoad` method. This method gets called the first time the view controller is loaded, which takes place well before the table will try to populate itself, so you'll be safe to create it here.

You're also going to need a way of passing the array of data around the application. This process requires a property that can be accessed by the various methods that will need access to the data.

Let's get started. Open the `STViewController.h` file (shown in Figure 1–8) and begin by creating the property.

> **NOTE:** To save space from now on, I'm not going to show the full Xcode interface—just the code that you'll need to enter.

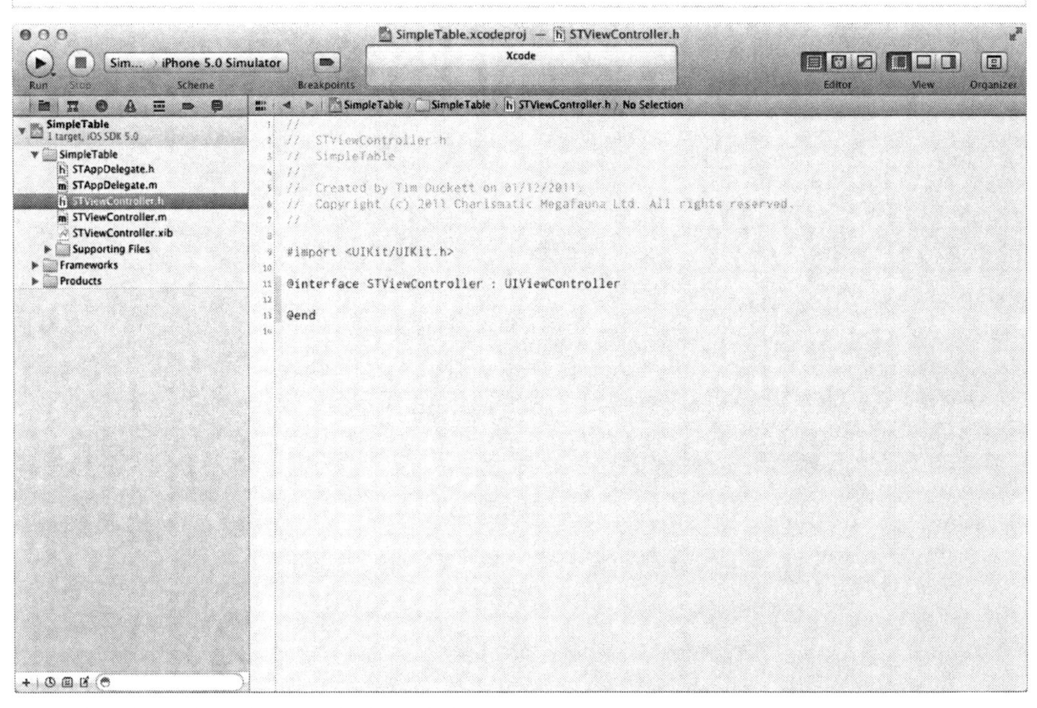

Figure 1–8. *Editing the* `STViewController.h` *file*

Add in a declaration for the property so that the code looks like Listing 1–1.

Listing 1–1. *Declaring the Property*

```
#import <UIKit/UIKit.h>

@interface STViewController : UIViewController

@property (nonatomic, strong) NSMutableArray *tableData;  // holds the table data

end
```

Save this file and then switch to the implementation file.

TIP: In Xcode 4, you can flip quickly between the `.h` and `.m` files with the Ctrl + Command + Up Arrow key combination, or by clicking the filename in the breadcrumb display at the top of the code editor then selecting the file from the drop-down menu that appears.

First, you'll need to synthesize the `tableData` property. Add the following line after `@implementation STViewController`:

```
@synthesize tableData;
```

Now you're going to create the actual data array itself. In the `View lifecycle` section of the `STViewController.m` file, you'll need to find the `viewDidLoad` method.

Our data array will be a simple array of ten `NSStrings`, each with a number. Add the code shown in Listing 1–2.

Listing 1–2. *Creating the Data Array*

```
- (void)viewDidLoad
{
    // Run the superclass's viewDidLoad method
    [super viewDidLoad];

    // Create the array to hold the table data
    self.tableData = [[NSMutableArray alloc] init];

    // Create and add 10 data items to the table data array
    for (NSUInteger i=0; i < 10; i++) {

        // The cell will contain a string "Item X"
        NSString *dataString = [NSString stringWithFormat:@"Item %d", i];

        // Here the new string is added to the end of the array
        [self.tableData addObject:dataString];

    }

    // Print out the contents of the array into the log
    NSLog(@"The tableData array contains %@", self.tableData);

}
```

Having created the `tableData` array in the `viewDidLoad` method, you'll need to clean up after yourself. There's no right or wrong place to do this. However, I've developed a habit: if I create an object in one method that needs to persist, I try to put the cleanup code in a corresponding method.

Because you create the `tableData` array in the `viewDidLoad` method, you can clean it up in the `viewDidUnload` method. That's what the code in Listing 1–3 does.

Listing 1–3. *Cleaning Up*

```
- (void)viewDidUnload
{
    [super viewDidUnload];

    self.tableData = nil;
}
```

Let's run the application to see that data array being created. The user interface isn't much to write home about yet, but you'll be able to see the data that you're going to feed to the table.

Run the application in the Simulator by pressing Command + R or by choosing **Product ➤ Run**, and then take a look at the logger output:

```
YYYY-MM-DD HH:MM:SS.sss SimpleTable[21502:ef03] The tableData array contains (
    "Item 0",
    "Item 1",
    "Item 2",
    "Item 3",
    "Item 4",
    "Item 5",
    "Item 6",
    "Item 7",
    "Item 8",
    "Item 9"
)
```

A NOTE ABOUT MEMORY MANAGEMENT IN IOS 5

Newcomers to iOS often arrive having heard hair-raising tales of the hideous complexity of memory management in Objective-C. There's a school of thought that says that all "modern" languages should have baked-in memory management such as garbage collection, and managing memory manually is somehow old-fashioned, difficult, and a waste of time. Someone in Apple was obviously listening to that school of thought, because perhaps the single most-anticipated feature of iOS 5 was automatic reference counting (ARC).

Put simply, ARC uses some compiler magic to take care of all the memory management issues that you had to worry about in previous versions. Prior to iOS 5, in order to prevent memory leaks, you had to "balance" any `alloc`, `retain` or `copy` of an object with a corresponding `release` (or `autorelease`). Miss a release, and you had a potential memory leak. Over-release, and you risked crashing your app by sending messages to deallocated objects. Having ARC means this is no longer something you need to worry about; switch it on in the compiler, and memory management will be taken care of "automagically."

NOTE: Automatic reference counting is supported in only iOS 5 and Xcode versions 4.2 and above.

Creating the Table View

As it stands, the user interface for our application is a bit dull. You haven't added the table yet! This needs fixing.

Click the `STViewController.xib` file in the project explorer, and you'll see the NIB file open in the Interface Builder pane, as shown in Figure 1–9.

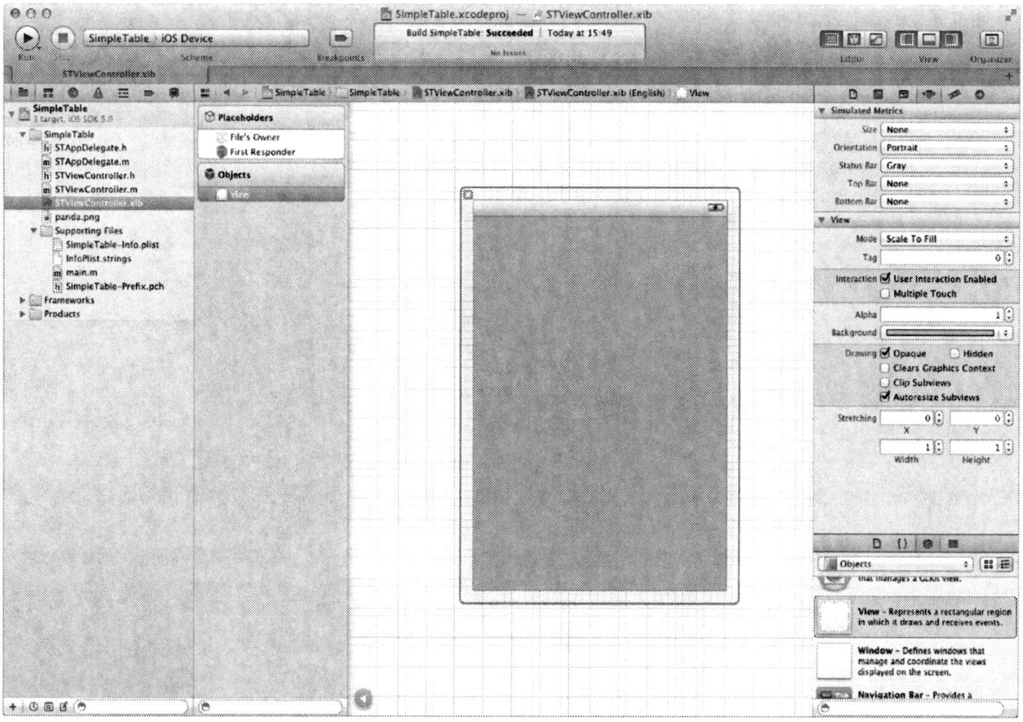

Figure 1–9. *Editing the NIB file in Interface Builder*

In the Objects browser at the bottom right, find the *Table View* item and drag it out onto the view in the center. By default, the table view will try to expand to fit the full view, but you need to resize it by grabbing the resize handles and making it smaller. Finally, grab a *Label* from the object browser and drop that onto the top of the view so it looks like Figure 1–10.

Figure 1–10. *Resizing the table view*

Believe it or not, that's all you need to do in order to implement the most basic table view. It won't display any data yet, because you haven't implemented the `UITableViewDataSource` protocol methods, and it certainly won't have any interactivity—but the app will run.

To prove this, run it again (Command + R), and marvel at our awesome application in the Simulator, as shown in Figure 1–11.

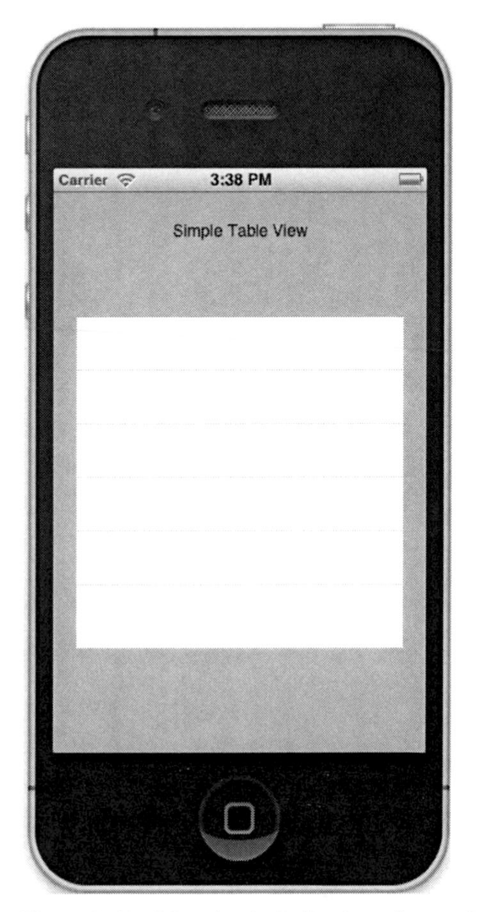

Figure 1–11. *A functional, albeit not very impressive, table-view application*

Okay—not all that impressive. Let's complete the wiring up of the table view so it actually *does* something.

Conforming to the Table View Protocols

The table view that you just created needs both a data source and a delegate. You need to conform our `STViewController` class to both the `UITableViewDataSource` and `UITableViewDelegate` protocols.

> **NOTE:** Data sources and delegates are covered in detail in Chapters 2 and 3.

You'll do this by editing the `STViewController.h` interface declaration in Listing 1–4.

Listing 1–4. *Conforming the Class to the `UITableDelegate` and `UITableDataSource` Protocols*

```
#import <UIKit/UIKit.h>

@interface STViewController : UIViewController <UITableViewDelegate, ➥
UITableViewDataSource>

@property (nonatomic, strong) NSMutableArray *tableData;
@property (nonatomic) int cellCount;

@end
```

This will tell the compiler to expect the required methods to have been implemented. You'll do this in a moment.

Wiring Up the Data Source and Delegate

Our `STViewController` object will be ready shortly, but the table view itself doesn't yet know that it will act as both a data source and a delegate. You need to connect the two together. There are two ways of doing this: visually (though Interface Builder) or in code. For this example application, you'll use Interface Builder, so click the NIB file to open it again.

Right-click the table-view object (either in the main Interface Builder or in the objects tree in the middle pane), and you'll see the Table View property "head-up display" (HUD), as shown in Figure 1–12.

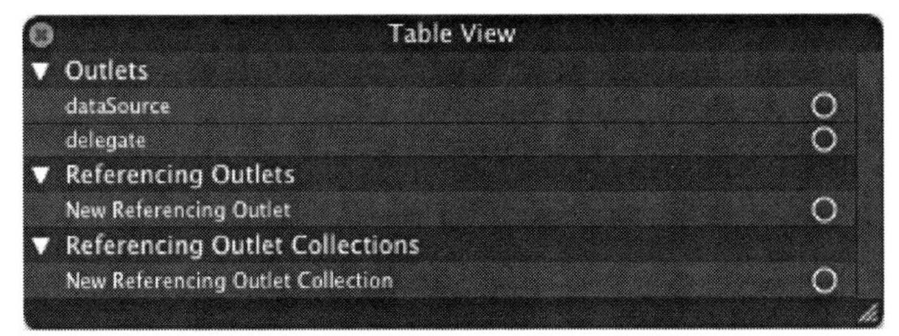

Figure 1–12. *The Table View property HUD*

It's showing the two Outlet properties that we're interested in: the `dataSource` and the `delegate`.

To connect these, mouse-over the circle to the right of the `dataSource` entry. The circle changes to a plus symbol. Click and drag from this symbol. A blue line extends out. Mouse-over the File's Owner item in the object tree, and it becomes highlighted in blue, as shown in Figure 1–13.

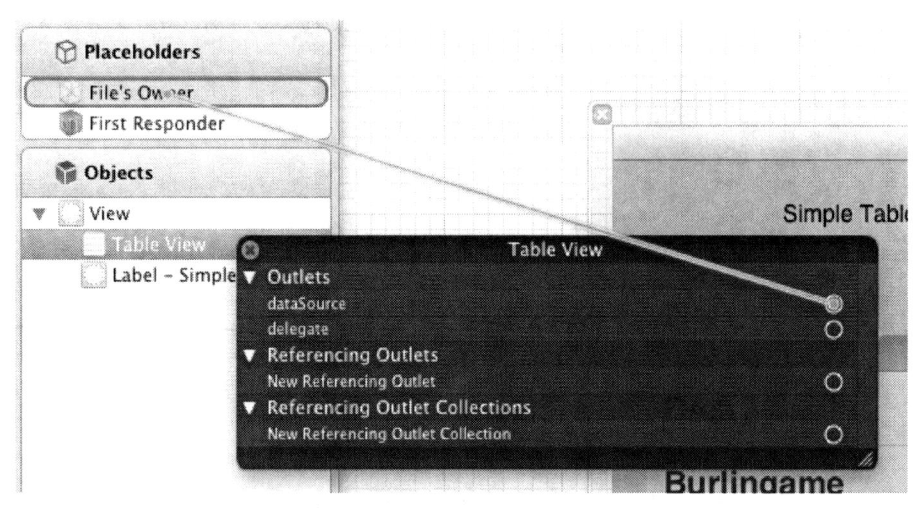

Figure 1–13. *Connecting the* `dataSource`

Release the mouse, and the `dataSource` is now connected. Next, repeat the same process for the `delegate`: drag from the plus symbol to File's Owner, drop, and connect.

The Table View properties HUD will now show that both the `dataSource` and the `delegate` are connected to the File's Owner, as shown in Figure 1–14.

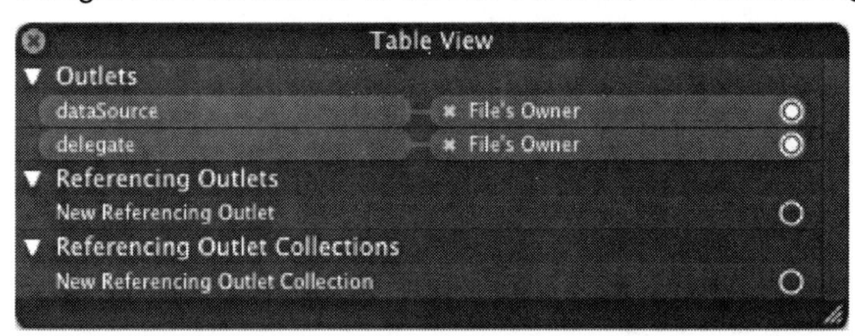

Figure 1–14. *The* `dataSource` *and* `delegate` *connected to File's Owner*

File's Owner in this context is the view controller for the view, our `STViewController` object.

Displaying the Data

Now that you have the table view wired up to its `delegate` and `dataSource`, you're in a position to start making it do something. A logical next step would be to get the table view to display its data.

As the table view draws itself, it asks its `dataSource` to provide cells that can then be displayed. You'll look at this process in a lot more detail in Chapter 3, but for now let's get those cells created.

The UITableViewDataSource protocol has two required methods and nine optional ones. Because this is a simple example, you're going to implement only the two required methods and one optional one.

The first required method—tableView:numberOfRowsInSection:—returns the number of rows that the section will eventually contain. The second required method—tableView:cellForRowAtIndexPath:—creates and returns the cell itself.

The optional method is numberOfSectionsInTableView:. It's optional in our app because we're using a table with a single section, and by default the number of sections in a table is 1. Later, when you look at more-complex sectional tables, this method definitely *will* be required, so I include it even though it's not strictly necessary.

numberOfSectionsInTableView:

You have a simple table with one section, so this method is going to be pretty trivial. Switch to STViewController.m, where you can create the numberOfSectionsInTableView: method, as shown in Listing 1–5.

Listing 1–5. ***The numberOfSectionsInTableView: Method***

```
#pragma mark - UITableViewDataSource

- (NSInteger)numberOfSectionsInTableView:(UITableView *)tableView {

    return 1;

}
```

> **NOTE:** The pragma line is a compiler directive. It's not used during compilation, but demarcates sections of the code during the writing process. If you pull down the breadcrumb menu at the top of the edit pane, you'll see that this line breaks up the list of methods and makes the code easier to navigate. Using this directive is not a big deal now, but as your classes grow, this can be a real lifesaver when trying to find a particular method among others.

tableView:numberOfRowsInSection:

In order to draw itself successfully, the table view needs to know how many rows are going to appear in the section (our simple table view has only one section). Earlier, you created an NSMutableArray to hold your data, and populated this with ten NSStrings. The section will have as many rows as there are elements in the NSMutableArray.

The NSArray class has a useful method for returning the number of elements in an array (this is inherited by instances of NSMutableArray, which is a subclass of NSArray):

```
[array count];
```

In STViewController.m, add the tableView:numbersOfRowsInSection: method, as shown in Listing 1–6.

Listing 1–6. *The tableView:numberOfRowsInSection: Method*

```
-(NSInteger)tableView:(UITableView *)tableView ➥
numberOfRowsInSection:(NSInteger)section {

    return [self.tableData count];

}
```

Pretty straightforward, yes?

tableView:cellForRowAtIndexPath:

Having figured out how many cells are going to be in the section, now it's time to create the cells. To begin, add the method in Listing 1–7 to STViewController.m, and then we'll step through what it does.

Listing 1–7. *The tableView:cellForRowAtIndexPath: Method*

```
- (UITableViewCell *)tableView:(UITableView *)tableView ➥
cellForRowAtIndexPath:(NSIndexPath *)indexPath {

    static NSString *cellIdentifier = @"Cell";

    UITableViewCell *cell = [tableView ➥
dequeueReusableCellWithIdentifier:CellIdentifier];

    if (cell == nil) {
        cell = [[UITableViewCell alloc] initWithStyle:UITableViewCellStyleDefault ➥
reuseIdentifier:CellIdentifier];
    }

    cell.textLabel.text = [self.tableData objectAtIndex:indexPath.row];

    return cell;
}
```

Let's start by looking at the method itself:

```
-(UITableViewCell *)tableView:(UITableView *)tableView ➥
cellForRowAtIndexPath:(NSIndexPath *)indexPath
```

This method returns an instance of UITableViewCell and takes two parameters:

- The tableView that is calling for the cell (Because this class might be the data source for numerous tables, it needs to identify which table it's dealing with.)
- An indexPath, which has a row property identifying the table row for which the cell is being requested

The first line of the method sets up a static NSString to act as a cell identifier:

```
static NSString *cellIdentifier = @"Cell";
```

TIP: The use of cell identifiers is something you'll explore in much more detail in Chapter 4. For now, you can get by thinking of this as a label that identifies the kind of cell you're dealing with. This table has only one kind of cell, hence the single identifier.

The next line attempts to find and return a cell with the correct `CellIdentifier` from the queue of cells that are ready for use:

```
  UITableViewCell *cell = [tableView ➥
dequeueReusableCellWithIdentifier:CellIdentifier];
```

Initially, there probably won't be any cells in the queue. In that case, the `dequeueReusableCellWithIdentifier:` method will return `nil`. That's checked in the `if` statement:

```
if (cell == nil) {
  cell = [[UITableViewCell alloc] initWithStyle:UITableViewCellStyleDefault ➥
  reuseIdentifier:CellIdentifier];
}
```

If `dequeueReusableCellWithIdentifier:` didn't return a cell, this code creates one with the `UITableViewCellStyleDefault` style, and gives it a reuse identifier label.

By this time, you have either a recycled cell from the queue, or you have created a brand new one. So you can configure the contents and return it to the calling method with the following:

```
cell.textLabel.text = [self.tableData objectAtIndex:indexPath.row];

return cell;
```

At this stage, you have some data and a table view, and you have wired up the methods that feed the table view with the data. Run the application, and you'll see our table resplendent with content, as in Figure 1–15.

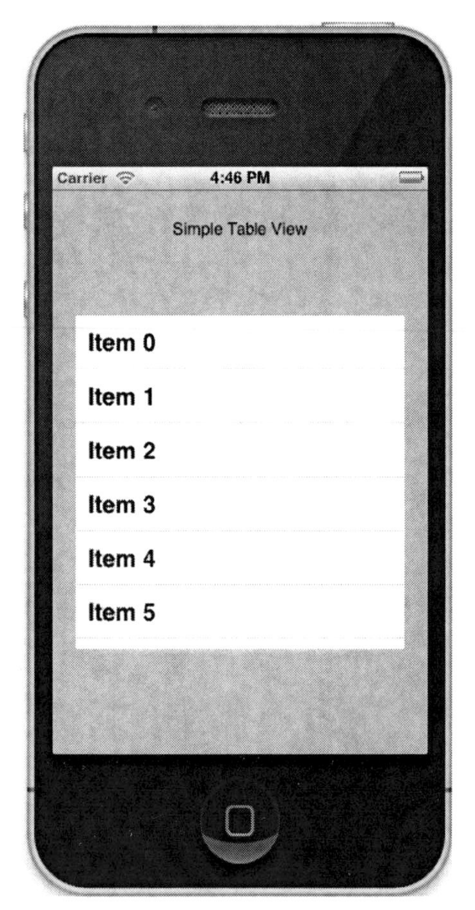

Figure 1–15. *The table replete with content*

On that triumphant note, it's time to make the table respond to some user input.

Adding Some Interactivity

You can legitimately feel quite pleased with yourself at this point. You have a table view that takes in data, displays it on the screen, and can scroll around (try scrolling the table if you haven't already). You can also select cells by tapping them, and the table view will highlight the selected row.

All of this functionality comes for free with an instance of `UITableView`, which saves us an awful lot of time getting a table view up and running. But eventually, you're going to want it to do much more. This is where the `UITableViewDelegate` comes in.

`UITableViewDelegate` provides a host of methods that allow the table and the cells (among other things) to react to user input. These methods support selecting, editing, reordering, and deleting cells, in addition to configuring how the table view looks. For the moment, you're going to take a look at just one of those methods, which enables a row to react to being tapped by the user.

tableView:didSelectRowAtIndexPath:

Our table view already responds in a somewhat limited way to user input. When you tap a cell, it highlights in blue. Behind the scenes, the table view makes a call to the delegate indicating two things—that a row has been selected, and which row that was.

If the delegate implements the `tableView:didSelectRowAtIndexPath:` method, it can use that to fire off some other activity. For example, in the iPhone's Contacts app, a view showing the contact's details will be displayed. In iTunes, the song shown in the row will start playing. And so on.

You're not going to do anything quite so ambitious here. When a row is tapped, you'll log the event into the debugger, and you'll pop up a modal dialog box showing which row has been tapped.

To begin, enter the method in Listing 1–8 into `STViewController`.

Listing 1–8. *The `tableView:didSelectRowAtIndexPath:` Method*

```
#pragma mark - UITableViewDelegate

- (void)tableView:(UITableView *)tableView didSelectRowAtIndexPath:➥
(NSIndexPath *)indexPath {

    NSLog(@"Table row %d has been tapped", indexPath.row);

    NSString *messageString = [NSString stringWithFormat:@"You tapped row %d",➥
 indexPath.row];

    UIAlertView *alert = [[UIAlertView alloc] initWithTitle:@"Row tapped"
                                                    message:messageString
                                                   delegate:nil
                                          cancelButtonTitle:@"OK"
                                          otherButtonTitles: nil];
    [alert show];

}
```

Let's unpack that method. The `tableView:didSelectRowAtIndexPath:` method doesn't return anything and takes two parameters:

- The `UITableView` instance that called the method (As with the data source, the delegate could respond to more than one table view and therefore needs to be able to distinguish between them.)
- The `indexPath` whose `row` property corresponds to the row that was tapped

First, you log that row number to the debugger:

```
NSLog(@"Table row %d has been tapped", indexPath.row);
```

TIP: Most developers spend as much time looking at the output of the debugger as they do actually writing code. To make the debugger console visible if it isn't already, do one of the following: choose **View ➤ Debug Area ➤ Show Debug Area** from the menu, or click the middle of the three View icons at the top left of the Xcode toolbar.

Then, using the row number, you create a message string to display in the alert view:

```
    NSString *messageString = [NSString stringWithFormat:@"You tapped row %d",↵
indexPath.row];
```

You then create that alert view:

```
    UIAlertView *alert = [[UIAlertView alloc] initWithTitle:@"Row tapped"
                                                     message:messageString
                                                    delegate:nil
                                           cancelButtonTitle:@"OK"
                                           otherButtonTitles: nil];
```

Next, you display it:

```
    [alert show];
```

Run the code by pressing Command + R (if the Simulator is still running, select the option to quit). Then tap a row at random. If all goes well, you'll see something like Figure 1–16.

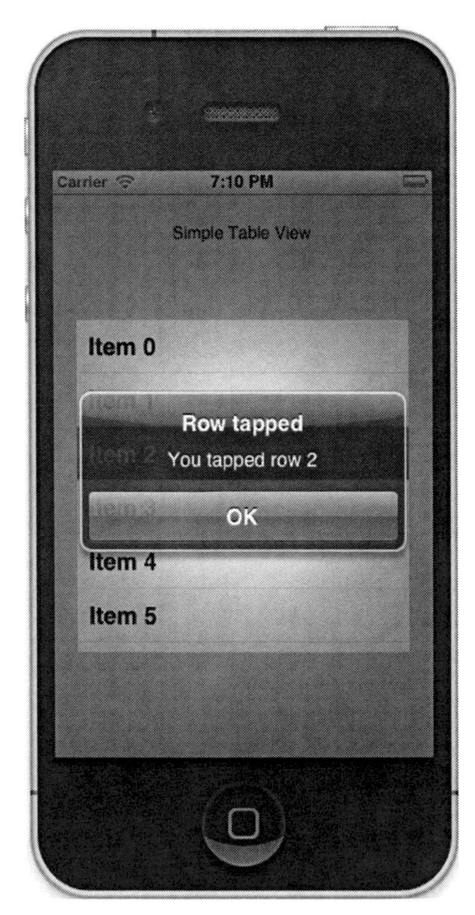

Figure 1–16. *Tapping a row*

Congratulations—that's a fully functional, responsive table you've just built there.

Understanding How the App's Objects Fit Together

Before you leave the SimpleTable app for more-adventurous exercises, it's worth looking at how the various objects fit together. The app has three main objects:

- The app delegate
- The view controller
- The view, which has the table view embedded within it

Figure 1–17 shows how the three objects relate, together with their outlets.

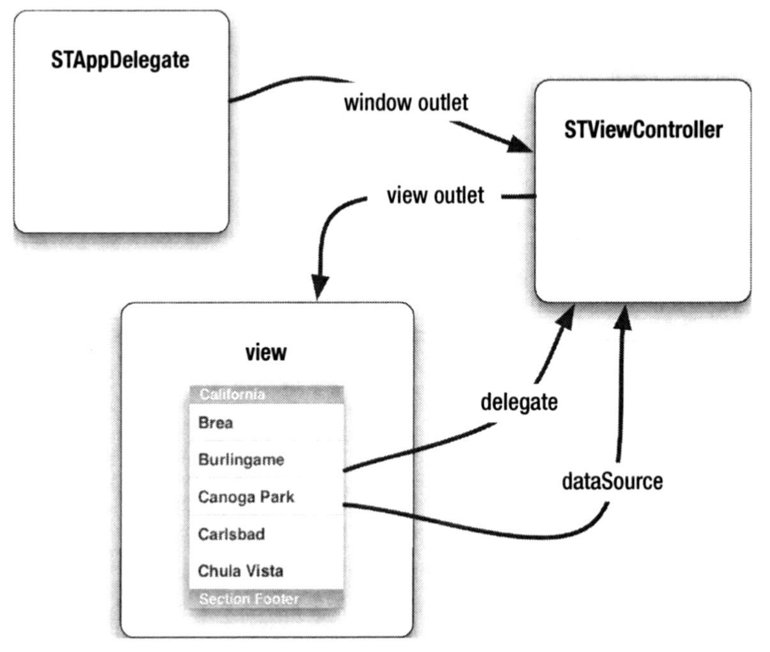

Figure 1–17. *The `SimpleTable` app object diagram*

The `STAppDelegate`'s `window` has a `rootViewController` property, which is connected to the `STViewController` object. This in turn has a `view` outlet, which is connected to the `view` object in the NIB file. Embedded in the NIB is the `UITableView` instance, which has `delegate` and `dataSource` properties. These are linked back to the `STViewController`.

Obviously, this is a pretty simple application, but as applications get more complex, it's worth spending time to sketch out an object diagram. If a picture's worth a thousand words, as the saying goes, an object diagram is worth at least a thousand lines of comments!

Summary

In this chapter, you've created a very basic table view stage by stage:

- To start, you created some data to display in the table.
- Then, using Interface Builder, you created an instance of `UITableView` in the window.
- The view controller conformed to the `UITableViewDataSource` and `UITableViewDelegate` protocols so that it could provide the data for the table, and the response to interaction.
- You implemented the code required to create cells for the table.
- Finally, you made the table react to user input.

From here, it's time to look in much more detail at how tables and cells are constructed, together with how they can be customized and made to respond to user interaction.

Chapter 2

How the Table Fits Together

In this chapter, you're going to take a whistle-stop tour of table views and the elements from which they're built. Although this chapter does not present a lot of code, it will provide a useful foundation later, when you start to customize table views.

Along the way, you'll look at the following:

- The types and styles of table views
- The anatomy and dimensions of table views
- `UITableView`'s relationship to the `UIScrollView` superclass
- Creation of table views in code and with Interface Builder
- Use of the `UITableViewController` class to take advantage of its template methods

Understanding Table Views

At its simplest, a *table view* is a list of items that can (often) be scrolled vertically. Because this is a common interface design pattern, UIKit provides a powerful suite of classes and protocols to make the creation and management of table views as simple and as effective as possible.

Table views can range from a very plain list created by using one of the standard styles provided by the SDK, to something so customized that it's barely recognizable as a table at all. Figure 2–1 shows some examples of table views.

Figure 2–1. *Examples of table views—the built-in Contacts app, the UK Train Times app, and the Path app*

The Contacts app is an example of an indexed table with section headings. The UK Train Times app uses grouped static rows, again with section headers. And the Path app takes the table view customization to extremes. This table view has two sections, together with a clock view that moves vertically as the table scrolls up and down. Despite the differences in visual appearance, all three of these apps are based around `UITableViews` and have identical interaction patterns.

Working with the UITableView Family

At the heart of the table view are the classes, protocols, and view objects that make up the members of the `UITableView` family:

- The `UITableView` and `UITableViewController` classes
- The `UITableViewDelegate` and `UITableViewDataSource` protocols
- The `UITableView` and `UITableViewCell` view objects

All six work together. The classes provide the core functionality for the table view, the protocols define various data and interaction methods, and the view objects provide the physical user interface.

The UITableView Class Hierarchy

The `UITableView` class is a subclass of `UIScrollView`, which in turn inherits from `UIView`, `UIResponder`, and ultimately `NSObject`, as shown in Figure 2–2.

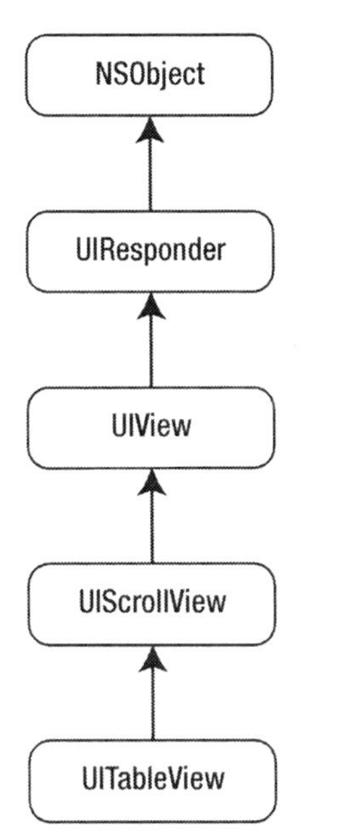

Figure 2–2. *The `UITableView` inheritance chain*

This means that `UITableView` benefits from much of the functionality provided by its parent classes. For example, `UIScrollView` provides the scrolling of the table, while `UIResponder` allows the table cells to respond to user touches and swipes.

> **NOTE:** In an attempt to reduce confusion, I'll use `UITableView` when I'm referring to the class, `tableView` when I'm referring to a specific instance of `UITableView`, and "table view" when I'm talking about table views in general.

Choosing the Type of Table View

Although their visual appearance can be customized to the point where it's almost difficult to recognize them as instances of the `UITableView` class at all, table views come in one of two basic forms: plain and grouped. These basic types have two variations: indexed and sectioned.

The Plain Table

The *plain table* is the basic vanilla incarnation of the `UITableView`. Figure 2–3 shows an example (with possibly the dullest content imaginable).

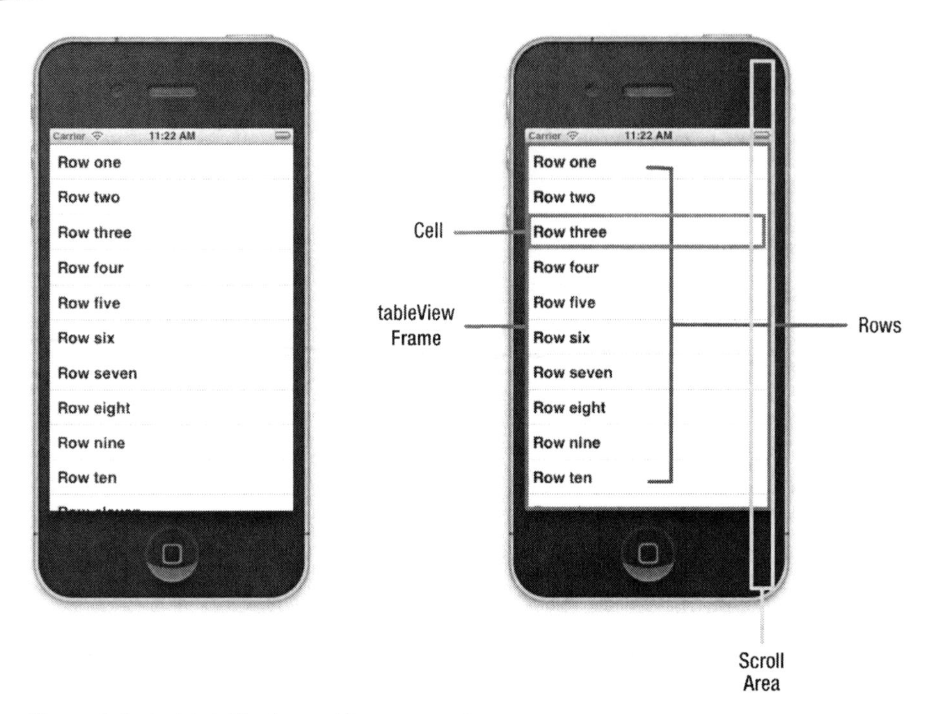

Figure 2–3. *A plain table view and its components*

The plain table is the version that is created by default, although the type can be specified:

```
    UITableView *tableView = [[UITableView alloc] initWithFrame:tvFrame ↵
style:UITableViewStylePlain];
```

If the number of rows in the `tableView` means that the table will scroll to reveal more rows, scroll indicators appear in the right-hand scroll area when the table is in motion.

The Indexed Table

The *indexed table* builds on the plain table by adding an extra navigation aid in the form of an index that appears on the right-hand side of the table view, adjacent to the scroll area. Figure 2–4 shows an example.

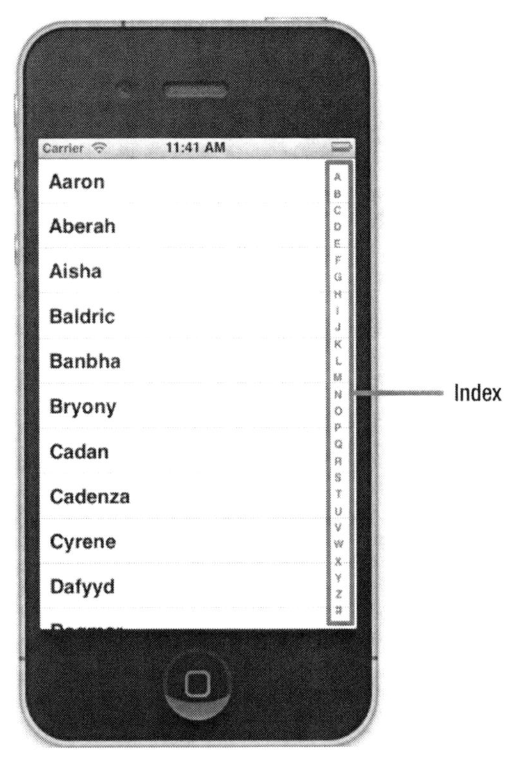

Figure 2–4. *An indexed table*

Implementing indexes involves `UITableViewDataSource` protocol methods, and is covered in detail in Chapter 6.

The Sectioned Table

The *sectioned table*, as its name suggests, groups its rows into sections. These sections can have headers. Figure 2–5 shows an example of relatively simple text headers, which could be replaced with complex `UIView` objects if needed.

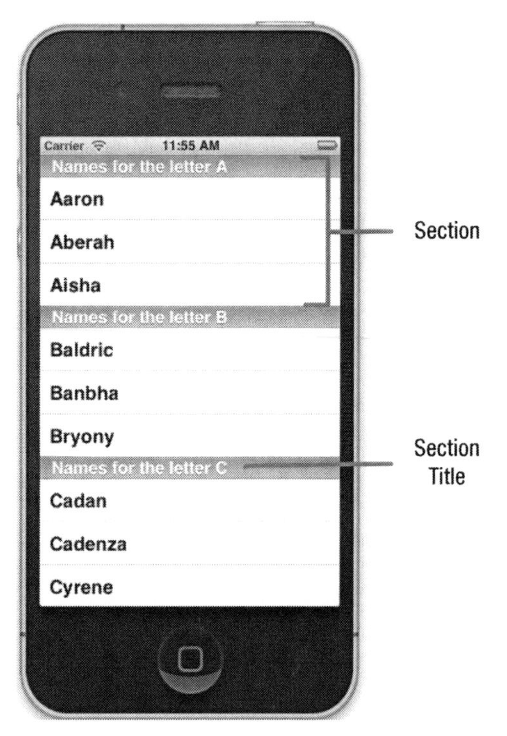

Figure 2–5. *A simple sectioned table*

This type of table view utilises several `UITableViewDataSource` protocol methods to configure the behavior of the sections, and is covered in Chapter 6.

The Grouped Table

The *grouped table* takes things one step further by separating the sections into a style that is distinct from the table view's background. Figure 2–6 shows an example.

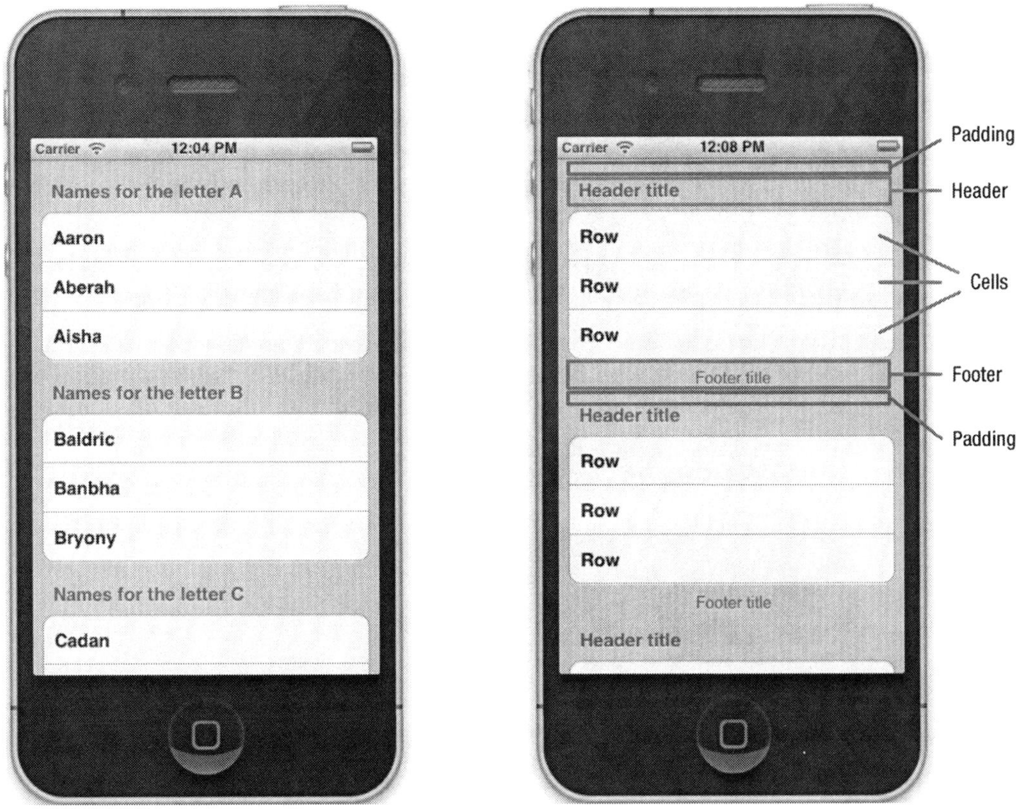

Figure 2–6. *A grouped table*

Each section has a header and footer. These are `UIViews`, and are returned by two `UITableViewDelegate` methods:

```
-(UIView *)tableView:tableView viewForFooterInSection:(NSInteger)section;
-(UIView *)tableView:tableView viewForHeaderInSection:(NSInteger)section;
```

Although you can manipulate the entire header and footer, often it's enough just to be able to set the titles. `UITableViewDataSource` has two methods to support this:

```
-(NSString *)tableView:tableView titleForHeaderInSection:(NSInteger)section;
-(NSString *)tableView:tableView titleForFooterInSection:(NSInteger)section;
```

If for any reason you need to find the dimensions of the headers and footers, these are returned (as `CGRect` values) by the following:

```
-(CGRect)rectForHeaderInSection:(NSInteger)section;
-(CGRect)rectForFooterInSection:(NSInteger)section;
```

The dimensions of the entire section (header, footer, and content) are available by calling the following:

```
-(CGRect)rectForSection:(NSInteger)section;
```

Setting TableView Dimensions

One way to visualize a `tableView` is to think of it as a window that provides a view of a conveyor belt of cells. The number of cells that are visible through the window depends on the size of the window—indicated by the `tableView`'s `frame` property—and the height of each cell. The `frame` property is a `CGRect` with height and width values.

The overall length of the conveyor belt—or more properly, the height of the `tableView` in pixels—is available through the `contentSize` property, which returns a `CGFloat`.

At the top and bottom of each "belt" of cells, you can add a `UIView` as a static header and footer. These are set through the `tableHeaderView` and `tableFooterView` properties, respectively. Figure 2–7 illustrates a `tableView`'s dimensions.

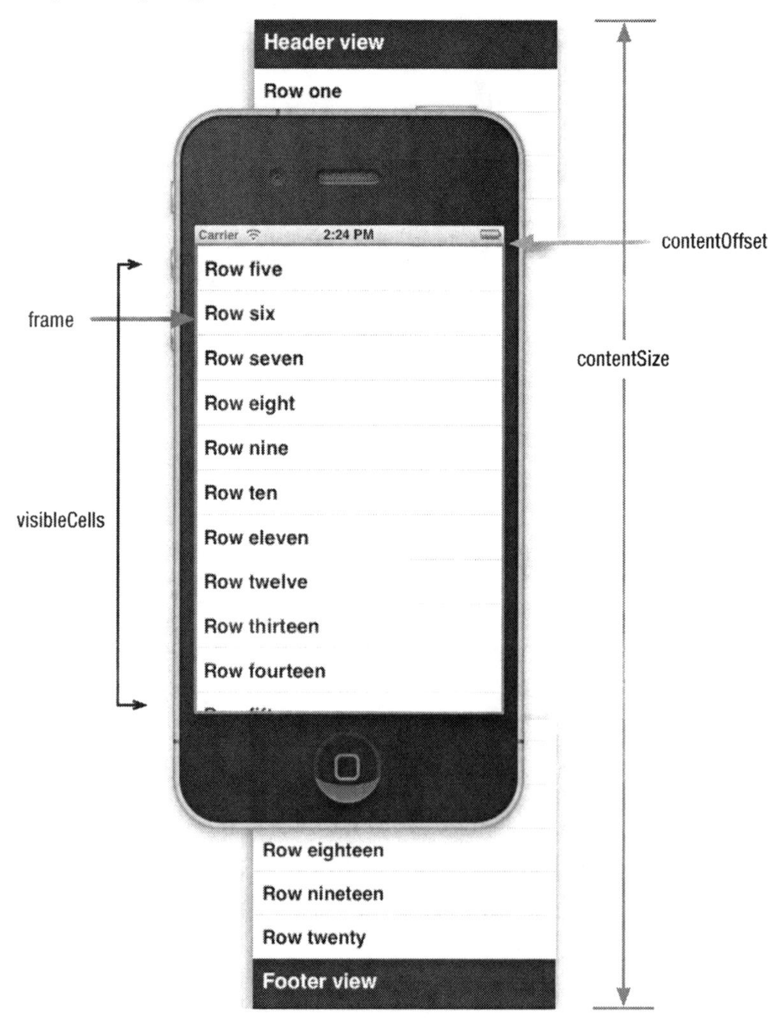

Figure 2–7. *The dimensions of a `tableView`*

To create the white-on-blue header and footers shown in the preceding example, you'd use something along the lines of Listing 2–1.

Listing 2–1. *Adding a Custom Header and Footer to a* `UITableView`

```
    UIView *tableHeaderView = [[UIView alloc] ➥
initWithFrame:CGRectMake(0, 0, 320, 50)];
    [tableHeaderView setBackgroundColor:[UIColor blueColor]];

    UIView *tableFooterView = [[UIView alloc] ➥
initWithFrame:CGRectMake(0, 0, 320, 50)];
    [tableFooterView setBackgroundColor:[UIColor blueColor]];

    UILabel *headerLabel = [[UILabel alloc] ➥
initWithFrame:CGRectMake(10, 10, 320, 25)];
    headerLabel.text = @"Header view";
    headerLabel.textColor = [UIColor whiteColor];
    headerLabel.font = [UIFont boldSystemFontOfSize:22];
    headerLabel.backgroundColor = [UIColor clearColor];

    UILabel *footerLabel = [[UILabel alloc] ➥
initWithFrame:CGRectMake(10, 10, 320, 25)];
    footerLabel.text = @"Footer view";
    footerLabel.textColor = [UIColor whiteColor];
    footerLabel.font = [UIFont boldSystemFontOfSize:22];
    footerLabel.backgroundColor = [UIColor clearColor];

    [tableHeaderView addSubview:headerLabel];
    [tableFooterView addSubview:footerLabel];

    [self.tableView setTableHeaderView:tableHeaderView];
    [self.tableView setTableFooterView:tableFooterView];
```

The cells that are visible at any given moment can be accessed en masse through the `tableView`'s `visibleCells` property. This is an `NSArray` and is updated as the table scrolls up and down.

Controlling the Background of a UITableView

Setting an image as the background of a `UITableView` is possible, albeit slight convoluted. There are four steps:

1. Set the `backgroundColor` property of your `tableView` to `clearColor`, so that the background image is visible.

   ```
   [myTableView setBackgroundColor:[UIColor clearColor]];
   ```

2. Create an instance of a `UIImageView` and set its `image` property to the image that you want to appear behind the table.

   ```
   UIImageView *tableBackgroundView = [[UIImageView alloc] ➥
   initWithImage:[UIImage imageNamed:@"myImage"]];
   ```

3. Set the UIImageView's frame property so that it's the same size as that of the tableView:

```
[tableBackgroundView setFrame: myTableView.frame];
```

4. Update the tableView's backgroundImage property to point to your new UIImageView object:

```
[myTableView setBackgroundView:tableBackgroundView];
```

What UITableView Inherits from UIScrollView

What does UITableView get from UIScrollView? The short answer to this is, "Everything that UITableView doesn't explicitly override.".This provides some useful UIScrollView and UIScrollViewDelegate methods and properties that are particularly relevant to the UITableView class.

contentSize indicates the full height that the table would be if all rows were created and populated at once. (In fact, unless the table is small, this very rarely happens because of UITableView's caching and queuing mechanism.) contentSize is calculated by adding the total height of all the rows, plus the header and footer views.

contentOffset indicates how far down the table has been scrolled from the top of the tableView's frame. For example, if the tableView's contentSize.height value is 1,000 pixels, and the table is scrolled halfway down, the contentOffset would be 500 pixels.

Two UIScrollViewDelegate methods are particularly useful if you want to know when your user is scrolling the table around. scrollViewWillBeginDragging is fired just before the tableView starts moving, and scrollViewDidScroll is called after the movement has stopped. This is where you could get the new contentOffset value and update anything that needed to change as a result.

NOTE: Although UITableView is a subclass of UIScrollView, table views can only scroll vertically.

Creating UITableViews

Any discussion of how to go about creating UITableViews has to come with a caveat: on their own, UITableViews don't really do very much. In order to become populated with data and interact with your user, they need the support of a class that implements the UITableViewDelegate and UITableViewDatasource protocols.

Having said that, in order to get a UITableView onto the screen, you need to be able to draw it. You have two options here: create it visually in a NIB file by using Interface Builder, or create it programmatically in code.

Creating a UITableView in Interface Builder

Creating a `UITableView` in Interface Builder is a massively challenging process:

1. Open your NIB file in Interface Builder.
2. Drag a `UITableView` from the Objects browser onto your view, as shown in Figure 2–8.

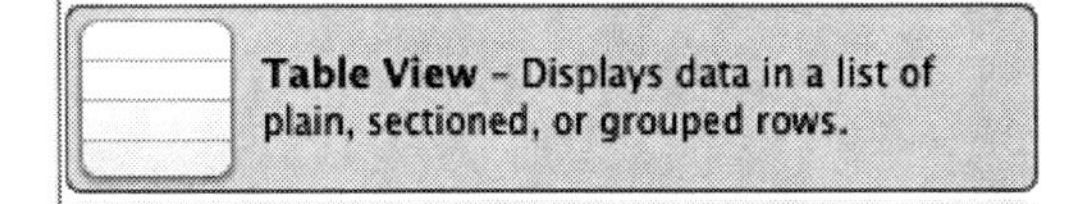

Figure 2–8. *The `UITableView` item in the Objects browser*

Okay, I lied. It's actually pretty straightforward. But there are a couple of details to take care of, so the process is worth stepping through.

Placing a UITableView into Another View

Although you'll often see table views full-screen, you're not restricted to that option. You can make your table views any size you want. This is pretty simple: drag the `UITableView` object onto the view in which it's going to appear, and adjust the size (see Figure 2–9).

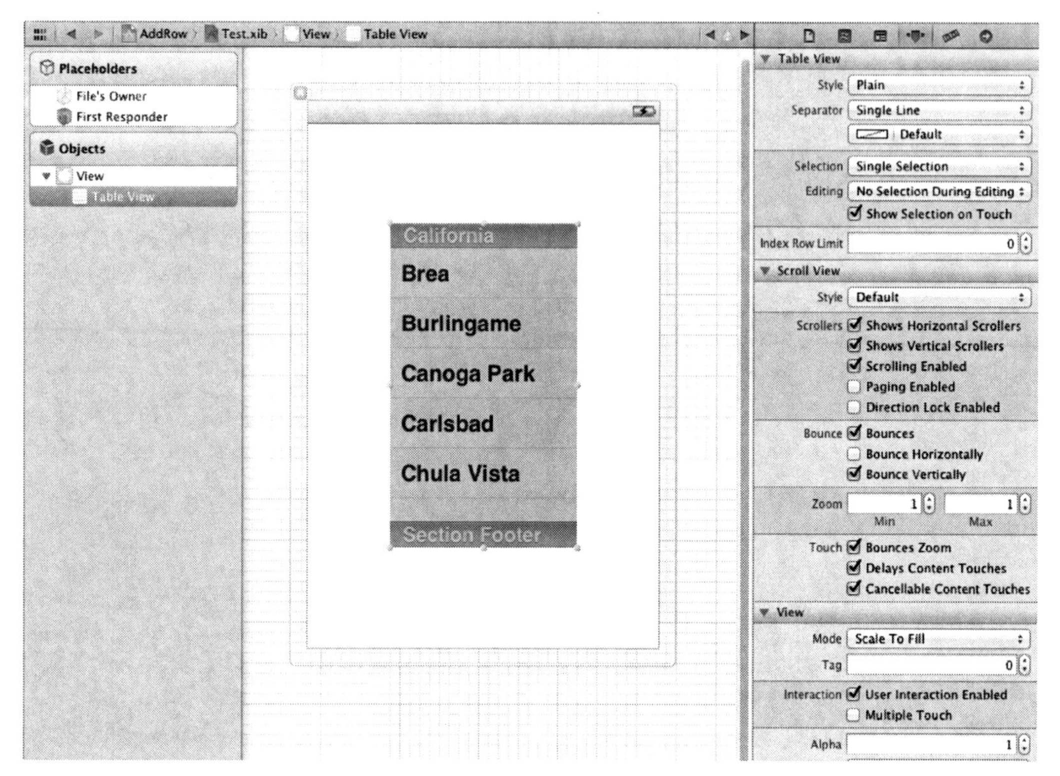

Figure 2–9. *Placing a `UITableView` into another view*

Placing a Full-Screen UITableView

If, on the other hand, your `tableView` will always be shown full-screen, there's not really much point in creating it as a child of another view that will never be shown.

The process in this scenario is slightly different:

1. Delete the existing view object from the NIB file.
2. Drag a `UITableView` object into the central area. The table view objects automatically expands to fill the full-screen view of 320 pixels by 480 pixels(see Figure 2–10).

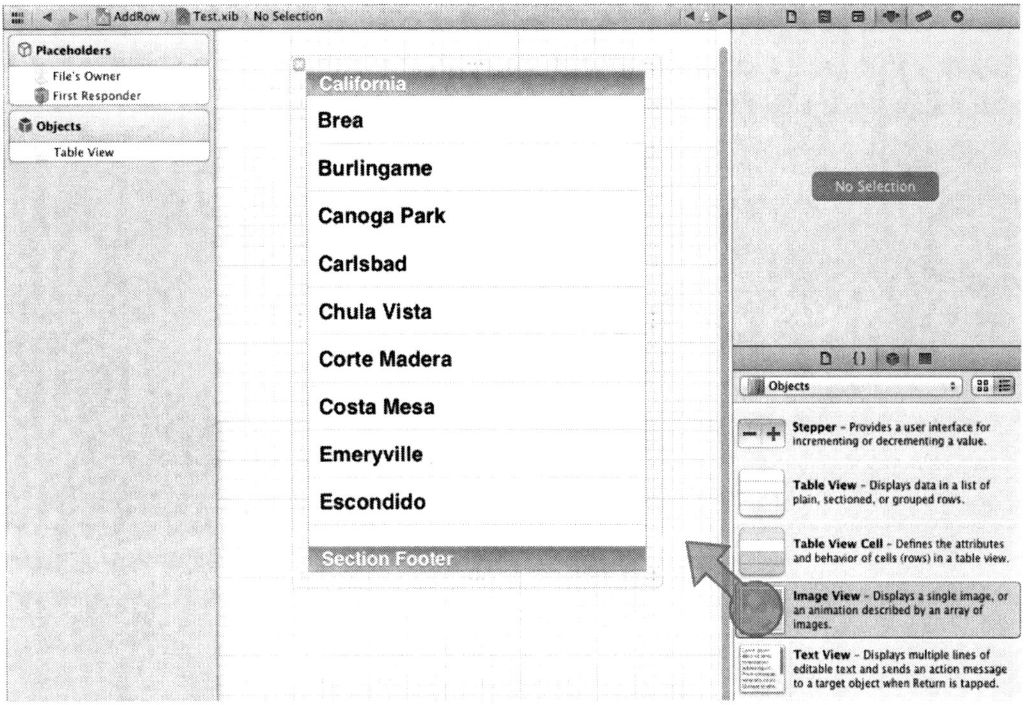

Figure 2–10. *Drag a `UITableView` object into the main area.*

3. Having removed the default view from the NIB file, you'll need to reconnect the File's Owner `view` outlet to the `tableView`. Ctrl-click the File's Owner icon in the Placeholders list and drag out to the `tableView`. Then release the mouse button, and select the View outlet from the pop-up list, as shown in Figure 2–11.

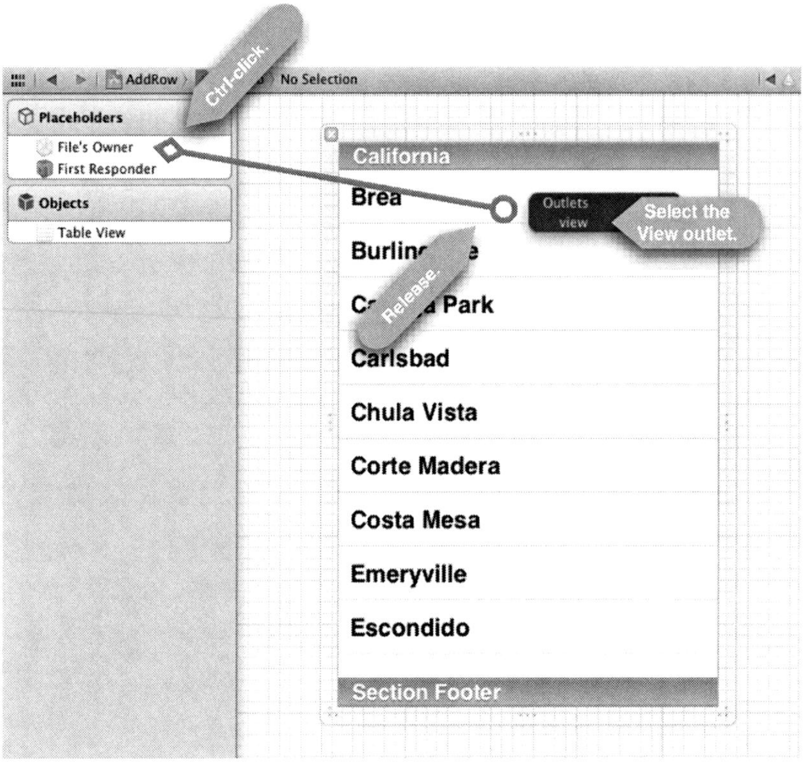

Figure 2–11. *Reconnecting the view outlet*

> **CAUTION:** It's easy to forget to reconnect the view outlet if you've deleted the object it was once connected to. If you don't reconnect, your app will crash with an error something along the lines of
>
> ```
> *** Terminating app due to uncaught exception 'NSInternalInconsistency
> Exception', reason: '-[UIViewController _loadViewFromNibNamed:bundle:]
> loaded the "PlainTable" nib but the view outlet was not set.'
> ```

4. After the `view` outlet is reconnected, you'll need to hook your new `tableView` up to its `dataSource` and `delegate`.

   The chances are that the class that will act as `dataSource` and `delegate` will also be the File's Owner. If that's the case, you can connect these by Ctrl-clicking and dragging from the table to the File's Owner icon and selecting `dataSource` and `delegate` from the pop-up options, shown in Figure 2–12.

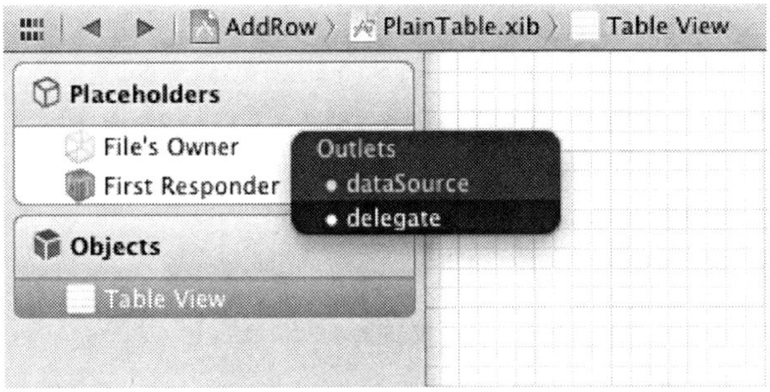

Figure 2–12. *Connecting the* `dataSource` *and* `delegate`

Creating a UITableView Programmatically

Following the maxim of *anything you can do in Interface Builder, you can also do in code*, the alternative way of creating a `UITableView` is to do so in code. It's a three-step process:

1. Create an instance of `UITableView` with a size and a style.
2. Set the new `tableView`'s `delegate` and `dataSource` properties.
3. Add the new `tableView` to the `superView`.

Listing 2–2 provides an example of how you could do this in a `UIViewController`'s `viewDidLoad` method.

Listing 2–2. *Adding a* `tableView` *Programmatically*

```
- (void)viewDidLoad
{
    [super viewDidLoad];
        // Do any additional setup after loading the view, typically from a nib.

    UITableView *tv = [[UITableView alloc] ➥
initWithFrame:self.view.frame style:UITableViewStylePlain];

    [tv setDelegate:self];
    [tv setDataSource:self];

    [self.view addSubview:tv];
    [tv reloadData];

}
```

> **CAUTION:** Having set the `delegate` and `dataSource` properties of your `tableView`, it will expect (nay, demand!) that the controller adopts the `UITableViewDelegate` and `UITableViewDataSource` protocols – in particular, that the `numberOfSectionsInTableView:`, `tableView:numberOfRowsInSection:` and `tableView:cellForRowAtIndexPath:` methods are implemented.
>
> If those protocols haven't been implemented correctly, the app will crash when the `tableView` is loaded, complaining that the `dataSource` hasn't returned a cell.

Creating a UITableView with UITableViewController

In order for a `tableView` to operate successfully, it needs a number of `UITableViewDelegate` and `UITableViewDataSource` methods to be implemented. Although Xcode's autocompletion helps with the typing, creating all the methods by hand will probably induce repetitive strain injury. Save your wrists, speed things up, and create a subclass of `UITableViewController` instead!

The process is delightfully simple. Instead of creating an instance of a vanilla `UIViewController`, drop down the subclass list and select `UITableViewController` instead, as shown in Figure 2–13.

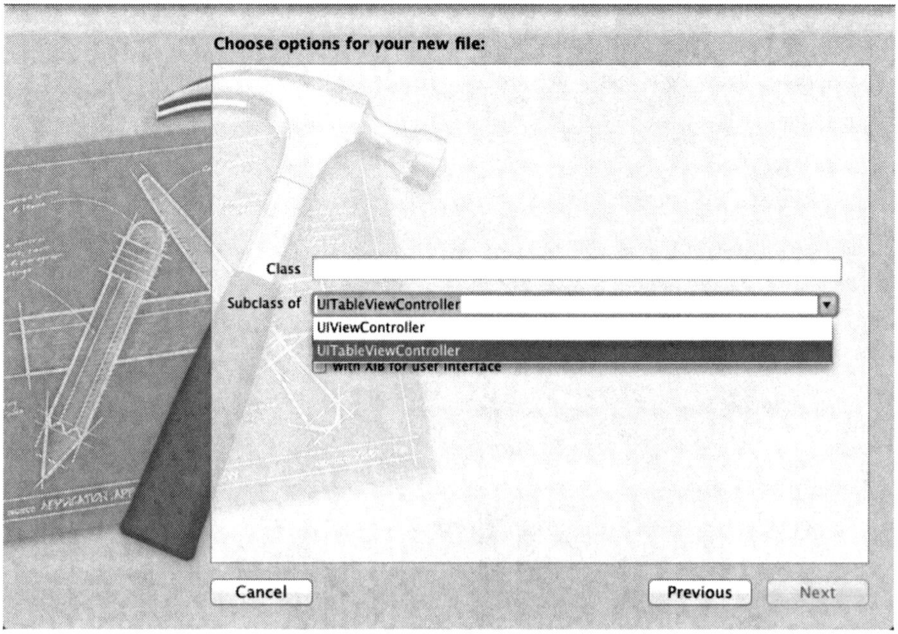

Figure 2–13. *Creating an instance of* `UITableViewController`

The new class files will be created as usual, but with some added extras. In addition to the usual `UIViewController` methods, you'll find some stubbed-out `UITableViewController` methods in the file (see Figure 2–14).

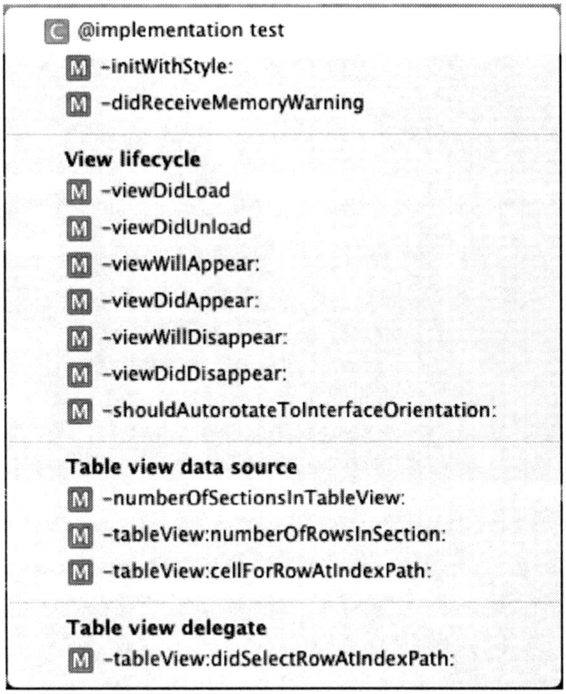

```
@implementation test
  -initWithStyle:
  -didReceiveMemoryWarning

View lifecycle
  -viewDidLoad
  -viewDidUnload
  -viewWillAppear:
  -viewDidAppear:
  -viewWillDisappear:
  -viewDidDisappear:
  -shouldAutorotateToInterfaceOrientation:

Table view data source
  -numberOfSectionsInTableView:
  -tableView:numberOfRowsInSection:
  -tableView:cellForRowAtIndexPath:

Table view delegate
  -tableView:didSelectRowAtIndexPath:
```

Figure 2–14. *The `UITableViewDataSource` and `delegate` methods*

This is the minimal subset of `UITableViewController`, `delegate`, and `dataSource` methods that you need to get going, and the class's header file declares it as conforming to the two protocols.

Xcode also provides a slew of other methods that are commented out:

```
-(BOOL)tableView:(UITableView *)tableView canMoveRowAtIndexPath:(NSIndexPath↩
 *)indexPath;

- (void)tableView:(UITableView *)tableView ↩
moveRowAtIndexPath:(NSIndexPath *)fromIndexPath toIndexPath:(NSIndexPath *)toIndexPath;

- (void)tableView:(UITableView *)tableView ↩
commitEditingStyle:(UITableViewCellEditingStyle)editingStyle ↩
forRowAtIndexPath:(NSIndexPath *)indexPath:

- (BOOL)tableView:(UITableView *)tableView ↩
canEditRowAtIndexPath:(NSIndexPath *)indexPath
```

None of these have to be implemented, but they're there as skeleton methods ready to be uncommented if you need them.

CAUTION: To remind you to complete the methods, Xcode includes compiler warnings in numberOfSectionsInTableView and tableView:numberOfRowsInSection. If you don't delete these, the compiler will moan at you when you build your project.

Summary

This short chapter introduced the anatomy and core components of the UITableView.

There are two basic styles of table view:

- Plain
- Grouped

Table views can also be split into sections, and provided with an index.

Although they can look different, the different types of table view have similar component parts and dimensions. They also inherit methods and properties from the UIScrollView parent class.

Like many of UIKit's components, it's possible to create UITableViews both visually—using Interface Builder—and programmatically. Anything that can be done with Interface Builder can also be done in code. Implementing the tableView's controller as a subclass of UITableViewController allows us to cut down on creating methods manually and use the templates that are provided.

In the next chapter, you'll learn how our newly created UITableView is fed with data, and how it works in conjunction with the UITableViewDelegate and UITableViewDataSource protocols.

Chapter 3

Feeding Data to Your Tables

When working with table views, it's important to bear in mind that on their own, they are able to do very little. Just as it takes a small army of ground staff (not to mention the flight crew!) to get an airliner off the tarmac and into the skies, so `tableViews` need the help and support of other objects in order to function properly.

One of the main parts of building `tableViews` is getting the objects to play nicely together, so this chapter covers the following:

- Where the table gets its data, and how you get it there
- An initial look at how the table handles interaction
- How the table keeps track of sections and cells
- An overview of the architecture patterns that the `UITableView` classes exploit

Some of this chapter's content might feel somewhat abstract and theoretical—but sticking with it is worthwhile. Developing your expertise with iOS (and `tableViews` especially!) often requires dealing with situations where you find yourself thinking, "Where the heck did *that* come from?" Figuring out what *that* is, and *where* it came from is generally a case of understanding the design patterns that iOS uses—some of which are covered in this chapter.

UITableView and Delegation

On its own, the `UITableView` is a pretty puny creature. Although it handles the display and scrolling of cells itself, it relies on external support for pretty much everything else.

That's not a weakness, though. By passing off the `UITableView`'s responsibility for other functions to external objects, you end up with code that's much more modular, robust, and easier to debug. The process of passing off that responsibility is known as *delegation*.

Understanding Delegation

Delegation is an application design pattern in which one object sends messages to a second object. Figure 3–1 illustrates this pattern, which can occur in a couple of scenarios:

- The first object is notifying the second that some event is about to occur, is occurring, or has occurred.
- The first object is asking the second object for input.

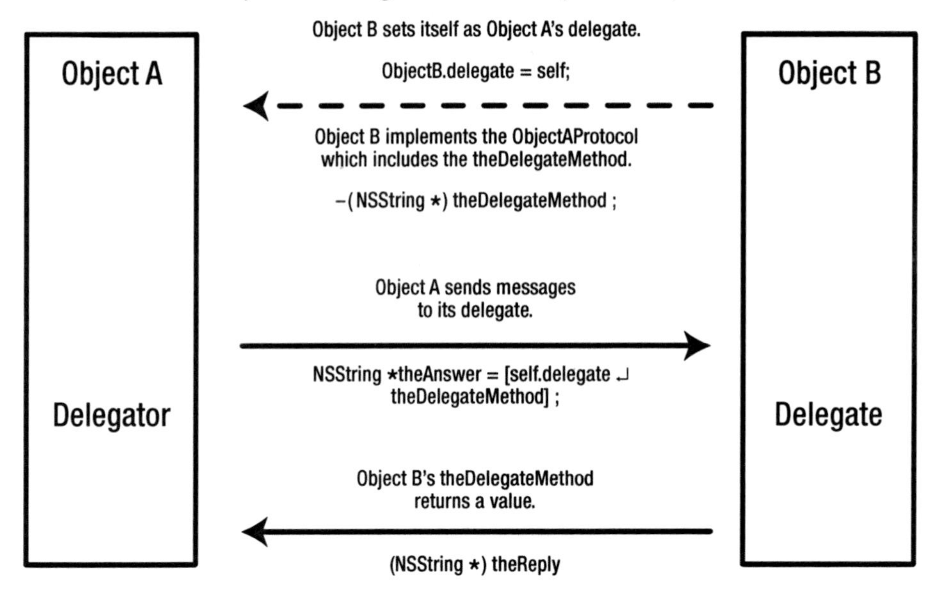

Figure 3–1. *The delegation pattern*

Those are pretty dry descriptions, so let's look at a couple of examples.

tableView:didSelectRowAtIndexPath

When a row in a table is selected, the `tableView` sends the `tableView:didSelectRowAtIndexPath` message to its `delegate` with two parameters: the `tableView`, and the `indexPath` of the selected row. The `delegate` can then respond to the selection event, either by doing something to the `tableView` or by triggering some external action.

For example, tapping a cell often causes a detail view to be loaded, so the `tableView:didSelectRowAtIndexPath` method would look similar to Listing 3–1.

Listing 3–1. *An Example* `tableView:didSelectRowAtIndexPath` *Method*

```
- (void)tableView:(UITableView *)tableView didSelectRowAtIndexPath: ➥
(NSIndexPath *)indexPath {

    DetailViewController *detailViewController = [[DetailViewController alloc] ➥
initWithNibName:@"DetailView" bundle:nil];

    [self.navigationController pushViewController:detailViewController animated:YES];

}
```

tableView:cellForRowAtIndexPath

You've met the `tableView:cellForRowAtIndexPath` method several times before. When the `tableView` is ready to display a cell, it asks its `dataSource` to return a `UITableViewCell` for the specified `indexPath` so that the cell can then be displayed inside the table itself.

The `dataSource` object will implement the `tableView:cellForRowAtIndexPath` method, as shown in Listing 3–2.

Listing 3–2. *A* `tableView:cellForRowAtIndexPath` *Method*

```
- (UITableViewCell *)tableView:(UITableView *)tableView ➥
cellForRowAtIndexPath:(NSIndexPath *)indexPath {

    static NSString *cellIdentifier = @"cellIdentifier";

    UITableViewCell *cell = [tableView ➥
dequeueReusableCellWithIdentifier:cellIdentifier];

    if (cell == nil) {
        cell = [[[UITableViewCell alloc] initWithStyle:UITableViewCellStyleDefault ➥
reuseIdentifier:cellIdentifier] autorelease];
    }

    // cell properties will be configured here

    return cell;
}
```

The point of all this is that by separating out the functionality, you can split view concerns from model concerns and use a controller to coordinate the two.

Setting Delegates

Objects and delegates don't just get together magically—there needs to be an explicit connection. Objects that have delegates have a `delegate` property, which can be set in code. Alternatively, you can use Interface Builder to do the same thing visually.

In the case of `UITableViews`, you can also set both `delegate` and `dataSource` by using Interface Builder. You Ctrl-click the `tableView` and then drag the connection to the File's Owner icon (see Figure 3–2).

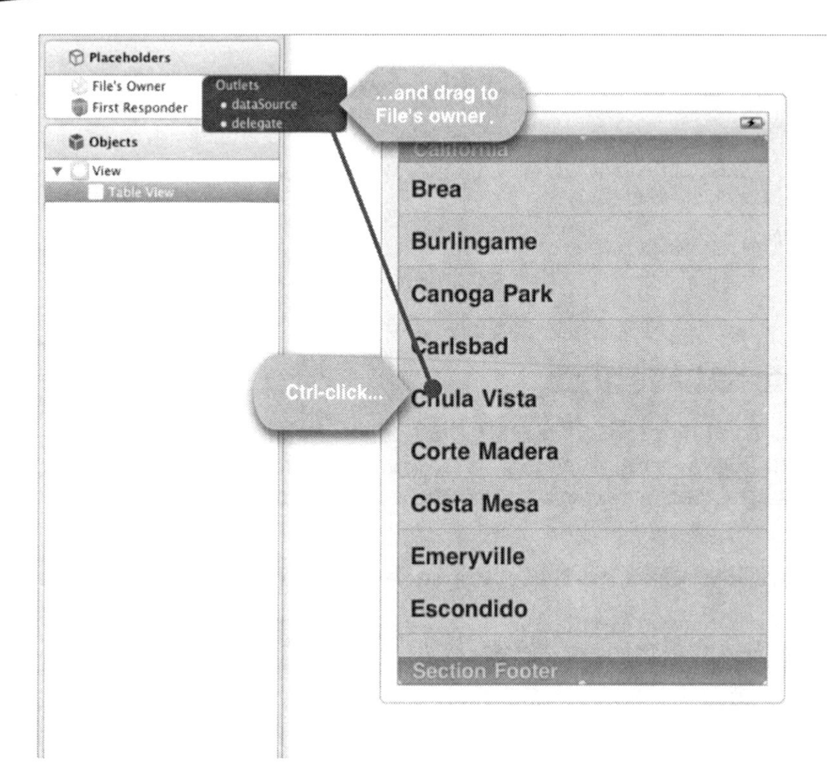

Figure 3–2. *Connecting `UITableView` `dataSource` and `delegate` properties in Interface Builder*

It's common for a `tableView`'s controller class to also be the `dataSource` and the `delegate`, although there's no reason why that has to be the case. If you have a number of table views being supplied by the same data source, for example, it might make more sense to create a stand-alone object to act as the data source for some or all of them.

The same can also be true of delegates. Admittedly, it's relatively unusual in the case of table views, but elsewhere in the iOS SDK, delegates are frequently external objects.

Getting an object and its delegate to play nicely together can feel a bit intricate at first, so it's worth taking a quick look at how this is done.

Wiring Up an Object with a Delegate

Think back for a moment to our two example objects (see Figure 3–3).

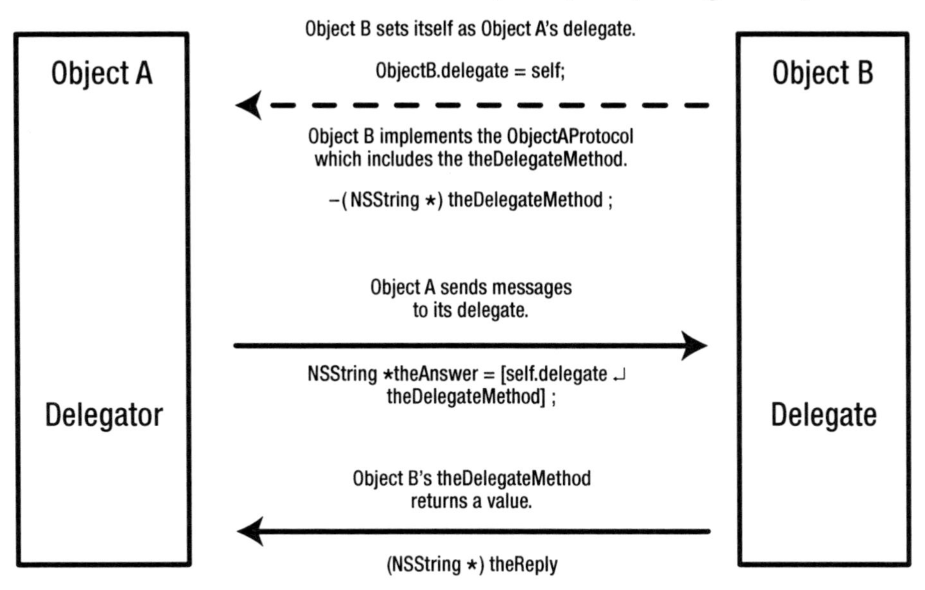

Figure 3–3. *The delegate pattern, again*

In order for `objectB` to act as `objectA`'s `delegate`, you need some way of connecting the two. This requires setting the `delegate` property of `objectA` to point to the instance of its delegate class, in this case `objectB`.

If `objectA` exposes a property called `delegate`, as shown here:

```
@property (nonatomic, weak) id delegate;
```

Then the object that's going to act as the delegate can set itself as `objectA`'s `delegate`:

```
objectA.delegate = self;
```

There's a subtlety here that's important to be aware of. Although `objectA` is the object with the `delegate` property, it's `objectB` that sets itself as `objectA`'s delegate.

This leads to an interesting memory management–related side effect, which you'll need to bear in mind. Although `objectB` has been set as `objectA`'s `delegate`, `objectA` will be unaware if `objectB` goes out of existence. `objectA` will continue to send messages to what it *thinks* is its `delegate`. As long as that delegate object exists, obviously that's not a problem. However, if the `delegate` object disappears, `objectA` will send messages to a nonexistent object, and the program will crash.

To prevent this, it's important to make sure that `objectB` will set `objectA`'s `delegate` property to `nil` anytime there's a risk of `objectB` disappearing. (It was `objectB` that set itself as `objectA`'s delegate, remember, so the onus is on `objectB` to clean up after itself, so to speak.) The best place to do this is within objectB's dealloc method, because this is the last thing called before the object winks out of existence:

```
-(void)dealloc {
    // objectB's dealloc method

    objectA.delegate = nil;
    [super dealloc];
}
```

Although sending a message to nil won't actually do anything—the message is simply discarded—at least it won't cause your program to fall over completely.

You hopefully have noticed that the delegate property looks a little different from the way that you've been setting up properties to this point:

```
@property (nonatomic, weak) id delegate
```

Specifically, it's a weak property of type id.

The type is id because objectA doesn't have any way of knowing what type of object might eventually become its delegate. In fact, nor does it care—so long as the object conforms to the objectA delegate protocol, it doesn't actually matter. (Protocols are covered in the following section.) id is a generic type, so any object type will do.

The property is weak (as opposed to strong) because objects *must not* retain their delegates. If they do, you run the risk of causing a retain loop. objectB will retain objectA as long as it's acting as objectA's delegate, and will release objectA when it sets objectA's delegate property to nil when it's deallocated. But if objectA retains objectB, objectB won't go out of existence because its retain count will never reach zero.

Defining Protocols

Methods are defined in protocols so that objects and their delegates know the methods that each is expected to implement and respond to. A *protocol* is simply a list of methods—sometimes required, and sometimes optional—that an object promises to implement.

If a protocol method is required, the object adopting the protocol must implement it. Otherwise, the compiler will complain, and the project won't build. Optional methods are, well, optional, so the compiler won't moan if they are missing.

Protocols are defined either in a stand-alone protocol header file, or in a class's header file. In both situations, they're defined as a list of methods, demarked by the @protocol compiler directive. The list is split into @required and @optional sections.

Listing 3–3 shows the UITableViewDataSource protocol methods defined in UITableView.h (I've removed the comments to save space).

Listing 3–3. *The* `UITableViewDataSource` ***Protocol***

```
@protocol UITableViewDataSource<NSObject>

@required

- (NSInteger)tableView:(UITableView *)tableView ➥
numberOfRowsInSection:(NSInteger)section;

- (UITableViewCell *)tableView:(UITableView *)tableView ➥
cellForRowAtIndexPath:(NSIndexPath *)indexPath;

@optional

- (NSInteger)numberOfSectionsInTableView:(UITableView *)tableView;

- (NSString *)tableView:(UITableView *)tableView ➥
titleForHeaderInSection:(NSInteger)section;
- (NSString *)tableView:(UITableView *)tableView ➥
titleForFooterInSection:(NSInteger)section;

- (BOOL)tableView:(UITableView *)tableView canEditRowAtIndexPath:(NSIndexPath ➥
*)indexPath;

- (BOOL)tableView:(UITableView *)tableView canMoveRowAtIndexPath:(NSIndexPath ➥
*)indexPath;

- (NSArray *)sectionIndexTitlesForTableView:(UITableView *)tableView;

- (NSInteger)tableView:(UITableView *)tableView sectionForSectionIndexTitle:(NSString ➥
*)title atIndex:(NSInteger)index

- (void)tableView:(UITableView *)tableView ➥
commitEditingStyle:(UITableViewCellEditingStyle)editingStyle ➥
forRowAtIndexPath:(NSIndexPath *)indexPath;

- (void)tableView:(UITableView *)tableView moveRowAtIndexPath:(NSIndexPath ➥
*)sourceIndexPath toIndexPath:(NSIndexPath *)destinationIndexPath;

@end
```

This tells us that although the `UITableViewDataSourceProtocol` defines a myriad of methods, only two of them have to be implemented in order for the table to function. The rest are optional.

> **NOTE:** Strictly speaking, in order to work, a `tableView` needs to know the number of sections it has. You'll notice that the `UITableViewDataSource` protocol lists `numberOfSectionsInTableView` as an optional method, which seems a little counterintuitive. A `tableView` gets around this by assuming that unless the `dataSource` says otherwise, the table view has just the one section.

ACCESSING PROTOCOL DEFINITIONS IN XCODE

When you implement a protocol method in your classes, that method needs to be implemented exactly as it's defined in the protocol. That can lead to a lot of typing, so it's a lot easier (and safer) to copy the method name directly from the protocol itself. You'll end up spending a *lot* of time checking protocol documentation, so here's a quick way of accessing it:

If you hold down the Option key and hover the mouse cursor over the protocol name in an Xcode window, the cursor changes to a "Mickey hand," and the name becomes a hyperlink. Clicking that link pops up a summary window

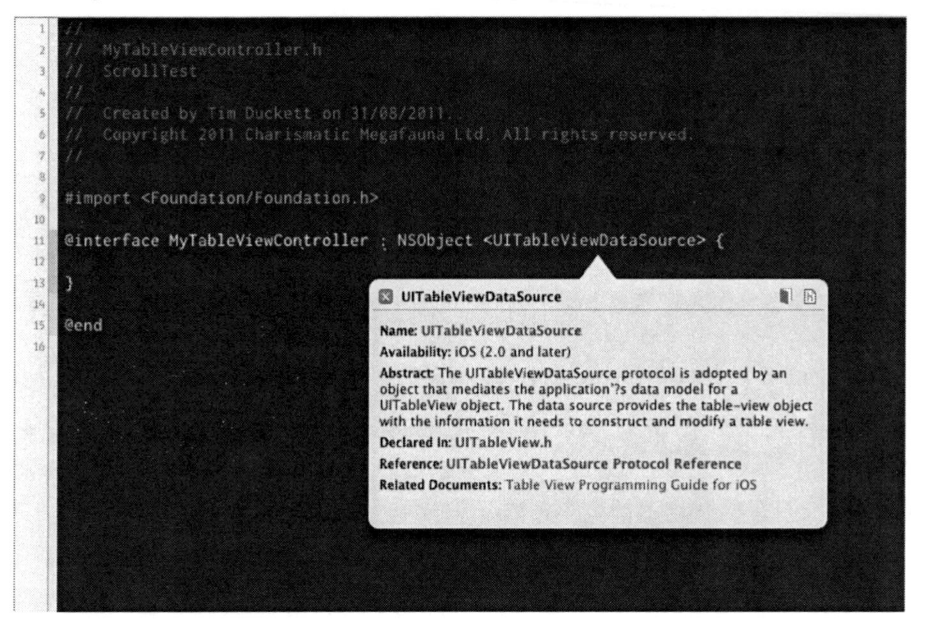

Clicking any of the highlighted terms opens either the help file in the Xcode Organizer, or the relevant code file itself.

Using UITableView's Delegate Methods

`UITableView` uses the delegate pattern to obtain data from its `dataSource` and to handle user interaction and table configuration (see Figure 3–4). Despite the name, a `tableView`'s `dataSource` is a form of a delegate—just one with specific responsibilities.

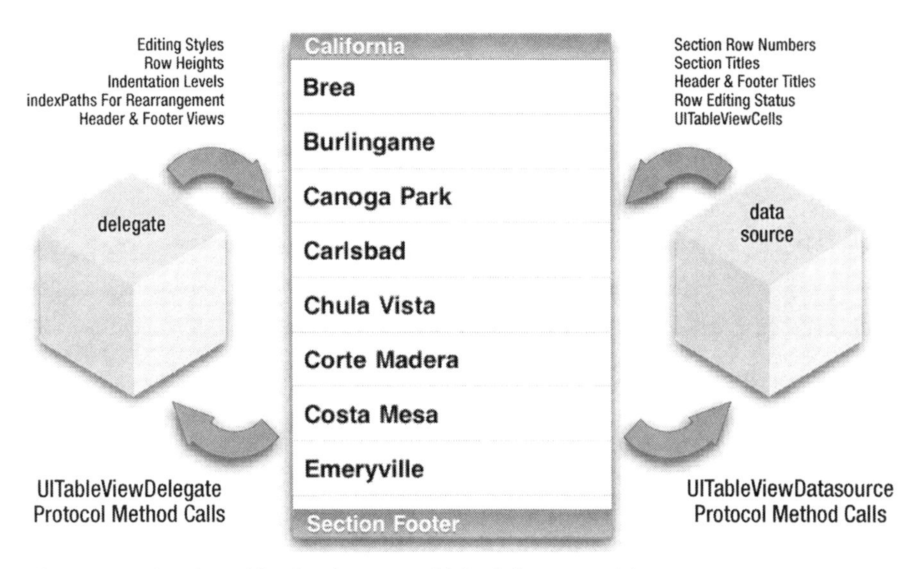

Figure 3–4. *How the `tableView` interacts with its `delegate` and `dataSource`*

Using UITableViewDelegate Methods

The `UITableViewDelegate` handles the following:

- Configuring the `tableView`'s rows
- Configuring the header and footer of sections
- Managing selection of rows
- Editing rows
- Managing accessory views
- Reordering rows

Table 3–1 shows the methods available in the `UITableViewDelegate` protocol.

Table 3–1. *UITableViewDelegate protocol methods*

Method	Purpose	Returns
tableView:willBeginEditingRowAtIndexPath	Fires when the cell is about to go into editing mode.	None
tableView:didEndEditingRowAtIndexPath	Fires when the table leaves editing mode.	None
tableView:editingStyleForRowAtIndexPath	Returns the editing style that should be used (none, insert, or delete).	UITableViewCellEditingStyle
tableView:willSelectRowAtIndexPath	Fired as the cell is selected with a touchUpInside event. didSelectRowAtIndexPath is called immediately after this method.	NSIndexPath
tableView:didSelectRowAtIndexPath	Fires when the user selects the cell at the provided indexPath by tapping it. This is a commonly implemented method that is often used to trigger the appearance of another view controller, or to toggle a check mark in the cell.	None
tableView:willDeselectRowAtIndexPath	Fires just before a row is deselected. (This fires only if a cell has already been selected.)	NSIndexPath
tableView:didDeselectRowAtIndexPath	Fires when the row is deselected (either programmatically or because another row has been selected). Often used to change the visual state of the cell after it's been deselected (for example, removing a highlight color).	None
tableView:accessoryButtonTappedForRowWithIndexPath	Fires when the user taps the accessory button that's displayed in a row. Will typically trigger some sort of response—for example, displaying a new viewController.	None
tableView:heightForHeaderInSection	Returns the height (as a CGFloat value) for the header of the provided section.	CGFloat
tableView:heightForFooterInSection	Similar to the heightForHeader method, this returns the header height as a CGFloat.	CGFloat

Method	Purpose	Returns
tableView:view ForHeaderInSection	Provides a UIView for use as the section's header. This and the corresponding footer method allow the headers and footers of sections to be customized.	UIView
tableView:view ForFooterInSection	The footer counterpart of the viewForHeaderInSection method.	UIView
tableView:indentationLevelFor RowAtIndexPath	Returns the level of indentation required for the row at that index path.	NSInteger
tableView:shouldIndent WhileEditingRowAtIndexPath	Determines whether the cell's background view should be indented while the cell is in editing mode (to make space for the editing control).	BOOL
tableView:targetIndexPath ForMoveFromRowAtIndexPath: toProposedIndexPath	Returns the indexPath indicating where a row is to be relocated, during cell reordering.	NSIndexPath
tableView:titleFor DeleteConfirmationButton ForRowAtIndexPath	Allows the title of the Delete button to be customized with a different label. (For example, 'Remove' or 'Revoke' etc)	NSString
tableView:willDisplayCell: forRowAtIndexPath	Fired just before the cell is drawn, which provides an opportunity to override any properties that have been set by the tableView (for example, background color or selection state). After this method has been fired, you're limited to setting the cell's frame and alpha properties.	None

Data Sources

Data sources have a pretty straightforward role in life: they provide data and information about data, and handle manipulation of data.

The Key Information Required By a UITableView

A UITableView needs three key pieces of information in order to successfully draw itself and its cells:

- The number of sections in the table
- The number of rows in the section
- The cells that belong in the rows within the sections.

The dataSource exists to provide this information.

Getting the Number of Sections in the Table

A simple table has only one section, so table views will assume this is 1 unless the numberOfSectionsInTableView method is implemented and returns something different.

Although numberOfSectionsInTableView is an optional method, I tend to always implement it so that it's there. Because this is the first method that gets called, you can also speed things up by returning 0 if the dataset for your table is empty—after which the tableView assumes that it's not going to get any additional data, and stops asking.

Getting the Number of Rows in the Section

Assuming that there's data to display, the numberOfRowsInSection method is called. The tableView calling the method supplies the section number as an integer, and the method returns the number of rows (also as an integer).

Getting Cells That Belong in This Row of This Section

Creating cells to be displayed is at the heart of setting up the tableView. This is where your code will need to return an instance of a UITableViewCell for the tableView to display, each time the tableView:cellForRowAtIndexPath: method is called..

The tableView will provide the section and row numbers as an indexPath, and it's up to your cellForRowAtIndexPath method to retrieve the data from the model, create the cell, and return it as quickly as possible.

How the Key Information Is Obtained by the Table

The conversation between the four objects involved – the view controller that contains the tableView, the tableView itself, and the delegate and dataSource objects belonging to the tableView – takes place in a specific order. This is illustrated in Figure 3–5.

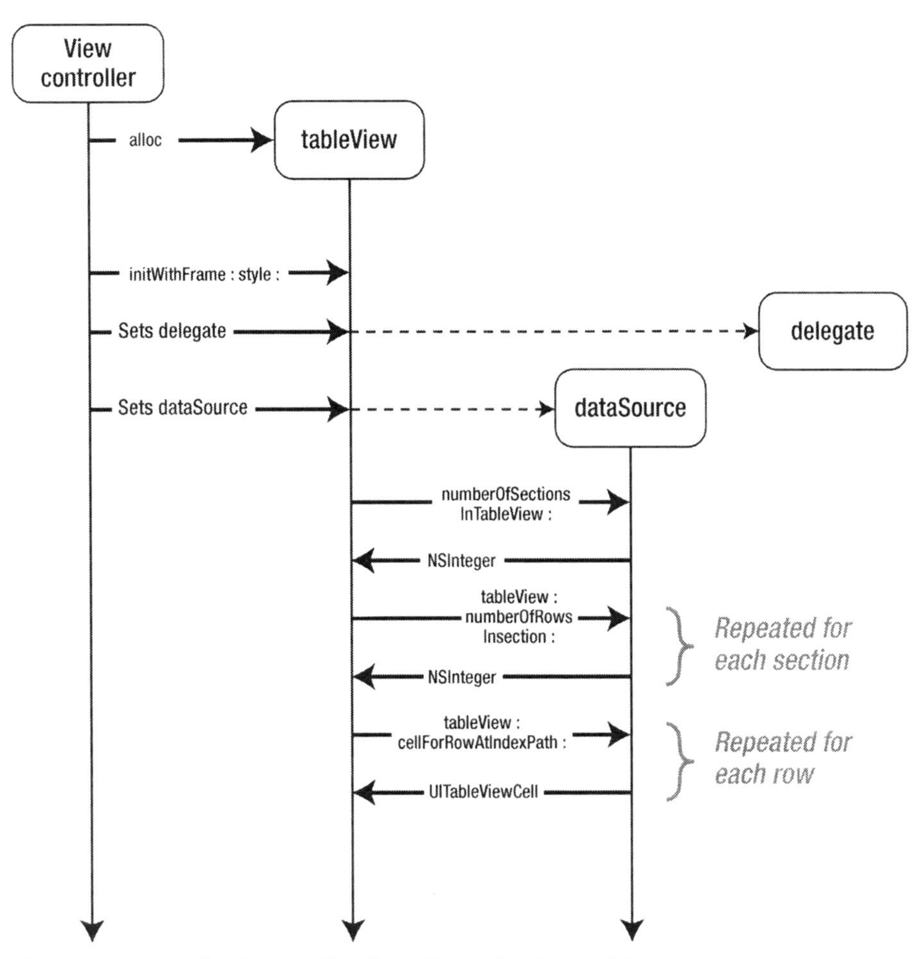

Figure 3–5. *Messaging Between View Controller,* `tableView`*, and* `datasource`

1. First, the view controller allocates and instantiates the `tableView`, and then sets the `delegate` and `dataSource` properties.
2. Once in existence, the `tableView` asks the `dataSource` for the number of sections for itself, and the `dataSource` replies with an `NSInteger` value.
3. Then the `tableView` provides a reference to itself and a section number in an `indexPath` instance, and asks the `dataSource` for the number of rows in that section. Again, the `dataSource` replies with an `NSInteger`.
4. Finally, the `tableView` provides a reference to itself and the row number in an `indexPath` object, and asks the `dataSource` to supply the cell for that row. The `dataSource` replies with an instance of a `UITableViewCell`.

After your dataSource can provide these three pieces of information, your tableView is in business. These three methods, and the other eight dataSource methods, are defined in the UITableViewDataSource protocol.

Cell, Section, and Row-Related UITableViewDataSource Methods

Three main methods, listed in Table 3–2, are concerned with providing exactly those three pieces of information. Two of the methods are required.

Table 3–2. *Cell, Section And Row Methods Of The UITableViewDataSource Protocol*

Method	Purpose	Returns	Required?
numberOfSectionsInTableView	Returns the number of sections in the table view	NSInteger	No
tableView:numberOfRowsInSection	Returns the number of rows in the given section	NSInteger	Yes
tableView:cellForRowAtIndexPath	Returns a UITableViewCell for the row provided	UITableViewCell	Yes

Although the tableView needs to know the number of sections required, the default value is 1, which is why you'll often see numberOfSectionsInTableView omitted for simple tables.

Title and Index-Related UITableViewDataSource Methods

There are four methods that create and manage the table's titles and indexes. Table 3–3 lists these methods.

Table 3–3. *UITableViewDataSource Protocol Title And Section Methods*

Method	Purpose	Returns
tableView:titleForHeaderInSection	Returns the header title for the given section	NSString
tableView:titleForFooterInSection	Returns the footer title for the given section	NSString
sectionIndexTitlesForTableView	Returns an array of titles for the index list that appears down the right-hand side of an indexed table (for example, A, B, C, D, and so on)	NSArray
tableView:sectionForSectionIndexTitle:atIndex	Returns the index number of the section with the given title and section title index	NSInteger

Insertion, Removal, and Reordering-Related UITableViewDataSource Methods

The remaining UITableViewDataSource protocol methods handle inserting, deleting, and reordering rows within the tableView. Table 3–4 lists these methods.

Table 3–4. *Insertion, Removal and Reordering-related UITableViewDataSource methods*

Method	Purpose	Returns
tableView:canEditRowAtIndexPath	Returns a Boolean value that depends on whether the given row is flagged as being editable. If this method isn't implemented, the tableView assumes that *all* rows can be edited.	BOOL
tableView:canMoveRowAtIndexPath	Returns a Boolean value that depends on whether the given row is flagged as being able to move within the table.	BOOL
tableView:moveRowAtIndexPath: toIndexPath	Instructs the dataSource to move a row from one location to another. This method would also need to update the underlying data model if the change is to persist.	void
tableView:commitEditingStyle: forRowAtIndexPath	Instructs the dataSource to commit the insertion or deletion of a row by calling the insertRowsAtIndexPath:withRowAnimation or deleteRowsAtIndexPath:withRowAnimation tableView methods.	void

The Thing to Bear in Mind About dataSource Methods

Although table views look simple enough on the surface, there's a lot going on underneath. Key to a good user experience is scrolling that is smooth and instantaneous. One of the main complaints you'll hear about iPad rivals, for instance, is that their scrolling stutters and is jerky.

In order for the table view to scroll smoothly, your dataSource must be prepared to provide data *as soon as it's asked for*. Delays in returning data mean delays in drawing the cells—and that means jerks and stutters in the user interface.

Making the data available immediately can have various forms—caching data queries being an obvious one. And needless to say, retrieving live tableView data from a network source is a *spectacularly* bad idea.

If your data isn't available immediately, it'll probably be necessary to provide placeholder information and go back to update missing values later, when the data becomes available.

UITableView has three sets of methods that can be used for this – reloadData reloads the whole table, while reloadRowsAtIndexPath updates specific rows. reloadSectionIndexTitles and reloadSections:withRowAnimation: update the specified sections.

All About indexPaths

Table views describe their layouts in terms of instances of the NSIndexPath class. Technically, these are representations of paths to nodes within a collection of nested arrays.

However, that's an extremely complicated description of what NSIndexPath objects are in the context of tableViews, so I'd stick to thinking of them in much more simple terms. As far as a tableView is concerned, an indexPath has two properties: a section and a row, shown in Figure 3–6. Both of these are instances of NSUIntegers.

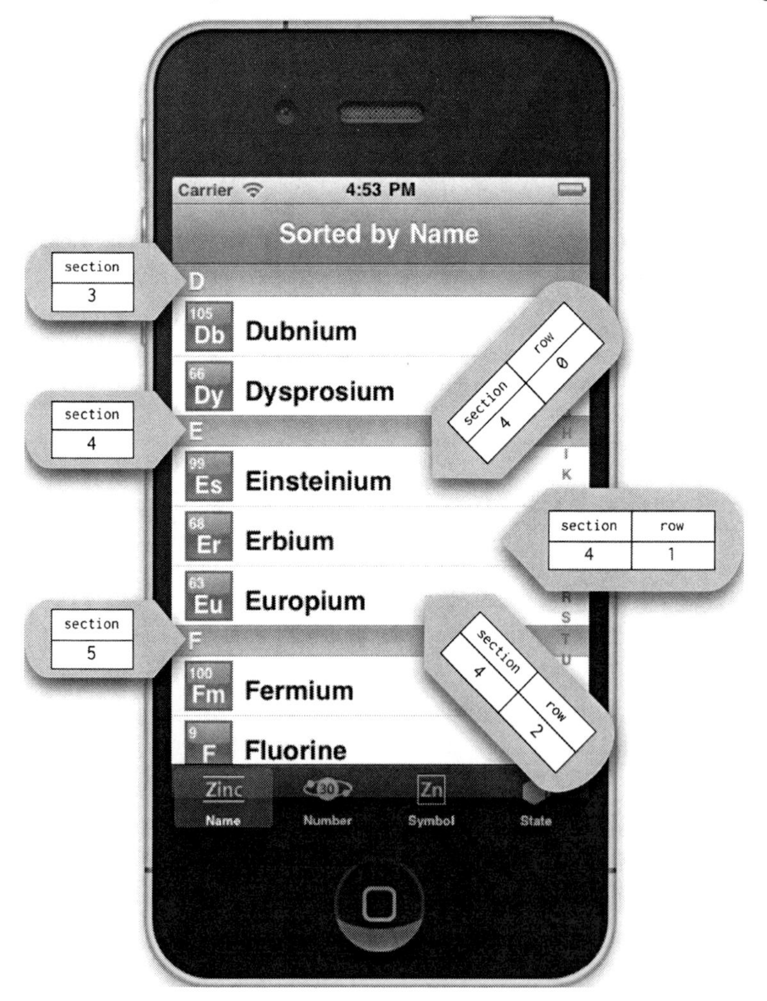

Figure 3–6. *indexPath sections and rows*

As you can see, the table uses indexPaths to identify sections and rows. The iPhone Simulator is running Apple's The Elements sample code, and it's scrolled down to the elements beginning with the letter *D*.

The elements are grouped in sections according to their first letter. Because D is the fourth letter of the alphabet, the elements beginning with D appear in section 3 (remember, indexPath numbering, as with NSArrays and so on, starts at 0).

There happen to be three elements beginning with the letter *E* (including the fantastically named *einsteinium*—atomic weight 252, discovered in 1952—the app has all the details). These are placed in rows 0, 1, and 2 (again, indexPath rows start at 0). This allows each row to be uniquely identified in the table. In the case of einsteinium, it's found in the indexPath with section == 3 and row == 0.

Creating indexPaths is somewhat fiddly, so the UITableView class extends NSIndexPath with a category that provides some convenience methods for creating indexPaths with sections and rows. One of these is indexPathForRow:inSection. Here's a (somewhat contrived) example of the kind of thing you could do to locate a specific cell:

```
-(void)findEinsteiumCellContents {

    NSIndexPath *einsteinIndexPath = [NSIndexPath indexPathForRow:1 inSection:3];

    UITableViewCell *einsteinCell = [theTableView ↵
cellForRowAtIndexPath:einsteinIndexPath];

    NSString *elementName = einsteinCell.textLabel.text;

    NSLog(@"The element name is %@", elementName);
}
```

The Model-View-Controller Design Pattern

To the untutored eye, an iOS application opened in Xcode looks like a mess of code. With a bit of familiarity, though, it's possible to discern that different aspects of the application have different functions.

At the front end, the user interface presents information to, and receives input from, the user. We typically think of a "user" as being a human, but the analogy still works if the user is in fact another system—as would be the case if the interface were an API.

Behind the scenes, virtually all applications contain data of some form or another. Sometimes that data is sourced externally—for example, the HTML that a web browser displays. Other times, the data is maintained internally to the application. Storing application state such as high scores is an example.

Sitting between the two, you need some logic—the application logic—to get and present data to the user interface, and to receive and process input from the user. You also need logic to manage the internal state of the application.

That "division of labor" has been formalized into an application architecture pattern called the *model-view-controller* pattern, illustrated in Figure 3–7. It divides the application into three areas:

- *Views*: In iOS terms, these are the views (or interfaces) that are created in Interface Builder, or programmatically within the code.
- *Controllers*: These provide the application's internal logic. These tend to be easier to spot in iOS apps, because they often have names such as `ScoreTableViewController`.
- *Models*: These manage the data within the application. A model can be as simple as an `NSArray` containing some `NSStrings`, or could be a full-blown Core Data setup.

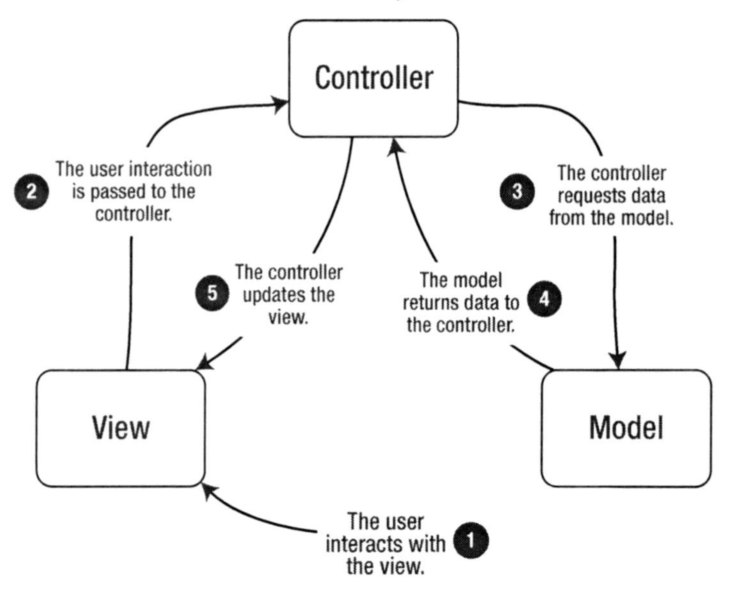

Figure 3–7. *The model-view-controller pattern*

Crudely speaking, the controllers fetch and process data from the models that gets passed to the views for consumption by the user. The user interacts with the views, and the results of those interactions are handled by the controllers.

Various analogies have been rolled out to illustrate the model-view-controller pattern, but the one that works best for me is the process that goes into making a movie.

Before you can go watch a movie, someone needs to write it. So the process starts with a screenwriter pouring out his soul over a typewriter and creating a script. That's the model: it's the source of the data that will later be used to create the cinematic experience.

In order to bring the script to life, you need actors. (Okay, the analogy breaks down slightly if you're thinking about the latest Pixar blockbuster, but animated characters still need voices, right?) They're the views, responsible for presenting the data of the script to the audience (via the medium of the camera, of course).

The person who sits between the writer and the actors—the controller in our programming analogy—is the director. The director is responsible for interpreting the script and telling the actors how to go about presenting it.

There's room for analogic subtlety here, as well. Good actors will take the director's direction along with the script's dialogue and add their own interpretation that takes the performance from something resembling a tree to one that will win them an Oscar.

That's where our interfaces come in. Consider the graceful gradients and subtle shading of the iOS interface, versus the, well, less-graceful and less-subtle interfaces of certain mobile devices that weren't designed in Cupertino...

Why Use the Model-View-Controller Pattern?

At first, the MVC pattern might seem like an unnecessary complication, especially for small applications. But thinking about—and building—applications in this way brings some benefits:

- *Modularity*: Each functional element of the application manages its own area of concern. The models deal with reading and writing of data, while the views handle presenting the information. This means that changes to one functional element don't necessarily affect others. You could completely change the underlying database engine, for example, and the views would remain the same..
- *Multiple views*: Consider the differences in the user interface between the iPhone and the iPad. If your application's logic was embedded in the views, you'd need to create it twice—once for the smaller screen of the iPhone, and again for the bigger screen of the iPad. By sticking with the MVC pattern, the same set of models and controllers can feed *both* versions of the interface.
- *Efficiencies*: Separating out the layers of the application allows for tricks such as threading and background processing. You can kick off a data-retrieval process while the views are still loading, for example, to take advantage of the iOS device's multitasking capabilities.

MVC and iOS

iOS is a model-view-controller-centric framework, although compared to many SDKs—particularly web frameworks—the MVC nature of iOS is sometimes a bit hidden. This will be especially the case if you've come to iOS from web frameworks such as Rails, Django, or Symfony. These make the separation of each layer very obvious. Each one has a set of files in separate directories called `models`, `views`, and `controllers`.

iOS, on the other hand, is more subtle. You can create views with XIB files, which are clearly views. But you can also create views programmatically with code inside view controllers, and that's where things start to get potentially confusing. Similarly, a `tableView's` data comes from a model, but that model could be as "extracted" as a SQLite database managed by Core Data, or as "embedded" as an `NSArray` created in the `viewDidLoad` method inside a view controller!

The key to staying sane with MVC in the iOS world is to remember that MVC is a conceptual framework, rather than something more absolute, such as a set of directories. If you bear in mind that the table's data comes from a model, and that model is actually the `NSArray` I mentioned, you'll still be thinking (and working) in an MVC way.

MVC and tableViews

The obvious question is now, "How does MVC fit with `UITableViews?`"

Fortunately, the answer is relatively straightforward. The table itself is the view. It presents the user interface and intercepts user interaction such as taps and scrolling flicks.

The data that the table presents comes from the model. As I mentioned, that could be as simple as a single `NSArray` that you create as you load the view, or something a lot more complex involving Core Data or information retrieved from an external network source.

The controller elements are the object(s) that act as the `tableView's delegate` and `dataSource`. The delegate receives messages from the `tableView` and deals with events such as a user tapping or swiping a cell. The `dataSource` "feeds" the table its data by retrieving it from the model.

Summary

This chapter has covered a lot of fairly heavy conceptual stuff, but all of the concepts tie back into `UITableViews` in some way. The data that is displayed by the `tableView` is provided by the `dataSource`, while the user's interaction with the `tableView` is handled by the `delegate`. Both of these are examples of the delegation design pattern, while the division of labor between the `tableView`, its controllers, and the underlying data is the model-view-controller architecture pattern in action.

Both the `dataSource` and `delegate` functions are defined by their respective protocols, `UITableViewDataSource` and `UITableViewDelegate`. Building a `tableView` is a process of implementing (at least) the required methods, and often some of the optional ones as well.

Armed with an understanding of where the table data comes from, and how the table handles interactions, you're ready to dive into the details and start the process of customization.

Chapter 4

How the Cell Fits Together

In this chapter, you're going to take a detailed look at cells and how they work. In order to be able to customize them, it's important to understand the anatomy of cells, and how they're created and reused.

You'll see the following:

- The internal structure of a cell
- The standard cell types that come for free with `UITableView`
- The configuration of default cell content
- The use of accessory views
- The creation and reuse of cells

This covers everything you need to know in order to create default-styled cells and perform basic configuration of them. Configuring cells is often a case of knowing when to intervene in the creation and reuse process. Later in Chapters 8 and 9, you'll build on this when you create customized cells.

Understanding the Anatomy of a UITableViewCell

The first thing to bear in mind about `UITableViewCells` is that they are `UIView` objects. The `UITableViewCell` class inherits from `UIView`, which means that most of the features of `UIViews` are available to you in `UITableViewCells`. Figure 4–1 shows the class hierarchy of `UITableViewCell`.

Because `UIView` inherits in turn from `UIResponder`, this also means that it's possible to interact with cells by using gestures. I'll show you some of the effects that this enables in Chapter 10.

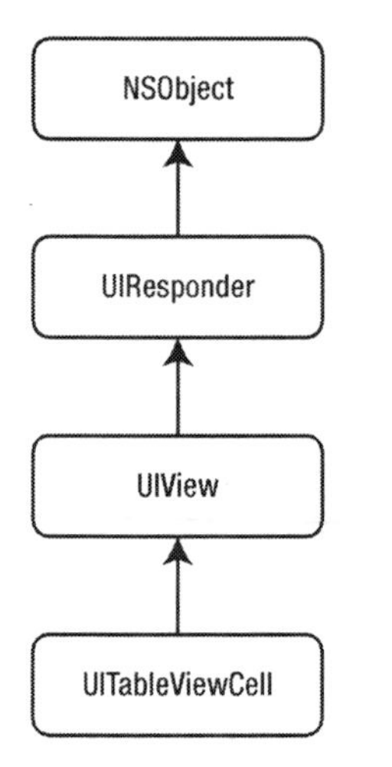

Figure 4–1. *The class hierarchy of* `UITableViewCell`

Basic Structure of the Cell

The vanilla cell has four component parts, shown in Figure 4–2:

- A *frame* and *bounds*, which describe the cell's location and size
- The *cell content*
- An optional *accessory view*
- An automatically placed *editing control*, which appears when the cell is in editing mode

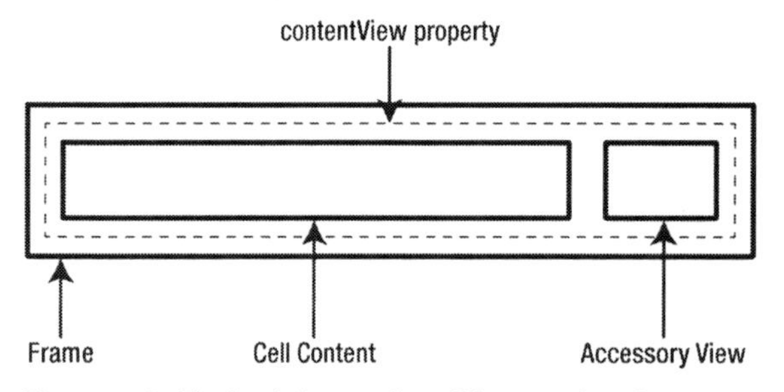

Figure 4–2. *The basic layout of a cell in normal mode*

The content of the cell can be accessed en masse through the `contentView` property, which is a `UIView`. You can add and remove subviews, and the `contentView` will take care of moving things around to allow the editing control to fit.

When switched to editing mode, the cell's `contentView` is reduced in width by about 40 points, and an editing control is inserted at the left side, as shown in Figure 4–3.

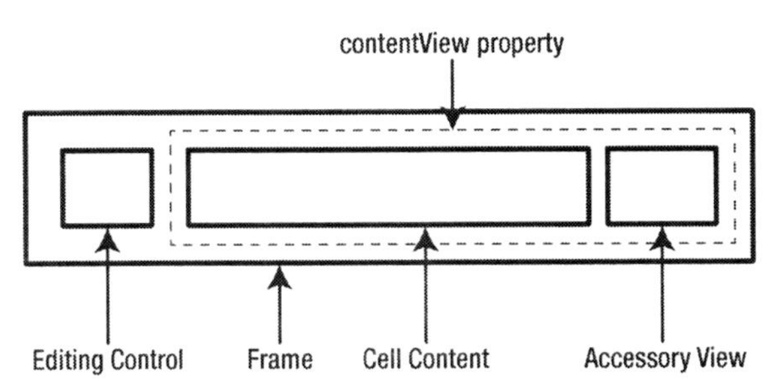

Figure 4–3. *The basic layout of a cell in editing mode*

The editing control can be either a green insertion control or a red deletion control.

> **NOTE:** When designing custom cells that will be edited, it's important to make sure that the layout of the content view can cope with being automatically resized. Chapter 8 covers this topic.

Content and Accessory Views

Content and accessory views are instances of `UIView`, which means that they have all the properties and methods of a "normal" `UIView`. You'll be exploiting these properties and methods when you go on to create customized cells.

Working with Standard Cell Types

`UITableViews` come with four standard cell types, and for many applications these may be all you need. The four styles have constant names, which unfortunately aren't particularly descriptive:

- `UITableViewCellStyleDefault`
- `UITableViewCellStyleValue1`
- `UITableViewCellStyleValue2`
- `UITableViewCellStyleSubtitle`

This section details the four types and then shows you how to select the one you want.

Using UITableViewCellStyleDefault

As the name suggests, `UITableViewCellStyleDefault` is the default cell style for a standard, out-of-the-box `UITableView`. It provides three areas (shown in Figure 4–4):

- A `UIImageView` called `imageView` at the left end of the cell. This is optional; if an image view isn't present in the cell, the cell content will align to the left.

- A `UILabel` called `textLabel`, which holds the cell content.
- An optional `UIView` called `accessoryView` that can show one of the standard accessory view indicators, a custom image by adding a `UIImageView` as a `subView`, or a control such as a UIButton.

As with all the other standard cell styles, the `textLabel` can be formatted by changing the `UILabel` properties such as font, text alignment and color, and so on. Although the layout of the default cells may be fixed, this formatting does enable you to apply some degree of customization.

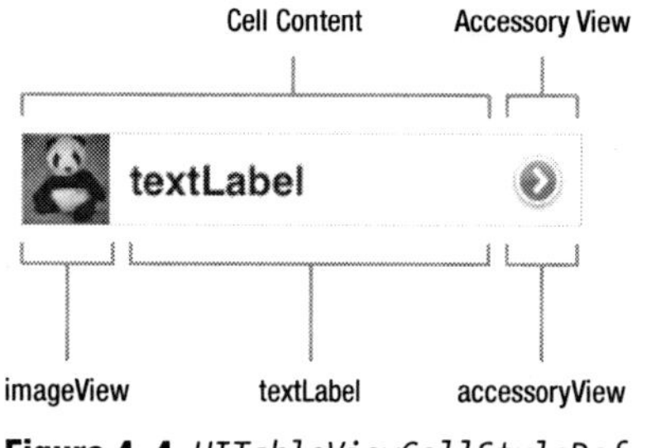

Figure 4–4. *UITableViewCellStyleDefault*

The content of the textLabel is accessed through its `text` property:

```
cell.textLabel.text = @"textLabel";
```

Similarly, the image is set by accessing the `imageView`'s `image` property:

```
cell.imageView.image = [UIImage imageNamed:@"panda"];
```

Using UITableViewCellStyleValue1

The `Value1` cell style is similar to the `Default` type, but includes an extra, optional `UILabel` called `detailTextLabel` and an optional `imageView`. Figure 4–5 shows an example.

Figure 4–5. *UITableViewCellStyleValue1*

The textLabels will attempt to handle restricted space but won't always result in the desired effect, as shown in Figure 4–6. If the automatic results aren't acceptable, this might be a cue for you to think about implementing a custom cell style.

Figure 4–6. *Truncation of cell content*

Using UITableViewCellStyleValue2

The Value2 cell style is virtually identical to the Value1 style, with the exception that the default weight of the textLabel and detailTextLabel are altered, and there's no imageView. Figure 4–7 shows an example.

textLabel detailTextLabel

Figure 4–7. *UITableViewCellStyleValue2*

Other than in the built-in Contacts app, I can't ever recall seeing an example of UITableViewCellStyleValue2 in the wild—but it's there if you need it.

Using UITableViewCellStyleSubtitle

The fourth default type is another variation of the other three. It combines textLabel and detailTextLabel with an optional imageView. Figure 4–8 shows this default cell with an image, and Figure 4–9 shows it without an image.

textLabel
detailTextLabel

Figure 4–8. *UITableViewCellStyleSubtitle with an image*

textLabel
detailTextLabel

Figure 4–9. *UITableViewCellStyleSubtitle without an image*

Selecting a Default Style

The four standard cell types are associated with a UITableViewCellStyle enum constant, which are defined in the UITableViewCell class's header file:

```
typedef enum {
  UITableViewCellStyleDefault,
  UITableViewCellStyleValue1,
  UITableViewCellStyleValue2,
  UITableViewCellStyleSubtitle
  UITableViewCellStyle;
}
```

You can set the cell style when the tableView's dataSource creates a new cell with the cellForRowWithIndexPath method (as shown in Listing 4–1).

Listing 4–1. *The cellForRowWithIndexPath Method*

```
  - (UITableViewCell *)tableView:(UITableView *)tableView ➥
cellForRowAtIndexPath:(NSIndexPath *)indexPath {

  static NSString *cellIdentifier = @"Cell";
```

```
  UITableViewCell *cell = [tableView ➥
dequeueReusableCellWithIdentifier:cellIdentifier];

  if (cell == nil) {
    cell = [[UITableViewCell alloc] initWithStyle:UITableViewCellStyleDefault➥
reuseIdentifier:CellIdentifier];
  }

  // cell is configured here
  return cell;
}
```

The key part is UITableViewCell's initWithStyle method, which instantiates a new cell instance with one of the four standard styles:

```
  cell = [[UITableViewCell alloc] initWithStyle:UITableViewCellStyleDefault➥
reuseIdentifier:CellIdentifier];

  cell = [[UITableViewCell alloc] initWithStyle:UITableViewCellStyleValue1➥
reuseIdentifier:CellIdentifier];

  cell = [[UITableViewCell alloc] initWithStyle:UITableViewCellStyleValue2➥
reuseIdentifier:CellIdentifier];

  cell = [[UITableViewCell alloc] initWithStyle:UITableViewCellStyleSubtitle➥
reuseIdentifier:CellIdentifier];
```

The new cell will be returned with the appropriate style, after which you can customize the various properties.

Configuring the Default Cell's Content

A UITableViewCell of one of the four default types has a whole range of properties that you can access to configure the content. This section presents four key properties—textLabel, detailTextLabel, imageView, and contentView—and then shows an example of using them.

textLabel

The textLabel property is a UILabel, with text that can be changed – this is generally used as the cell's "main title":

```
cell.textLabel.text = @"The main cell text";
```

detailTextLabel

detailTextLabel is also a UILabel, with text that can be changed – this can act as a "subtitle" for the cell:

```
cell.detailTextLabel.text = @"The cell subtitle";
```

imageView

The cell's `imageView` is a `UIImageView` – it has an `image` property that can be passed a `UIImage`, which is then displayed in the cell:

```
cell.imageView.image = [UIImage imageNamed:@"avatar.png"];
```

contentView

The cell's `contentView` is a `UIView` to which subviews can be added:

```
[cell.contentView addSubview:theView];
```

You'll look at `contentView` in much more detail in Chapter 8.

A common mistake is to try to access these properties directly:

```
cell.textLabel = @"Some text";    // This won't work!
```

In order to ensure that the table is as responsive as possible, it's a good idea to make sure that any images are scaled before adding them to the cell. If cells need to rescale images before displaying them, jerky scrolling of the table can result.

Formatting Text in Default Cell Types

Here's an example of setting these properties in practice:

```
cell.textLabel.textColor = [UIColor blueColor];
cell.detailTextLabel.font = [UIFont fontWithName:@"TimesNewRomanPSMT" size:12];
cell.detailTextLabel.textColor = [UIColor redColor];
```

This code results in the cell shown in Figure 4–10. I wouldn't necessarily advise using this frankly hideous combination of fonts and colors, but you get the idea.

Figure 4–10. *Example cell formatting*

Working with Accessory Views

`UITableViewCell` provides three types of accessory views (well, four if you count `None` as a type). Accessory views are displayed at the right-hand end of the cell. You can also add your own custom accessory view. These are `UIViews`, which either act as a hint to the user that touching the cell will result in some kind of action, or show some information about the cell state.

Tapping an accessory view causes the `tableView` to call the delegate's `accessoryButtonTappedForRowWithIndexPath` method. This allows you to trigger actions such as pushing in a new view controller.

As an alternative to using a default accessory views, you can provide a custom view of your own, or place a control such as a `UIButton` into a custom view.

Using UITableViewCellAccessoryDisclosureIndicator

The `DisclosureIndicator` acts as a hint that touching the cell will result in another table view being displayed, to drill down into a data hierarchy. Figure 4–11 shows how this appears:

Item 1 >

Figure 4–11. *UITableViewCellAccessoryDisclosureIndicator*

Using UITableViewCellAccessoryDetailDisclosureIndicator

The fact that `DetailDisclosureIndicator` looks like a button is a hint that touching the cell will result in the display of more data. The display might be another table view, but could be another view of a different type.

When it's tapped, a `DetailDisclosureIndicator` sends the `tableView:accessoryButtonTappedForRowWithIndexPath` message to the table's `dataSource`. Figure 4–12 shows this:

Item 1

Figure 4–12. *UITableViewCellAccessoryDetailDisclosureIndicator*

Using UITableViewCellAccessoryCheckmark

The check mark, shown in Figure 4–13, shows that the cell has been selected, either by the user tapping the row or by some data field behind the scenes. This provides a way of selecting and deselecting one or more items in a list. It's a very common user interface pattern for setting configuration items, for example.

Item 1 ✓

Figure 4–13. *UITableViewCellAccessoryCheckmark*

Using UITableViewCellAccessoryNone

As the name suggests, `UITableViewCellAccessoryNone` doesn't display any accessory view. Figure 4–14 shows an example. Setting this accessory type removes any previously set accessory. You might use this view because there's no further information below this level—or because the cell was previously selected and showed a `UITableViewCellAccessoryCheckmark`.

Item 1

Figure 4–14. *UITableViewCellAccessoryNone*

Setting the Accessory View Type

The cell's accessory view is set with the accessoryType property:

```
cell.accessoryType = UITableViewCellAccessoryTypeCheckmark;
```

Listing 4–2 presents a snippet of code that shows how you might toggle a check mark on and off, depending on the value of some data.

Listing 4–2. *Toggling a Cell's Accessory Type*

```
NSString *dataItem = [tableData objectAtIndex:indexPath.row];

if ( [dataItem isEqualToString:@"some string"] ) {

  cell.accessoryType = UITableViewCellAccessoryCheckmark;

} else {

  cell.accessoryType = UITableViewCellAccessoryNone;

}
```

Apple provides guidelines about which accessory type should be used for what purpose. Although I've never heard of an app being rejected from the App Store because disclosure indicators were used in a nonstandard way, doing so runs the risk of confusing your users. It's probably best to stick with the default behaviors unless there's a very good reason not to.

Using an Accessory View to Show Cell Selection State

Using the presence or absence of a cell accessory view is a perfectly valid way of showing whether a cell is selected. But there is a "gotcha" that can very easily get you if you're not careful.

Think back to the model-view-controller pattern for a moment. Cells are views, and the data that populates the cell exists in the model(s). When you switch a selection indicator on and off, you're doing that to the view—*not* the model.

Cells themselves don't have state. Remember, even in a tableView of 99,999 rows, only about 11 cells are created. If you want the selection state to persist the next time that data point is displayed, you *must* update the external data model and then set the selection indicator accordingly.

Similarly, if you set the accessory view state of a cell that is then recycled from the cache, it'll arrive back at the table in the same state as it had when the cell was dumped into the cache. That's why it's important to reset accessory views (and later, any controls or views that you've included in your custom cells) every time a row is updated.

Listing 4–3 presents a code snippet from one of my apps—a networked game called TeaWars—that demonstrates this in practice. The table displays a list of peer devices. In the next step, the user can select the ones they want to connect to. Tapping the row fires the `didSelectRowAtIndexPath` method, which adds that client ID to an `NSMutableArray` called `listOfPlayers`.

As the cells are popped and pushed in and out of the cache, the `cellForRowAtIndexPath` method checks whether the peer exists in the `listOfPlayers` array. If it does, it must have been selected, so the cell needs a `UITableViewCellAccessoryCheckmark`. (The `_sessionManager` object handles the network communication, so it's not really relevant to this example.)

Listing 4–3. *Toggling Cell Selection*

```
#pragma mark -
#pragma mark TableViewDelegate methods

- (UITableViewCell *)tableView:(UITableView *)tableView ➥
cellForRowAtIndexPath:(NSIndexPath *)indexPath {

    static NSString *cellIdentifier = @"cellIdentifier";

    UITableViewCell *cell = [tableView
dequeueReusableCellWithIdentifier:cellIdentifier];

    if (cell == nil) {
        cell = [[UITableViewCell alloc] initWithStyle:UITableViewCellStyleDefault➥
 reuseIdentifier:cellIdentifier];
        cell.accessoryType = UITableViewCellAccessoryNone;
    }

    // Retrieve the ID of the relevant connected client
    NSString *peerID = [_sessionManager.connectedClients ➥
objectAtIndex:indexPath.row];

    // Retrieve the displayName of the peer
    cell.textLabel.text = [_sessionManager.gkSession displayNameForPeer:peerID];

    // If this peerID is contained in the listOfPlayers, it's been selected
    // so show the checkmark in the cell
    if ( [listOfPlayers containsObject:peerID] ) {
        cell.accessoryType = UITableViewCellAccessoryCheckmark;
    } else {
        // The peer ID isn't in the list, so it's not selected
        cell.accessoryType = UITableViewCellAccessoryNone;
    }

    return cell;
}
```

Creating Custom Accessory Views

Because the cell's `accessoryView` is an instance of `UIView`, it's a pretty trivial task to assign your own custom `UIView` to the cell:

```
  cell.accessoryView = [[UIImageView alloc] ↩
initWithImage:[UIImage imageNamed:@"foo.png"]];
```

As with the cell's imageView, it's best to make sure any accessoryView image is sized and scaled correctly first. You're not just restricted to images, though – the accessoryView can be a useful place to insert controls such as UIButtons.

Creating and Reusing Cells

Having looked at the various default cell styles that are available, you're probably impatient to start creating custom cell styles of your own. Before you move on to that, though, it's a good idea to explore in more detail how cells are created and managed by the table view itself. Creating custom cells is often a process of knowing when to intervene in the "standard" processes—so knowing what those processes are will help you to figure out what's going on and why.

Memory Limitations

iOS devices pack a lot into small packages. But even though the iPhone and iPad have something like 256,000 times the memory of the Apollo Lunar Module's onboard computer, memory is still a constraint. The small form-factor of the devices means there's a limit to the amount of RAM that can be crammed into the casing. As an iOS developer, the memory footprint of your apps is something you need to remain aware of.

Apps with very small tables, like our SimpleTable app, don't pose much of a problem. We had only 10 rows. But if the app's data comes from a bigger source, you could have thousands—if not millions—of rows. Dealing with that data en masse could quickly overwhelm the limited memory that iOS devices have.

Speed and Smoothness

When the iPhone was first launched back in 2007, one thing that reviewers were consistently blown away by was the smoothness of the interface. Flick a table view, and it smoothly scrolls up and down—no stuttering, hesitation, or jerkiness. Interfaces that don't respond smoothly are *incredibly* obvious to the user (and jerky interface response is one of the main criticisms of iPhone and iPad rivals).

Making content move around smoothly onscreen isn't too big a challenge to today's powerful graphics processors. Making a table (or indeed, any scrolling interface) run smoothly mainly requires that data can be retrieved fast enough to be moved onto the screen, without the screen having to wait for it. Delays in fetching data manifest themselves as stuttering or hesitating scrolling views.

Just-in-Time Creation and Recycling

So, how does iOS deal with limited memory and a need for smoothness and speed? The solution to both problems is ingenious. `UITableViews` take advantage of an important fact: although a table might have thousands of cells, only a few are visible to the user at any one time.

First, `UITableViews` use a *just-in-time* approach to creating cells. A new cell is created just before it's required. Each cell is then ready to be displayed, but not so soon that the device memory becomes clogged with cells that aren't yet needed.

Second, after a cell is no longer visible, it's *dequeued* into a cache for reuse. Taking a preexisting cell and updating its content is both quicker and less memory-intensive than creating one afresh. Instead of creating a brand new cell, the `tableView` will dequeue and recycle an existing cell, updating its content just before it's displayed onscreen.

The Table View's "Conveyor Belt"

All this can seem a little abstract, so a visual analogy can help. You can think of the `tableView` as something like a conveyor belt inside a box – the user can move the belt backwards and forwards with a control button. A small section of the belt is visible through a window in the top of the box.

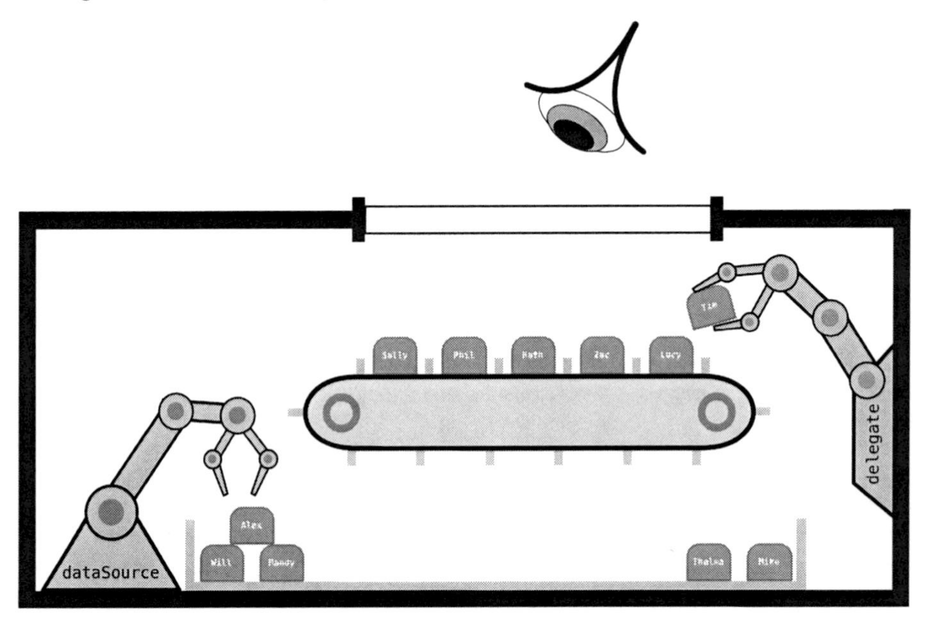

Figure 4–15. *The cell production process*

The conveyor belt has slots into which different types of cells can be placed. As the cells reach either end of the conveyor belt, they fall into a tray underneath.

Inside the box, and next to the conveyor stand two robot arms. One, called `delegate`, has the job of placing cells into the slots. Just before the user winds the belt to move an empty slot underneath the window, `delegate` tells a second robot arm called `dataSource`—the type of cell that is needed to fill that slot. `dataSource` reaches into the tray and sees whether it can retrieve a discarded cell. If there aren't any discarded cells in the tray, `dataSource` quickly builds a new one.

After it has a cell—either new or recycled—`dataSource` quickly scribbles the `textLabel` onto the cell and hands it to `delegate`. `delegate` puts the cell onto the belt, and it appears beneath the window just in time as the user cranks the handle.

How the "Conveyor Belt" Process Is Built in Code

Fortunately for those of us building and configuring table views, a lot of this conveyor-belt action takes place behind the scenes. The heavy lifting is done by the `cellForRowAtIndexPath` method.

If you've created a new `UITableViewController` subclass by using the built-in template, the subclass is virtually ready to use out of the box. Listing 4–4 provides the template version with some comments I've added so that it relates to our conveyor-belt analogy.

Listing 4–4. *The "Conveyor Belt" Code*

```
// the tableView asks the dataSource robot to create and return
// a cell to fit into the indexPath.row slot

- (UITableViewCell *)tableView:(UITableView *)tableView ↵
cellForRowAtIndexPath:(NSIndexPath *)indexPath
{
    static NSString *CellIdentifier = @"theIdentifier";

    // the dataSource robot reaches into the tray
    // and tries to find an old cell with the right cell identifier

    UITableViewCell *cell = [tableView ↵
dequeueReusableCellWithIdentifier:CellIdentifier];

    if (cell == nil) {

        // there wasn't an old cell in the tray, so the dataSource robot has
        // to create a new cell from scratch

        cell = [[UITableViewCell alloc] ↵
        initWithStyle:UITableViewCellStyleDefault reuseIdentifier:CellIdentifier];
    }

    // The dataSource robot now sets up the cell
    // Configures the cell...

    // and hands it over to the tableView robot
    return cell;
}
```

Identifying Cells with the cellIdentifier

It's important to bear in mind that tables can display numerous types of cells in the same `tableView`. Later you'll exploit this to create highly customized tables. The `tableView`, therefore, needs some way of identifying each type, which is the job of the `cellIdentifier`.

The `CellIdentifier` is simply an arbitrary `NSString` that is unique to each cell type. When a new cell is created, it's "tagged" with the `cellIdentifier`. Behind the scenes, the `dataSource` uses this `cellIdentifier` to do the following:

- Drop the discarded cell into the right queue for later reuse
- Retrieve a cell of the right type from a queue when the `tableView` requests a new cell

Figure 4–16 shows a somewhat contrived example with two cell types alternating on odd and even rows.

textLabel
textLabel detailTextLabel
textLabel
textLabel detailTextLabel
textLabel
textLabel detailTextLabel

Figure 4–16. *Cell alternation*

The table was produced by the code in Listing 4–5.

Listing 4–5. *Creating Alternating Cell Types*

```
- (UITableViewCell *)tableView:(UITableView *)tableView ➥
cellForRowAtIndexPath:(NSIndexPath *)indexPath {

    NSString *CellIdentifier;

    if ( (indexPath.row % 2) == 0 ) {
        CellIdentifier = @"rowOdd";
    } else {
        CellIdentifier = @"rowEven";
    }

    UITableViewCell *cell = [tableView ➥
dequeueReusableCellWithIdentifier:CellIdentifier];

    if (cell == nil) {

        switch ( [CellIdentifier isEqualToString:@"rowOdd"] ) {
            case YES:
                cell = [[UITableViewCell alloc] ➥
```

```
initWithStyle:UITableViewCellStyleDefault reuseIdentifier:cellIdentifier];
                break;

            case NO:
                cell = [[UITableViewCell alloc] ↵
initWithStyle:UITableViewCellStyleValue2 reuseIdentifier:cellIdentifier];
                break;

            default:
                break;
        }

    }

    cell.textLabel.text = @"textLabel";
    cell.detailTextLabel.text = @"detailTextLabel";

    return cell;
}
```

Stepping through Listing 4–5, the first task is to create a string for use as the cell identifier:

```
NSString *cellIdentifier;
```

The identifier is used to determine whether the row is odd or even. We can use the modulo function to divide the `indexPath.row` by 2. If the modulus is zero, the row is even; otherwise, it's odd. The cell identifier can then be set accordingly:

```
if ( (indexPath.row % 2) == 0 ) {
    cellIdentifier = @"rowOdd";
} else {
    cellIdentifier = @"rowEven";
}
```

We then try to dequeue a reusable cell with the cell identifier for this row:

```
UITableViewCell *cell = [tableView ↵
dequeueReusableCellWithIdentifier:cellIdentifier];
```

If one doesn't exist, we have to create one of the appropriate type. The code uses a `switch` statement to create a `UITableViewCellStyleDefault` if the row is odd, and a `UITableViewCellStyleValue2` if it's even:

```
if (cell == nil) {

    switch ( [cellIdentifier isEqualToString:@"rowOdd"] ) {

    case YES:
      cell = [[UITableViewCell alloc] ↵
initWithStyle:UITableViewCellStyleDefault reuseIdentifier:cellIdentifier];
        break;

    case NO:
      cell = [[UITableViewCell alloc] ↵
initWithStyle:UITableViewCellStyleValue2 reuseIdentifier:cellIdentifier];
        break;
```

```
    default:
      break;
        }

  }
```

Having created the right kind of cell, then it's simply a case of configuring it:

```
cell.textLabel.text = @"textLabel";
cell.detailTextLabel.text = @"detailTextLabel";
```

Finally, you return it to the tableView:

```
return cell;
```

CELL CACHING AND REUSE IN PRACTICE

You might be wondering how efficient this cell recycling process actually is. Here's a quick experiment that should hopefully convince you just how ingenious this is.

You'll tweak the SimpleTable app that you created in Chapter 1 and create a *lot* of rows—99,999 of them, in fact. Then as the `tableView` creates each new cell, you'll increment a counter and output this to the debugger so you can keep track of how many cells have been created in total. The results may surprise you.

First, amend the `STViewController`'s header file to add a new instance variable that you'll use to track the number of cells:

```
@interface STViewController : UIViewController ↩
<UITableViewDelegate, UITableViewDataSource>

@property (nonatomic, strong) NSMutableArray *tableData;
@property (nonatomic) NSUInteger cellCount;  // property to hold cell count

@end
```

Then synthesize the properties, and amend the `viewDidLoad` method to increase the number of items in the tableData array:

```
- (void)viewDidLoad
{
    // Run the superclass's viewDidLoad method
    [super viewDidLoad];

    // Set the cell count to zero
    self.cellCount = 0;

    // Create the array to hold the table data
    self.tableData = [[NSMutableArray alloc] init];

    // Create and add 99,999 data items to the table data array
    for (NSInteger i=0; i < 99999; i++) {

        // The cell will contain a string "Item X"
        NSString *dataString = [NSString stringWithFormat:@"Item %d", i];

        // Here the new string is added to the end of the array
        [self.tableData addObject:dataString];
```

```
    }

    // Print out the number of items in the array to the log
    NSLog(@"The tableData array contains %d items", [self.tableData count]);
    NSLog(@"There are %d cells initially", self.cellCount);

}
```

Finally, alter the `cellForRowAtIndexPath` method so that it increments and displays the cell count:

```
- (UITableViewCell *)tableView:(UITableView *)tableView ↵
cellForRowAtIndexPath:(NSIndexPath *)indexPath {

  static NSString *cellIdentifier = @"cellIdentifier";

  UITableViewCell *cell = [tableView ↵
dequeueReusableCellWithIdentifier:cellIdentifier];

  if (cell == nil) {

      // A new cell has been created, so increment the counter
      self.cellCount ++;

      // create the new cell
      cell = [[UITableViewCell alloc] initWithStyle:UITableViewCellStyleDefault ↵
reuseIdentifier:cellIdentifier];

  }

  cell.textLabel.text = [self.tableData objectAtIndex:indexPath.row];

  // log the cell count
  NSLog(@"There are now %d cells", self.cellCount);

  return cell;
}
```

Run the app. Scroll up and down the table, and take a look at the results in the debugger:

```
SimpleTable[17766:ef03] The tableData array contains 99999 items
SimpleTable[17766:ef03] There are 0 cells initially
SimpleTable[17766:ef03] There are now 1 cells
SimpleTable[17766:ef03] There are now 2 cells
SimpleTable[17766:ef03] There are now 3 cells
SimpleTable[17766:ef03] There are now 4 cells
SimpleTable[17766:ef03] There are now 5 cells
SimpleTable[17766:ef03] There are now 6 cells
SimpleTable[17766:ef03] There are now 7 cells
SimpleTable[17766:ef03] There are now 7 cells
SimpleTable[17766:ef03] There are now 8 cells
SimpleTable[17766:ef03] There are now 8 cells
```

No matter how far down the table you scroll, you'll see that the `tableView` never creates more than about eight cells.

Side Effects of Cell Reuse and Caching

Although caching and reusing cells dramatically reduces memory use and speeds up the table, some potential side effects can cause problems. When the unused cells are dumped into the queue, they're queued *as is*. In other words, their content and attributes remain in exactly the same state as when the cell was created.

This can cause interesting display issues, with seemingly "old" cells creeping into the middle of the table. This can be reasonably obvious when it happens with cell data, but it can catch you unaware if you're customizing other cell attributes such as selection state.

To prevent this, it's vitally important to reset the cell's content every time it's used—regardless of whether it's a new or dequeued cell.

There are three places where you can amend cell content:

- `cellForRowAtIndexPath`: As we've already seen, this is where you'll do most of the cell's configuration—setting content items based on the data returned by the `tableView`'s model and so on.
- `prepareForReuse`: This method gets called on the cell in the background just before it's returned to the delegate by `dequeueReusableCellWithIdentifier`. You can override this method if needed, but for performance reasons, Apple recommends that you reset only noncontent cell attributes here (editing and selection states, for example) and change content only in `cellForRowAtIndexPath`.
- `willDisplayCell:forRowAtIndexPath`: After the cell is created with `cellForRowAtIndexPath`, there's one last chance to tweak it before the `tableView` actually draws it to the screen. Just before this happens, the `tableView` will tell the delegate that it's about to draw a cell for a particular row—and at this point, you can change state-based properties such as selection and background color.

One technique I have seen suggested on forums is to create each cell with a unique `cellIdentifier`. Although that may work for very small tables, it's an incredibly bad idea if you're populating a table with a significant number of cells. By creating unique `cellIdentifiers`, you're preventing the caching and reuse of cells, so the memory footprint of your app will be significantly higher than it otherwise would be.

Summary

In this chapter, you've looked in depth at how cells are structured, created, and reused. You've also seen how cells can be configured beyond their default look by using just the default elements. Successfully customizing cells depends on knowing when to override the default processes, so you've learned how the table view creates and manages cells for us.

By understanding what's possible with basic customizations, you can then use this information to go further. In Chapter 8, you'll use this knowledge to build completely customized cells, and build on this further in Chapter 9. In Chapter 10, you'll improve the way that users can interact with cells.

Chapter 5

Using Tables for Navigation

Navigation controllers are an almost ubiquitous feature of the iOS user interface. They enable a user to manage the navigation through a hierarchy of content, moving through the tree of content items in a simple and consistent way.

Examples of this kind of user interface pattern abound. The iPhone's built-in Contacts app is a classic example of this. Contacts are displayed in a table view, and tapping a row pushes in a view with details their details as shown in Figure 5–1.

Figure 5–1. *The built-in iPhone Contacts app*

This user interface pattern is so common that the iOS SDK provides a controller for this specific purpose that handles the heavy lifting of the navigation for you. This chapter will show you how to create and configure a navigation-based app with `UINavigationController`.

This is done in five steps:

1. Creating the skeleton structure of the app
2. Creating some example data to feed the `UINavigationController`
3. Building the detail view
4. Linking the `UINavigationController` with the detail view
5. Tweaking the `UINavigationController` to customize its appearance.

The approach that I take here is a little unusual, in that you would usually create a navigation controller-based app using the template that Xcode provides. That's fine, but the template does an awful lot for you, and it hides significant detail about how the various pieces fit together.

Building the app from scratch, by contrast, will give you a good understanding of the anatomy of a navigation controller.

The Navigation Controller Interface Pattern

The way in which navigation controllers fit together with the application structure always reminds me of Russian dolls. Views fit inside controllers, which fit inside windows; at first it can seem unfeasibly complicated.

Navigation controllers act in a similar way to the page history and forward and back buttons of a web browser. As you visit each new page, that page is added to the browser's history. The forward and back buttons allow you to move up and down the list of pages that you've visited. That's the pattern used by the Contacts app, shown in Figure 5–2.

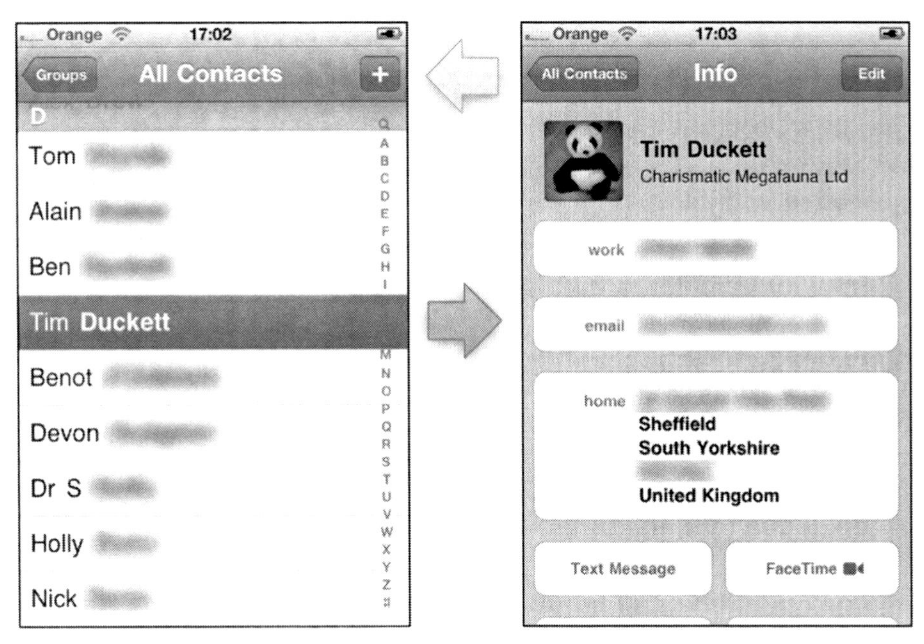

Figure 5–2. *Pushing and popping views*

Instead of a list of pages, the navigation controller is basically a stack of view controllers. The top-most view controller in the stack is visible, so in order to display a new view controller, you push that onto the top of the stack. Visually, the new view controller usually appears to slide in from the right, as in Figure 5–3.

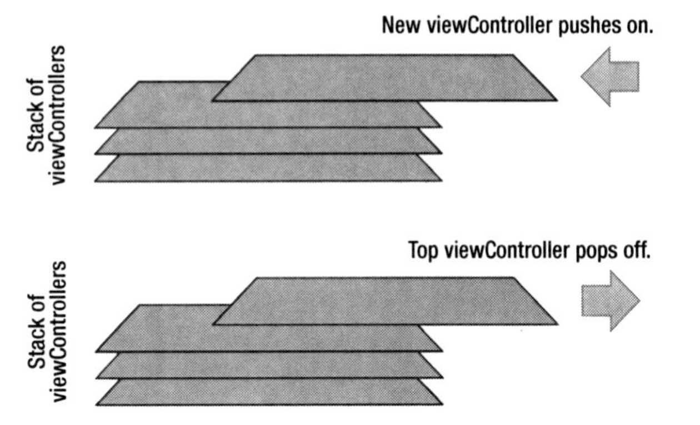

Figure 5–3. *Pushing and popping view controllers into the navigation controller stack*

When you want to navigate "backwards," you pop the current view controller off the stack to expose the one underneath. The top-most view controller usually appears to slide off to the right.

Introducing the UINavigationController

The Apple iOS documentation describes a `UINavigationController` as a "container for several other views," which is as good a way of describing it as I can think of. Shown in Figure 5–4, it gives you a top navigation bar and an optional toolbar at the bottom.

There's also space for bar button items on the navigation bar. Between the top and bottom bar there's a space for your custom content to be loaded into: it's into this space that you'll push and pop view controllers.

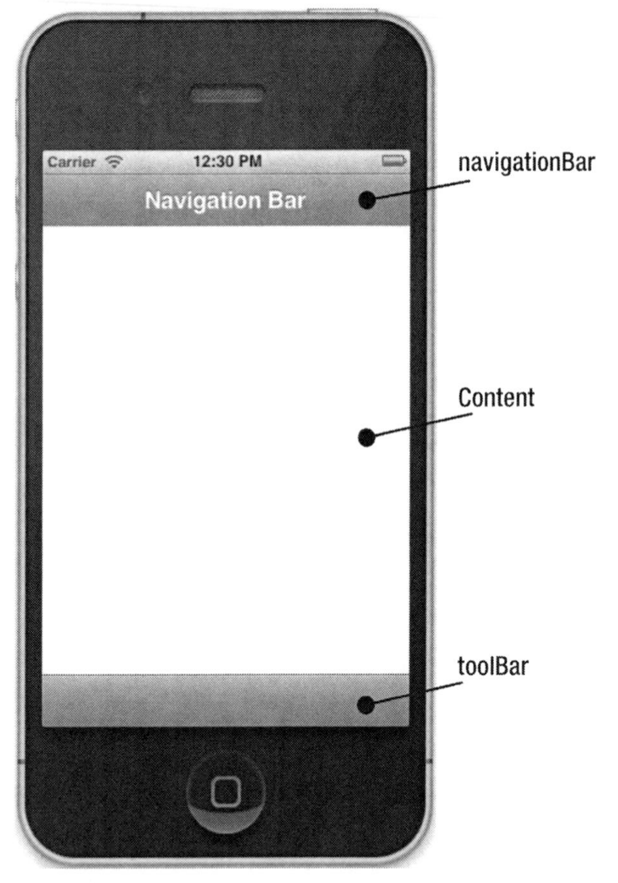

Figure 5–4. *The components of UINavigationController*

Interacting with the content inside the view controllers—tapping on a row, tapping on a button, and so on—is the cue to call the `UINavigationController`'s `pushViewController:animated:` and `popViewController:animated:` methods.

As well as moving through the stack of view controllers one by one, you can also head straight to the top of the stack by calling `UIViewController`'s `popToRootControllerAnimated:` method.

And finally, pushing (or popping) to a specific view controller is achieved by the `popToViewController:animated` method, which takes a parameter of type `UIViewController` through which you can indicate which controller you're after.

NOTE: Although using `UITableViews` with `UIViewControllers` is by far and away the most common scenario, it's worth remembering that the view controllers you push and pop can be *any* kind of view controller.

You're not restricted to using a table at the top level; you could just as easily push in the next view by tapping on say, a `UIButton`, as you could by tapping on a row in a `tableView`. Use whatever will provide the user experience that you're trying to deliver.

THE NAVIGATION CONTROLLER EXAMPLE APPLICATION

Illustrating the function of the `UINavigationController` really calls for an example application that is a bit more complex than the SimpleTable app that we've been using as our example so far. To do this, I've built a relatively simple app to use as the basis of this chapter. It's far from being something that you'd want to buy from the App Store, but it'll do for these purposes.

If you've got kids (or even if you haven't and you've got friends who have) you'll know that one of the most important decisions you can make before the little bundle of joy arrives is deciding on a name. Get it wrong, and you could condemn your offspring to an educational lifetime of teasing in the playground. Don't get it right, and Great Aunt Agatha will cut you out of her will for not continuing the family tradition of all first-born males being named Algernon.

To help you navigate through this minefield, what you need (of course!) is an iOS app: enter the oh-so-imaginative titled Baby Names. Although this most emphatically won't win any awards for either design or ground-breaking functionality, it gives us something to work with.

Creating a Navigation Controller App

Probably because navigation controller-based apps are so common, most versions of Xcode ship with a template for creating this type of app. These give you a lot of the plumbing readymade to speed you on your way.

I'm going to take the back-to-basics approach, though, and build the app entirely by hand. That's not because there's anything wrong with the app templates, but if you start from scratch you'll end up with a much better feel for how all the pieces fit together.

Start by creating a new app in Xcode (**File ➤ New ➤ New Project**) that uses the "Single View Application" template as shown in Figure 5–5.

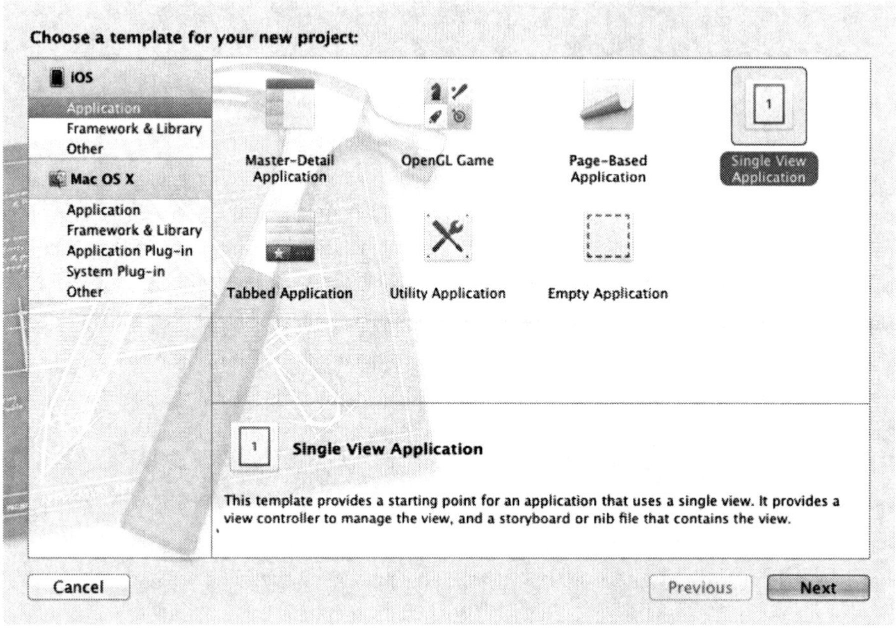

Figure 5–5. *Xcode's new application dialog*

> **TIP:** The selection of default templates that ship with Xcode tends to alter from version to version (this book was written using Xcode 4.2).
>
> Your version of Xcode may look different from this, but among the templates there'll be one that creates a skeleton application with a single view; that's the one we're after.

Name the application `BabyNames` and save it to the folder of your choice. Give the project a class prefix of `BN` and make sure that Automatic Reference Counting is enabled. You'll end up with an app containing:

- An app delegate, called `BNAppDelegate`
- A view controller, called `BNViewController`
- A nib file for the view controller

As you progress through building the app you will create some extra view controllers, objects classes, and nib files, so you may want to set up some groups in Xcode to keep the various files organized, displayed in Figure 5–6. It's up to you whether to do this in your apps, but I find it helps keep things organized as the project expands.

Figure 5–6. *Creating groups in the app*

Having created the app skeleton, the next step is to create some sample data.

Creating the Name Class

Although the look and feel of the app is built up step by step, there's no reason why the data model can't be created straight away. In fact, having a good idea of how the data will be structured from the outset can help figure out how the interface should work.

At the core of the app are names. So core, in fact, that you're going to create a `BNName` class with the following attributes (see also Figure 5–7).

- `nameText` - A string containing the name itself
- `gender` - A string containing a gender flag M, F, or U (for unisex)
- `derivation` - A string containing some text about the derivation of the name
- `iconName` - A string containing the filename of the name's icon
- `notes` - A string containing some explanatory notes about the name

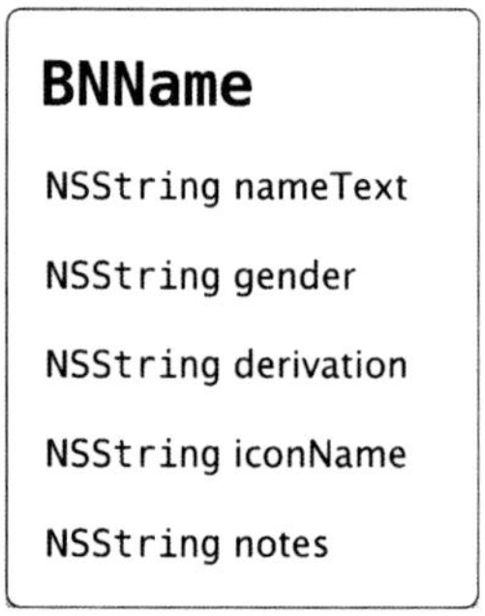

BNName

NSString nameText

NSString gender

NSString derivation

NSString iconName

NSString notes

Figure 5–7. *The BNName object*

Let's get this underway. Highlight the `Models` group in the navigator area and Ctrl or right-click. In the context menu that pops up, select the **New File** option. You'll be presented with a selection of templates for the new file (see Figure 5–8).

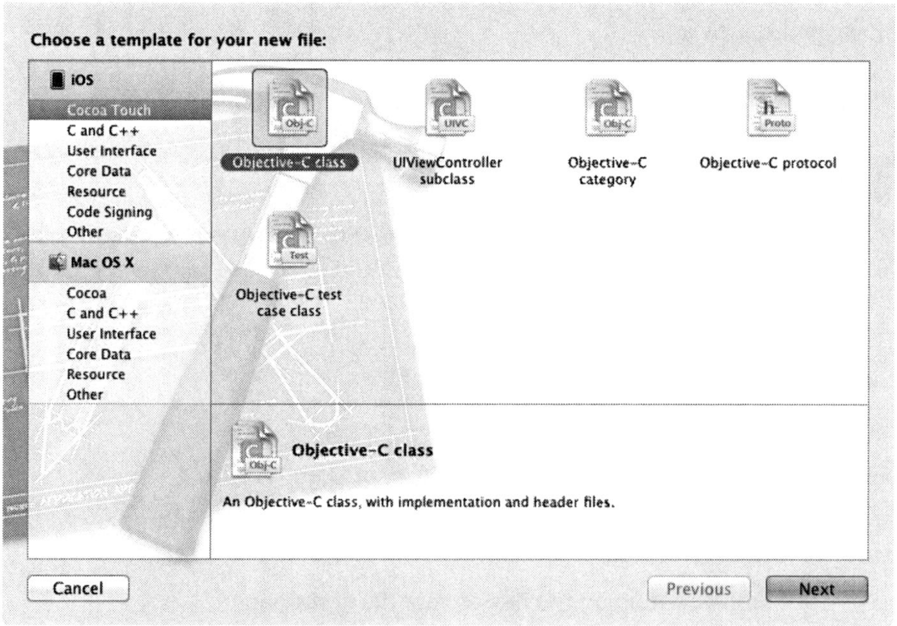

Figure 5–8. *Xcode's New File templates*

Select `Objective-C class` and click next (see Figure 5–9). You need to create a subclass of `NSObject`, which should be the default option in the drop-down list.

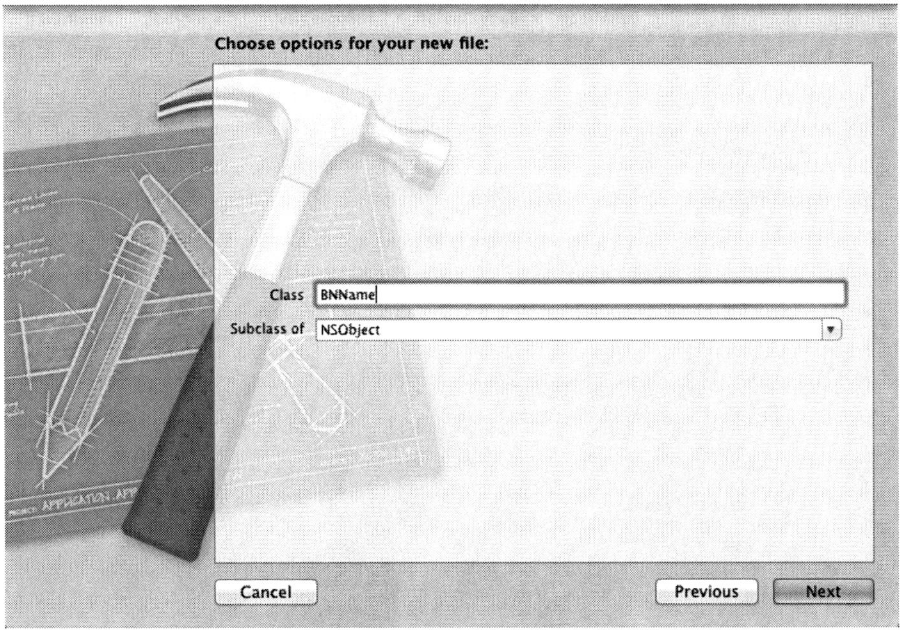

Figure 5–9. *Selecting the subclass of the new object*

Call the new file `BNName`, click **Next**, and make sure that the tick-box to add the file to the `BabyNames` target is selected. See Figure 5–10.

Figure 5–10. *Naming and saving the new class*

The new class `BNName` will be created, and the header and implementation files will appear in the navigator (Figure 5–11).

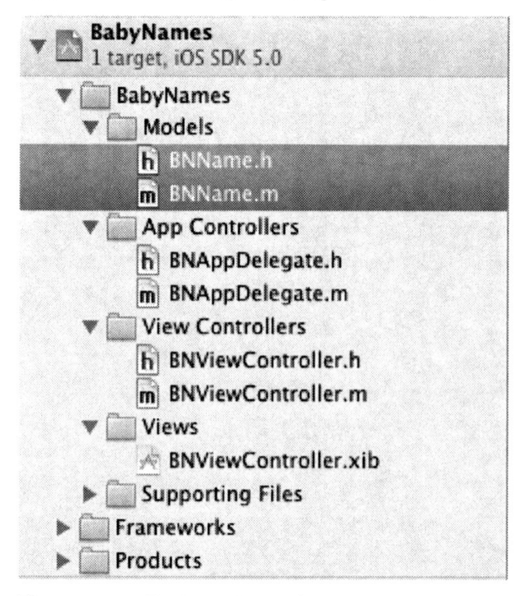

Figure 5–11. *The new class's files*

TIP: If you ticked the "Create local git repository for this project" option when you created the project, you'll see symbols appearing to the right of filenames. These show each file's source control status: new files show a status of A (indicating they need to be added to the repository). Files with a status of M have been modified.

Support for the Git version control system was introduced with Xcode 4. It's out of the scope of this book, but if you're not using source control with your projects, I'd *strongly* recommend investigating it.

Now you need to configure our new class. Open up the BNName.h file, and add the class's properties as shown in Listing 5–1.

Listing 5–1. *BNName.h*

```
#import <Foundation/Foundation.h>

@interface BNName : NSObject

@property (nonatomic, strong) NSString *nameText;
@property (nonatomic, strong) NSString *gender;
@property (nonatomic, strong) NSString *derivation;
@property (nonatomic, strong) NSString *icon;
@property (nonatomic, strong) NSString *notes;

@end
```

Switch to BNNames.m and complete the implementation as shown in Listing 5–2:

Listing 5–2. *BNName.m*

```
#import "BNName.h"

@implementation BNName

@synthesize nameText;
@synthesize gender;
@synthesize derivation;
@synthesize iconName;
@synthesize notes;

- (id)init
{
    self = [super init];
    if (self) {
        // Initialization code here.
    }

    return self;
}

@end
```

At the moment, the BNName class doesn't need any methods, so you're done with it for now.

Creating Some Dummy Data

Having created a BNName class, the next stage is to create some dummy data that we can use for prototyping purposes. You need a model to feed the tableView with data; this is created as the app starts up.

Switch to BNAppDelegate.h, and add a property to hold an NSMutableArray for the table data:

```
@property (nonatomic, strong) NSMutableArray *tableData;
```

You also need to synthesize this array in the implementation file:

```
@synthesize tableData;
```

Then switch to the BNViewController and add and synthesize the corresponding property for the table data:

```
@property (nonatomic, strong) NSArray *tableData;
```

Initially, you're going to create instances of BNName with nonsense data so you've got some data with which you can test out our app. To do this, you need to create a method called createNameWithNonsenseData that returns—well—a name filled with random data.

Then in the AppDelegate's application:didFinishLaunchingWithOptions: method you'll load the tableData array with a suitable number of nonsense names. As the view controller is instantiated, the names are passed into its tableData property.

First add a declaration for createNameWithNonsenseData to the BNAppDelegate.m file. It also needs the header for the BNName class importing, as shown in Listing 5–3:

Listing 5–3. *Adding the Method Declaration to BNAppDelegate.m*

```
#import "BNAppDelegate.h"
#import "BNViewController.h"
#import "BNName.h"

@interface BNAppDelegate()

    -(BNName *)createNameWithNonsenseDataWithIndex:(int)index;

@end

@implementation BNAppDelegate

... implementation continues ...
```

Now add the new method at the bottom of the file, shown in Listing 5–4.

Listing 5–4. *Creating Random Names*

```
-(BNName *)createNameWithNonsenseDataWithIndex:(int)index {

    BNName *randomDataName = [[BNName alloc] init];

    NSArray *namesArray = [[NSArray alloc] initWithObjects:@"Abigail", @"Ada", ↵
@"Adelaide", @"Abel", @"Algernon", @"Anatole", @"Barbara", @"Bertha", @"Brunhilda", ↵
```

```
@"Barton", @"Ben", @"Boris", @"Calista", @"Cassandra", @"Constance", @"Caspar", ↵
@"Clive", @"Corey", @"Danica", @"Dido", @"Dora", @"Darnell", @"Dexter", @"Dunstan",  ↵
@"Duncan",  nil];

    NSArray *genderArray = [[NSArray alloc] initWithObjects:@"Boy", @"Girl",↵
 @"Unisex", nil];

    NSArray *notesArray = [[NSArray alloc] initWithObjects:@"'Prosperous and joyful'. ↵
A popular name in Victorian times.", @"'Bright fair one'. A term of endearment used ↵
by the Irish", @"'Son of the furrows; ploughman' One of the twelve apostles", @"One ↵
who is graceful and charming", @"'Spear'. A warrior who wielded her spear to the ↵
detriment of her enemies", nil];

    NSArray *derivationArray = [[NSArray alloc] initWithObjects:@"Celtic", ↵
 @"Germanic", @"Old English", @"Latin", @"Greek", nil];

    NSArray *iconArray = [[NSArray alloc] initWithObjects:@"icon1.png", @"icon2.png", ↵
@"icon3.png", @"icon4.png", @"icon5.png", nil];

    int genderCount = [genderArray count];
    int notesCount = [notesArray count];
    int derivationCount = [derivationArray count];
    int iconCount = [iconArray count];

    randomDataName.nameText = [namesArray objectAtIndex:index];
    randomDataName.gender = [genderArray objectAtIndex:(arc4random() % genderCount)];
    randomDataName.derivation = [derivationArray objectAtIndex:(arc4random() % ↵
derivationCount)];
    randomDataName.iconName = [iconArray objectAtIndex:(arc4random() % iconCount)];
    randomDataName.notes = [notesArray objectAtIndex:(arc4random() % notesCount)];

    return randomDataName;

}
```

NOTE: You don't need to use this data. I picked the values pretty much at random. There's enough *lorem ipsum* in the world without me adding to it!

Having gained the ability to create instances of BNName filled with random data, you can now store these in the tableData array.

Switch back up to the application:didFinishLaunchingWithOptions: method and amend it to fill up the tableData array as shown in Listing 5–5.

Listing 5–5. *Creating the Random Data*

```
- (BOOL)application:(UIApplication *)application
didFinishLaunchingWithOptions:(NSDictionary *)launchOptions
{
    self.window = [[UIWindow alloc] initWithFrame:[[UIScreen mainScreen] bounds]];

    // Create dummy data

    NSUInteger numberOfNames = 25;
```

```
    self.tableData = [[NSMutableArray alloc] initWithCapacity:numberOfNames];

    // Create a temporary array of tableData
    for (NSUInteger i = 0; i < numberOfNames; i++) {

        // Create a new name with nonsense data
        BNName *tempName = [self createNameWithNonsenseDataWithIndex:i];

        // Add it to the temporary array
        [self.tableData addObject:tempName];

    }

    self.viewController = [[BNViewController alloc] initWithNibName:➥
@"BNViewController" bundle:nil];

    self.window.rootViewController = self.viewController;
    [self.window makeKeyAndVisible];
    return YES;
}
```

Connecting Up the Table View

As it stands, the app doesn't actually display any content when it launches. Let's fix that by adding in a `tableView`, and getting it to load the data. Switch to `BNViewController.xib`, click on the `View` item in the objects list and drag in a **Table View** so that it fills the entire view, as demonstrated in Figure 5–12.

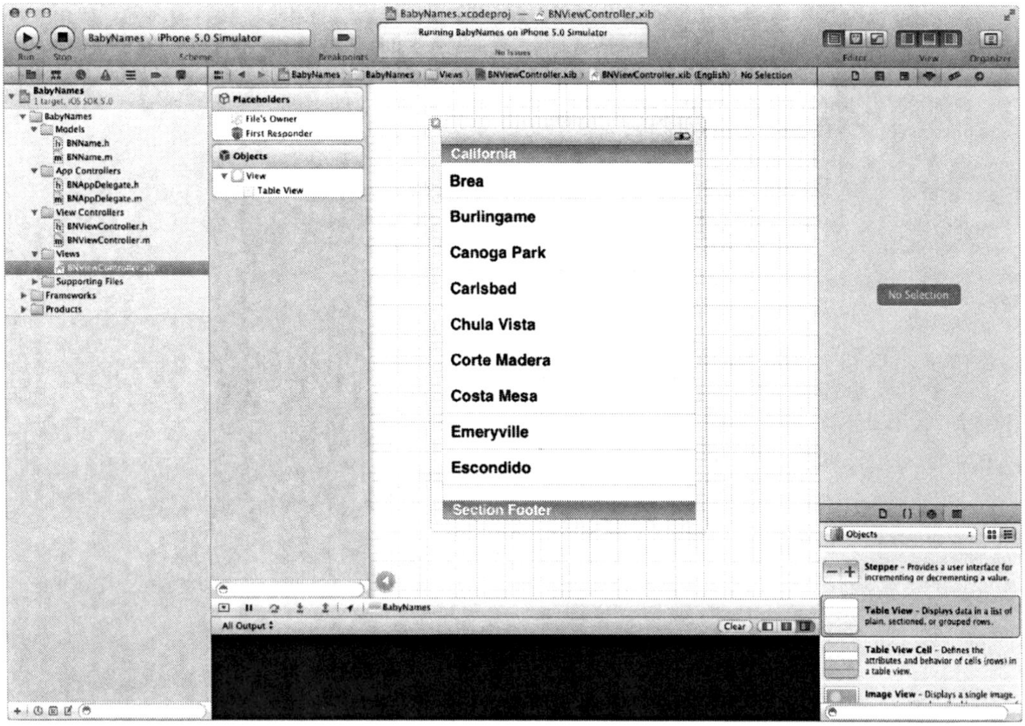

Figure 5–12. *Adding a tableView to the view*

Now connect the new tableView to a property in the view controller. Click the "Show Assistant" button in the Editor section of the toolbar to bring up BabyNamesViewController.h in the Assistant pane. Right-click and drag out from the tableView to underneath the tableData property declaration. When the "Insert outlet or outlet collection" hint pops up, release the mouse button. In the pop-up control, enter theTableView in the name field as shown in Figure 5–13.

Figure 5–13. *Adding the tableView property*

Click Connect and Xcode will add in the property for you:

```
@property (strong, nonatomic) IBOutlet UITableView *theTableView;
```

Now connect up the tableView's dataSource and delegate. Right-click and drag from the table to File's Owner in the Placeholders list, and then select Datasource from the popup. Repeat the same process and select Delegate. See Figure 5–14.

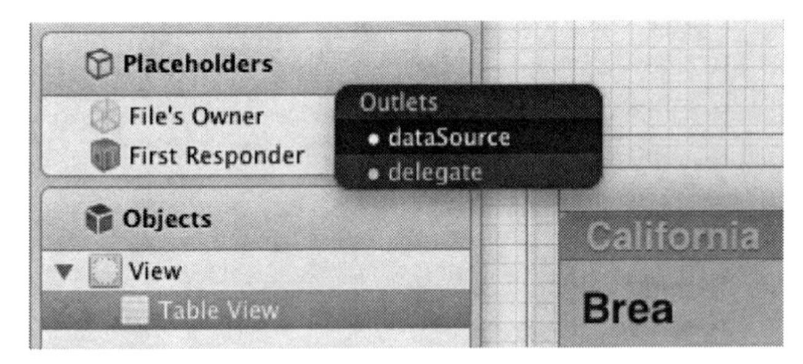

Figure 5–14. *Connecting the dataSource and delegate*

The next stage is to conform the controller to the two `UITableView` protocols, `UITableViewDelegate` and `UITableViewDataSource`. Switch to `BNViewController`'s header file and add the protocol declarations as shown in Listing 5–6.

Listing 5–6. *Adding the Protocol Declarations*

```
#import <UIKit/UIKit.h>

@interface BNViewController : UIViewController <UITableViewDelegate,  ↵
 UITableViewDataSource>

@property (nonatomic, strong) NSArray *tableData;
@property (strong, nonatomic) IBOutlet UITableView *theTableView;

@end
```

The final step of wiring up the table is to add the mandatory `UITableViewDataSource` methods to `BNViewController`: first, `tableView:numberOfRowsInSection`. For the moment, it can simply return `0`, as shown in Listing 5–7.

Listing 5–7. *The `tableView:numberOfRowsInSection:` Method*

```
- (NSInteger)tableView:(UITableView *)tableView numberOfRowsInSection:↵
(NSInteger)section {

    return 0;

}
```

and then `tableView:cellForRowAtIndexPath`, shown in Listing 5–8:

Listing 5–8. *The `tableView:cellForRowAtIndexPath:` Method*

```
- (UITableViewCell *)tableView:(UITableView *)aTableView ↵
cellForRowAtIndexPath:(NSIndexPath *)indexPath {

    static NSString *cellIdentifier = @"BabyNameCell";

    UITableViewCell *cell = [tableView↵
 dequeueReusableCellWithIdentifier:cellIdentifier];

    if (cell == nil) {
        cell = [[UITableViewCell alloc] initWithStyle:UITableViewCellStyleDefault ↵
reuseIdentifier:cellIdentifier];
    }
```

```
    return cell;
}
```

Run the app to check everything's wired up correctly, and you should see an empty table, as in Figure 5–15.

Figure 5–15. *The empty table*

> **TIP:** If at this point Xcode falls over with an error complaining about code signing, check that you're running the app on the Simulator rather than any devices that might be connected to your Mac. The drop-down list next to the **Run** and **Stop** buttons should be showing **iPhone 5.0 Simulator**.

Feeding the Table with Data

Having wired up the table, now let's get some data in it.

Earlier, you created an NSMutableArray called tableData in the appDelegate. You will use this to populate the corresponding tableData property of the BNViewController, then feed this data to the tableView.

Switch to BNAppDelegate's implementation file and add the line below to the application:didFinishLaunchingWithOptions: method as shown in Listing 5–9:

```
// Pass the array of dummy names into the view controller
self.viewController.tableData = (NSArray *)self.tableData;
```

Listing 5–9. ***The application:didFinishLaunchingWithOptions: Method***

```
- (BOOL)application:(UIApplication *)application
didFinishLaunchingWithOptions:(NSDictionary *)launchOptions
{
    self.window = [[UIWindow alloc] initWithFrame:[[UIScreen mainScreen] bounds]];

    // Create dummy data

    NSUInteger numberOfNames = 25;

    self.tableData = [[NSMutableArray alloc] initWithCapacity:numberOfNames];

    // Create a temporary array of tableData
    for (NSUInteger i = 0; i < numberOfNames; i++) {

        // Create a new name with nonsense data
        BNName *tempName = [self createNameWithNonsenseDataWithIndex:i];

        // Add it to the temporary array
        [self.tableData addObject:tempName];

    }

    self.viewController = [[BNViewController alloc] ➥
 initWithNibName:@"BNViewController" bundle:nil];

    // Pass the array of dummy names into the view controller
    self.viewController.tableData = (NSArray *)self.tableData;

    self.window.rootViewController = self.viewController;
    [self.window makeKeyAndVisible];
    return YES;
}
```

The BNAppDelegate's tableData is a mutable array so that the dummy data can be added to it, whereas the BNViewController's property is an (immutable) NSArray. To "convert" from the mutable to immutable form, you need to cast the NSMutableArray to an NSArray as the property is assigned:

```
self.viewController.tableData = (NSArray *)self.tableData;
```

Now you can alter BNViewController's tableView:numberOfRowsInSection: method:

```
- (NSInteger)tableView:(UITableView *)tableView numberOfRowsInSection:➥
(NSInteger)section {

    if (self.tableData != nil) {
   return [self.tableData count]
   }

return 0;

}
```

The tableData array contains a number of BNName objects. In order to work with these, you have to tell the view controller about the BNName class, so add a #import statement to the top of the file:

```
#import "BNName.h"
```

And now you can update the tableView:cellForRowAtIndexPath: method as shown in Listing 5–10.

Listing 5–10. ***The Updated*** *tableView:cellForRowAtIndexPath:* ***Method***

```
-(UITableViewCell *)tableView:(UITableView *)tableView➥
 cellForRowAtIndexPath:(NSIndexPath *)indexPath {

    static NSString *cellIdentifier = @"BabyNameCell";

    UITableViewCell *cell = [tableView➥
 dequeueReusableCellWithIdentifier:cellIdentifier];

    if (!cell) {
        cell = [[UITableViewCell alloc] ➥
initWithStyle:UITableViewCellStyleDefault reuseIdentifier:cellIdentifier];
    }

    // Extract the BNName object from the tableData
    BNName *tempName = [self.tableData objectAtIndex:indexPath.row];

    // Update the cell's textLabel
    cell.textLabel.text = tempName.nameText;

    return cell;

}
```

This should be fairly self-explanatory: for each row in the table, the BNName object is extracted from the array. The cell's textLabel property is set with the BNName's nameText value. Run the app, and you'll start to see the data, as shown in Figure 5–16.

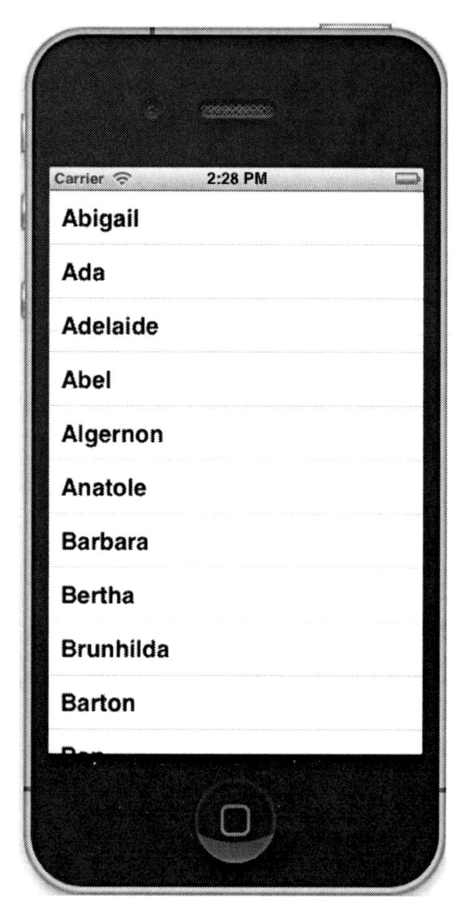

Figure 5–16. *Data appears in the table!*

Building the Detail View

When the users click on a Name row in the table, the app will present them with a details screen with the information for that name. The `UINavigationController` will handle the process of pushing the detail view in, but before it can do this you need to create a details view.

As the app is still at the proof-of-concept stage, you can make this as simple or as detailed as you like. I've made a very (very!) basic version to use as a starting point. Either way, you need to add a new view controller.

Highlight the View controllers group in the Navigator, right-click, and add a new file. Choose the `UIViewController` subclass, and call the file `BNDetailViewController`. Don't forget to check the "`With XIB for user interface`" option to create a nib file. Open `BNDetailViewController.xib` and add the controls that you need.

Then amend the `BNDetailViewController.xib` file to create properties and ivars for all the controls in your view.

My work of art looks like that in Figure 5-17.

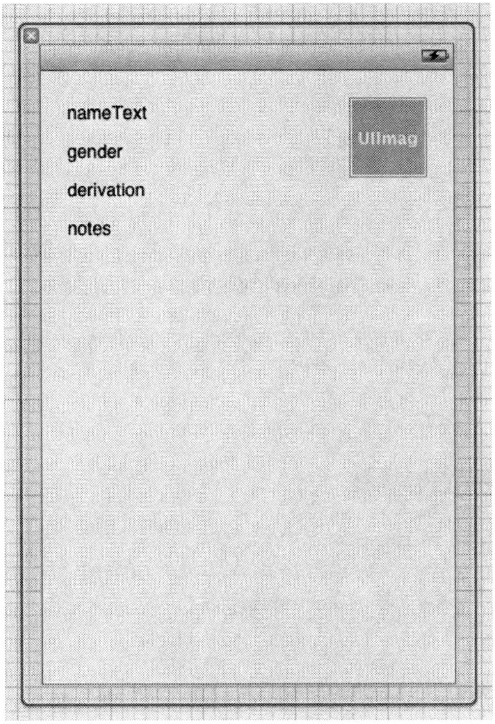

Figure 5–17. *A very basic detail view*

I've also added a property to allow the selected Name to be passed over to the `BNDetailViewController`. Your header file will depend on the controls you've placed on your view. Mine looks like that in Listing 5–11.

Listing 5–11. *BNDetailViewController.h*

```
//  BNDetailViewController.h
#import <UIKit/UIKit.h>
@class BNName;

@interface BNDetailViewController : UIViewController

@property (nonatomic, retain) BNName *BNName;
@property (retain, strong) IBOutlet UILabel *nameTextLabel;
@property (retain, strong) IBOutlet UILabel *genderLabel;
@property (retain, strong) IBOutlet UILabel *derivationLabel;
@property (retain, strong) IBOutlet UILabel *notesLabel;
@property (retain, strong) IBOutlet UIImageView *iconImageView;

@end
```

And the top of my corresponding `BNDetailViewController.m` like that in Listing 5–12.

Listing 5–12. *The Top of* `BNDetailViewController.m`

```
//  BNDetailViewController.m

#import "DetailViewController.h"
#import "BNName.h"

@implementation DetailViewController

@synthesize BNName;
@synthesize nameTextLabel;
@synthesize genderLabel;
@synthesize derivationLabel;
@synthesize notesLabel;
@synthesize iconImageView;
```

Now switch to the `BNDetailViewController.xib` file, add the view controls and connect them to the relevant outlets.

Having created a view controller and a layout for the detail screen, this is the point where you can introduce the navigation controller.

Implementing the Navigation Controller

Implementing the navigation controller is a process of replacing the app's initial table view with a `UINavigationController`, then loading the table view into this. At the moment, the code in the app delegate that manages the initial view looks like Listing 5–13.

Listing 5–13. *The Current Initial View Code*

```
    self.window = [[UIWindow alloc] initWithFrame:[[UIScreen mainScreen] bounds]];

    // Create dummy data
    // ...

    self.viewController = [[BNViewController alloc] ➥
 initWithNibName:@"BNViewController" bundle:nil];

    // Pass the array of dummy names into the view controller
    self.viewController.tableData = (NSArray *)self.tableData;

    self.window.rootViewController = self.viewController;
    [self.window makeKeyAndVisible];
    return YES;
```

A diagram or two can help make sense of this. Let's start by looking at Figure 5–18, which displays how this app currently sets up its visual interface.

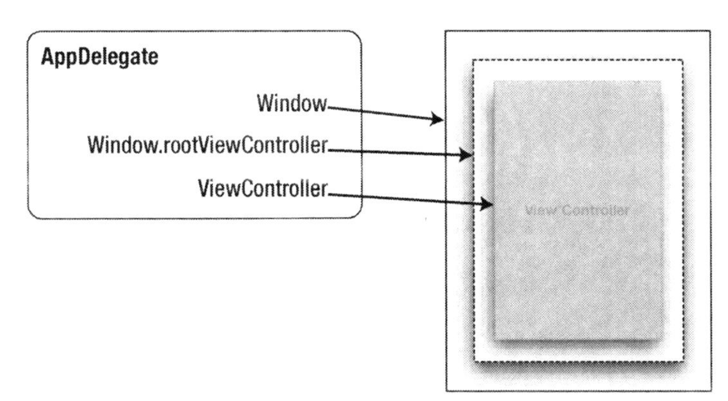

Figure 5–18. *How the app delegate instantiates the user interface*

The app delegate has a `window` property that is created using the bounds of `UIScreen`'s `mainScreen` property. This window is where the visible user interface for the app has to fit. In effect, it's a virtual reference in software to the physical screen of the device.

The window property has a `rootViewController` property, which you can think of as the frontmost slot in the window into which a view controller can be placed.

> **CAUTION:** There's a potential source for confusion here due to some less-than-consistent naming conventions in iOS. Both the app delegate and `UINavigationControllers` have a property called `rootViewController`. They've both got broadly similar purposes, but they're **NOT** the same thing. Make sure you know what context you're dealing with when thinking about `rootViewController` properties.

The app delegate also has a `viewController` property. An instance of the `BNViewController` is instantiated from the nib file, and then assigned to the `viewController` property.

At this point you have got two things: a way of referencing the physical screen (via the `window` property) and a `viewController` object. To make the `viewController` visible, you simply insert the `viewController` object into the window's `rootViewController` property. That's at the top of the stack, so it's the one that's visible on the device screen.

How the Navigation Controller Is Wired Up

The process for a navigation controller app is similar, but subtly different. Instead of filling the window with the `viewController`, you create a `UINavigationController` object and put that in the `window`. Then you take the `viewController` that we had to start with and put that inside the navigation controller. See what I mean about Russian dolls?

Figure 5–19 shows how this hangs together in practice.

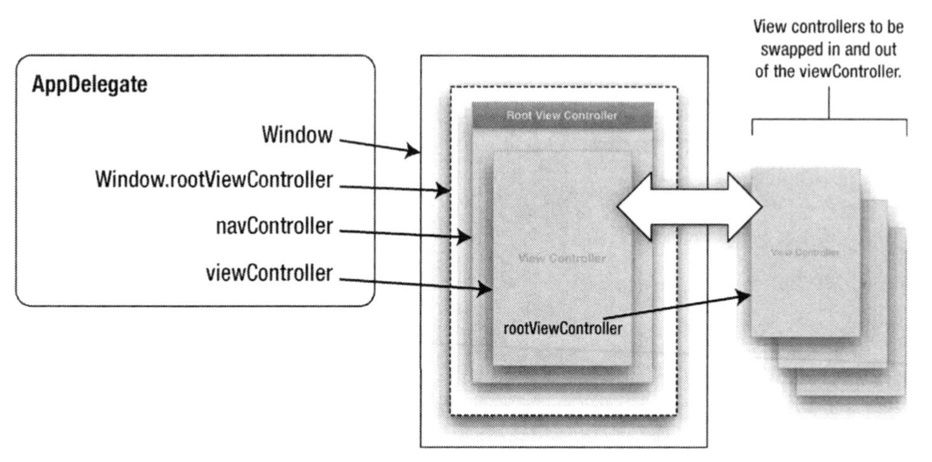

Figure 5–19. *How the navigation controller fits into the picture*

The corresponding code from the app delegate is shown in Listing 5–14:

Listing 5–14. *The Updated Code*

```
- (BOOL)application:(UIApplication *)application ➥
didFinishLaunchingWithOptions:(NSDictionary *)launchOptions
{
    self.window = [[UIWindow alloc] initWithFrame:[[UIScreen mainScreen] bounds]];

    // Create dummy data
    // ...

    // Create an instance of BNViewController
    BNViewController *bnViewController = [[BNViewController alloc]  ➥
 initWithNibName:@"BNViewController" bundle:nil];

    // Pass the array of dummy names into the BNViewController
    bnViewController.tableData = (NSArray *)self.tableData;

    // Create an instance of UINavigationController called navController
    // and set the bnViewController as its RootViewController
    UINavigationController *navController = [[UINavigationController alloc] ➥
 initWithRootViewController:bnViewController];

    // Make the navController the rootViewController
    self.window.rootViewController = navController;

    [self.window makeKeyAndVisible];
    return YES;

}
```

Just before you run the app, make one more tweak. Switch back to `BNViewController`'s implementation file, find the `viewDidLoad` method, and add this line to the bottom:

```
    self.title = @"Baby Names";
```

If you run the app now, you'll see that the table is still there, but now it sits inside a navigation controller that provides a top bar. The title of the view controller displayed in the navigation controller's content area is shown in the top bar (see Figure 5–20).

Figure 5–20. *The navigation controller with the table inside*

Linking the Navigation Controller and Detail Views Together

The app is getting close, but tapping on the cells still doesn't cause the detail view to magically appear. In order for this to happen, you need to implement the `tableView`'s `didSelectRowAtIndexPath:` method.

Switch to `BNViewController.m` , and import the `BNDetailViewController`'s header file:

```
#import "BNDetailViewController.h"
```

Then as in Listing 5–15, add the `tableView:didSelectRowAtIndexPath:` method in the table delegate section:

Listing 5–15. *The* `tableView:didSelectRowAtIndexPath:` *Method*

```
-(void)tableView:(UITableView *)tableView ↩
didSelectRowAtIndexPath:(NSIndexPath *)indexPath {

    BNDetailViewController *detailViewController = [[BNDetailViewController alloc] ↩
 initWithNibName:@"BNDetailViewController" bundle:nil];

    [self.navigationController pushViewController:detailViewController animated:YES];

}
```

To kick things off, you need to create an instance of the `BNDetailViewController`:

```
    BNDetailViewController *detailViewController = [[BNDetailViewController alloc] ↩
 initWithNibName:@"BNDetailViewController" bundle:nil];
```

And push this onto the navController:

```
    [self.navigationController pushViewController:detailViewController animated:YES];
```

Run the app now, and tap on a row: the `BNDetailViewController` will slide in from the right, and tapping the "back" button will slide it out again as shown in Figure 5–21.

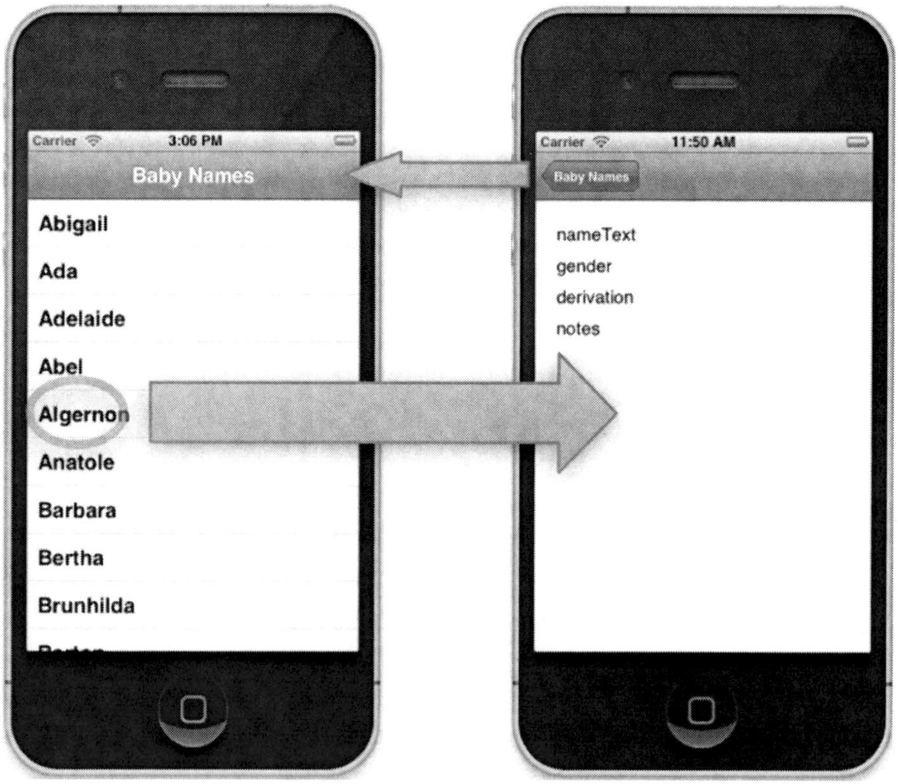

Figure 5–21. *Navigation from list to detail and back again*

One minor bit of housekeeping remains: when the detail view is removed and the tableView reappears, you'll need to deselect the previously selected row. The BNViewController's viewWillAppear: and viewDidAppear: methods are fired just before and just after the detail view is removed, so you can use the viewDidAppear: to remove the selection highlight from the row, as shown in Listing 5–16.

Listing 5–16. *The viewDidAppear: Method*

```
- (void)viewDidAppear:(BOOL)animated
{
    [super viewDidAppear:animated];

    NSIndexPath *selectedIndexPath = [self.theTableView indexPathForSelectedRow];

    [self.theTableView deselectRowAtIndexPath:selectedIndexPath animated:YES];

}
```

First, you need to get hold of the indexPath of the currently selected row (which is the same as it was when the detail view was pushed in), and then use this to call the tableView's deselectRowAtIndexPath:animated: method.

If you pass in YES as the animated: parameter, the highlight will be removed with a gentle fade effect.

Wiring Up the Detail

Although the animated navigation is impressive, the lack of real content on the detail view is less so. Let's fix that in the tableView:didSelectRowAtIndexPath: method.

Before it can show any detail, you need the BNName object that the selected row is displaying so that it can be passed into the BNDetailViewController object:

```
detailViewController.BNName = [self.tableData objectAtIndex:indexPath.row];
```

Now, as in Listing 5–17, you can update the BNDetailViewController's UILabels in its viewDidLoad method.

Listing 5–17. *The Updated viewDidLoad Method*

```
- (void)viewDidLoad
{
    [super viewDidLoad];
    // Do any additional setup after loading the view from its nib.
    self.nameTextLabel.text = self.BNName.nameText;
    self.genderLabel.text = self.BNName.gender;
    self.derivationLabel.text = self.BNName.derivation;
    self.notesLabel.text = self.BNName.notes;
}
```

Finally, let's add some icons to the app. In my detail view, I've added a UIImageView outlet that's 65 pixels square. The appDelegate's dummy data method randomly allocates one of four icons to the BNName instance, so there needs to be four corresponding files added to the project.

Adding images to an Xcode project is best done with the **File ➤ Add Files To Project** menu option. To keep things organized, I tend to add assets such as images into a group along the lines of Figure 5–22.

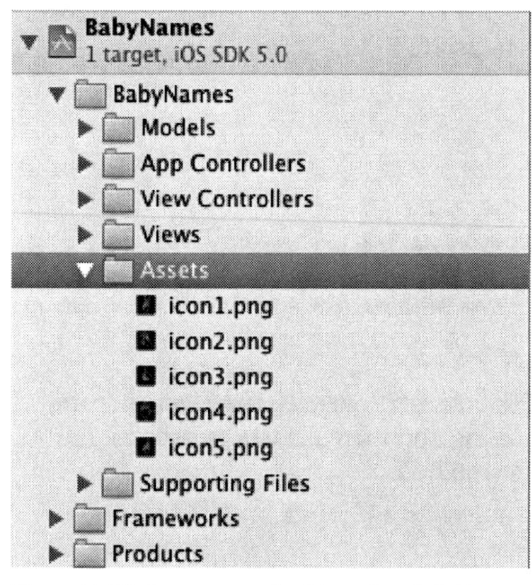

Figure 5–22. *Images organized in an Assets folder*

Having got some icons, wire up that `UIImageView` outlet in `BNDetailViewController`'s `viewDidLoad` method:

```
self.iconImageView.image = [UIImage imageNamed:self.BNName.iconName];
```

Run the app, tap on a row, and now you'll see the detail for that name as in Figure 5–23.

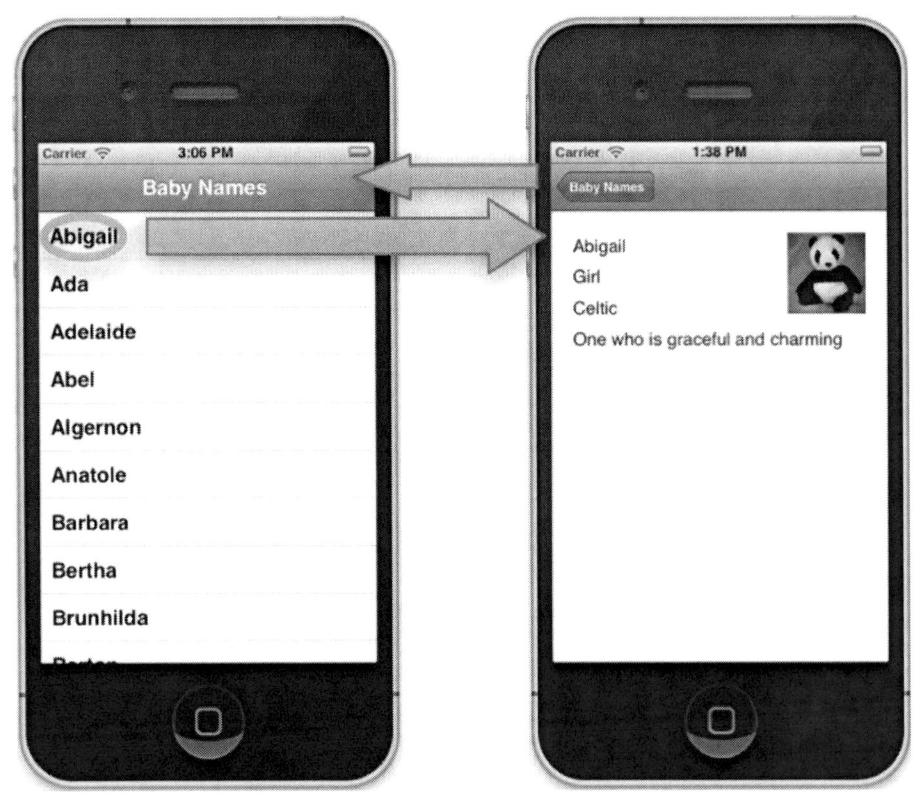

Figure 5–23. *The name detail view*

Although this certainly isn't going to win any awards for user interface design, you've now got the navigation controller, table view, and detail view controllers wired up and playing nicely together.

Summary

In this chapter you've wired together a `UINavigationController`-based app from scratch. The app delegate loads the navigation controller. The navigation controller loads the table view. The table view provides the relevant row, and asks the navigation controller to push in the detail view for the row's content.

Having put the structure and the basic function of the app together, you can adapt this to drive the table with any suitable model as the data source. The structure of that data will determine how you'll handle drilling into the detail, and using the techniques that are explored in Chapter 8 onwards, you can customize the look and feel of the table to match your app's design.

Chapter 6

Indexing, Grouping, and Sorting

Although UITableView is efficient at managing large quantities of data, the user interface is constrained by the physical size of the device. By the time a table displays more than 10 or 12 rows, its labels and controls have become too small to easily work with.

If a table contains a lot of data, the user might also have to perform a lot of scrolling, which doesn't make for a good user experience. Fortunately, some UITableView facilities are available to improve the organization of the data presented by the table view.

Using Indexed Tables

An *indexed table* is fundamentally the same as a plain-style table, but with an index running down the right hand edge, as you saw in Chapter 2. Typically, this index displays letters or numbers, which the user can tap to automatically scroll the table to the relevant section, without having to scroll manually.

This is how apps such as the built-in Contacts application work. When the app opens, you're at the top of the list of names beginning with A. Tapping Z will rapidly scroll the app down to the bottom of the list.

Indexed tables rely on two elements: an array of strings to act as index entries that will be displayed down the right-hand edge, and data that is organized into sections corresponding to the index entries. In the case of the Contacts app, names are organized alphabetically in sections—a section for names beginning with *A*, a section for names beginning with *B*, and so on.

Although there needs to be a corresponding section for each entry in the index, the titles of the section headers don't have to be the same as the index strings themselves. In the Contacts app, the section headers and indexes *are* the same, but you can be more flexible if you need to be.

CAUTION: Apple's iOS Human Interface Guidelines advise against using table indexes in conjunction with in-cell controls, because the index will tend to obscure the right-hand side of the cells.

Using Sectioned and Grouped Tables

Sections take the organized presentation of data one stage further, and introduce the concept of grouping the rows together, as you learned in Chapter 2. These can be presented either by dividing the table view by section headers or by splitting the table up into groups.

Splitting the rows into distinct groups helps break up the information, and makes it easy to see the separate groups when scrolling through a long table, as shown in Figure 6–1.

Figure 6–1. *Sectioned and grouped table styles*

Although the visual presentation is quite distinct, both sectioned and grouped tables use the same underlying data structure. The data for each section or group is stored in an "inner" array, which in turn is stored in an "outer" array that organizes all the sections and groups together.

NOTE: If you're using a grouped table, you wouldn't typically use an index. Although there's nothing in Apple's Human Interface Guidelines *explicitly* prohibiting it, an index does tend to look strange because of the way that it overlaps with the grouped table's background.

Creating a Simple Indexed Table

Before you dive into the complex stuff, let's take a look at putting together a very simple indexed table, shown in Figure 6–2. This table consists of a list of names, one for each letter of the alphabet. The names are sorted into sections, and there's an index list for navigation.

To keep the example simple, each section has only one name, so there's no need to sort the data for each section. You'll look at sorting the rows in the next section of this chapter.

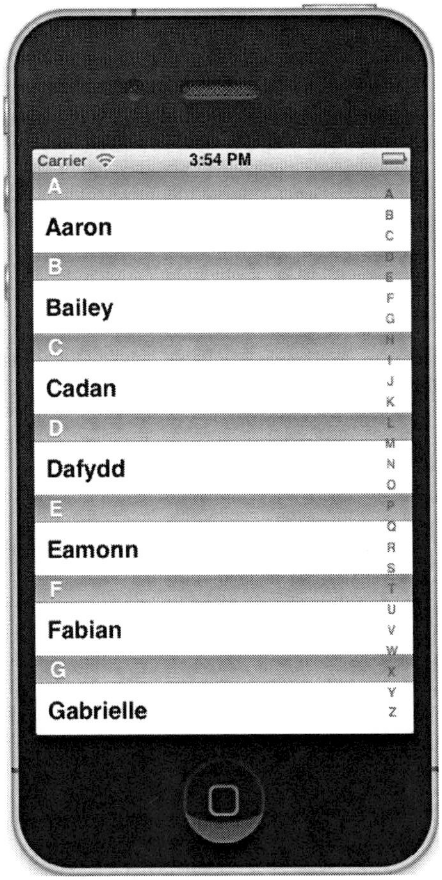

Figure 6–2. *The simple indexed table*

Start by creating a new project based on the Single View Application template. This will provide you with a skeleton application containing an `AppDelegate`, a view controller class, and a XIB file.

Setting Up the Basic Table

The Single View Application template gives us a very basic skeleton app, with an `AppDelegate` and a single view controller. At the moment, that view controller is an empty view (if you run the app at this stage, it's a blank, gray screen).

To get the initial table view up and running, you'll need to do two things:

1. Conform the view controller to the `UITableViewDelegate` and `UITableViewDataSource` protocols.
2. Add the `tableView` to the NIB file.

Setting up the view controller is easy enough. In the header file, add the two protocol names to the interface:

```
@interface ViewController : UIViewController <UITableViewDelegate, ↵
UITableViewDataSource>
```

Then open the view controller's NIB file, and drag a Table view from the Objects browser into the NIB's view. It will snap to the full extent of the view as you release the mouse button.

Finally, link the new table view to the controller by Ctrl-clicking it and dragging the connection line out to the File's Owner icon in the Placeholders list. Click the `dataSource` item in the HUD pop-up, and repeat the process again to connect the `delegate`.

Creating the Source Data

To start, you're going to need two sources of data:

- The objects to display in the table rows
- The objects to display as the index titles

These will be stored in two `NSArray` properties. The view controller will also need to act as a `delegate` and a `data source` for the table view, as shown in Listing 6–1.

Listing 6–1. *The View Controller's Header File*

```
#import <UIKit/UIKit.h>

@interface ViewController : UIViewController <UITableViewDelegate, ↵
UITableViewDataSource>

@property (nonatomic, strong) NSArray *tableData;
@property (nonatomic, strong) NSArray *indexTitlesArray;

@end
```

Both properties will need to be synthesized in the implementation file.

To keep this example as simple as possible, you'll use an array of 26 names for the table data, and an array of the letters of the alphabet for the index titles. One place to set this up is in the view controller's `viewDidLoad` method, shown in Listing 6–2.

Listing 6–2. *The View Controller's `viewDidLoad` Method*

```
- (void)viewDidLoad
{
    [super viewDidLoad];
    // Do any additional setup after loading the view, typically from a nib.
    self.tableData = [[NSArray alloc] ➥
initWithObjects:@"Aaron",@"Bailey",@"Cadan",@"Dafydd",@"Eamonn",@"Fabian",➥
@"Gabrielle",@"Hafwen",@"Isaac",@"Jacinta",@"Kathleen",@"Lucy",@"Maurice",➥
@"Nadia",@"Octavia",@"Padraig",@"Quinta",@"Rachael",@"Sabina",@"Tabitha",➥
@"Uma",@"Valentina",@"Wallis",@"Xanthe",@"Yvonne",@"Zebadiah",nil];


    NSString *letters = @"A B C D E F G H I J K L M N O P Q R S T U V W X Y Z";
    self.indexTitlesArray = [letters componentsSeparatedByString:@" "];

}
```

The `indexTitlesArray` uses `NSString`'s handy `componentsSeparatedByString` method to take a string of letters, separated by spaces, and return an array of the original string split at each space. That's a *lot* quicker than typing `@"a", @"b", @"c"` and so on.

Feeding the Table with Data

To create an indexed table, the `tableView`'s `dataSource` and `delegate` have a little bit more work to do than you've seen in previous examples.

The `tableView:cellForRowAtIndexPath` method is identical to ones that you've seen before, as you can see in Listing 6–3.

Listing 6–3. *The `tableView:cellForRowAtIndexPath` Method*

```
-(UITableViewCell *)tableView:(UITableView *)tableView ➥
cellForRowAtIndexPath:(NSIndexPath *)indexPath {

    static NSString *cellIdentifier = @"cellIdentifier";
    UITableViewCell *cell = [tableView
dequeueReusableCellWithIdentifier:cellIdentifier];

    if (!cell) {
        cell = [[UITableViewCell alloc] initWithStyle:UITableViewCellStyleDefault➥
reuseIdentifier:cellIdentifier];
    }

    cell.textLabel.text = [self.tableData objectAtIndex:indexPath.section];

    return cell;

}
```

In previous simple tables with a single section, the number of rows in the section was the number of rows in the source data. This made the numberOfRowsInSection method very simple. If the table's data were stored in an NSArray called tableData, for example, the method would look like Listing 6–4.

Listing 6–4. *A simple numberOfRowsInSection Method*

```
-(NSInteger)tableView:(UITableView *)tableView numberOfRowsInSection: ↩
(NSInteger)section {
    return [self.tableData count];
}
```

In our indexed table, you need to know how many rows will appear in each of the sections so that the numberOfRowsInSection method can return this data. Because this is a simple example with one name per letter of the alphabet, you can hack this by simply returning 1, as shown in Listing 6–5.

Listing 6–5. *The Actual numberOfRowsInSection Method*

```
-(NSInteger)tableView:(UITableView *)tableView ↩
numberOfRowsInSection:(NSInteger)section {
    return 1;
}
```

Having established the number of rows in each section, and creating a cell for each row, there are four things you need to do to get the indexing side of things working:

- Return the number of sections in the table.
- For each section, return the title for that section's header so that it can appear above the cells.
- Return an array of strings to use as the index so that this can be displayed down the right-hand side of the table.
- For each string in the index, figure out which section that string relates to so that the table can jump to the appropriate one.

Let's tackle these one by one.

Returning the Number of Sections in the Table

To return the number of sections in the table, you need the numberOfSectionsInTableView method. This will be the same as the number of entries in the index titles, as shown in Listing 6–6.

Listing 6–6. *The numberOfSectionsInTableView Method*

```
- (NSInteger)numberOfSectionsInTableView:(UITableView *)tableView {

    return [self.indexTitlesArray count];

}
```

Creating the Title for the Section Header

The section headers will appear above the rows in that section. The appearance of the header can be customized, but the default is a gray bar, as shown in Figure 6–3.

Figure 6–3. *The default section header*

You need to supply a section header for each section, but these headers don't necessarily have to be the same as the index entries.

Our section headers *will* be the same as the index entries, so we can use the section number to access the object at that index of the `indexTitlesArray`, as shown in Listing 6–7.

Listing 6–7. *The `titleForHeaderInSection` Method*

```
-(NSString *)tableView:(UITableView *)tableView ↵
titleForHeaderInSection:(NSInteger)section {

    return [self.indexTitlesArray objectAtIndex:section];

}
```

Building the Index

The index is built up from an array of `NSStrings`. Strictly speaking, these could be of any length, but there are fairly obvious space constraints. You're best keeping the strings to no more than about three letters.

Providing the data for the index is simply a case of returning the array, as shown in Listing 6–8.

Listing 6–8. *The `SectionIndexTitlesForTableView` Method*

```
-(NSArray *)sectionIndexTitlesForTableView:(UITableView *)tableView {

    return self.indexTitlesArray;
}
```

Matching the Index to the Section

When an element in the index is tapped, the `tableView` will automatically scroll so that the heading for the corresponding section is at the very top of the table. Fortunately, the `tableView` handles working out how far to scroll, but you do need to give it a helping hand by telling it which table section corresponds to which index. Listing 6–9 shows how to achieve this.

Listing 6–9. *The* `tableView:sectionForSectionIndexTitle:atIndex` ***Method***

```
- (NSInteger)tableView:(UITableView *)tableView sectionForSectionIndexTitle: ➥
(NSString *)title atIndex:(NSInteger)index {

    return [self.indexTitlesArray indexOfObject:title];

}
```

Putting this all together will result in a table that looks like Figure 6–4.

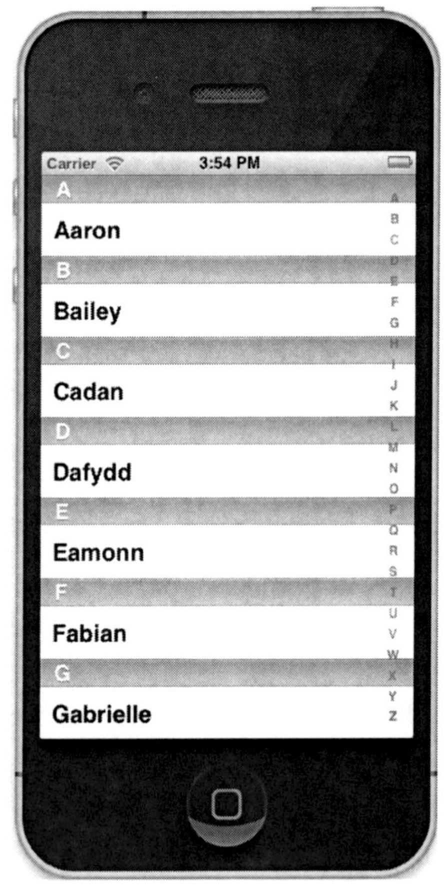

Figure 6–4. *A very simple indexed table*

It's worth noting that you don't have to use indexes and sections together. If you want an indexed table without section headers, don't implement the `tableView:titleForHeaderInSection` method, and your table will be a simple indexed one, as shown in Figure 6–5.

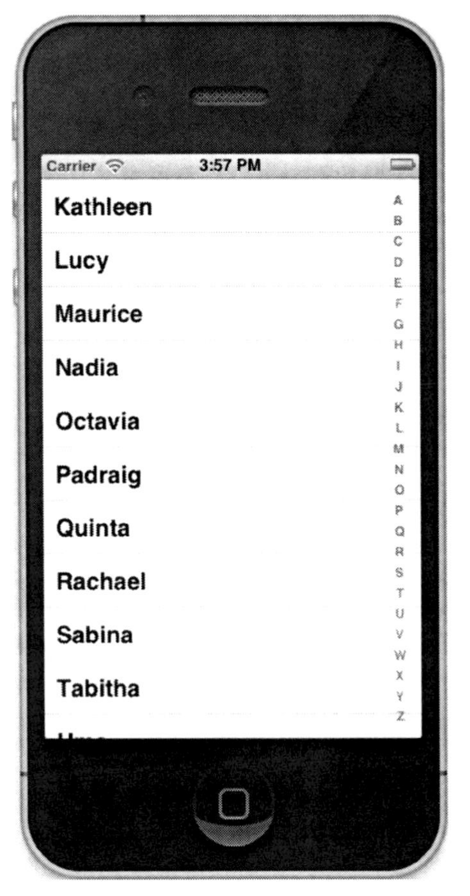

Figure 6–5. *An indexed table without section headings*

Similarly, you can remove the index by omitting the `sectionIndexTitlesForTableView` method.

Building Practical Sectioned Tables

The simple table that you've built so far will hopefully have given you a feel for how an indexed and sectioned table fits together—but it was a very simple example. In reality, your apps are likely to have far more complex data, with correspondingly complex implementations.

In this section, you're going to build a more complex example with data that can support the table types in Figure 6–6.

Figure 6–6. *The all-singing, all-dancing tables*

The app is going to implement several new features:

- Loading source data from a property list (plist) file
- Using the `UILocalizedIndexedCollation` class to automate the creation of section headers and index lists
- Creating section headers conditionally, based on the index

Creating the Data for a Table with Sections and Indexes

To feed an indexed table, you need three sets of data:

- An array of strings for the table's index
- Data for each section header
- Data for the rows in each section

The easiest way to supply the latter two is with an array of arrays. The outer array organizes the sections, and contains the inner arrays that hold the data for the rows.

The inner arrays are sorted so that the rows appear in order. The outer array is sorted so that the sections appear in order. Figure 6–7 shows the example.

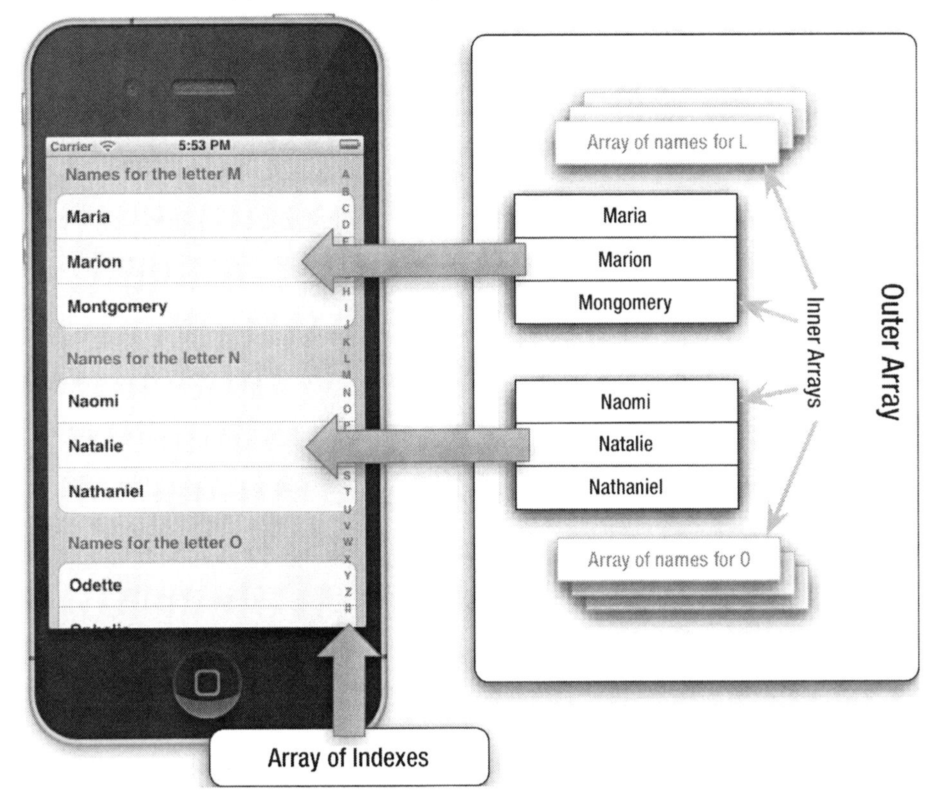

Figure 6–7. *How the table gets fed data*

The data objects in the inner arrays don't necessarily have to be ordered, but that's usually the case.

There are two ways to create the data for an indexed table:

- Manually, by creating an array of arrays yourself
- Using the `UILocalizedIndexedCollation` class to do much of the heavy lifting for you

Which method you use is a matter of personal preference and the dictates of the app you're building, so I'll cover both.

Arrays of Arrays

Creating the data structure manually is a two-stage process:

1. Create the inner arrays and populate them with their objects.
2. Add the inner arrays into the outer array.

There's an implicit assumption here that you'll be adding the objects into the arrays (and the inner arrays into the outer array) in the order that you want them to appear in the table. If this isn't the case, you can sort them before they're needed. You'll look at this in a moment.

Listing 6–10 provides a very simple (and very contrived) example of how you might create an array of arrays.

Listing 6–10. *The Simplest Possible Array of Arrays*

```
-(NSArray *)createArrayOfArrays{

    // Create the inner arrays
    NSArray *innerArrayA = [NSArray arrayWithObjects:@"A1", ↵
@"A2", @"A3", @"A4", nil];
    NSArray *innerArrayB = [NSArray arrayWithObjects:@"B1", ↵
@"B2", @"B3", @"B4", nil];
    NSArray *innerArrayC = [NSArray arrayWithObjects:@"C1", ↵
@"C2", @"C3", @"C4", nil];
    NSArray *innerArrayD = [NSArray arrayWithObjects:@"D1", ↵
@"D2", @"D3", @"D4", nil];
    NSArray *innerArrayE = [NSArray arrayWithObjects:@"E1", ↵
@"E2", @"E3", @"E4", nil];

    // Create the outer array
    NSArray *outerArray = [[NSArray alloc] initWithObjects:
                            innerArrayA,
                            innerArrayB,
                            innerArrayC,
                            innerArrayD,
                            innerArrayE,
                            nil];

    return outerArray;

}
```

Although this approach is perfectly functional, it's not the most flexible—especially because you're in charge of sorting the arrays into the order that they're needed. Fortunately, iOS provides the snappily named `UILocalizedIndexedCollation` class that automates a lot of the process for us.

UILocalizedIndexedCollation

The `UILocalizedIndexedCollation` class provides some convenience methods that can help create data structures for indexed tables. To quote Apple's class reference:

> *The `UILocalizedIndexedCollation` class is a convenience for organizing, sorting, and localizing the data for a table view that has a section index.*

The class works with an array of row objects, and sorts, organizes, and localizes the data into a form that's ready for the table view.

It's a four-stage process:

1. Create an instance of a `UILocalizedIndexCollation` object. This provides an array called `sectionTitles` that contains the alphabet for the current locale setting. (This will automatically adjust, so you don't need to worry about what it contains.)
2. Create the array structure—an outer array for the sections, and an inner array for each of your `sectionTitles`.
3. For each object in the array of row objects, use `UILocalizedIndexCollation`'s `sectionForObject` method to determine which inner array the object should be placed in.
4. After placing all the row objects into their respective inner arrays, use `UILocalizedIndexCollation`'s `sortedArrayFromArray` method to sort the inner array into order.

In each case, `UILocalizedIndexCollation` will use the relevant locale to figure out how the row objects should be organized and sorted—which means you don't need to know your S from your ß...

LOCALIZATION IN PRACTICE

A the name suggests, the `UILocalizedIndexedCollation` class handles a lot of the heavy lifting involved in localizing your app, and is dependent on the localization settings of your application bundle. This allows the class to handle the different ordering requirements of various languages.

For example, an app that uses US English as its locale will return 27 results in its `sectionTitles` array: one each for A to Z, and one for numbers that appear in the list as #. If you're using one of the Scandinavian locales, however, you'll also automatically get an entry for the Ø character—so the class can save a lot of time and effort.

iOS localization is even clever enough to support non-Latin character sets. When using the Traditional Chinese locale, for example, the class will sort the entries by the number of strokes in the Chinese character.

There is extensive support for localization in iOS, but it's a big topic in its own right. Check out the Introduction to Internationalization Programming Topics guide in the Xcode documentation for more details.

All this *sounds* like a lot of work, but it's not bad as it seems. By using `UILocalizedIndexCollation`, you'll put the app in Figure 6–6 together in short order.

Creating the All-Singing, All-Dancing Table

Creating the app is a four-step process:

1. Create a new app from the Single View Application template.
2. Create some data to display in the table. To provide a bit of variety, you'll use a plist file to provide the raw data.
3. Add the `tableView` to the NIB file and conform the view controller class to `UITableView`'s `delegate` and `dataSource` protocols (which will be very familiar by now).
4. Extend the view controller class to implement the additional methods that handle the indexing and section handling for the table.

Creating the App from a Template

There's nothing new here. In Xcode, create a new project by choosing **File ➤ New ➤ New** Project, select the Single View Application template, and save the project somewhere suitable.

> **NOTE:** I've called my application NamesApp, and I've given it a class prefix of NA.

That will give you an `AppDelegate`, a subclass of `UIViewController` called `NAViewController`, and a NIB file.

Creating Some Data in a plist File

If you haven't met them before, property list (commonly abbreviated as *plist*) files are a useful way of storing data in a key-value structure. They serve a practically identical purpose to JavaScript Object Notation (JSON) files, but with a couple of iOS-specific advantages:

- Because plist files are a native iOS format, Xcode provides a nifty editor that makes creating and editing them a snap.
- iOS can read and write to plist files significantly faster than it can to an equivalent JSON file.

Plist files are stored in the application bundle, but you can create and edit them in much the same way as you would a class or a NIB file. To create a new plist for the table data, choose **File ➤ New ➤ New File**, and then select the Property List option from the Resource group, as shown in Figure 6–8.

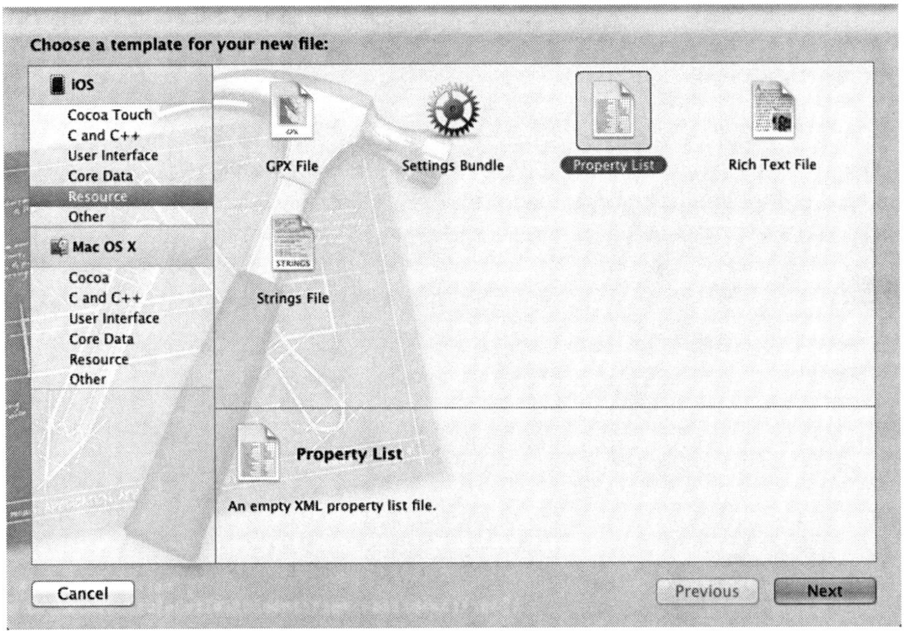

Figure 6–8. *Creating a new property list file*

Call the file **Names**, and click Create to create the file.

If you click the `Names.plist` file in the project explorer, you'll be presented with a blank file, with headings for Key, Type, and Value. To create a new key-value pair, Ctrl-click in the Source Editor and select the Add Row option, as shown in Figure 6–9.

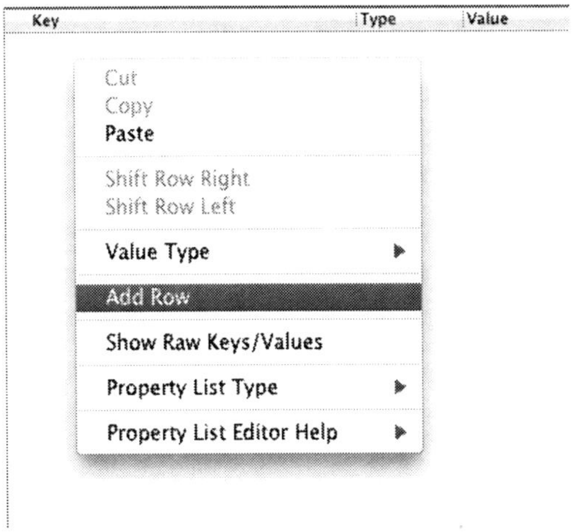

Figure 6–9. *Adding a new key-value pair*

A new, empty Key item will be added, as shown in Figure 6–10.

Figure 6–10. *The new key-value pair*

Various types of key-value pairs can be created, but the key thing to remember (labored pun intended) is that keys must be unique. You're going to create a list of names, so rather than a type string, you're going to need an array. Click the drop-down arrows next to String, and you'll see a pop-up list of types, shown in Figure 6–11.

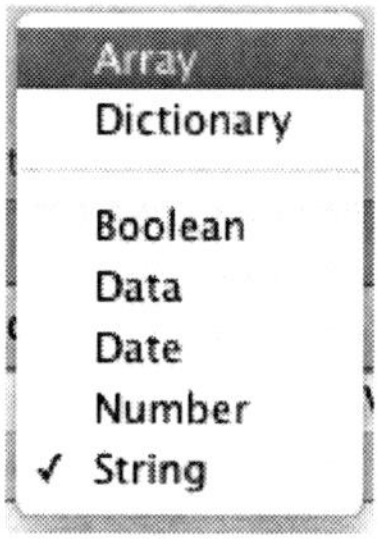

Figure 6–11. *The Types pop-up list*

Select the Array option, and the New Item key will change to an Array type. Double-click the New Item title and replace it with `names`.

Now you'll start adding Name values. Click the disclosure indicator in the Names row so that it's highlighted, and press Return. A new line with a name of Item 0 will appear underneath Names, as shown in Figure 6–12.

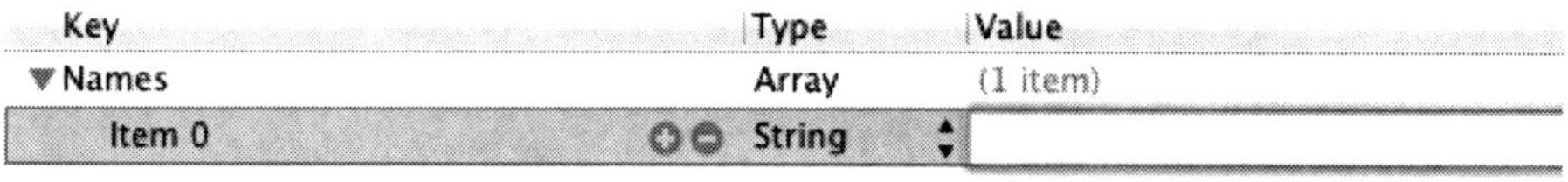

Figure 6–12. *Adding a new value*

In the Value field, type the first name. (I've used Aaron, but you use whatever takes your fancy.) Then press Return to save the new value. Press Return again, and you'll repeat the process.

Now you have two options: continue typing, or use the plist file from the source code on the Apress site. If you go for the second option, you'll end up with a plist that looks like Figure 6–13.

Key	Type	Value
names	Array	(78 items)
Item 0	String	Aaron
Item 1	String	Aberah
Item 2	String	Aisha
Item 3	String	Cadan
Item 4	String	Cadenza
Item 5	String	Cyrene
Item 6	String	Baldric
Item 7	String	Banbha
Item 8	String	Bryony
Item 9	String	Dafyyd
Item 10	String	Dagmar
Item 11	String	Dymphna
Item 12	String	Fabian
Item 13	String	Florence
Item 14	String	Frieda
Item 15	String	Eamonn
Item 16	String	Edith
Item 17	String	Eveline
Item 18	String	Gabriella
Item 19	String	Grant
Item 20	String	Gwyneth

Figure 6–13. *The source code's plist file*

Using the plist in Code

In order to use the data stored in the plist file, it has to be loaded and parsed before you can use it as the data source for the table view.

In the `NAViewController`'s header file, add an `NSArray` called `tableData` as a property, and then synthesize it in the implementation file. Now alter the `ViewController`'s `viewDidLoad` method to add the lines in Listing 6–11.

Listing 6–11. *Additional Code for* `viewDidLoad`

```
    NSBundle* bundle = [NSBundle mainBundle];

    NSString* plistPath = [bundle pathForResource:@"Names" ofType:@"plist"];

    NSDictionary *namesDictionary = [[NSDictionary alloc]  ↩
initWithContentsOfFile:plistPath];

    self.tableData = [namesDictionary objectForKey:@"names"];
```

This code performs three tasks:

- Locates the plist file in the application's main bundle
- Creates an `NSDictionary` from the contents of the plist file
- Loads the values held in the plist's names array into the `tableData` instance variable

Sorting Out the User Interface

Having started the creation of the data, it's time for a quick diversion into the user interface. Open the `NAViewController` XIB file and drag a `UITableView` onto the view, allowing it to fill the full view.

You have the option of setting the table's style to *plain* or *grouped*. Select the Table view in the Objects inspector, and then switch to the Attribute inspector if that isn't already shown.

If you wanted a grouped style, you could select the Grouped option from the Table View section at the top of the Attributes inspector, as shown in Figure 6–14.

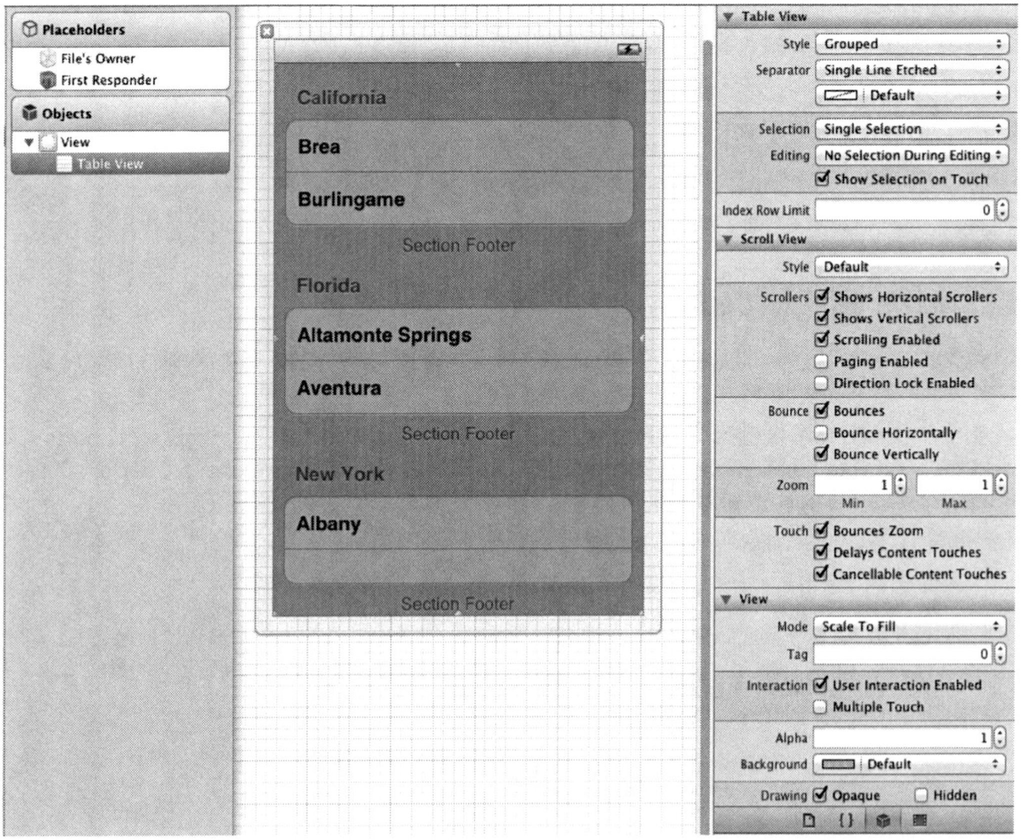

Figure 6–14. *Changing the `tableView`'s style to Grouped*

Now set the table's delegate and dataSource properties by connecting to the File's Owner: Ctrl-click the table and drag the connector up to the File's Owner icon. Select delegate from the HUD pop-up, and then repeat the process again to connect the dataSource property.

Finally, you'll need to conform the NAViewController class to the UITableView Delegate and dataSource protocols. Switch to the NAViewController.h file and then amend the class interface definition:

```
@interface NAViewController : UIViewController <UITableViewDelegate, ↵
UITableViewDataSource>
```

Extending the ViewController Class

Now it's time to start implementing the additional methods in the NAViewController class to set up the table.

The first step is to create another property, this time for the UILocalizedIndexedCollation object. Add the following to the header file, and then the corresponding synthesis in the implementation:

```
@property (nonatomic, strong) UILocalizedIndexedCollation *collation;
```

And instantiate it in the viewDidLoad method back in the implementation file:

```
self.collation = [UILocalizedIndexedCollation currentCollation];
```

Because there's a fair amount of code involved to set up the UILocalizedIndexedCollation, you'll put this in its own method. Add an @interface section to the implementation file:

```
@interface NAViewController()

    -(void)configureSectionData;

@end
```

Then add in property declarations (and corresponding synthesis) for two more arrays that you'll use shortly. The full header file should look like Listing 6–12.

Listing 6–12. ***The Full*** *NAViewController* ***Header File***

```
#import <UIKit/UIKit.h>

@interface ViewController : UIViewController <UITableViewDelegate, ↵
UITableViewDataSource>

@property (nonatomic, strong) NSArray *tableData;
@property (nonatomic, strong) UILocalizedIndexedCollation *collation;
@property (nonatomic, strong) NSMutableArray *outerArray;
@property (nonatomic, strong) NSArray *indexTitlesArray;

@end
```

And then call the configureSectionData method at the end of viewDidLoad, which should look like Listing 6–13.

Listing 6–13. *The Full `viewDidLoad` Method*

```
- (void)viewDidLoad
{
    [super viewDidLoad];
    // Do any additional setup after loading the view, typically from a nib.
    NSBundle* bundle = [NSBundle mainBundle];
    NSString* plistPath = [bundle pathForResource:@"Names" ofType:@"plist"];

    NSDictionary *namesDictionary = [[NSDictionary alloc] ➥
initWithContentsOfFile:plistPath];

    self.tableData = [namesDictionary objectForKey:@"names"];

    self.collation = [UILocalizedIndexedCollation currentCollation];

    [self configureSectionData];

}
```

Sorting the Data

Now it's time to create the `configureSectionData` method, shown in Listing 6–14.

Listing 6–14. *The `configureSectionData` Method*

```
-(void)configureSectionData {

    NSUInteger sectionTitlesCount = [collation.sectionTitles count];

    self.outerArray = [NSMutableArray arrayWithCapacity:sectionTitlesCount];

    for (NSUInteger index = 0; index < sectionTitlesCount; index++) {
        NSMutableArray *array = [NSMutableArray array];
        [self.outerArray addObject:array];
    }

    for (NSString *nameString in tableData) {
        NSInteger sectionNumber = [collation ➥
sectionForObject:nameString collationStringSelector:@selector(lowercaseString)];
        NSMutableArray *sectionNames = [outerArray objectAtIndex:sectionNumber];
        [sectionNames addObject:nameString];
    }

    for (NSUInteger index = 0; index < sectionTitlesCount; index++) {
        NSMutableArray *namesForSection = [outerArray objectAtIndex:index];
        NSArray *sortedNamesForSection = [collation sortedArrayFromArray:
namesForSection collationStringSelector:@selector(lowercaseString)];
        [self.outerArray replaceObjectAtIndex:index withObject:sortedNamesForSection];
    }

}
```

Let's step through this method.

The UILocalizedIndexCollation class provides a sectionTitles property that returns an NSArray of section titles relevant to the device's locale. If the device locale is set to US English, for example, sectionTitle will return the following:

```
(A,B,C,D,E,F,G,H,I,J,K,L,M,N,O,P,Q,R,S,T,U,V,W,X,Y,Z,#)
```

Next you get the count of sectionTitles, and assign that to an NSUInteger:

```
NSUInteger sectionTitlesCount = [collation.sectionTitles count];
```

Assuming for the sake of argument that there are 27 (A to Z plus #) sectionTitle objects, you then create the outer array with the same number of slots (27) for the inner arrays (one per section, remember):

```
self.outerArray = [NSMutableArray arrayWithCapacity:sectionTitlesCount];
```

Now it's time to create those inner arrays and add them to the outer array:

```
for (NSUInteger index = 0; index < sectionTitlesCount; index++) {
    NSMutableArray *array = [NSMutableArray array];
        [self.outerArray addObject:array];
}
```

After the arrays are ready, you can start the process of putting the row objects into the appropriate section. Iterating across each element in the tableData array, you feed that into UILocalizedIndexCollation's sectionForObject:collationStringSelector method:

```
for (NSString *nameString in tableData) {
    NSInteger sectionNumber = [collation sectionForObject:nameString↵
collationStringSelector:@selector(lowercaseString)];

    NSMutableArray *sectionNames = [outerArray objectAtIndex:sectionNumber];

        [sectionNames addObject:nameString];
}
```

This takes two arguments: the object that you want to allocate to the appropriate inner array, and a collationStringSelector that determines how each object should be evaluated.

This method has to return an NSString and can't take any arguments. Because the tableData array is full of NSString objects, you can use the lowercaseString method as the selector.

The sectionForObject:collationStringSelector method returns an NSInteger that is the index of the inner array into which the object should be placed. If the value of nameString that was being evaluated was Aaron, then this would return 0, while a value of Baldric would return 1, Cadan would return 2, and so on.

NOTE: If you were dealing with custom objects with their own properties, you would use one of those instead. You'd need to ensure that the custom object had an NSString property that could be used as the collation string selector. For example, if you had a Customer object with a range of properties including an NSString called customerName, the call to the sectionForObject:collationStringSelector method might look like the following:

```
NSInteger sectionNumber = [collation sectionForObject:theCustomer↩
collationStringSelector:@selector(customerName)];
```

Having obtained the sectionNumber, you use this to get a reference to the relevant inner array and add the nameString object to it:

```
NSMutableArray *sectionNames = [self.outerArray objectAtIndex:sectionNumber];

[sectionNames addObject:nameString];
```

After you've iterated across each nameString object in the tableData array, each one will have been placed into the relevant inner array, but in the order encountered in the plist file.—

If you're lucky, this might already be in the order that you want—alphabetized, for example—but it's just as likely to be random. So the next and final step is to iterate across each inner array in turn and sort the contents:

```
for (NSUInteger index = 0; index < sectionTitlesCount; index++) {

    NSMutableArray *namesForSection = [outerArray objectAtIndex:index];

    NSArray *sortedNamesForSection = [collation sortedArrayFromArray: ↩
namesForSection collationStringSelector:@selector(lowercaseString)];

            [outerArray replaceObjectAtIndex:index withObject:sortedNamesForSection];
}
```

The unsorted namesForSection array is fed into the sortedArrayFromArray method, which also takes a collationStringSelector argument, and the resulting sorted array stored in sortedNameForSection. The unsorted array is replaced in outerArray by the newly sorted version.

Configuring the Sections

With the data organized into the required structure, you're now in a position to set up the sections. There are five methods you need to implement:

- numberOfSectionsInTableView returns an NSInteger of the total number of sections in the table (see listing 6–15).
- titleForHeaderInSection returns an NSString that can be used as the title for each section (see listing 6–16).

- sectionIndexTitlesForTableView returns an NSArray containing NSStrings for each title in the index displayed down the right-hand edge of the table (see listing 6–17).
- sectionForSectionIndexTitle:atIndex takes three arguments: the tableView, the title, and index of the index title that has been selected by the user. This method returns an NSInteger for the corresponding section (see listing 6–18).
- numberOfRowsInSection returns the number of rows in the given section (in other words, the number of elements in the relevant inner array (see listing 6–19).

Listing 6–15. *numberOfSectionsInTableView*

```
- (NSInteger)numberOfSectionsInTableView:(UITableView *)tableView {
    return [self.collation.sectionTitles count];
}
```

This method returns the number of entries supplied by UILocalizedIndexCollation's sectionTitles method. If the device locale is set to US English, for example, this would return 27 (the letters A to Z plus # for numbered titles).

Listing 6–16. *titleForHeaderInSection*

```
-(NSString *)tableView:(UITableView *)tableView ➥
titleForHeaderInSection:(NSInteger)section {

    NSString *theLetter = [self.collation.sectionTitles objectAtIndex:section];

    if (![theLetter isEqualToString:@"#"]) {
        NSString *titleString = [NSString stringWithFormat:  ➥
@"Names for the letter %@", theLetter];
        return titleString;
    }

    return nil;

}
```

This method creates a custom NSString for each section A through Z, but doesn't create a section title for the # section.

Listing 6–17. *sectionIndexTitlesForTableView*

```
-(NSArray *)sectionIndexTitlesForTableView:(UITableView *)tableView {
    return self.collation.sectionTitles;
}
```

This method returns an NSArray of the section index titles for the table view, which are then displayed down the right-hand edge of the table. If you don't need an index (if, for example, you're using a grouped-style table), you can omit this method and an index won't be displayed.

Listing 6–18. *sectionForSectionIndexTitle*

```
- (NSInteger)tableView:(UITableView *)tableView ➥
sectionForSectionIndexTitle:(NSString *)title atIndex:(NSInteger)index {
```

```
        return [self.collation sectionForSectionIndexTitleAtIndex:index];
    }
```

This listing provides a cross-reference between the index at the right-hand edge of the table, and the appropriate section in the table itself. It returns the `NSInteger` of the section, which the table uses to scroll up or down to the appropriate location. If you're not using an index, this method isn't required.

Listing 6–19. *numberOfRowsInSection*

```
    -(NSInteger)tableView:(UITableView *)tableView numberOfRowsInSection:➥
    (NSInteger)section {

        NSArray *innerArray = [self.outerArray objectAtIndex:section];
        return [innerArray count];
}
```

This method returns the number of rows that are required to be displayed in a given section. This is the count of the number of elements in the appropriate inner array, so the first step is to get a reference to the array that is the *n*th object in the outer array (where *n* is the section number). `NSArray`'s `count` method then returns the number of elements in the inner array.

Finally, you'll need the `tableView:cellForRowAtIndexPath` method, shown in Listing 6–20.

Listing 6–20. *tableView:cellForRowAtIndexPath*

```
-(UITableViewCell *)tableView:(UITableView *)tableView➥
cellForRowAtIndexPath:(NSIndexPath *)indexPath {

    static NSString *cellIdentifier = @"cellIdentifier";

    UITableViewCell *cell = [tableView
dequeueReusableCellWithIdentifier:cellIdentifier];

    if (!cell) {
        cell = [[UITableViewCell alloc] ➥
initWithStyle:UITableViewCellStyleDefault reuseIdentifier:cellIdentifier];
    }

    // Get the inner array for this section
    NSArray *innerArray = [self.outerArray objectAtIndex:indexPath.section];

    // Get the name from the inner array
    NSString *theName = [innerArray objectAtIndex:indexPath.row];

    cell.textLabel.text = theName;

    return cell;

}
```

This gets the data for the row in two stages. First, it gets a reference to the array of content for the section in question (the names for the letter), and then gets the name string from the array based on the row.

Put all these together, and you'll end up with the table view in Figure 6–15.

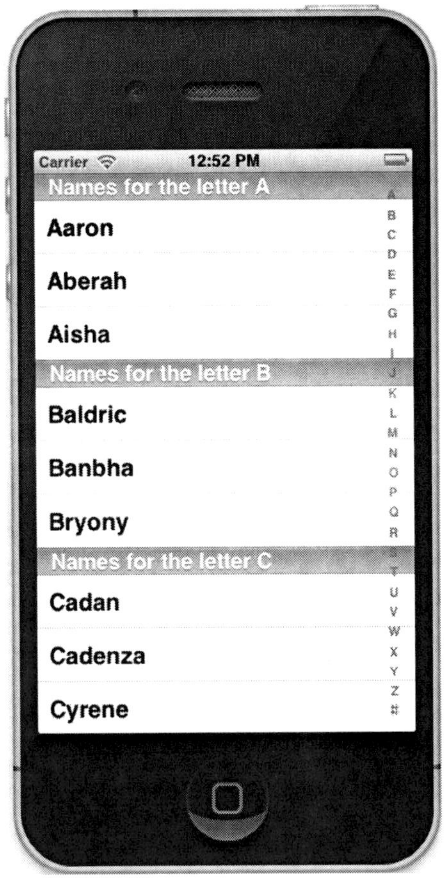

Figure 6–15. *The finished table view*

Creating Table and Section Header and Footer Views

Up until now, you've been customizing the section headers with simple text strings—but you don't have to stop there. The `tableView:viewForHeaderInSection` and `tableView:viewForFooterInSection` methods return `UIViews`—which means that anything you can put in a `UIView`, you can put in a section's header and footer.

Figure 6–16 shows where headers and footers appear and how they're repeated. Table headers and footers should be configured as the table loads, and the `viewDidLoad` method is a good place to do this. Section headers and footers are handled as the sections themselves are created.

Figure 6–16. *Table and section headers and footers*

Listing 6–21 produces the section header shown in figure 6–16 (`tableView` is an instance variable reference to the table itself).

Listing 6–21. *A Custom Section Header*

```
-(UIView *)tableView:(UITableView *)theTableView ➥
viewForHeaderInSection:(NSInteger)section {

    // Create header and footer views for the table
    UIView *sectionHeaderView = [[UIView alloc] initWithFrame: ➥
CGRectMake(0, 0, tableView.frame.size.width, 50.0)];
    sectionHeaderView.backgroundColor = [UIColor ➥
colorWithRed:1.0 green:0.7 blue:0.57 alpha:1.0];
    UILabel *headerLabel = [[UILabel alloc] initWithFrame: ➥
CGRectMake(15, 15, sectionHeaderView.frame.size.width,15.0)];
    headerLabel.backgroundColor = [UIColor clearColor];

    headerLabel.text = @"Section Header";
    [headerLabel setFont:[UIFont fontWithName:@"Courier-Bold" size:18.0]];
    [sectionHeaderView addSubview:headerLabel];
```

```
    return sectionHeaderView;
}
```

If you've implemented custom header and footers, you'll need to inform the table of their respective heights with the `heightForHeaderInSection` and `heightForFooterInSection` methods:

```
-(CGFloat)tableView:(UITableView *)tableView ➥
heightForHeaderInSection:(NSInteger)section {
    return 50.0;
}
```

The effects you can produce aren't limited to garish colors. Figure 6–17 shows an example from one of my apps. There are two sections in the table. Section 0 contains a single row with a static image, and section 1 is a series of custom cells containing sliders.

The "ruler" that provides the scale for the sliders is section 1's header. It contains a `UIImageView` of the ruler image. As the table scrolls up, the ruler scrolls up with it until it reaches the top of the table and then "sticks."

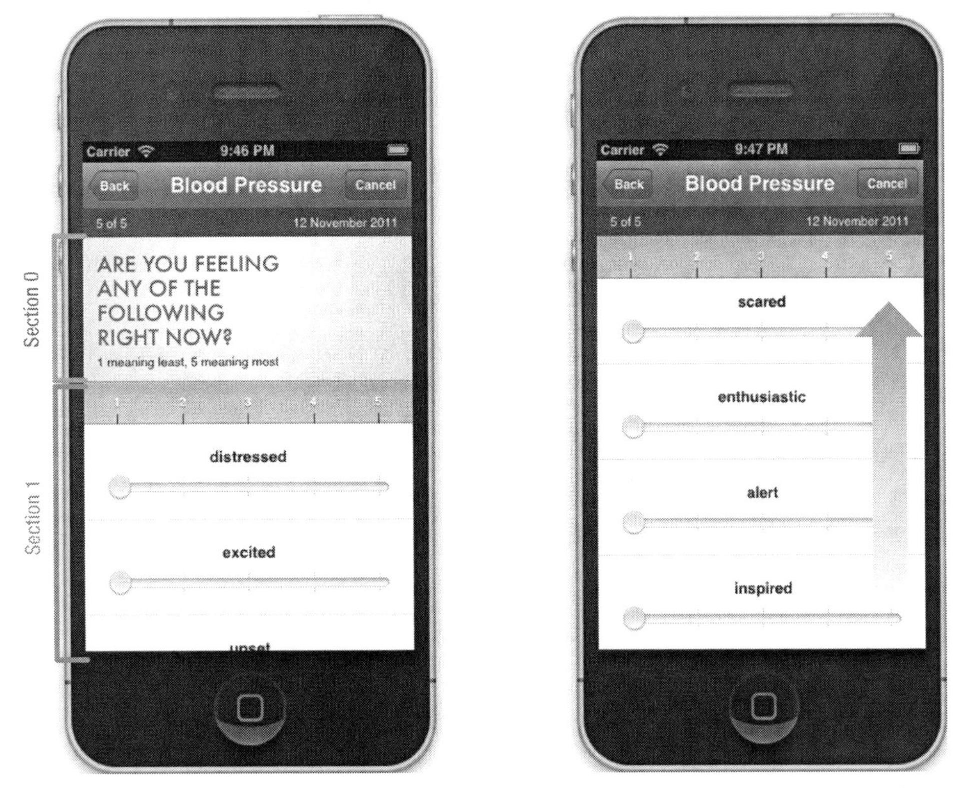

Figure 6–17. *An example of a custom section header: as the section1 header scrolls up, it is "pinned" to the top.*

The code to achieve this is pretty straightforward, as shown in Listing 6–22. It uses the `tableView:viewForHeaderInSection` method, which returns a `UIView` object in response to a given section number. As it stands here, the method will create and return a `UIView` containing a `UIImageView` object for section 1 in the table, and will return `nil` otherwise.

Listing 6–22. *Custom Section Headers in Action*

```
-(UIView *)tableView:(UITableView *)tableView
viewForHeaderInSection:(NSInteger)section {

    if (section == 1 ) {

        // Create section 1 header
        UIImageView *headerImage = [[UIImageView alloc] initWithImage:[UIImage
     imageNamed:@"sectionTwoHeader"]];

        UIView *headerView = [[UIView alloc] initWithFrame:
    CGRectMake(0, 0, headerImage.frame.size.width, ➥
headerImage.frame.size.height)];

        [headerView addSubview:headerImage];
    return headerView;

    }

    return nil;
}
```

NOTE: Adding controls such as UISliders to cells is covered in Chapter 10.

Moving the Table Programmatically

The table view scrolls around automatically in response to taps on an index entry, but it's also possible to move the table around programmatically.

NOTE: If you're reacting to user input through `UITableViewDelegate` methods such as `viewDidScroll` or `tableView:didSelectRowAtIndexPath:`, be aware that moving and selecting the table programmatically won't cause the delegate methods to be invoked—so you'll need to trigger them manually.

There are three main methods that can be used:

- `scrollToRowAtIndexPath:atScrollPosition:animated:`
- `scrollToNearestSelectedRowAtScrollPosition:animated:`
- `selectRowAtIndexPath:animated:scrollPosition:`

scrollToRowAtIndexPath:atScrollPosition:animated:

This method takes an IndexPath position—section *a*, row *b*—and scrolls to the appropriate place.

The second parameter controls where in the tableView the destination row should appear: top, middle, or bottom. There's a fourth option that aims to make the row visible with a minimum of movement. If the row is already visible, the table won't move at all. Otherwise, it will be scrolled to the nearest of the three alternatives.

You select the desired behavior by providing one of the four UITableViewScrollPosition values:

- UITableViewScrollPositionNone
- UITableViewScrollPositionTop
- UITableViewScrollPositionMiddle
- UITableViewScrollPositionBottom

The final parameter determines whether the table "zooms" to the desired row with some animation or moves there instantaneously. YES enables animations, and NO suppresses them.

scrollToNearestSelectedRowAtScrollPosition:animated:

This method is similar in terms of parameters, but will scroll the table to the nearest already-selected row, either with or without animations.

selectRowAtIndexPath:animated:scrollPosition:

This method allows a row to be selected programmatically, and optionally scrolls the table so that the selected row is located in the desired location in the tableView.

Passing in UITableViewScrollPositionNone has a different effect than with the previous two methods—the table won't scroll at all. If you want minimum scrolling, select the row with this method and then call scrollToViewAtIndexPath.

Finding the Current Scroll Position in the Table

There are occasions when you need to figure out how far down a table the user has scrolled. For example, the current (at the time of writing) version of the Path app displays a timestamp alongside the right-hand end of a table that slides up and down to indicate how far down the timeline you've gone (see Figure 6–18).

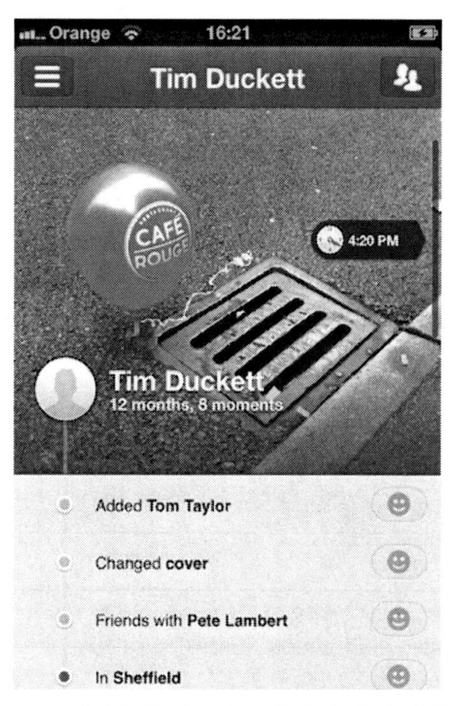

Figure 6–18. *The timestamp indicator in the Path app*

The Y position of this timestamp is proportional to how far down the table has scrolled—so how is that position calculated? The answer lies in the fact that `UITableView` is a subclass of `UIScrollView`, and so inherits all the properties and methods that `UIScrollView` provides.

The `contentOffset` property exposes how far from the origin the scroll view (or in this case, the table view) has been scrolled. If you had a table that was, say, 1000 pixels high when all its data was fully loaded, the `contentOffset`'s y value would gradually increase as the user scrolled down, until it reached a maximum of 1000 pixels.

Figuring out how tall the table is going to be is a little trickier, mainly because of the way that the table view handles building rows and loading data without the need for much "manual" intervention on your part when writing the code.

The trick is to wait until the all the table's data has been loaded—in other words, the table view knows how many rows and sections it has (and therefore how tall the content is going to be). Figuring out exactly when this has happened is difficult, especially if your table's data is very dynamic, but one option is to override the table view controller's `viewDidAppear` method something like this:

```
- (void)viewDidAppear:(BOOL)animated
{
    [super viewDidAppear:animated];

    maxTableHeight = self.tableView.contentSize.height;
    frameTableHeight = self.tableView.frame.size.height;
```

```
}
```

The table view's contentSize property is a CGSize. The height value is the total height of the table after all the rows have been loaded. The frame property is the size of the table in the NIB itself.

After you have these three values, you can use them to calculate the Y position of the timestamp and to update that as the table scrolls. UIScrollView has a series of delegate properties, including scrollViewDidScroll:

```
-(void)scrollViewDidScroll:(UIScrollView *)scrollView;.
```

If you conform your table view's controller to the UIScrollViewDelegate protocol and implement this method, it'll get called every time the table is scrolled. This is the point where you can perform the calculations and redraw the UIView that's moving around the screen.

Summary

In this chapter, you have looked at a couple of methods to improve the visual presentation of large amounts of data in table views. Breaking the data—and the table—into sections provides additional structure to the table, while indexes provide a means of quick navigation between sections.

Using the grouped table style further subdivides the information visually, which can help to emphasize the sections when scrolling around. Groups can be further enhanced with header and footer views.

Chapter 7

Selecting and Editing Table Content

Although some situations can be handled with read-only tables, you don't need to look too far to find others where tables need to be adaptable. Building tables that can handle selection and rearrangement—and can insert, update and delete new rows—is a common requirement.

In this chapter, we'll look at

- How to handle selection of rows in your tables
- How tables can be built to handle rearrangement of their data
- How tables can be used to create, edit, update, and delete items from their underlying data models

A Recap of the Model-View-Controller Pattern

Before getting into the mechanics of selecting, inserting, and deleting with a table view, you'll need to understand how these changes affect the underlying data that the table displays. This means understanding the model-view-controller (MVC) architecture pattern that you met back in Chapter 3. The `UITableView` is an example of an MVC architecture, which separates the front-end *views* from the back-end *models*.

That separation is described by the MVC pattern, which divides the application into three areas:

- *Views*: In iOS terms, these are the views (or interfaces) that are created in Interface Builder, or programmatically within the code. In `UITableView` terms, a view is the table itself, and the cells that form the rows of the table.

- Controllers: These represent the application's internal logic. In other words, the controller is the class or classes that control the display of data and interaction with the table—either because it's an entire subclass of `UITableViewController`, or because it's a `UITableViewController` delegate and/or data source.
- Models: These manage the data within the application. The model can be as simple as an `NSArray` containing some `NSStrings`, or could be a full-blown Core Data setup. However complex or simple, though, it's the model that supplies the data to be displayed in the `tableView`.

  Figure 7–1 illustrates the MVC pattern, which we saw earlier in Chapter 3.

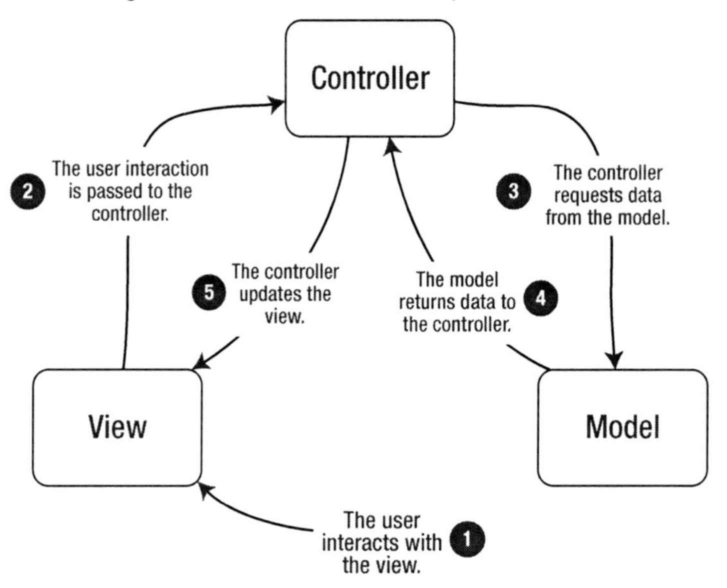

Figure 7–1. *The model-view-controller pattern*

As you can see, the controllers fetch and process data from the models that gets passed to the views for consumption by the user. The user interacts with the views, and the controllers handle the results of those interactions.

Why the Model-View-Controller Pattern Is Important

When working with `tableViews` that respond to user interaction in some way, it's important that you bear the MVC design pattern in mind. Cells have no memory—effectively, they're just envelopes for their contents. As soon as they're scrolled out of the visible view, they will either be recycled or will disappear entirely. Their state will either be lost—or worse, be inappropriately applied to the contents of the recycled cell.

To the user, this will seem as if the state of the cell isn't "sticky." If the user taps a row to set a value and display a check mark, the selection might change if the user scrolls up or down.

This applies not just to selections, but also to insertions, deletions, and reordering. Take a row deletion, for example. Your user taps the Edit button on the navigation bar and deletes a row. The `tableView` handles revealing the edit controls, removing the deleted row, and animating the "closing of ranks" as the rows move up to fill the empty space. As far as the user is concerned, the job is done—the row has gone, never to return.

But the underlying data in the model hasn't yet been altered by any of the user interface changes. If the table is reloaded (which is likely if it's part of a `UINavigationController`, for example), the original data will be reloaded, and the deleted row will appear again. Worse still, if a new row was apparently inserted, the information that the user provided will be lost.

The bottom line is that any changes that your user—or your app—makes in the views have to be reflected in the model in order for them to persist. The `tableView` will handle the adding and deleting and moving of rows (and if you've enabled the animations, it'll do a graceful job of it), but it's up to you to reflect the changes in your model.

Cell Selection

Unless the `tableView` is being used to display static information, at some point the user will interact with it and will need feedback. Cell selection is one part of providing that feedback.

What Selection Is For

There are two types of cell selection that you may need to implement, depending on the app's functionality:

- *Momentary selection*, to provide feedback to the user about which row they're in the process of interacting with
- *Persistent selection*, where you want to show which rows in the table are displaying items from the data model with a particular state (for example, objects that might have an "on" state)

Controlling Selection

You can control selection of rows in two ways: globally for the whole `tableView` or on a row-specific basis.

Global Selection

`UITableView` has an `allowsSelection` property, which can be set either in Interface Builder as you construct the view or programmatically at any point in the table's life cycle. Setting the `allowsSelection` property to `NO` disables row selection completely, so the table won't react to touches (other than scrolling).

There are a couple of reasons why you might want to disable selection entirely:

- Your table is only displaying data rather than allowing interaction with it.
- The table rows are being edited or rearranged, and selection would interfere with this process.

Understanding How Selection Works

There are four `UITableViewDelegate` methods that work together to provide selection functionality:

- `tableView:willSelectRowAtIndexPath:`

  This method is called after the user has touched down and lifted a finger (a `TouchUpInside` action, in other words), but before the `tableView:didSelectRowAtIndexPath:` method is called. By default, this method isn't implemented. Implementing this and returning `nil` will prevent the row selection from taking place.

- `tableView:didSelectRowAtIndexPath:`

  Assuming that the `tableView:willSelectRowAtIndexPath:` method didn't return `nil`, this is where you implement your custom behavior. The behavior can be presentational (displaying a check mark, for example) or can cause some kind of navigation action (for example, a `pushNavigationController` action).

- `tableView:willDeselectRowAtIndexPath:`

  This method is called only if an existing selection has been made. It returns the `indexPath` of the row that *should* be deselected—and so gives you the opportunity to deselect another row in place of the one that is currently selected. Try as I might, I've never been able to conjure up a scenario where this was required, but your mileage may vary. If you return `nil` from this method, the row won't be deselected, which effectively means you can "lock" selection if required.

- `tableView:didDeselectRowAtIndexPath:`

  This method tells the delegate that the row is now deselected. It's the place where you'd want to reverse any custom selection traits that you created. If you have a custom cell that shows selection by turning the `textLabel` green, for example, you would use the `tableView:didDeselectRowAtIndexPath:` method to change it back to the normal color.

TIP: If cell selection appears to lag behind the user's input, you might have inadvertently implemented `tableView:willDeselectRowAtIndexPath:` instead of `tableView:didSelectRowAtIndexPath:`. It's surprisingly easy to be tripped up by Xcode's autocompletion, and once the wrong method has been added to your code, it can be difficult to spot where the problem has been introduced.

Managing Row-Specific Selection

In addition to enabling or disabling selection at the global `tableView` level, you may also need to control it at the row level. For example, later in this chapter, you'll build a table that allows extra rows to be inserted by tapping an **Add New** row.

Depending on the requirements of your data model, you might want to disable this function.

By checking which row is being selected in the `tableView:willSelectRowAtIndexPath:` method, you can add conditional code to allow the selection of some rows and prevent the selection of others. That's shown in Listing 7–1.

Listing 7–1. *Checking Row Selection in* `tableView:willSelectRowAtIndexPath:`

```
-(NSIndexPath *)tableView:(UITableView *)tableView ↩
willSelectRowAtIndexPath:(NSIndexPath *)indexPath {

    NSUInteger rowToNotSelect = 3;

    if (indexPath.row == rowToNotSelect) {
        return nil;
    }

    return indexPath;

}
```

This code arbitrarily prevents the selection of row 3, and returns `nil` if it's row 3 that's being checked. You can also return an `indexPath` other than the value that was passed in if you wanted to select *another* row, rather than the one that was tapped. I haven't been able to think of any situation where you'd actually *want* to do that, but it's there if you need it.

Visualizing Selection

Visualizing the selection provides feedback to your user that their actions have been registered by the app. It can also provide a cue that something is about to happen or is taking place.

When the user taps a table row, the standard behavior turns the row's background blue and the `textLabel` white, as shown in Figure 7–2.

Figure 7–2. *The default row selection style*

There's also an alternative `UITableViewCellSelectionStyleGray` style, shown in Figure 7–3.

Two
Three
Four

Figure 7–3. *The gray selection style*

You may also want to disable the selection highlight completely if it will interfere with any custom selection behavior that you implement, in which case you can use `UITableViewCellSelectionStyleNone`.

All three styles are set by the cell's `selectionStyle` property. In most scenarios, you'd set this in the `tableView:cellForRowAtIndexPath:` method, for example:

```
cell.selectionStyle = UITableViewCellSelectionStyleGray;
```

Customizing Selection

You're not restricted to the standard white-on-blue or white-on-gray selection highlight styles. If you've customized the `tableView` cells, this highlighting style probably won't be appropriate anyway.

By adding custom code to the `tableView:didSelectRowAtIndexPath:` method, you can manipulate your cells as you see fit. Figure 7–4 shows an example from one of my apps.

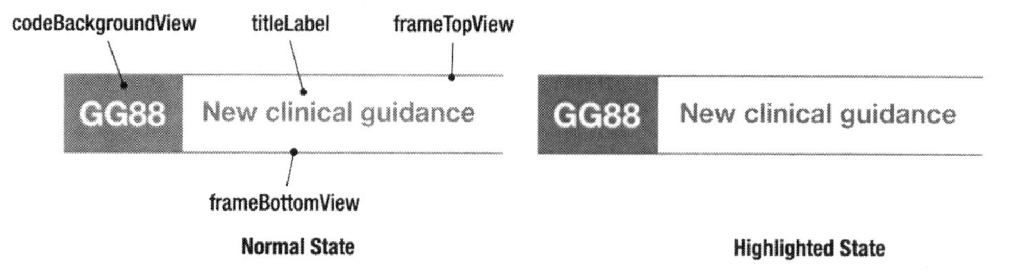

Figure 7–4. *A custom cell in normal and highlighted state*

The cell background and outlines are UIViews, so it's possible to manipulate their backgroundColor properties. They're set to orange in the cell's NIB file, and then switched to blue in the tableView:didSelectRowAtIndexPath: method:

```
// Set cell highlight
UIColor *blueColour = [UIColor colorWithRed:0.08 green:0.4 blue:0.58 alpha:1.0];
cell.codeBackgroundView.backgroundColor = blueColour;
cell.frameTopView.backgroundColor = blueColour;
cell.frameBottomView.backgroundColor = blueColour;
cell.titleLabel.textColor = blueColour;
```

TIP: One of the limitations of Interface Builder is that there's no line tool (or shape tools of any description, for that matter). This makes drawing lines awkward. One option is to include line graphics as UIImageViews, but that's quite expensive in rendering terms.

Another option is to place UIViews where the lines are required, and set the width (or height) to a very small value—say, 1 or 2 pixels. You can use the UIView's backgroundColor property to set the color of your "line." You're restricted to solid lines of a single color, but it's often a quicker process than creating line graphics in another package and importing them as images.

Handling Deselection

If you stick with the default selection behavior, deselection is handled for you. The white-on-blue or white-on-gray cell style will revert back to the default black-on-white.

If there's custom selection behavior in play, however, you'll need to handle that manually. This need can arise in two situations:

- When another cell has been selected. In this situation, you can add your deselection code to either the tableView:willDeselectRowAtIndexPath: or tableView:didDeselectRowAtIndexPath: method.
- When the selection is now irrelevant because some action has been performed—for example, after returning to the tableView from a detail view.

  This pattern can be seen in the Mail app. Tapping an e-mail in the list view slides in the e-mail content. After the content view is dismissed, the highlight is removed—slowly enough that you can see which e-mail you previously tapped, but not so slow that the selection lingers.

  In this situation, the selection is removed in the tableView's viewDidAppear method with UITableView's deselectRowAtIndexPath:animated: method.

Visualizing Persistent Selection

Visualizing persistent selection is required for one of two reasons:

- Your user is selecting multiple rows prior to some other action—for example, deleting records from the model.
- The selection reflects the underlying state of a property of the object that the row represents—for example, an item in a checklist has been "checked off."

Either way, you need a means of indicating selection that's distinct from the momentary selection indicating which row has been tapped.

Apple makes an overt point in the Human Interface Guidelines that selection traits associated with momentary selection shouldn't be used to indicate state. In other words, don't use the default cell highlighting options to indicate the state of the underlying data in the model. Doing so risks confusing your users, and is likely to get your app rejected from the App Store.

To show persistent selection, a couple of options are available:

- Use `UITableViewCell`'s built-in `accessoryView` to show a selection mark.
- Create some other visual indication in a custom cell.

Your options in the second scenario are limited only by taste and what it's possible to get a cell to do, so I'll concentrate on the first.

Using Selection Marks to Indicate Multiple Selections

The first point to note about indicating multiple selections is that that the table has to allow it. Prior to iOS 5, tables supported selection of only a single row at a time, which led to numerous work-around solutions. Someone at Apple must have noticed, because now this property (which is `NO` by default) allows a number of rows to be selected simultaneously.

This is controlled at the table level. You can set the property in Interface Builder, as shown in Figure 7–5.

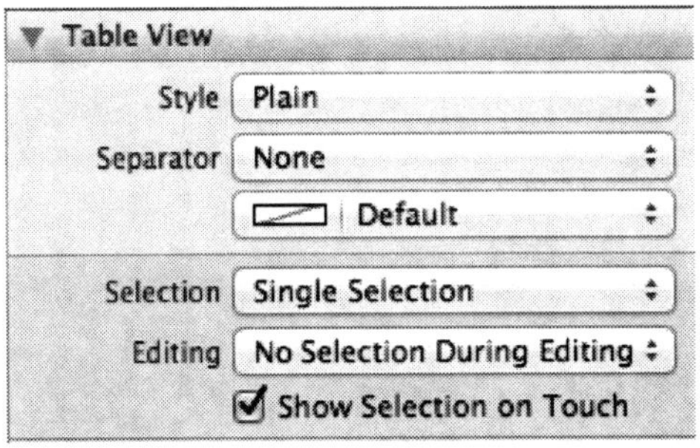

Figure 7–5. *Controlling table selection traits in Interface Builder*

Or you can set the property programmatically:

```
[tableView setAllowsSelection:YES];

[tableView setAllowsMultipleSelection:NO];
```

Working with Multiple Row Selections

After selection has taken place, the row (or rows) that have been selected can be accessed through two `tableView` properties:

- `indexPathForSelectedRow`
- `indexPathsForSelectedRows`

As their names suggest, they return `indexPaths`. The results returned are different, though, so it's important not to mix the two up (the names of the properties being so similar doesn't help here).

`indexPathForSelectedRow` returns a single `indexPath`. If only one cell is selected, this will be the `indexPath` that's returned, as you would expect. If more than one row is selected, `indexPathForSelectedRow` will return the *first* row that was selected.

`indexPathsForSelectedRows` returns an `NSArray` of `indexPaths` for *all* the rows that are selected. The `indexPath` objects in the array are in the order that the rows were selected—index 0 is the first row, index 1 is the second, and so on.

If no rows are selected at all, both these properties will return `nil`.

Visualizing Multiple Row Selection

There are basically two options when it comes to visualizing multiple row selections: using the default cell's accessory view or customizing your cell.

Which method to use will depend first on whether your cell has an accessory view. If you've created a custom subclass of `UITableViewCell`, it might not. Second, the method chosen depends on whether showing an indicator at the right-hand end of the cell is visually appropriate.

Using the Cell's Accessory View to Show a Selection Mark

The default `UITableViewCell` (shown in Figure 7–6) has an accessory view at its right-hand end, which is often used to indicate that selecting the row will cause some kind of action—for example, pushing in a detail view.

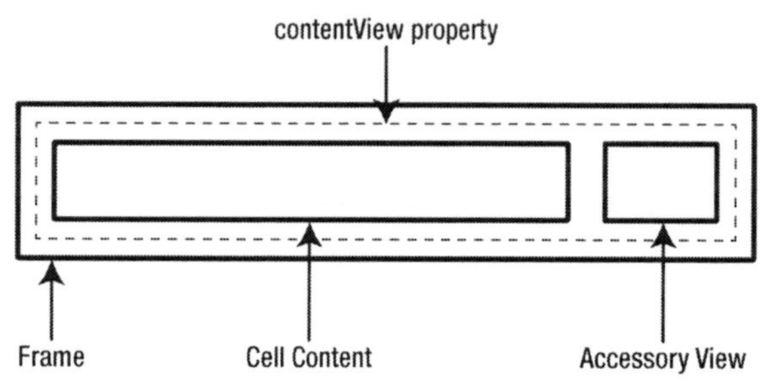

Figure 7–6. *The default accessory view*

The accessory view is exposed in two ways:

- As the cell's `accessoryType` property, which can be set to one of the four `UITableViewCellAccessoryType` values
- As a `UIView` property, which can be customized directly

Listing 7–2 is an example of a `tableView:cellForRowAtIndexPath:` method that displays the default tick mark when an object property is set.

Listing 7–2. *An Example `tableView:cellForRowAtIndexPath:` Method*

```
-(UITableViewCell *)tableView:(UITableView *)tableView➥
 cellForRowAtIndexPath:(NSIndexPath *)indexPath {

    static NSString *cellIdentifier = @"cellIdentifier";

    UITableViewCell *cell = [tableView➥
 dequeueReusableCellWithIdentifier:cellIdentifier];

    if (!cell) {
        cell = [[UITableViewCell alloc] initWithStyle:UITableViewCellStyleDefault➥
 reuseIdentifier:cellIdentifier];
    }

    MyObject *theObject = [tableData objectAtIndex:indexPath.row];

    if (theObject.isSelected == YES) {
        cell.accessoryType = UITableViewCellAccessoryCheckmark;
    } else {
        cell.accessoryType = UITableViewCellAccessoryNone;
    }

    cell.textLabel.text = theObject.name;

    return cell;

}
```

Assuming that three of the myObjects have their selected property set to YES, the result would appear as in Figure 7–7.

Two	✓
Three	✓
Four	✓

Figure 7–7. *The default selection tick mark*

Using the Cell's Accessory View to Show a Custom View

Because the accessory view is exposed as a UIView property, it can be manipulated accordingly. Listing 7–3 is a code snippet showing how you could set the accessoryView property to display an image.

Listing 7–3. *Inserting an Image into the Accessory View*

```
    UITableViewCell *cell = [tableView cellForRowAtIndexPath:indexPath];
    UIImage *accessoryImage = [UIImage imageNamed:@"accessory"];
    UIImageView *accessoryImageView = [[UIImageView alloc]↵
 initWithImage:accessoryImage];
    [accessoryImageView setFrame:CGRectMake(0, 0, 28.0, 28.0)];

    cell.accessoryView = accessoryImageView;
```

Showing Selection in Other Ways

You're not restricted to using accessory views to show selection, especially if you're implementing custom cells. Virtually any combination of images, text formatting, or area highlighting can be used, depending on your inclination and the needs of the project. Whatever you decide to do, you'll need to implement it in either tableView:willSelectRowAtIndexPath: or tableView:didSelectRowAtIndexPath:.

Handling Deselection After Multiple Selection

If you've implemented custom selection (either by an accessory view method or by something more adventurous), you're also responsible for handling the deselection process. Basically, this means undoing whatever selection trait you supplied when the row was selected. There are two places where this can be done: tableView:willDeselectRowAtIndexPath: and tableView:didDeselectRowAtIndexPath:. In either case, the row in question is located at the indexPath provided.

Here's an example of how you might handle this to *reverse* the effect of the code in Listing 7.3.

```
    -(void)tableView:(UITableView *)tableView didDeselectRowAtIndexPath:↵
(NSIndexPath   *)indexPath {
```

```
    UITableViewCell *cell = [tableView cellForRowAtIndexPath:indexPath];
    cell.accessoryView = nil;

}
```

Selection Dos and Don'ts

There are a few of things to bear in mind when configuring row selection:

- Don't use selection to indicate the state of the row's object. Selection works at the view level of the MVC hierarchy, so it's independent of the model.
- Unless multiple selections are allowed, always programmatically deselect the previously selected row before a new row is selected.
- If the response to the row selection is to push a new view onto the display (for example, if you have a navigation controller that pushes on a detail view), always programmatically deselect the previous rows after the detail view is dismissed. This will ensure that the rows aren't still highlighted after the detail view is popped off the view stack, but provides a visual cue as to which row the detail view referred to.

Responding to Selections with More Detail

Selection of a row by the user generally requires some kind of response in return. These can be broadly categorized in one of two patterns:

- The selection results in the display of additional data, either by "drilling down" into a navigation hierarchy or displaying some form of detail view.
- The selection reflects some kind of choice on the part of the user and results in the update of a model.

A common pattern is to push in a new view of some description—a navigation view that reveals another `tableView` enabling drill-down into the information hierarchy, for example, or a detail view that contains more information about the row that was tapped.

Listing 7–4 is an example of that second process.

Listing 7–4. *An Example of a `tableView:didSelectRowAtIndexPath:` Method*

```
-(void)tableView:(UITableView *)tableView didSelectRowAtIndexPath:➥
(NSIndexPath *)indexPath {

    NSString *selectedName = [self.tableData objectAtIndex:indexPath.row];

    DetailViewController *detailViewController = [[DetailViewController alloc]➥
 initWithNibName:@"DetailView" bundle:nil];
    detailViewController.name = selectedName;
```

```
    [detailViewController setModalTransitionStyle:UIModalTransitionStyleFlipHorizontal];
    [self presentViewController:detailViewController animated:YES completion:nil];

}
```

This is a `UITableViewDelegate` method that takes two parameters: a reference to the `tableView` itself and the `IndexPath` that has been selected.

The first task is to get a reference to the object in the model that corresponds to the row that's been selected. Bear in mind that it's the row that's been selected, and not the model object itself:

```
NSString *selectedName = [tableData objectAtIndex:indexPath.row];
```

In this situation, the table's model is an `NSArray` of strings, so it's simply a case of getting the string that resides at the corresponding index.

After you have a reference to the selected object, the code instantiates an instance of a `DetailViewController`, having first deselected the row. It then sets the `DetailViewController`'s name property, and pushes in the new view with a modal transition.

Design Patterns and UITableViews

In addition to architectural design patterns such as MVC, there are also interaction patterns. Whereas architectural patterns help you consider how to structure and build an application, interaction patterns can help to manage what you do with it.

After you've used the MVC pattern to build the table, the question arises, "What are you going to do with the data that the table contains?" Clearly, the user will read the content of the cells, but what then? What sort of user behaviors do we need to anticipate?

A useful pattern to use when thinking about data and how to work with it is *create, read, update, delete*, or *CRUD* for short. This is most commonly used when working with records in a database, but it's also applicable when considering what might happen to a row in a `UITableView`.

Read

In database terms, *reading* is concerned with retrieving records from the database, usually with some kind of SQL `SELECT` query. In `UITableView` terms, you can think of reading as the process of getting data out of the model and into the table itself through methods such as `tableView:cellForRowAtIndexPath:`. We've covered this in detail elsewhere, so you don't need to trouble yourself much with the Read action.

Create

In addition to displaying information, table views are often used to enable the user to create and enter new information. The Contacts app is a good example of this: tapping the + button at the top of the list of names causes a modal view containing a form for a new contact to be pushed in from the bottom of the screen. The form that arrives in response to tapping + isn't part of the tableView itself, but after the new Contact object has been created, the `tableView` does have to react to that and insert the new row at the appropriate place.

Update

The Contacts app allows existing contact information to be updated by selecting a contact and then tapping the Edit button. Again, this isn't, strictly speaking, a `tableView` concern until the amended data is saved, at which point it may be necessary to rearrange the rows to cope with the changed data.

A more `tableView`-specific action would be the user wanting to rearrange rows or sections. The `UITableView dataSource` and `delegate` protocols provide a number of methods to support this, which you'll look at later in this chapter.

Delete

An equally common interaction pattern is deleting an entire record. The iPhone's Notes app, shown in Figure 7–8, enables the deletion of notes by swiping left or right in the row to reveal a Delete control. Tapping Delete animates the removal of the row, which slides away to the left, after which the rows below are scrolled up to fill the gap.

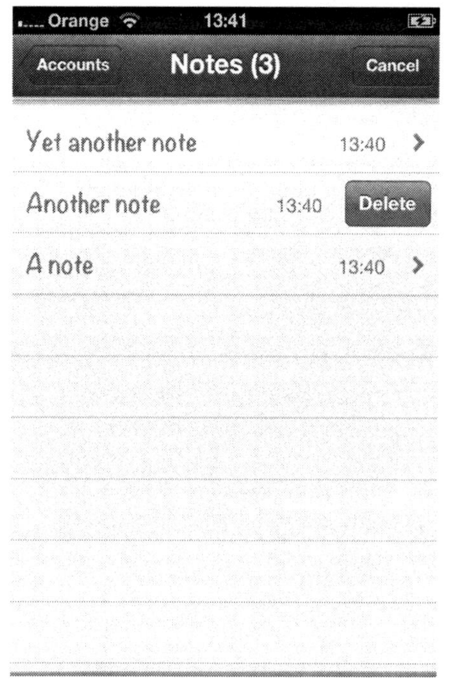

Figure 7–8. *Deleting a note*

All these functions and animations come for free though the built-in `UITableViewDelegate` methods. We'll start by looking at the actions that have the greatest impact on the tableView itself: inserting new rows and deleting existing ones.

> **NOTE:** If your table view controller is a subclass of `UITableViewController`, you'll get a lot of insertion and deletion behavior for free courtesy of the `UITableViewController` superclass. That's great as far as implementing the functionality is concerned, but not that helpful if you're trying to figure out how things work so you can adapt them later. Therefore, I'm working through this section with a generic `UIViewController` and adding the table view functionality in manually.

Inserting and Deleting Rows

As you'll probably be expecting by now, inserting and deleting rows is a multistage process that involves the `tableView`, the `delegate`, and the `dataSource` working in tandem with each other.

The process involves the following:

1. Putting the table into editing mode.
2. For each row, checking whether editing is allowed and displaying the editing controls if it is
3. Responding to the user's touches on the editing controls by sending a message to the `dataSource`
4. Updating the model
5. Updating the table's rows

The sequence of events, and the passing of messages between `tableView`, `dataSource`, and `delegate`, is illustrated in Figure 7–9.

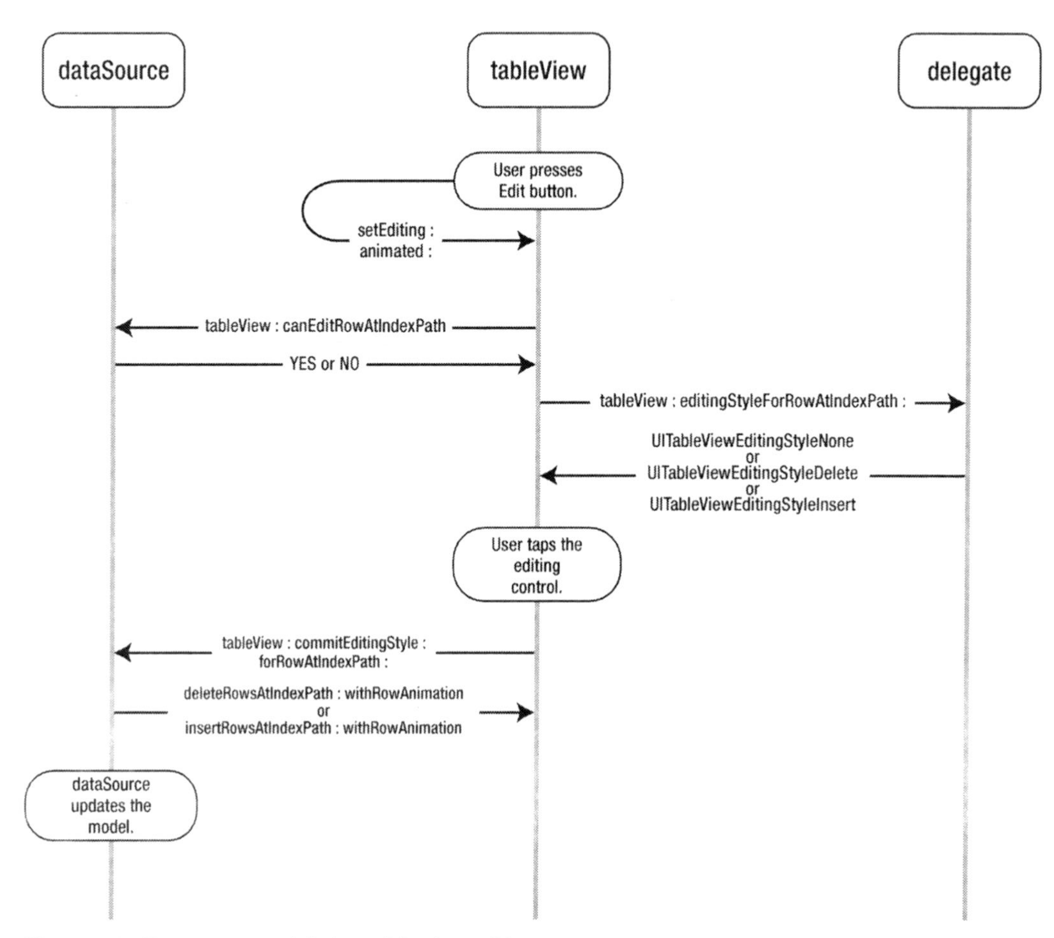

Figure 7–9. *Messages passed during `tableView` editing*

At first glance, this looks horrendously complicated. It's actually not that bad, as you'll see as you step through it.

THE SAMPLE APP

If you want to follow along with the upcoming examples, you will need a simple table to experiment with. I'm not going to go into detail about how to do that (hopefully you can build a table after having read this far!) but a couple of specifics are worth mentioning:

- Because tables with editing functions are often found in `UINavigationControllers`, I've implemented the table view inside a navigation controller.
- The `tableView`'s data model is deliberately simple, so that the data doesn't overshadow the more relevant matters of editing, updating, and deleting.

Creating a UINavigationController-based table

To create the UINavigationController-based table, I've taken the standard Single View Application template provided by Xcode and amended the AppDelegate to create a UINavigationController with a tableView inside.

This is how the revised AppDelegate's applicationDidFinishLaunchingWithOptions: method now looks:

```
- (BOOL)application:(UIApplication *)application➥
 didFinishLaunchingWithOptions:(NSDictionary *)launchOptions
{
    self.window = [[UIWindow alloc] initWithFrame:[[UIScreen mainScreen] bounds]];

    // Override point for customization after application launch.

    UIViewController *vC = [[ViewController alloc] initWithNibName:@"ViewController"➥
 bundle:nil];

    UINavigationController *navController = [[UINavigationController alloc]➥
 initWithRootViewController:vC];

    self.window.rootViewController = navController;

    [self.window makeKeyAndVisible];

    return YES;
}
```

The main points to note are as follows:

- I've created a UIViewController called ViewController with a NIB file containing a UITableView. This tableView has ViewController set as its delegate and dataSource.
- In the applicationDidFinishLaunchingWithOptions method, an instance of ViewController is instantiated as the vC object.
- After the vC object has been created, I instantiate an instance of UINavigationController and initiate it with vC as its rootViewController.
- After the navController is created, it's set as the AppDelegate's window's rootViewController (not to be confused with the rootViewController property of the UINavigationController—they're completely separate).
- As a result, the ViewController instance is displayed inside the UINavigationController, which is in turn displayed inside the application's main window.

Creating the sample table's data model

The data model for this app is very simple. It's just an NSMutableArray of NSStrings, which gets created in ViewController's viewDidLoad method:

```
- (void)viewDidLoad
{
    [super viewDidLoad];
```

```
        // Do any additional setup after loading the view, typically from a nib.

    self.navigationItem.title = @"Row insertion";
    self.navigationItem.rightBarButtonItem = self.editButtonItem;


    self.tableData = [[NSMutableArray alloc] initWithObjects:@"One", @"Two", @"Three",

}
```

There are a couple of other setup-related tasks in this method. The following sets up the title of the navigation bar:

```
self.navigationItem.title = @"Row insertion";
```

This code creates an Edit button:

```
self.navigationItem.rightBarButtonItem = self.editButtonItem;
```

The overall effect is shown in Figure 7–10.

Figure 7–10. *The customized navigation bar*

Putting the Table into Editing Mode

The first step is to put the table into editing mode, which is invoked by sending the message `setEditing:animated:` to the table view:

```
[tableView setEditing:YES animated:YES];
```

Normally this would be done in response to a button tap. If you were using a `UINavigationController`, the `UINavigationBar` at the top of your screen comes with a handy Edit button baked in. You could set this up in the `viewDidLoad` method:

```
self.navigationItem.rightBarButtonItem = self.editButtonItem;
```

This gives you not only an Edit button at the top right of the navigation bar, but one that will automatically toggle between Edit (before the table goes into editing mode) and Done (while the table is in editing mode). The effect is shown in Figure 7–11.

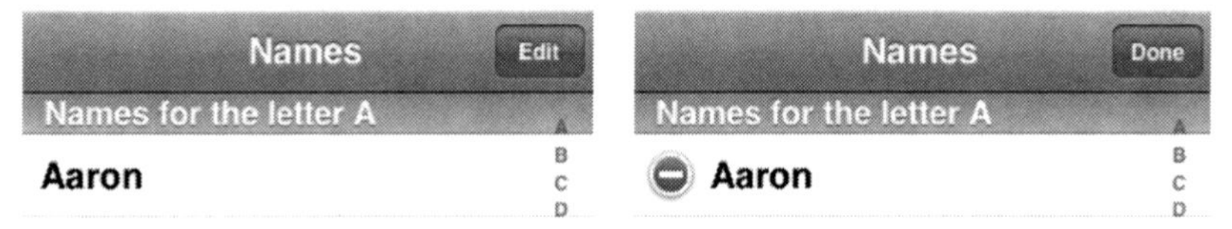

Figure 7–11. *The toggling Edit button*

If you're not using a `UINavigationController`, you'll need to add a button that calls the `setEditing:animated:` selector, and then handle the toggling between Edit and Done modes manually.

Listing 7–5 shows an example of adding an Edit button.

Listing 7–5. *Adding an Edit Button*

```
    editButton = [UIButton buttonWithType:UIButtonTypeRoundedRect];
    [editButton setFrame:CGRectMake(0, 49, 60, 30)];
    [editButton setTitle:@"Edit" forState:UIControlStateNormal];
    [editButton addTarget:self action:@selector(startTableEditMode:)➥
 forControlEvents:UIControlEventTouchUpInside];
    [self.view addSubview:editButton];
```

Then you'll need to implement the `setEditing:animated` method in Listing 7–6.

Listing 7–6. *The `setEditing:animated:` Method*

```
-(void)setEditing:(BOOL)editing animated:(BOOL)animated {

    [super setEditing:editing animated:animated];

    [theTableView setEditing:editing animated:animated];

}
```

And Listings 7–7 and 7–8 show how you could call the `setEditing:animated` method and toggle the button's title and action.

Listing 7–7. *Putting the Table into Edit Mode*

```
-(IBAction)startTableEditMode:(id)sender {
    [self setEditing:YES animated:YES];
    [editButton setTitle:@"Done" forState:UIControlStateNormal];
    [editButton removeTarget:nil action:NULL ➥
forControlEvents:UIControlEventAllEvents];
    [editButton addTarget:self action:@selector(endTableEditMode:)➥
 forControlEvents:UIControlEventTouchUpInside];
}
```

Listing 7–8. *Taking the Table out of Edit Mode*

```
-(IBAction)endTableEditMode:(id)sender {
    [self setEditing:NO animated:YES];
    [editButton setTitle:@"Edit" forState:UIControlStateNormal];
    [editButton removeTarget:nil action:NULL forControlEvents:UIControlEventAllEvents];
    [editButton addTarget:self action:@selector(startTableEditMode:)➥
 forControlEvents:UIControlEventTouchUpInside];
}
```

Controlling Whether Rows Can Be Edited

After the table is in editing mode, the table view will then ask the data source whether each row should be editable. If the `tableView:canEditRowAtIndexPath:` method is implemented, this is called for each row in turn. Listing 7–9 shows how you could use this method to prevent a specific section from being edited.

Listing 7–9. *Controlling Whether a Section or Row Can Be Edited*

```
-(BOOL)tableView:(UITableView *)tableView canEditRowAtIndexPath:➥
(NSIndexPath *)indexPath {
    if (indexPath.section == 0) {
        return NO;
```

```
    }

    return YES;
}
```

If the tableView:canEditRowAtIndexPath: method returns NO, the row won't be indented. Figure 7–12 shows the effect of this.

Figure 7–12. *Preventing editing of an entire section*

If the tableView:canEditRowAtIndexPath: isn't implemented, the table view assumes that each row *can* be edited. In effect, the default return value is YES.

Controlling Each Row's Editing Style

Having established whether a row can be edited, the table view then asks the delegate which editing style each row should use:

```
-(UITableViewCellEditingStyle)tableView:(UITableView *)tableView↵
 editingStyleForRowAtIndexPath:(NSIndexPath *)indexPath {
```

```
    return UITableViewCellEditingStyleDelete;
}
```

If the `tableView:editingStyleForRowAtIndexPath:` method is implemented, it will return one of three possible options:

- `UITableViewCellEditingStyleDelete`: This causes the deletion control to be inserted at the left-hand end of the cell.
- `UITableViewCellEditingStyleInsert`: This causes the insertion control to be inserted at the left end of the cell.

- `UITableViewCellEditingStyleNone`: Somewhat unsurprisingly, this does not insert an editing control.

As with `tableView:canEditRowAtIndexPath:`, if the `tableView:editingStyleForRowAtIndexPath:` isn't implemented, the `tableView` will assume that all cells will be deletable and return `UITableViewCellEditingStyleDelete` as the default value.

Inserting additional rows is a little more involved, so we'll cover that later in this chapter.

Dealing with Row Deletions

If you've been following along so far, your table will look like Figure 7–13, with an Edit button, cells that display Delete controls when the table goes into editing mode, and a Delete button that appears at the end of the row when the Delete control is tapped.

Figure 7–13. *Progress so far*

However, tapping that Delete button is something of an anticlimax. Nothing happens.

When the Delete button is tapped, the `tableView` sends the `tableView:commitEditingStyle:forRowAtIndexPath:` message to the data source. It takes three parameters:

- A reference to the `tableView` itself (in case the data source needs to distinguish between a number of `tableViews`)
- The `UITableViewCellEditingStyle` of the control that's just been tapped—in this case, `UITableViewCellEditingStyleDelete`
- An `indexPath` object locating the row in question

When the data source receives the `commitEditingStyle:forRowAtIndexPath:` message, it needs to do two things:

1. Update the tableView's model by deleting the object represented by the row in the table. Remember that the table itself is just a view, and unless we actually delete the object from the model, it will reappear in the table the next time the table gets reloaded.

2. Send the tableView:deleteRowsAtIndexPath:withRowAnimation: message to the tableView so that it updates the table display. In this case, because we're dealing with a Delete, it will animate the deleted cell sliding off to the left, and then move the cells below it up to close the gap.

Listing 7–10 shows how this might be done.

Listing 7–10. *Implementing the commitEditingStyle: Method*

```
-(void)tableView:(UITableView *)tableView commitEditingStyle:↩
(UITableViewCellEditingStyle)editingStyle forRowAtIndexPath:(NSIndexPath *)indexPath {

    if (editingStyle == UITableViewCellEditingStyleDelete) {

        [self.tableData removeObjectAtIndex:indexPath.row];

        NSArray *indexPathArray = [NSArray arrayWithObject:indexPath];

        [tableView deleteRowsAtIndexPaths:indexPathArray↩
 withRowAnimation:UITableViewRowAnimationAutomatic];

    }

}
```

There's a reasonable amount going on here. First, you need to check what kind of action is required (you'll be adding the insert action shortly).

If it's a delete, you need to remove the object in question from the data model. In this simple instance, it's just a case of removing an object from an array, but in a more complex app, this might require a database deletion:

```
[tableData removeObjectAtIndex:indexPath.row];
```

Then, as tableView:deleteRowsAtIndexPath:withRowAnimation: takes an array of NSIndexPath objects, you need to quickly stuff the indexPath parameter into an NSArray:

```
NSArray *indexPathArray = [NSArray arrayWithObject:indexPath];
```

Finally, you can send that message to the tableView:

```
[tableView deleteRowsAtIndexPaths:indexPathArray↩
withRowAnimation:UITableViewRowAnimationAutomatic];
```

There's a range of table cell insertion and deletion animations to choose from. These are listed in Table 7–1.

Table 7–1. *The `UITableViewRowAnimation` Options*

UITableViewRowAnimation Type	Effect
`UITableViewRowAnimationFade`	Rows fade in and out.
`UITableViewRowAnimationRight`	Inserted rows slide in from the right; deleted rows slide out to the right.
`UITableViewRowAnimationLeft`	Inserted rows slide in from the left; deleted rows slide out to the left.
`UITableViewRowAnimationTop`	Inserted rows slide down from the bottom of the row above; deleted rows slide up toward the bottom of the row above.
`UITableViewRowAnimationBottom`	Inserted rows slide up from the top of the cell below; deleted rows appear to be covered by the row below sliding up.
`UITableViewRowAnimationNone`	Inserted rows simply appear; deleted rows simply disappear.
`UITableViewRowAnimationMiddle`	Cells are inserted and deleted with an accordion-style effect.
`UITableViewRowAnimationAutomatic`	The `tableView` automatically chooses an appropriate animation style (available only in iOS 5 and later).

It's worth noting that the `Top`, `Bottom`, and `Middle` styles can produce some bizarre effects if you try to apply them to rows at the very top or bottom of the `tableView`. For that reason, iOS 5 introduced `UITableViewRowAnimationAutomatic`, which automatically applies the correct top, bottom, or middle style depending on which row is being animated. This saves a lot of work, so unless you have a very good reason to do otherwise, it's the way to go. Don't try to use this style if you're targeting devices running iOS 4.*x*, though, because it will crash the app until you wrap it in conditional code that checks the OS version.

"Swipe"-style Row Deletions

In addition to the "tap-Edit-and-then-tap-the-Delete-control-and-then-tap-the-Delete-button" method of deleting rows, `UITableView` provides another method. Swiping from side to side in the cell will cause a Delete button to slide in from the right-hand side. Tapping the button will then call the `commitEditingStyle` method as usual.

Because it's a user-initiated action, the call to `tableView:commitEditingStyle:forRowAtIndexPath:` is bracketed by two other calls: `tableView:willBeginEditingRowAtIndexPath:` and `tableView:didEndEditingRowAtIndexPath:`.

There are a couple of reasons why I think this is a Bad Idea, and you shouldn't implement it:

- It is hidden functionality. Until the user swipes over the row, there's no indication that this action will trigger any effect. Neither is it intuitive how to cancel the action. Tapping elsewhere in the cell will do so, but that runs the risk of accidentally tapping the Delete button by mistake.
- Using a swipe in a row to trigger the Delete action means that this action isn't available for other, potentially more useful actions, such as revealing controls "underneath" the row. (Yes, I *know* this contradicts my first point, but if you're going to use "hidden" gestures to trigger actions, at least make the actions the most useful ones!)

There's a counterargument, of course. The swipe-to-delete method is a standard part of iOS table views that's used extensively in apps such as Mail, so users may tend to expect it. Apple's user interface designers are very clever people, and they clearly think it's okay.

However, if I *have* managed to convince you that enabling swipe-to-delete is a Bad Thing, here's how to disable it. Swiping in the cell triggers the `tableView:editingStyleForRowAtIndexPath:` method. By default, this always returns `UITableViewCellEditingStyleDelete`.

If you want to restrict cell editing unless the table is in editing mode, you can test for this before returning the editing style. That's what Listing 7–11 does.

Listing 7–11. *Disabling Swipe-to-Delete*

```
-(UITableViewCellEditingStyle)tableView:(UITableView *)tableView ➥
 editingStyleForRowAtIndexPath:(NSIndexPath *)indexPath {

    if (self.editing) {
        return UITableViewCellEditingStyleDelete;
    }

    return UITableViewCellEditingStyleNone;

}
```

Unless the table is in editing mode (that is, `self.editing == YES`), this method will return `UITableViewCellEditingStyleNone`, preventing the Delete control from being shown.

Dealing with Row Insertions

If your app needs to handle row deletions, there's a fair chance it will also need to deal with row insertions. This process is not too dissimilar to dealing with deletions:

1. Put the table into editing mode.
2. Check whether the row can be edited.
3. Return the editing style for the row in question (in this case, `UITableViewEditingStyleInsert`).

4. Handle whatever actions are needed to create a new object model—for example, presenting a modal data entry view.
5. Commit the editing action with `tableView:commitEditingStyle:➥ forRowAtIndexPath:` and then update the model.
6. Update the table by inserting a row with `insertRowAtIndexPath:withAnimation:`.

The first two steps we've already covered with the deletion process. The third is a little more involved, so let's look at it.

A common requirement is a need to insert a new row to the end of a table or a section. There are a couple of ways that this could be approached. One option is to place an Add button onto the navigation bar in a similar way to the Edit/Done button that you saw earlier.

The downside to this approach is that you may already have an Edit button in place—or you might not have a navigation bar at all. In this case, a different approach is needed: placing the call to action into the table itself, as shown in Figure 7–14.

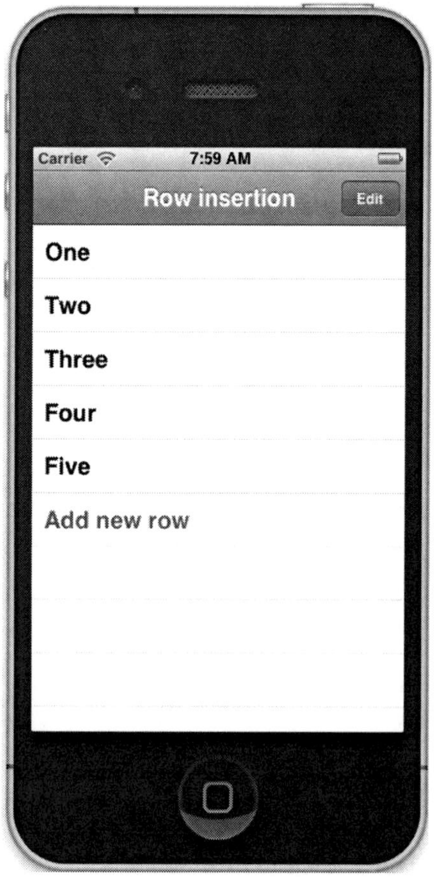

Figure 7–14. *The call to action in the table*

Tapping the Add New Row row when the table is not in editing mode will switch it into editing mode. Tapping any other row will result in the "normal" row selection actions.

Regardless of how the table entered editing mode, the Add New Row row will show an Insert control, while all the other rows will show a Delete control (shown in Figure 7–15).

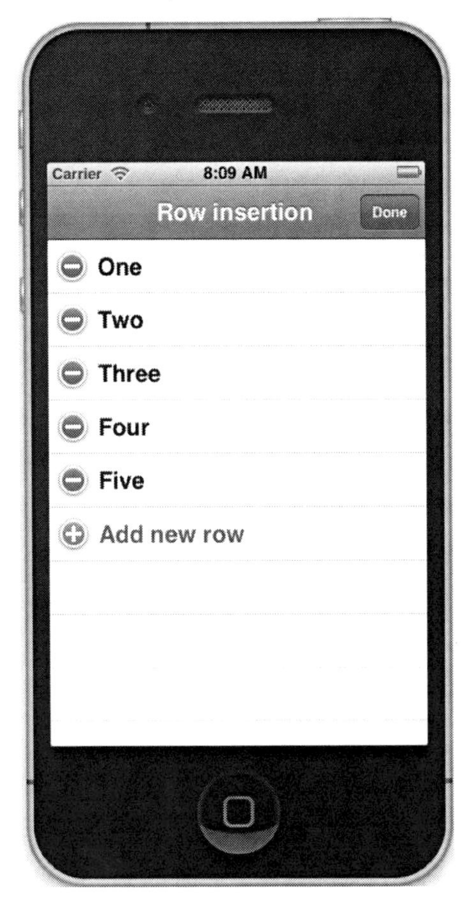

Figure 7–15. *The table in editing mode*

Amending the Data Model

Because you're going to be adding and removing objects to and from the data model, it will need to be mutable. As before, this means an NSMutableArray, which is shown in Listing 7–12.

Listing 7–12. *The viewDidLoad Method*

```
- (void)viewDidLoad
{
    [super viewDidLoad];
        // Do any additional setup after loading the view, typically from a nib.
```

```
    self.navigationItem.title = @"Row insertion";
    self.navigationItem.rightBarButtonItem = self.editButtonItem;

    self.tableData = [[NSMutableArray alloc] initWithObjects:@"One", @"Two", @"Three",

}
```

The Add New Row item needs to appear in the last row. One option is to add this to the data model itself, but that would violate the separation of the model from the view. The "cleaner" alternative is to add the row when the table gets reloaded. First, you'll need to tell the table to expect an extra row, as shown in Listing 7–13.

Listing 7–13. ***The Updated*** *`tableView:numberOfRowsInSection:`* ***Method***

```
-(NSInteger)tableView:(UITableView *)tableView numberOfRowsInSection:➥
(NSInteger)section {
    return [self.tableData count] + 1;
}
```

And then add the extra row in the `tableView:cellForRowAtIndexPath:` method, as shown in Listing 7–14.

Listing 7–14. ***The Updated*** *`tableView:cellForRowAtIndexPath:`* ***Method***

```
-(UITableViewCell *)tableView:(UITableView *)tableView➥
 cellForRowAtIndexPath:(NSIndexPath *)indexPath {

    static NSString *cellIdentifier = @"cellIdentifier";

    UITableViewCell *cell = [tableView➥
 dequeueReusableCellWithIdentifier:cellIdentifier];

    if (!cell) {
        cell = [[UITableViewCell alloc] initWithStyle:UITableViewCellStyleDefault➥
 reuseIdentifier:cellIdentifier];
    }

    if (indexPath.row == [self.tableData count]) {

        cell.textLabel.text = @"Add new row";
        cell.textLabel.textColor = [UIColor darkGrayColor];

    } else {

        cell.textLabel.text = [tableData objectAtIndex:indexPath.row];

    }

    return cell;

}
```

The magic happens after the cell is created. If the method is dealing with the last row (in other words, the `indexPath`'s row value is the same as the number of items in the data model), then the `cell.textLabel.text` property is set to Add New Row.

NOTE: Bear in mind that while `indexPath` values start from `0`, counting the number of elements in the data model starts from 1. Hence—usually—the `indexPath`'s `row` value for the final item in the table will be `([tableData count] - 1)`. If the `indexPath`'s `row` value equals `[tableData count]`, you're actually one row *beyond* the end of the array, and therefore need to insert the Add New Row item here.

Working with the New Row

Having created the new row, you now have to handle the user interaction. When the row is tapped, you want the table to enter editing mode, which means revising the `tableView:didSelectRowAtIndexPath:` method in Listing 7–15.

Listing 7–15. ***The*** `tableView:didSelectRowAtIndexPath:` ***Method***

```
-(void)tableView:(UITableView *)tableView didSelectRowAtIndexPath:(NSIndexPath↵
 *)indexPath {

    if (indexPath.row == [self.tableData count]) {

        // put table into edit mode
        [self setEditing:YES animated:YES];

    } else {

        // Handle "normal" selection

    }

}
```

Again, you test to see whether the selected row is the one at the end of the table. If it is, you override the default `setEditing:animated:` method to put the cell into editing mode, as shown in Listing 7–16.

Listing 7–16. ***The Custom*** `setEditing:animated:` ***Method***

```
-(void)setEditing:(BOOL)editing animated:(BOOL)animated {

    [super setEditing:editing animated:animated];
    [theTableView setEditing:animated animated:animated];

}
```

You will need to amend the `tableView:editingStyleForRowAtIndexPath:` method to supply the insertion control to the last row (shown in Listing 7-17).

After the table is in editing mode, it's up to the user to either edit something with the Delete or Insert controls, or take the table out of editing mode. If they do the latter, you don't need to worry about responding to their action. The updated `setEditing:animated:` method will handle that. An editing action, on the other hand, is something you need to handle.

Listing 7-17.

```
-(UITableViewCellEditingStyle)tableView:(UITableView *)tableView
editingStyleForRowAtIndexPath:(NSIndexPath *)indexPath {

    if (self.editing) {

        if (indexPath.row == [self.tableData count]) {
            return UITableViewCellEditingStyleInsert;
        } else {
            return UITableViewCellEditingStyleDelete;
        }

    }

    return UITableViewCellEditingStyleNone;

}
```

Tapping a row's control will fire the `tableView:commitEditingStyle:forRowAtIndexPath:` method, supplying references to the `tableView` itself, the row that was tapped, and the type of control.

There are two possibilities here: a `UITableViewCellEditingStyleDelete` or a `UITableViewCellEditingStyleInsert`. If it's a `delete`, then you'll handle that as you did previously: remove the object from the relevant index of the data model and then delete the row from the table.

An `insert`, on the other hand, needs the opposite approach. First, you'll need a new object. For demonstration purposes, you'll create an `NSString` containing a date stamp:

```
NSString *theObjectToInsert = [NSString stringWithFormat:@"%@", [NSDate date]];
```

Then, this new object needs to be added to the data model. It's important that this takes place *before* the table gets updated, because the table will need to determine the number of rows it now has in order to be able to insert the new row:

```
[tableData addObject:theObjectToInsert];
```

`NSMutableArray`'s `addObject` inserts the new object at the end of the existing array, but you could of course insert it at a particular position with `insertObject:atIndex:`.

Now that you have the new object safely stored in the data model, you can insert the new row into the table. You'll want this to appear in the penultimate row—above Add New Row, but below the existing rows (along the lines of Figure 7–16).

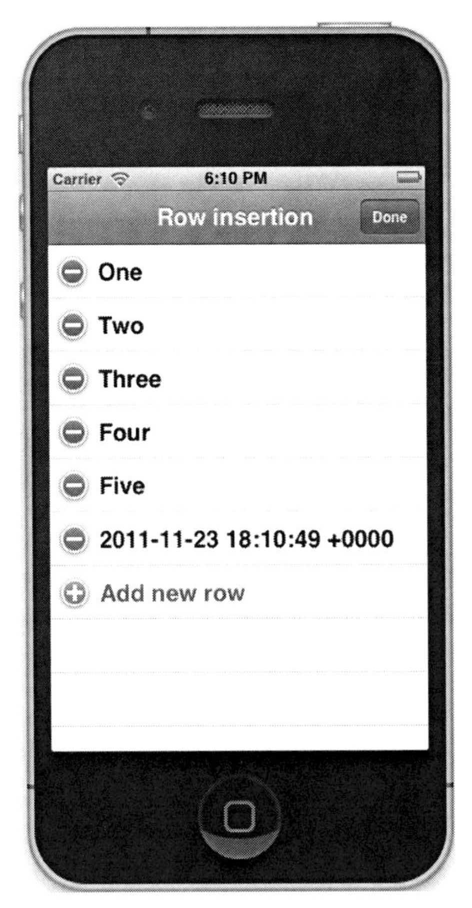

Figure 7–16. *The newly inserted row*

UITableView's insertRowsAtIndexPath:withRowAnimation: takes an NSArray of IndexPath objects where new rows are required, and calls the tableView's cellForRowAtIndexPath: method to fill them.

It'll automatically shift existing rows down. Our table currently has five rows, and our indexPath.row value is 4 (remember, table rows are zero-indexed.) Inserting a new row at indexPath.row 4 will cause whatever's currently in that row to be shifted down to the new indexPath.row 5.

```
[tableView insertRowsAtIndexPaths:indexPathArray↵
 withRowAnimation:UITableViewRowAnimationAutomatic];
```

The UITableViewRowAnimationAutomatic value will force the tableView to take care of moving existing rows around to keep the animation seamless.

Putting that all together (with a little bit of refactoring to keep the method tidy) looks like Listing 7–18.

Listing 7–18. *The Completed `commitEditingStyle:` Method*

```
-(void)tableView:(UITableView *)tableView commitEditingStyle:➥
(UITableViewCellEditingStyle)editingStyle forRowAtIndexPath:(NSIndexPath *)indexPath {

    NSArray *indexPathArray = [NSArray arrayWithObject:indexPath];

    if (editingStyle == UITableViewCellEditingStyleDelete) {

        [self.tableData removeObjectAtIndex:indexPath.row];
        [tableView deleteRowsAtIndexPaths:indexPathArray➥
 withRowAnimation:UITableViewRowAnimationAutomatic];

    } else if (editingStyle == UITableViewCellEditingStyleInsert) {

        NSString *theObjectToInsert = [NSString stringWithFormat:@"%@", ➥
[NSDate date]];
        [tableData addObject:theObjectToInsert];
        [tableView insertRowsAtIndexPaths:indexPathArray➥
 withRowAnimation:UITableViewRowAnimationAutomatic];

    }

}
```

Rearranging Tables

In addition to inserting and deleting rows and sections, you can also rearrange them, both programmatically and through user actions.

The rearrangement process is similar to the insertion and deletion process, as shown in Figure 7–17:

1. The table enters editing mode
2. The `tableView`'s `delegate` is consulted about the permissibility of moving the row
3. The row gets moved
4. The data model is updated.

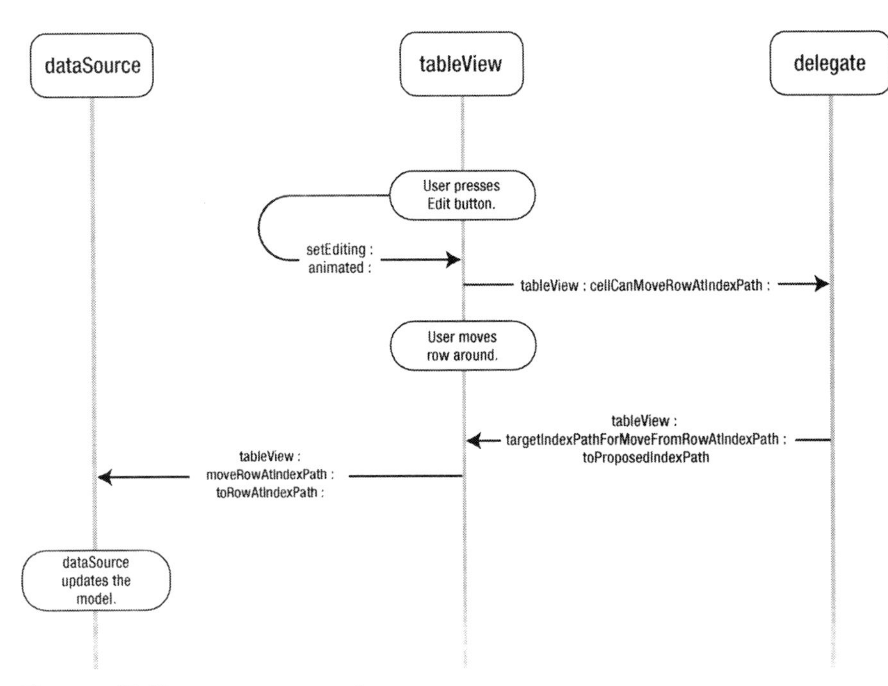

Figure 7–17. *The row rearrangement process*

Entering Editing Mode

In order to rearrange rows, the table needs to be in editing mode. As with deletions, there are two ways of doing this. In the case of `UITableViewController` subclasses, the user can tap the navigation bar's Edit button or override the `tableView`'s `setEditing:animated:` method.

Checking Whether Rows Can Be Moved

As the `tableView` enters editing mode, it asks the delegate whether each visible row can be moved by calling the `tableView:canMoveRowAtIndexPath:` method. This returns either `YES` or `NO`. Returning `NO` will enable you to "lock" particular rows into place.

For example, if you have an Add New Row row at the bottom of the table, it doesn't make sense to be able to move this. Listing 7–19 shows how you'd "lock" this row into place.

Listing 7–19. *The `tableView:canMoveRowAtIndexPath:` Method*

```
-(BOOL)tableView:(UITableView *)tableView canMoveRowAtIndexPath:➥
(NSIndexPath *)indexPath {

    if (indexPath.row == [self.tableData count]) {
        return NO;
    }

    return YES;
}
```

Moving Rows Around

After the table is in editing mode and the rows are flagged as movable, the Reordering control appears at the right-hand end of the cell, as in Figure 7–18.

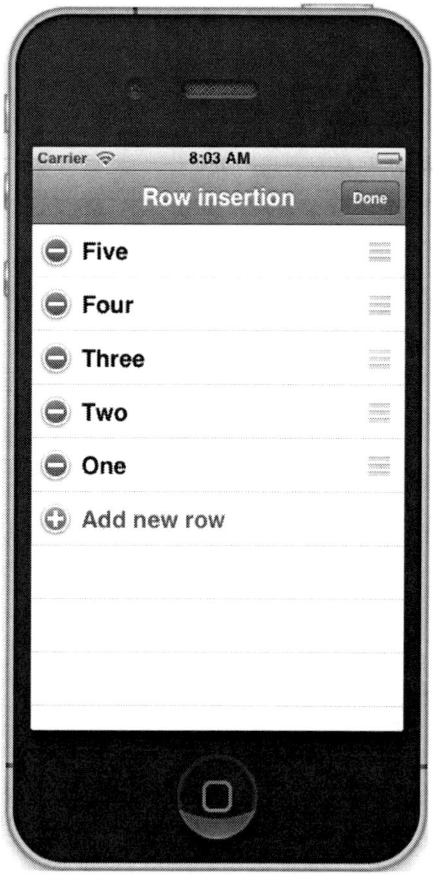

Figure 7–18. *The table in editing mode (and rearranged)*

Touching the Reordering control will cause the row to be animated away from the table and become draggable. As the row passes over other rows, the `tableView` will animate the shuffling around to make room.

Can the Row Be Moved to Here?

In addition to controlling whether rows can be moved at all, `UITableView`'s delegate can also control whether a row can be moved to a particular location.

As the row in motion passes over the static rows in the table, the `tableView` will call the `tableView:targetIndexPathForMoveFromRowAtIndexPath:toProposedIndexPath:` method.

(This is probably the method that's responsible for critics of Objective-C complaining about long-winded method names.)

This method takes three parameters: a reference to the `tableView` itself, the original `indexPath` of the row that's being moved, and the `indexPath` that has just been moved over. The `tableView` doesn't know yet whether the user is going to release the Reordering control and "drop" the cell into place, so this method will be called repeatedly as the row in motion moves over `indexPath` positions as it travels up and down the table.

If the row can be moved to this position, the method simply returns the `proposedDestinationIndexPath` to confirm that this move is permissible.

You can use this method to complement "freezing" the Add New Row row to the bottom of the table. In addition to not wanting to move the Add New Row row, you also want to prevent the user from moving another row to the very bottom. Figure 7–19 shows what you're trying to avoid.

Figure 7–19. *Not allowed!*

You can implement this by checking whether the proposed indexPath is the end of the table. If it is, you can "send" the row back to where it came from by returning sourceIndexPath. If it isn't, the move can be allowed by returning proposedDestinationIndexPath. Listing 7–20 shows this in action.

Listing 7–20. *Preventing a Move to the End of the Table*

```
-(NSIndexPath *)tableView:(UITableView *)tableView↵
 targetIndexPathForMoveFromRowAtIndexPath:(NSIndexPath *)sourceIndexPath↵
 toProposedIndexPath:(NSIndexPath *)proposedDestinationIndexPath {

    if (proposedDestinationIndexPath.row == [self.tableData count]) {
        return sourceIndexPath;
    }

    return proposedDestinationIndexPath;

}
```

Updating the Model

After completing the shuffling of rows, the user will take the table out of editing mode either by tapping the Done button on the navigation bar or by tapping whatever custom control you implemented.

At this stage, it's vital to remember that all the changes have taken place only in the view. The underlying data model has not been updated with the changes. Unless you explicitly update the model, the changes won't persist.

This could manifest itself in a couple of ways. The next time the table is reloaded, the rows will have reverted to their original ordering. Worse, if your table has more rows than can be displayed at once, as the table scrolls, you'll get some extremely weird ordering effects appearing.

If the delegate has allowed the move, the tableView will call its delegate's tableView:moveRowAtIndexPath:toIndexPath: method. This takes three parameters: the usual reference to the tableView itself; the indexPath of the source row, and the indexPath of the destination row.

How you go about rearranging the model is obviously dependent on how your model is implemented. In our simple example, you can exploit NSMutableArray's insertObject:atIndex: and removeObjectAtIndex: methods, as shown in Listing 7–20.

Listing 7–20. *Updating the Model with Rearranged Objects*

```
-(void)tableView:(UITableView *)tableView moveRowAtIndexPath:↵
(NSIndexPath *)sourceIndexPath toIndexPath:(NSIndexPath *)destinationIndexPath {

    [tableData insertObject: [tableData objectAtIndex:sourceIndexPath.row]↵
 atIndex:destinationIndexPath.row];
    [tableData removeObjectAtIndex:(sourceIndexPath.row + 1)];

}
```

This method first grabs the object from the donor row and inserts it at the destination. If you just left things there, you'd end up with two copies of the original object. The `insertObject:atIndex:` method inserts a new index at the specified index, moves the other objects beyond the insertion down by one, and inserts a copy of the object from the source `indexPath`.

Enabling Batch Insertion and Deletion

In most user-controlled situations, rows will be affected one by one. You can, however, combine a number of insertion or deletion commands by wrapping them into a block:

```
[tableView beginUpdates];

// do lots of
// insertions and deletions here

[tableView endUpdates];
```

This takes care of a lot of heavy lifting for you. The manipulation of the `tableView` and the data model will take place in the sequence you specify, but you don't need to worry about tracking the changes as you go along.

This is quite subtle and quite powerful. If you delete row 1 of the table, then what was row 2 will move up to become row 1. So now you have to refer to row 1 to affect what was previously row 2, and so on. The update block handles this for you. If you delete row 1 and then delete row 2 within the block, *row 2* will refer to the original row 2.

You mustn't call any methods that will update the `tableView` within an update block (`reloadData` and so on). If you do, you have to handle the animations yourself.

Summary

In this chapter, you've looked at how tables can be extended from being presenters of static, unreactive data to handle user input through selection traits.

You've also seen how tables can be used to rearrange data and to facilitate the updating of the underlying data model.

Finally, you took things to their logical conclusions and extended the tables still further to allow users to add, amend, and delete information from the data model—taking the table from being a read-only view to a fully interactive component.

Chapter 8

Improving the Look of Cells

Using UITableView's built-in standard cell types is a great way to get up and running quickly. But pretty soon you're going to run up against the limitations of the standard look and feel and want to move beyond the typical layouts.

Creating and using custom cells isn't difficult, and builds on all the topics that we've covered so far. There are three main ways of customizing cells:

- Adding subviews to the cell's contentView
- Creating a custom cell in a NIB by using Interface Builder
- Creating a custom subclass of UITableViewCell

The three methods complement each other. In this chapter, you'll look at the first two. Then in Chapter 9, you'll take a detailed look at custom subclasses.

The two approaches in this chapter are different ways to achieve much the same result, but there's a certain amount of commonality between them. This chapter's examples include some repetition in order so it's possible to compare the two techniques.

Customizing Cells

When it comes to customizing cells, you can take three approaches:

- Add subviews to the cell's contentView.

  The entire content of the cell can be accessed through the contentView property. When the cell is created by the cellForRowAtIndexPath method, you can create and add your controls as subviews to contentView.

Your new subviews can work alongside the built-in subviews, or you can ignore the built-in subviews completely. If you don't set the built-in subviews, they will not be inserted into the cell.

- Create a custom cell in a NIB by using Interface Builder.

  Using Interface Builder, you can lay out the cell controls visually in a NIB, and then load that file when the cell is created by `cellForRowAtIndexPath`.

  Then with a bit of additional code to access your custom controls, it's possible to set their values programmatically.

- Create a subclass of `UITableViewCell` and override `layoutSubViews`.

  As an alternative to Interface Builder's visual approach, you can subclass `UITableViewCell` and lay out the custom cell's content in code—either overriding the `layoutSubviews` method or drawing the cell with `drawRect`.

Which Method Should I Use?

The short answer is—it depends! There's no right or wrong way to customize cells. Which approach is best depends on a combination of what you're trying to achieve, how comfortable you are working with code versus laying out views visually (and vice versa), and how quickly you need to get your code up and running.

Adding Subviews to the Cell's contentView

The cell's contents sit inside a `UIView` called `contentView`, shown in Figure 8–1. Although `contentView` itself is read-only—meaning you can't replace it—you can add and remove subviews to and from it.

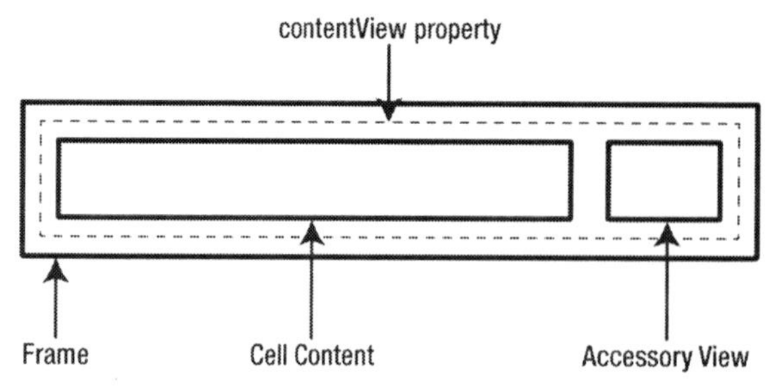

Figure 8–1. *The cell's layout*

These subviews can be any control or component that inherits from `UIView` itself—including labels, controls, text fields, images, and so on.

You add a custom view when a new cell is created for the first time, and that view will then be in place if and when the cell is subsequently recycled.

This means that if you're adding content into the custom view that will vary with each row—a label, an image, and so on—these need to be set for each and every row. The implication here is that you need to be able to reach back inside the custom view, as it were, to access the properties in order to set them.

The approach to take is to think of your custom view in two parts:

- *Creating the structure*: Setting the size and position of the elements that you're going to add to the cell's `contentView` in each new cell
- *Updating the content*: Configuring the properties of the custom elements you've added to the `contentView` as each row is updated

TIP: If you don't explicitly reference the standard cell contents—**`textLabel`**, **`detailTextLabel`**, **`imageView`**, and **`accessoryView`**—then they won't be inserted into the cell and won't get in the way of your custom layout.

VIEWS AND THEIR HIERARCHY

One aspect of iOS that often causes confusion is how `UIViews` relate to each other. All this talk of adding subviews—but to where? And what?

The key concept to understanding `UIViews` is that they form a hierarchy, shown in Figure 8–2.

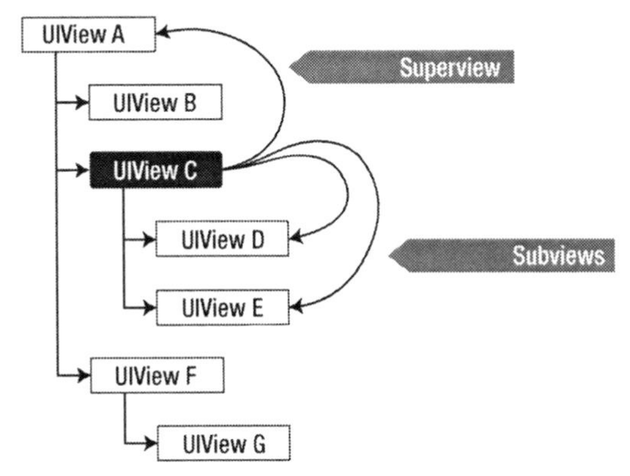

Figure 8–2. *The view hierarchy*

Each `UIView` can have a parent—or `superView`—and one or many `subViews`. Visibility of `subViews` is tied to their `superView`, so setting the visibility of `UIView C` to `hidden` would also cause `UIViews D` and `E` to disappear.

Each `UIView` has a property called `subViews`, which is an `NSArray` containing any `UIViews` for which this `UIView` instance is the parent, or `superView`—see Figure 8–3.

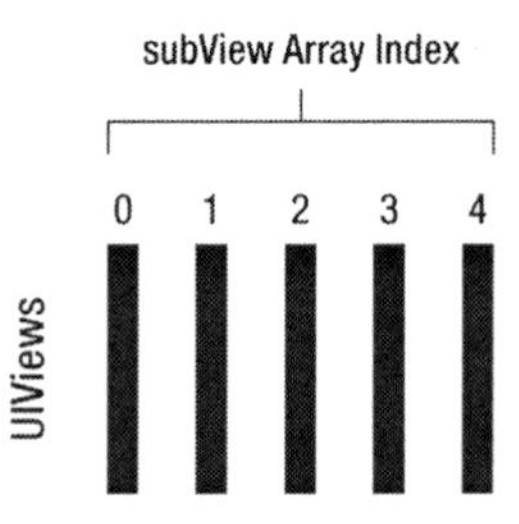

Figure 8–3. *Views in a subView array*

You can access each subView for a UIView by iterating through its array of subViews:

```
for (UIView *theSubView in parentView.subViews) {
  // do something to theSubView
}
```

Similarly, each UIView has a superView property that is a reference to the "parent" view. In Figure 8–2, the superView of view C would be view A, and view C would have two views in its subViews array: views D and E.

If you're creating complex layouts with multiple views, subviews, and superviews, it's worth keeping some diagrams sketched to show how each view relates to the others. That can prevent much confusion later.

Creating the Elements in the Cell

The first step has to take place as each cell is created. This occurs in the dataSource's tableView:cellForRowAtIndexPath method, shown in Listing 8–1.

Listing 8–1. *Where Custom Subview Creation and Updating Takes Place*

```
- (UITableViewCell *)tableView:(UITableView *)tableView ➥
cellForRowAtIndexPath:(NSIndexPath *)indexPath {

    static NSString *cellIdentifier = @"cellIdentifier";

    UITableViewCell *cell = [tableView ➥
dequeueReusableCellWithIdentifier:cellIdentifier];

    if (cell == nil) {

       cell = [[UITableViewCell alloc] initWithStyle:UITableViewCellStyleDefault ➥
reuseIdentifier:cellIdentifier];

          //
          // Create the structure here
          //

    }

    //
    // configure the cell & custom content here
    //

    return cell;
```

```
}
```

As an example, Listing 8–2 shows how you could go about creating and customizing a `UILabel` and an `imageView` in each cell.

Listing 8–2. *Creating the `UILabel`*

```
  - (UITableViewCell *)tableView:(UITableView *)tableView ➥
cellForRowAtIndexPath:(NSIndexPath *)indexPath {

    static NSString *cellIdentifier = @"cellIdentifier";

    UITableViewCell *cell = [tableView ➥
dequeueReusableCellWithIdentifier:cellIdentifier];

    if (cell == nil) {

        cell = [[UITableViewCell alloc] initWithStyle:UITableViewCellStyleDefault ➥
reuseIdentifier:cellIdentifier];

        // Create a new label with the size we need
        UILabel *myLabel = [[UILabel alloc] init];
        myLabel.frame = CGRectMake(75, 10, 200, 25);

        // Set the label's tag value
        myLabel.tag = 1020;

        // Add the new label to the contentView
        [cell.contentView addSubview:myLabel];

    }

    //
    // configure the cell & custom content here
    //

    return cell;

}
```

This should all be familiar, with the possible exception of setting the label's tag value. I'll show you what we do that for in a moment.

Creating the image view is a very similar process, shown in Listing 8–3.

Listing 8–3. *Creating the `imageView`*

```
if (cell == nil) {

        cell = [[UITableViewCell alloc] initWithStyle:UITableViewCellStyleDefault ➥
reuseIdentifier:cellIdentifier];

        // Create a new label with the size we need
        UILabel *myLabel = [[UILabel alloc] init];
        myLabel.frame = CGRectMake(75, 10, 200, 25);

        // Set the label's tag value
        myLabel.tag = 1020;
```

```
        // Add the new label to the contentView
        [cell.contentView addSubview:myLabel];

        // Create the frame for the image view
        CGRect myImageFrame = CGRectMake(10, 10, 50, 25);

        // Create the image view itself
        UIImageView *myImageView = [[UIImageView alloc]↩
initWithFrame:myImageFrame];

        // set the tag
        myImageView.tag = 1010;

        // Add it to the contentView
        [cell.contentView addSubview:myImageView];

    }
```

Updating the Content

The preceding code will ensure that every new cell will be created with a `UILabel` and a `UIImageView` inside it, ready for configuration as each row is updated.

At this point, you meet what might seem like a bit of a stumbling block. After the subviews that you created are inserted into the cell's `contentView`, you can no longer access them directly to update them. They're effectively subsumed into the cell's `contentView`, which doesn't have any properties or outlets that you can use to update them.

This is where the tags come in. Updating the content is a two-step process:

1. Getting a reference to the custom label and `imageView` inside the cell's `contentView`, which you do by referencing their tags.
2. Updating the content of the controls.

Tagging Controls in the Cell

Every `UIView` control has an associate `tag` property, which can be set either in Interface Builder, or dynamically in code. The `tag` is simply an integer value that uniquely identifies each element—with one very important caveat. You're in charge of the `tag`'s uniqueness.

Let me say that again, for emphasis. The *control doesn't care about what its* `tag` *value is*, and *the view doesn't care if the* `tag` *is unique*. If you need to identify each control uniquely, the `tag`s need to be unique. You can get some very strange results if that's not the case.

Setting the `tag` of a control can be done in the View section of the Attributes inspector (shown in Figure 8–4).

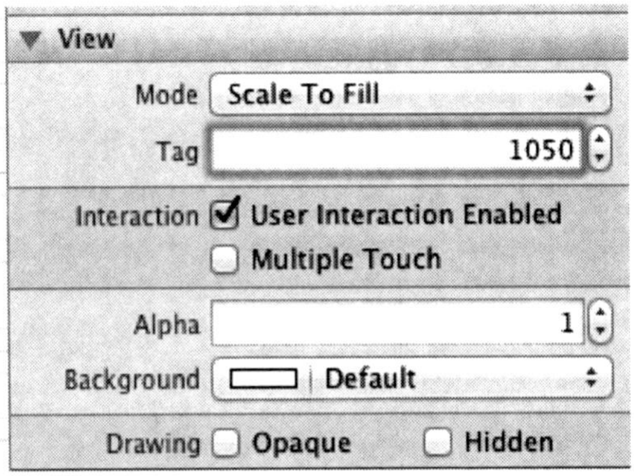

Figure 8–4. *Setting a control's tag*

Alternatively, the tag's value can be set in code:

```
[myControl setTag:1050];
```

There are a couple of tricks I use to keep track of control tags within NIB files:

- Start the numbering at a large value, and leave "space" in the numbering for additional tags. I've gotten into the habit of starting tag numbering at 1000, and incrementing by 10 for each tag.
- Keep the tag numbering consistent with the layout of the NIB. For example, if you have four UILabels in a line, give the top one the tag 1000, the second 1010, the third 1020, and so on.

After you've finished with the NIB file, the next challenge is keeping track of tag numbers in your classes. This is where enumerations come into their own.

Enumerations (enums) allow you to associate integer values with what are effectively text labels. One way of thinking about them is as a kind of compile-time global find-and-replace (this will make Objective-C purists wince, through.)

enums need to be defined before they're used. I tend to put them at the top of my implementation files so I know where to find them, although you will also find them placed above the first method where they're used.

```
#import "TableNavViewController.h"
#import "TableNavAppDelegate.h"

enum {
    kCustomCellTitleLabel = 1000
};

@implementation TableNavViewController
```

Then as the file is compiled, any instances of the enum (in this case kCustomCellTitleLabel) will be replaced by whatever integer follows. So if you have the following code:

```
UILabel *myLabel = (UILabel *)[nib viewWithTag:kCustomCellTitleLabel];
```

The compiler will interpret this as follows:

```
UILabel *myLabel = (UILabel *)[nib viewWithTag:1000];
```

Starting an enum with k just indicates it's a constant. You don't need to do this, but you'll see this done a lot in Apple code that defines constants. It's a hangover from days of yore.

By using enums inline in your code rather than the actual tag values themselves, you're doing several things:

- You're making your code significantly more readable, because it's far more obvious what the control does.
- You're making any use of the wrong tag much more obvious.
- You're providing a record of all your tags at the top of your implementation file (or wherever you choose to place them), keeping everything neatly together.

Casting controls

You'll notice that the line that creates your UILabel has a slightly strange syntax. You're *casting* the UIView in the NIB with the tag 1050 into a UILabel. If this is something new to you, fear not—it's not as arcane as it sounds.

The viewWithTag method returns a UIView, which will respond to all the methods defined for the UIView class. The problem is that the view with tag 1050 is actually a UILabel, and you want to set its textLabel property.

UIView doesn't have a text property. If you try to send a text message to an instance of UIView, the compiler will (rightly) complain that the UIView won't respond, and the program will crash when the message is sent.

The work-around is something of a cheat. What you're doing in the line

```
UILabel *myLabel = (UILabel *)[nib viewWithTag:1050];
```

is telling the compiler that the view with tag 1050 is actually a UILabel. Technically speaking, you're casting it from a UIView to a UILabel. This reassures the compiler enough for it to allow you to set the view's text property:

```
myLabel.text = @"Some custom text";
```

However, the compiler takes your word that the control really is a UILabel. It won't check whether that's actually the case. If it's not—and you mistakenly try to set its textLabel property—then although the compiler won't complain, the program will most certainly crash.

Tracking down these kinds of bugs can be painful, so this is one reason why it pays to be very careful with tags. It's all too easy to incorrectly assign a tag to the wrong control.

Putting It all Together

Putting all these steps together, Listing 8–4 shows what your `cellForRowAtIndexPath` will now look like. (Having suggested that you use `enums`, I'm defining static constants here.)

Listing 8–4. *The Full `contentView` Approach*

```
- (UITableViewCell *)tableView:(UITableView *)tableView ↵
cellForRowAtIndexPath:(NSIndexPath *)indexPath {

    static NSString *cellIdentifier = @"cellIdentifier";

    static const int kLabel = 1010;        // constant for the label tag
    static const int kImage = 1020;            // constant for the imageView tag

    UITableViewCell *cell = [tableView ↵
dequeueReusableCellWithIdentifier:cellIdentifier];

    if (cell == nil) {

        cell = [[UITableViewCell alloc] initWithStyle:UITableViewCellStyleDefault ↵
reuseIdentifier:cellIdentifier];

        CGRect myImageFrame = CGRectMake(10, 10, 50, 25);
        UIImageView *myImageView = [[UIImageView alloc] initWithFrame:myImageFrame];
        myImageView.tag = kLabel;
        [cell.contentView addSubview:myImageView];

        UILabel *myLabel = [[UILabel alloc] init];
        myLabel.frame = CGRectMake(75, 10, 200, 25);
        myLabel.tag = kImage;
        [cell.contentView addSubview:myLabel];

    }

    UIImageView *myImageView = (UIImageView *)[cell viewWithTag:kLabel];
    [myImageView setImage:[UIImage imageNamed:@"cellimage.png"]];

    UILabel *myLabel = (UILabel *)[cell viewWithTag:kImage];
    myLabel.text = [tableData objectAtIndex:indexPath.row];

    return cell;
}
```

Creating Custom Cells Visually Using Interface Builder

Adding subviews to the cell's `contentView` can quickly lead to a lot of code—and unless you're good at mentally translating between the cell's layout and the coordinates in the code, that code can be difficult to follow.

An alternative approach is to use the power and flexibility of Interface Builder to create a custom cell in a NIB file, and use this to create a completely customized cell whenever a new one is required.

I don't subscribe to the school of thought that maintains, *"Real developers don't use visual tools."* If you find it quicker and easier to design your custom cells with a visual layout tool (and subject to the following caveat), go right ahead. What counts, after all, is getting the job done.

The Stages of Creating Cells Visually

Creating custom cells visually with Interface Builder is a multistage process:

1. Create a new NIB file, and lay out the cell using Interface Builder.
2. Ensure that both the NIB and the `tableView`'s `dataSource` are using the same cell identifier.
3. Create controls inside your new cell.
4. Assign tags to the controls so they can be accessed from the outside world.

Those four steps will give you a custom cell that can be created when required using `tableView:cellForRowAtIndexPath`. After you have an instance of that custom cell, you can then manipulate the controls according to the values of the data in your table's model.

Laid out like this, it seems like a lot of work. In reality, it's a very quick process to get the housekeeping tasks out of the way so you can get on with creating the cell itself.

Creating a New NIB File

First, you're going to need a new NIB file. From the File menu, choose the New File option, or type Command + N.

From the templates (shown in Figure 8–5), select the View option and then tap Next. You'll need to select iPhone as the Device Family, and then give the NIB file a name.

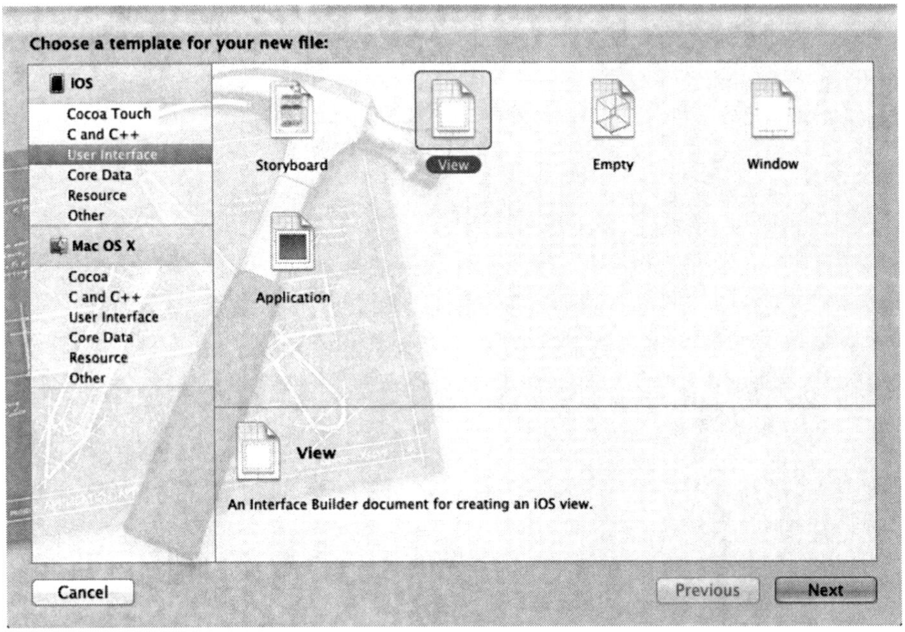

Figure 8–5. *Creating the new view*

The view will be created with an empty full-screen view (see Figure 8–6), which you don't need. Select that in the object list and delete it by pressing Backspace, and you'll be left with an empty NIB.

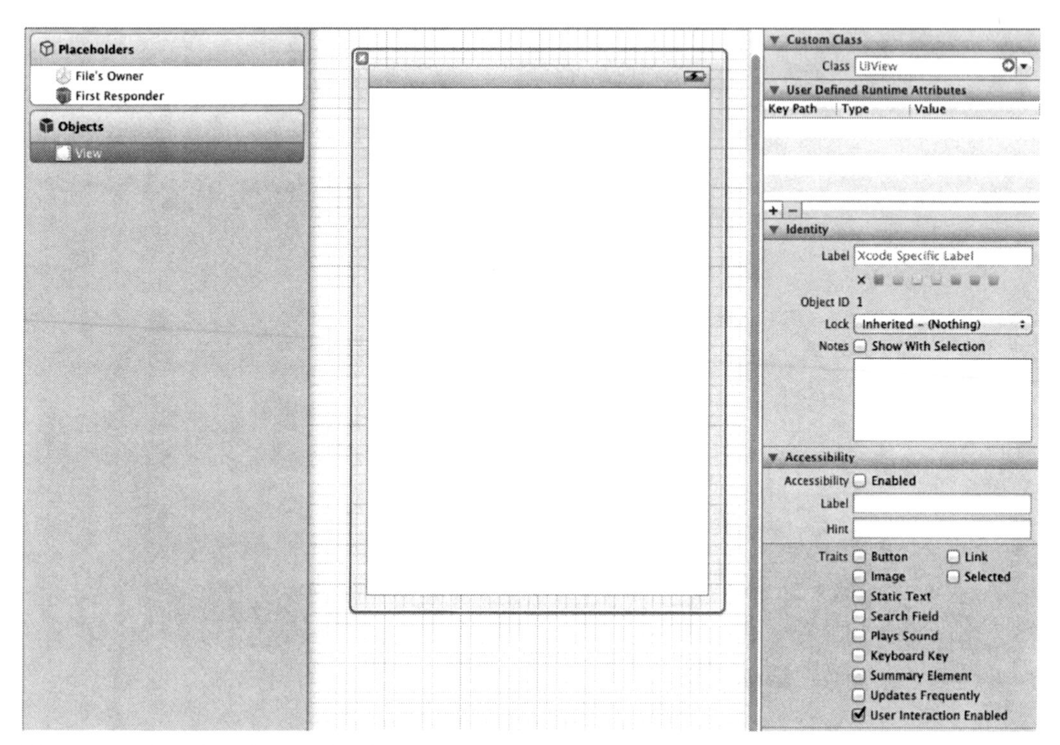

Figure 8–6. *The default view, ready to be deleted*

To create the cell, scroll down through the Objects browser at the right, and drag a Table View Cell out into the center panel, as shown in Figure 8–7.

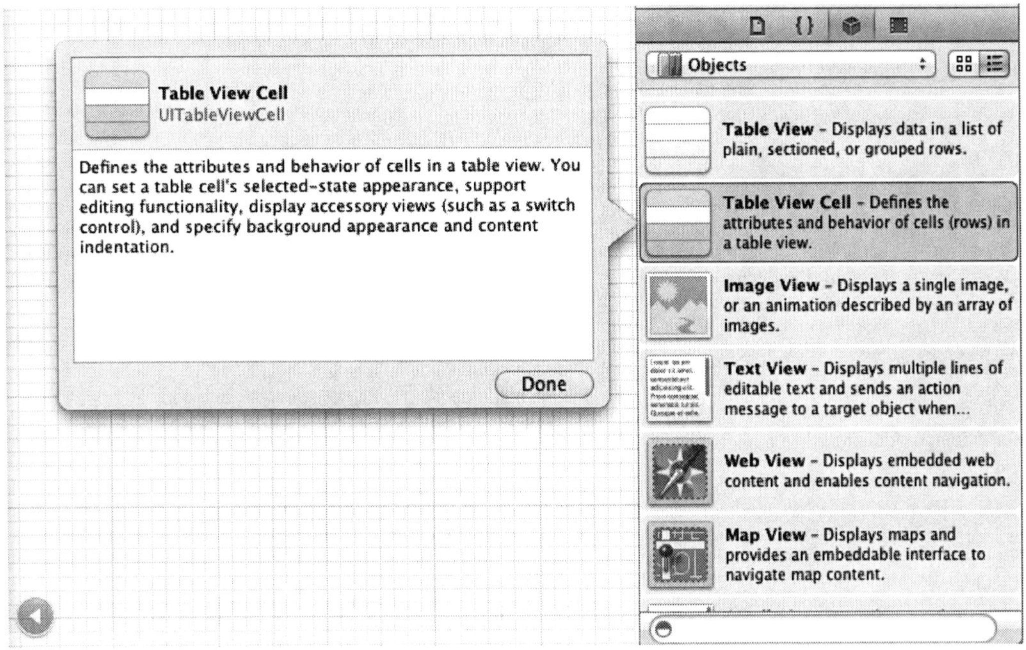

Figure 8–7. *Selecting the Table View Cell*

That will create a new, empty cell with the default height and width, shown in Figure 8–8.

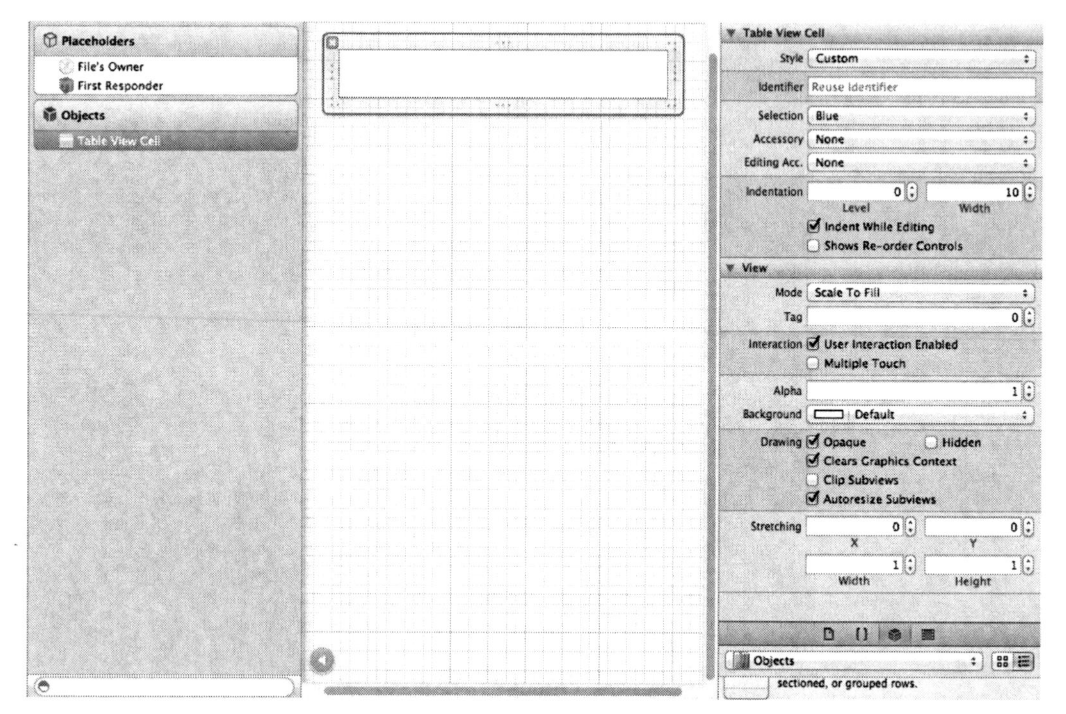

Figure 8–8. *The new cell, ready for customization*

CAUTION: The default cell that's created when you drag it out of the Objects list is 320 pixels wide and 44 pixels high. Unless you tell it otherwise, the **tableView** will assume that all cells are this height. Therefore, if you change the height of the custom cell, you'll need to let the **tableView** know about this.

UITableView's **tableViewDelegate** has a **tableView:heightForRowAtIndexPath** method that returns a **CGFloat** value for the row height in pixels:

```
-(CGFloat)tableView:(UITableView *)tableView  ➥
heightForRowAtIndexPath:(NSIndexPath *)indexPath {
    return 100;
}
```

Creating tables with a range of cell heights is possible but comes with some potentially significant performance overheads. If all cells are the same height, the tableView is able to skip the need to constantly recalculate "housekeeping" dimensions—and that can speed things up considerably.

If your data is variable, for performance purposes you're generally better off building the cell to the maximum dimensions it needs to be, and laying the contents out to make best use of the space available.

Because this is a subclass of `UIView`, you can drag and drop other controls into this cell in exactly the same way as if you were creating a full-screen view. However, before you get carried away, there are a couple of housekeeping activities you could get out of the way first.

Setting Up the Cell's Identifier

Earlier, in the `tableView:cellForRowAtIndexPath` method, you defined a `reuseIdentifier` that the `tableViewController` could use to keep track of dequeued cells for reuse. In the code, this is simply an arbitrary `NSString`. If there's only one type of cell to keep track of, I tend to call this `cellIdentifier` simply so its purpose is really obvious.

What you call yours really doesn't matter. What *is* important is that you associate whatever the reuse identifier is going to be with the kind of custom cell that it's going to refer to.

If you select the Table View Cell item in the Objects list, and then open the Attributes inspector, you'll see an Identifier option as the second item in the list (see Figure 8–9).

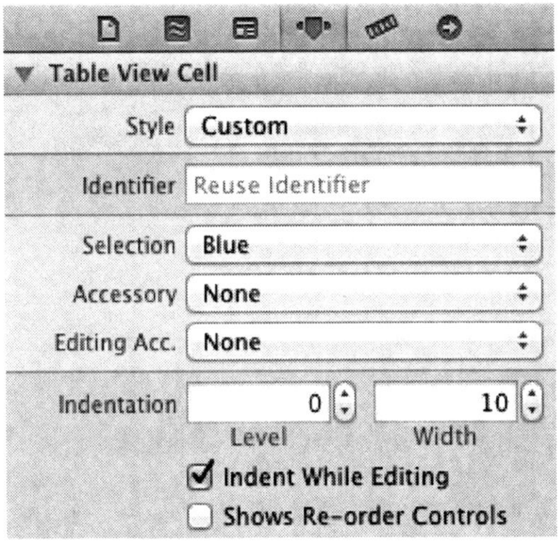

Figure 8–9. *The cell's Reuse Identifier setting*

Unsurprisingly, this is a reference to the `reuseIdentifier` in the code. Because you defined an `NSString` with the contents `cellIdentifier` in the `tableView:cellForRowAtIndexPath` method, this is what you'll need to enter here.

Creating the Cell's Content

Finally, after all that, you're ready to start laying out the cell's contents. Because the cell is an instance of `UIView`, you can put in a cell pretty much anything you can put in a plain ol' `UIView`. Your choice is limited only by your imagination, what the cell needs to do, and the controls at your disposal. Figure 8–10 is a very simple layout that will be used in the next steps of this example.

TIP: You're not limited to static content such as **UILabels** and **UIViews**. You can also place controls such as **UIButtons**, **UISwitches**, and **UISliders** into cells. This is covered in Chapter 10.

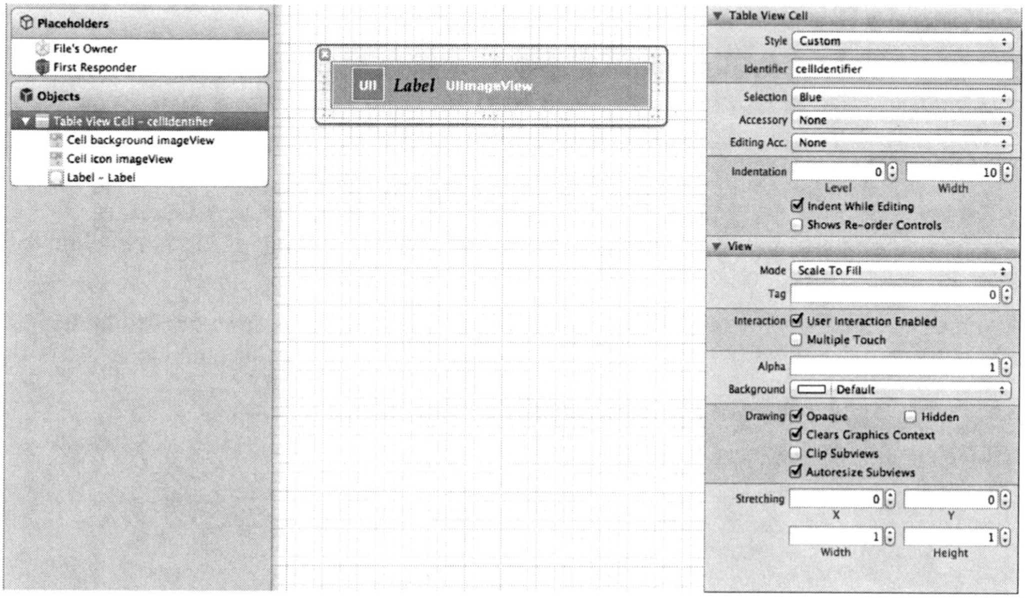

Figure 8–10. *An example custom cell layout*

Assigning Tags to Controls

Earlier in the chapter, you were assigning tags to cell content by setting each object's `tag` property in code. That's not an option when using Interface Builder, because you need the tag to get a reference to the control.

Tag attributes can be set in the View section of the Attributes inspector (see Figure 8–11).

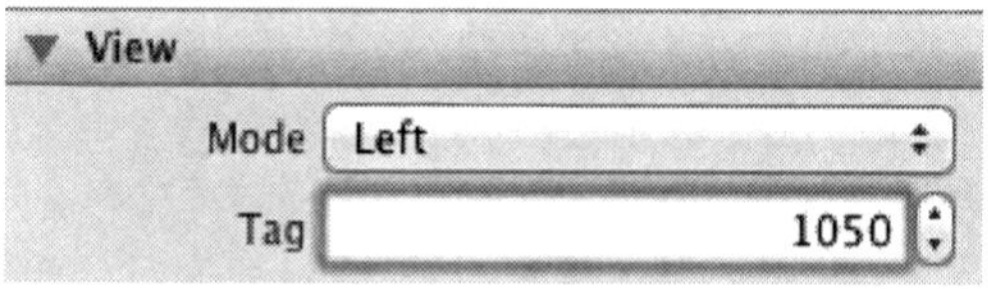

Figure 8–11. *The Tag field in Interface Builder*

This has the same effect as

```
[myControl setTag:1050];
```

would have in code.

Referencing Tagged Controls

After your controls are tagged, this leads to the obvious question: how do you go about using them?

Earlier in this chapter, I mentioned that each UIView has a property called subViews, which is an NSArray containing all the subviews related to the parent. Because all view controls are ultimately subclasses of UIView, it's entirely legitimate to think of them as instances of UIViews, and not to care about whether they're UILabels or UITextViews and so on.

This means that you can think of your custom cell as being a UIView (remember, UITableViewCell inherits from UIView) with a property called subviews, which is an NSArray of all the controls inside the cell.

The top-level UIView—the UITableViewCell itself—will be the object at index 0 in that array (which can also be accessed using the objectAtIndex:0 method).

Loading the cell from the NIB file is a two-stage process:

```
UINib *theNib = [UINib nibWithNibName:@"NewCell" bundle:nil];
cell = [[theNib instantiateWithOwner:self options:nil] objectAtIndex:0];
```

After you have accessed the cell itself, it's possible to exploit UIView's viewWithTag method to get a reference to the controls that need setting:

```
UILabel *myLabel = (UILabel *)[cell viewWithTag:1050];
myLabel.text = @"Some custom text";
```

(Remember from earlier in this chapter that viewWithTag returns a UIView object, so in order to configure a UILabel (for example), you'll need to cast it from a UIView to a UILabel.)

Creating Cells at Runtime

Cells are returned to the tableView on demand from the dataSource. This is the job of the tableView:cellForRowAtIndexPath method, which either returns a previously created cell from the cache or creates a brand-new instance.

So far, you've been creating instances of standard cell types—UITableViewCellStyleDefault and so on. Now that you've created a custom cell in a NIB file, rather than creating a standard cell, you'll load the custom cell from the NIB file and configure its controls.

In iOS 5, Apple introduced a "short-cut" method of creating cells from NIBs, which I'll show in a moment. But at the time of this writing, you're more likely to see code that looks very similar to the "default" tableView:cellForRowAtIndexPath method, shown in Listing 8–5.

Listing 8–5. *Creating a Custom Cell from a NIB File*

```
- (UITableViewCell *)tableView:(UITableView *)tableView ➥
cellForRowAtIndexPath:(NSIndexPath *)indexPath {

    static NSString *cellIdentifier = @"cellIdentifier";

    UITableViewCell *cell = [tableView ➥
 dequeueReusableCellWithIdentifier:cellIdentifier];

    if (cell == nil) {
       UINib *cellNib = [UINib nibWithNibName:@"CustomCell" bundle:[NSBundle ➥
 mainBundle]];
        cell = [[cellNib instantiateWithOwner:self options:nil] objectAtIndex:0];

    }

    // Configure the cell's contents
    //  ...

    return cell;
}
```

Most of this is the process that you've seen before. You create a cell identifier string and attempt to get a cell with a corresponding identifier from the cache, to save creating a new cell from scratch.

If that isn't possible, instead of creating a new cell by using `UITableViewCell`'s `initWithStyle:reuseIdentifier` method, you're doing something slightly different.

`[UINib nibWithName:@"CustomCell" bundle:[NSBundle mainBundle]]` is pretty self-explanatory. It will attempt to locate and load the NIB file called `customCell`. (The `.xib` file extension is implied, so doesn't need to be specified.)

`NSBundle` is a reference to the location of the program's code and resources in the file system—similar, but not exactly analogous to the directory on disk where your Xcode project lives. `mainBundle` returns the `NSBundle` object associated with the contents of the application itself. Think of it as being the contents of the .app file.

Assuming that the NIB file can be located, `[cellNib instantiateWithOwner:self options:nil]` returns an `NSArray` of the contents. `objectAtIndex:0` returns a reference to the object in the array with an index value of 0.

In the case of a NIB file containing a `UITableViewCell` that in turn contains controls, the cell itself will be at the top of the "tree" and have an index of 0 (see Figure 8–12 for an illustration).

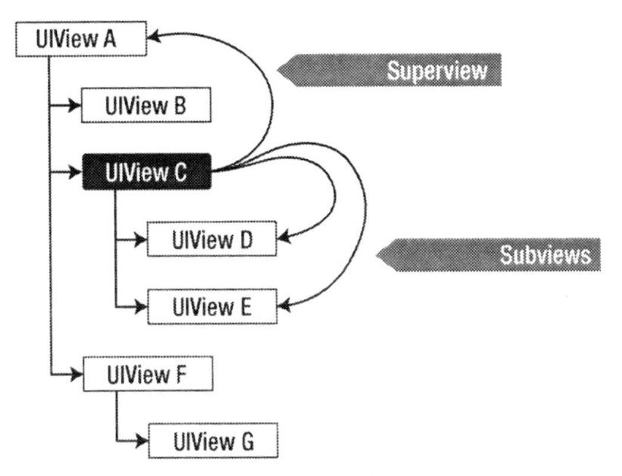

Figure 8–12. *An example view hierarchy*

Having either created a new cell, or retrieved one from the NIB file, it's time to configure the controls that it contains:

```
UILabel *myLabel = (UILabel *)[cell viewWithTag:1050];
 myLabel.textLabel.text = [self.tableData objectAtIndex:indexPath.row];
```

New in iOS 5!

In iOS 5, Apple introduced a "short-cut" method of instantiating cells from NIB files that has three stages:

1. Declaring a property for the cell identifier
2. Registering the NIB object that contains the cell, and associating that with the cell identifier
3. Creating the cell itself (and then customizing the controls as usual)

Registering the NIB object needs to happen only once during the lifetime of the controller, so an obvious place to put the code is in the `viewDidLoad` method of the `tableView`'s controller:

```
cellIdentifier = @"CustomCell";

[tableView registerNib:[UINib nibWithNibName:@"customCell" bundle:nil] ➥
forCellReuseIdentifier:cellIdentifier];
```

This takes two parameters:

- A reference to an instance of `UINib`, which you get by passing in `UINib`'s `nibWithNibName` method
- The `NSString` cell identifier that was previously created

After the NIB is registered for use as a cell, the `dequeueReusableCellWithIdentifier` method will do one of two things:

- If there's a cached cell available for reuse, it will be dequeued and can be accessed through the cell variable.
- If there isn't a cell available for reuse, `dequeueReusableCellWithIdentifier` will create one from the registered NIB.

Both of these things take place behind the scenes, so there's now no longer any need to do the check for the cell's existence manually. `dequeueReusableCellWithIdentifier` will handle all that for you. Listing 8–6 shows this in action.

Listing 8–6. *Creating a Custom Cell from a NIB File, the iOS 5 Way*

```
- (UITableViewCell *)tableView:(UITableView *)tableView↩
 cellForRowAtIndexPath:(NSIndexPath *)indexPath {

UITableViewCell *cell = [tableView dequeueReusableCellWithIdentifier:cellIdentifier];

    // Configure the cell's contents
    //  ...

    return cell;
}
```

Putting It All Together

Having gone through the detail, let's put this all together in a complete `tableView:cellForRowAtIndexPath` example.

The custom cell that this code utilizes (shown in Figure 8–13) lives in a NIB file called `CustomCell.xib`, and has an identifier of `cellIdentifier` and three controls:

- A `UIImageView` that holds the cell's background image and has the tag `1010`
- A `UIImageView` that holds the cell's icon image and has the tag `1020`
- A `UILabel` that will hold the cell's text content and has the tag `1030`

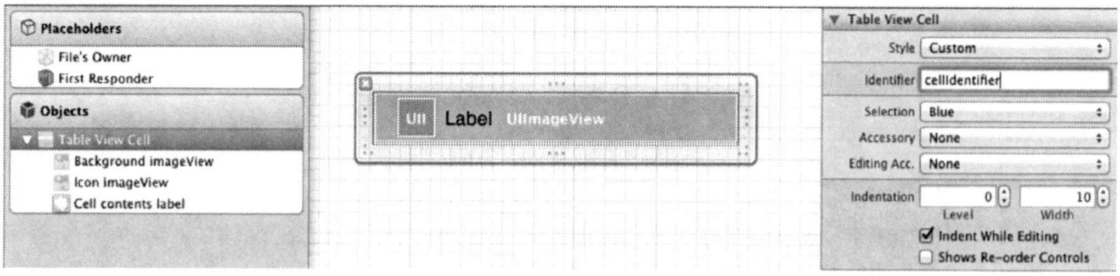

Figure 8–13. *The custom cell*

The corresponding `tableView:cellForRowAtIndexPath` method will look like Listing 8–7.

Listing 8–7. *The Complete* `tableView:cellForRowAtIndexPath` *Method*

```
- (UITableViewCell *)tableView:(UITableView *)tableView↵
 cellForRowAtIndexPath:(NSIndexPath *)indexPath {

    UITableViewCell *cell = [tableView↵
 dequeueReusableCellWithIdentifier:cellIdentifier];

    UILabel *cellLabel;
    cellLabel = (UILabel *)[cell viewWithTag:1000];
    cellLabel.text = [tableData objectAtIndex:indexPath.row];

    UIImageView *cellIcon = (UIImageView *)[cell viewWithTag:1010];
    cellIcon.image = [UIImage imageNamed:@"cellIcon"];

    UIImageView *cellBackground = (UIImageView *)[cell viewWithTag:1020];
    cellBackground.image = [UIImage imageNamed:@"cellBackground"];

    return cell;
}
```

When a cell is required, the `tableView` will ask its `dataSource` for a cell via the `tableView:cellForRowAtIndexPath` method. It'll supply a reference to itself, and the index path for the section and row that the cell will be used to fill.

The `dataSource` will return a dequeued cell from the cache (or create one behind the scenes) based on the cell identifier string you supply to indicate the type of cell you're after.

By this point, you have either recycled an existing cell or created a brand new one. Now you can use tags to get references to the custom controls within the cell, casting from generic `UIView` objects to instances of the specific control that you're trying to configure. The values come from the `tableView's` model—in this case, an array called `tableData`.

Finally, having created/retrieved and configured the cell, you return it to the `tableView` ready to be displayed.

Handling Cell Resizing

In Chapter 7, you looked at the various changes that take place when selecting and editing table content—and spent a lot of time looking at the controls that are added to the cell when the table goes into editing mode. This begs the question: how should a customized cell react to changes in shape, either because of the table entering editing mode, or because the entire device has been rotated?

There are two types of events that can cause cell resizing:

- Putting a table into editing mode, which causes the editing and/or reordering controls to be displayed
- Rotating the device from portrait to landscape, and vice versa

Both types of events will cause the cells to resize—in the first instance, because the cell needs to display more "furniture," and in the second, because the cell has to adapt to a new table width.

Handling Editing

As you saw earlier, the table goes into editing mode when the `setEditing:animated` method is called. At this point, if the cell is editable (and/or the row can be rearranged), the additional cell controls are inserted, as shown in Figure 8–14.

From this...

... to this

... or this

Figure 8–14. *Changing from normal to editing mode*

The deletion or insertion control appears at the left end of the cell, and the rearrangement control (if applicable) appears at the right. This means that the content of the cell has to move right to accommodate the deletion or insertion control, and potentially shrink to accommodate the rearrangement control.

When the deletion/insertion controls appear, the row appears to move right, with the accessory view moving off-screen if applicable.

In both situations, the cells' `contentViews` will automatically alter the width value of their `frames`.

Assuming that your `tableView` is the full width of the screen (that is, 320 pixels in portrait mode, or 480 pixels in landscape), then the new default width of the cells' `contentViews` is shown in Table 8–1. (Bear in mind that these are the defaults. Hard-coding the dimensions isn't best-practice.)

Table 8–1. `contentView` *Widths*

Mode	Portrait Orientation `contentView` width	Landscape Orientation `contentView` Width	Difference
Row One	320 pixels	480 pixels	-
Row One ›	300 pixels	460 pixels	-
⊖ Row One	288 pixels	448 pixels	–12 pixels
⊖ Row One ≡	257 pixels	417 pixels	–12 pixels for insert/delete controls –31 pixels for rearrangement control

Reacting to Editing

The standard `UITableViewCell` styles do a reasonable job of handling the change in `contentView` size. The `textLabel` control is an instance of `UILabel`, which has a property called `lineBreakMode` that allows you a degree of control over how the text is truncated when the `contentView`'s size reduces.

Figure 8–15 shows the default behavior.

A row with lots of content ›
Not so much content ›
Virtually none ›

⊖ A row with lots of cont...
⊖ Not so much content
⊖ Virtually none

Figure 8–15. *Default content truncation*

If you've customized the cell by adding things to the `contentView`, then you're in charge of handling the resizing of whatever those things are.

There are two ways of doing this - the hard way is to obtain the new size of the `contentView` and calculate what the new sizes of your custom `UIViews` and subclasses should be. Alternatively, you could take the easy route and use `autoresizingMasks`.

Autoresizing Masks—Springs and Struts

Autoresizing masks can be set either in Interface Builder or in code. They use the concepts of *springs* and *struts*. By default, a view is held in place relative to its `superView` by struts that don't change their length. Springs, on the other hand, do change their length to allow the view's coordinates to change.

Figure 8–16 shows how they're displayed in the Properties pane in Interface Builder.

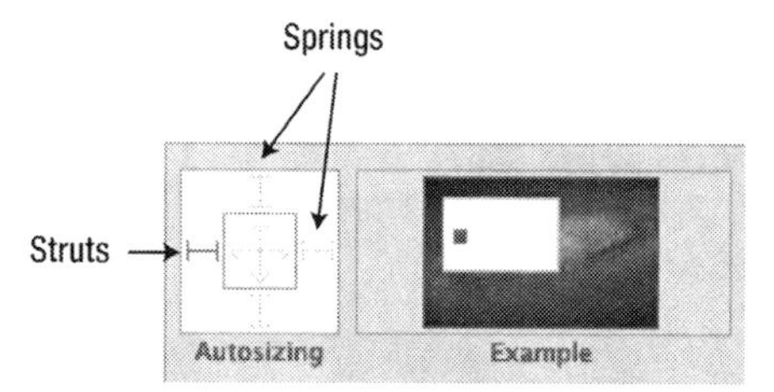

Figure 8–16. *Springs and struts*

The best way to understand springs and struts is to whip up an app and play around with them. Figures 8–17 and 8–18 show how springs and struts constrain view movement.

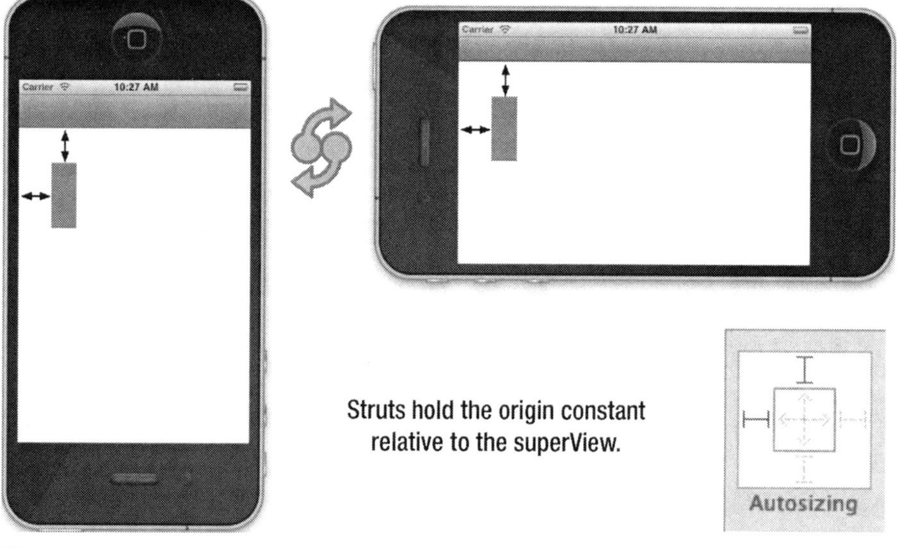

Figure 8–17. *The effect of struts*

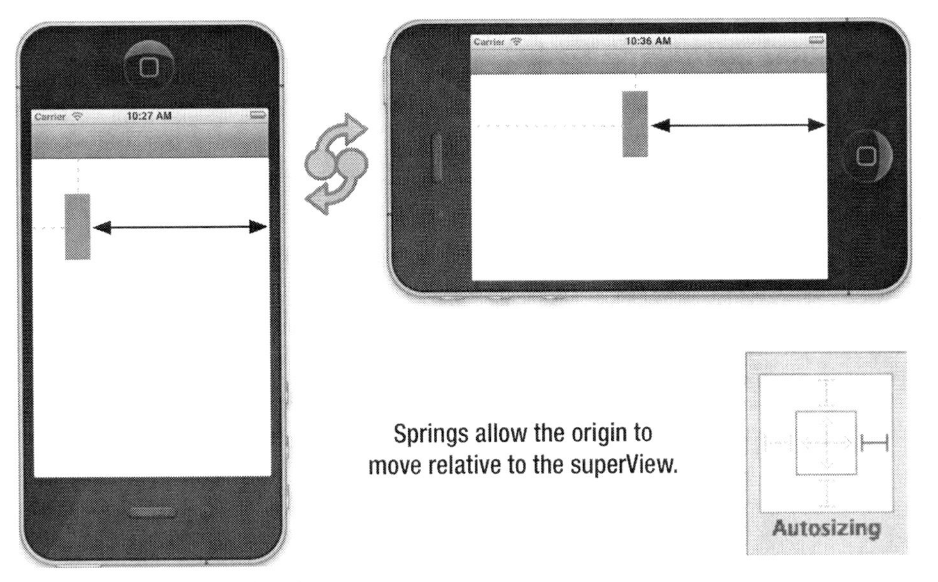

Figure 8–18. *The effect of springs*

Autoresizing Masks—Widths and Heights

By default, the width and height of a view is fixed absolutely. Neither value will change if the `superView`'s dimensions alter. Changing width and height struts into springs will allow the view's proportions to change, relative to the `superView`.

In Figure 8–19, the red view is 50 percent of the `superView`'s height; and 50 percent of the `superView`'s width. Setting the height and width struts means these proportions will remain constant.

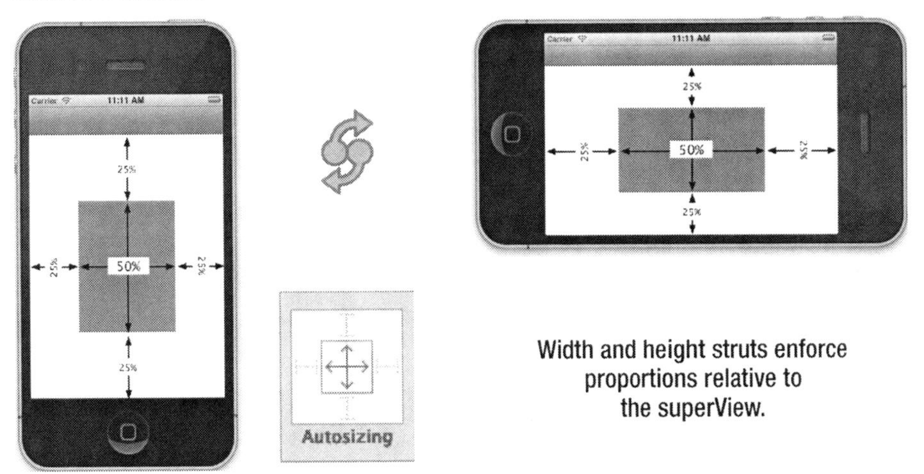

Figure 8–19. *Height and width remain proportional to the `superView`.*

Setting Struts and Springs in Code

Struts and springs can also be set in code with the appropriate `UIViewResizing` mask. These are shown in Figure 8–20.

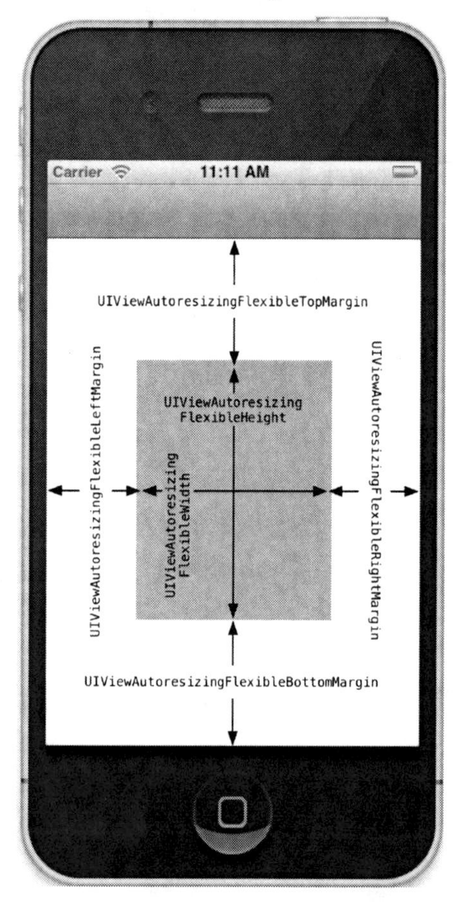

Figure 8–20. *`UIViewAutoResizing` masks*

Listing 8–8 is a hypothetical example that adds a custom `textLabel` in place of the built-in one and adds a background image.

Listing 8–8. *A Hypothetical `cellForRowAtIndexPath` Method*

```
- (UITableViewCell *)tableView:(UITableView *)tableView↵
 cellForRowAtIndexPath:(NSIndexPath *)indexPath
{
    static NSString *cellIdentifier = @"Cell";

    UITableViewCell *cell = [tableView↵
 dequeueReusableCellWithIdentifier:cellIdentifier];
    if (cell == nil) {
        cell = [[UITableViewCell alloc] initWithStyle:UITableViewCellStyleDefault↵
 reuseIdentifier:CellIdentifier];
```

```
    }

    // Configure the cell's background
    UIImageView *gradient = [[UIImageView alloc] initWithImage:[UIImage➥
 imageNamed:@"gradient"]];
    [cell.contentView addSubview:gradient];

    // Configure the cell's label
    UILabel *theLabel = [[UILabel alloc] initWithFrame:CGRectMake(10, 0, 300, 44)];
    theLabel.text = [_tableData objectAtIndex:indexPath.row];
    theLabel.font = [UIFont fontWithName:@"Helvetica-Bold" size:23];
    theLabel.backgroundColor = [UIColor clearColor];
    [cell.contentView addSubview:theLabel];

    cell.accessoryType = UITableViewCellAccessoryDisclosureIndicator;

    return cell;
}
```

Because there is no explicit setting of theLabel's autoresizingMask, it will default to UIViewAutoresizingNone. Figure 8–21 shows what happens when the tableView enters editing mode.

Figure 8–21. *What happens in editing mode*

Not a very compelling user experience, is it?

You can fix this by setting the autoresizingMask to UIViewAutoresizingFlexibleWidth:

```
theLabel.autoresizingMask = UIViewAutoresizingFlexibleWidth;
```

Now the table view will look like Figure 8–22.

Figure 8–22. *Improved with the aid of UIViewAutoresizingFlexibleWidth*

Handling Rotation Events

When it comes to building your table views to handle rotation events, perhaps the first question you need to ask is whether the view *should* support rotation in the first place.

There are a couple of factors to take into account here:

- Does presenting more-discrete pieces of information (for example, more rows in portrait orientation) enhance the user experience? Or can you exploit the additional horizontal space to show extra details about each row?
- If the table view fits into a larger hierarchy of views, do the preceding and subsequent views support (or require) landscape orientation? If they do, does the table view need to support landscape in order to fit elegantly with its neighbors?

There aren't any *definitely* right answers to either question. The bottom line is that if you think showing the table view in landscape orientation will enhance the user experience of your app, then you need to support it. If it won't, then you shouldn't.

Orientation Types

An iPhone or iPad can be rotated into one of four orientations, shown in Table 8–2.

Table 8–2. *The Available Device Orientations*

	UIInterfaceOrientationPortrait
	UIInterfaceOrientationLandscapeRight
	UIInterfaceOrientationPortraitUpsideDown
	UIInterfaceOrientationLandscapeLeft

Rotation is controlled through UIViewController's shouldAutorotateToInterfaceOrientation method. It takes a UIInterfaceOrientation parameter, and returns YES if the view controller should support that orientation. For example, if you wanted to support portrait and upside-down, you'd implement the following:

```
- (BOOL)shouldAutorotateToInterfaceOrientation:(UIInterfaceOrientation)➥
interfaceOrientation {

    return (interfaceOrientation == UIInterfaceOrientationPortrait) ||➥
 (interfaceOrientation == UIInterfaceOrientationPortraitUpsideDown);

}
```

Rotation events are announced through a series of UIViewController methods. Assuming that shouldAutorotateToInterfaceOrientation will allow the rotation, two methods are called in sequence:

```
-(void)willRotateToInterfaceOrientation:(UIInterfaceOrientation)toInterfaceOrientation➥
```

```
duration:(NSTimeInterval)duration;
```

This method takes the orientation that the device is about to enter as a parameter, and so now is your opportunity to update any views that need to react to the transition.

After the rotation has completed, a second method is called:

```
- (void)didRotateFromInterfaceOrientation:➥
(UIInterfaceOrientation)fromInterfaceOrientation
```

This method takes the previous orientation as a `UIInterfaceOrientation` parameter.

Summary

This chapter has covered two of the three main ways of creating and configuring custom `tableView` cells:

- Adding subviews to the cell's `contentView`, and configuring these in the `cellForRowAtIndexPath` `dataSource` method
- Designing a cell from scratch by using Interface Builder, and configuring the custom controls in code when the cell is loaded from its NIB file

The third approach—which is the most flexible, but also the one that requires most work to set up—is to create a custom subclass for each type of cell that your `tableView` requires. That's what the next chapter covers.

Chapter 9

Creating Custom Cells with Subclasses

In Chapter 8, you looked at two of the three main ways of creating and configuring custom UITableViewCells:

- Adding subviews to the cell's built-in contentView
- Creating a custom cell from scratch and instantiating it from a nib file.

The third approach – which provides the greatest flexibility, albeit at the cost of slightly more complexity – is to create a custom subclass of UITableViewCell.

The main reasons for using this approach is that you need multiple types of cell in the same table, or you want a level of control over the contents that is awkward to achieve by adding subviews.

In this chapter, we will look at the different ways of creating custom cells with UITableViewCell subclasses. It will cover:

- How to subclass UITableViewCell
- Using subclasses with nib files
- Handling selection in cell subclasses
- Customizing the cell by overriding layoutSubviews
- Creating cells with a custom contentView

Why Create a Custom Cell Subclass?

Creating a custom cell through the approach of using a custom subclass gives you complete flexibility over the layout. You're starting with a blank canvas (or blank view, at least), so how the cell looks is entirely up to you.

The trade-off is that this method is slightly more complex – for a start, you'll have to create a custom subclass of `UITableViewCell`. However, don't let that put you off – my experience is that it's all too easy to spend significant amounts of time trying to get the desired results using one of the "lighter" methods, when in fact it would have been quicker to reach straight for a custom subclass.

Creating custom subclasses also enables the creating of multiple types of cell in the same table – this can give your visual design a much greater degree of freedom than if you had to shoehorn dissimilar data into a single cell type.

As you'd expect, there are two approaches you can use – the "visual" approach, involving creating a custom cell in Interface Builder; and the "code" approach that creates and configures the cell entirely in code.

Both processes, though, have a couple of common steps at the outset.

The Process of Creating Custom Cells

Creating custom cells with a subclass of `UITableViewCell` is a 6-stage process, with two common steps at the outset regardless of which approach you're taking:

1. With a pencil and paper, design the layout of your custom cell. This isn't a compulsory step, but having an idea of how the cell will fit together on paper tends to pay dividends in the long run.
2. Create a class for each type of custom cell that inherits from `UITableViewCell` and implement properties for the dynamic view objects that you are going to create in your cell.

Then, either:

3. Build your cell in Interface Builder, and add populate it with the view objects that you need – labels, views, images and so on.

Or:

3. In the custom subclass, layout the cell in code by overriding the `layoutSubviews` or `initWithStyle:` methods.
4. Add any custom initialization code that the class needs to function.
5. When the table needs to fill a row with a custom cell, instantiate an instance of your custom `UITableViewCell` subclass in the `dataSource's` `tableView:cellForRowAtIndexPath:` method, and set the dynamic properties according to the data.
6. Rinse and repeat as required!

As you can see, it's really not all that complicated a process. Keep in mind a couple of subtleties as you build your custom cell (see the note below for details of those) and you'll find that this is actually a quick and flexible process.

SOME PERFORMANCE-RELATED FACTORS TO BEAR IN MIND

When creating a subclass of `UITableViewCell`, there are a couple of performance-related factors to bear in mind in order to maximize the performance of your table:

- **Be wary of building cells that are expensive for the graphics engine to render**. Although the GPUs (graphics processing units) built into the iPhone and iPad provide breathtaking performance considering the size of the devices, they aren't infallible. In particular, be careful with transparency and alpha values – if the GPU has to calculate how much of a lower layer can be seen through the transparency mask of an upper layer, this can result in a serious performance hit. This is covered in more detail in Chapter 10.
- **Don't violate the principles of MVC.** Your custom cell is a view, and as such should only be concerned with displaying content. If you need to undertake any kind of code-based configuration of that content – concatenating strings, or adding values for example – that should take place in the datasource, not in the view.

Having mentioned these two caveats, don't let them put you off trying to push the boundaries of what's possible. The members of the iOS device family are high-performance little beasts, so you'll most likely be surprised at what's possible before you start to push at the limits of their capabilities.

Designing Your Cell

When designing a custom cell, I put down my Magic Mouse and reach for a pencil and some (squared) paper. That's what works for me – your approach may differ – but I find that if I start trying to design a cell in Interface Builder, two problems quickly emerge.

Firstly, Interface Builder tends to push me in the direction of "pixel perfection" before I've decided on what the cell is actually going to do. The fact that you can (relatively) easily line things up exactly means it's very tempting to spend your time doing just that, at the expense of thinking about the overall design.

Secondly, I become frustrated by the limitations of Interface Builder quite quickly. It looks like it should have the same level of fine-detailed control over layout as a tool like Photoshop, but it simply doesn't. If laying out designs in Photoshop is precision surgery with a scalpel, then Interface Builder can sometimes feel like painting a brick wall with a broom.

NOTE: To illustrate the process of creating custom cells, and using multiple types of cell in the same table, I'm going to create a somewhat-contrived example with two types – one cell type for even-numbered rows, and one cell type for odd-numbered rows.

Creating the Class for the Custom Cell

The new custom cells that you are going to create will be instances of a subclass of `UITableViewCell`. This means that when you create them, they will have all the functionality of a "standard" `UITableViewCell`, but with the opportunity to add additional functions of your own.

To illustrate this process, I'm going to create two `UITableViewCell` subclasses – which I'll call `OddCell` and `EvenCell` - so that eventually the table will have two distinct types of cell with differing layouts.

Creating the Subclasses

The first step is to create the subclasses (Figure 9–1). In XCode, ctrl-click the group in which you want to create the new class and select "New File" from the pop-up window.

Then, select the `Objective-C class` icon from the `Cocoa Touch` group, and click `Next`.

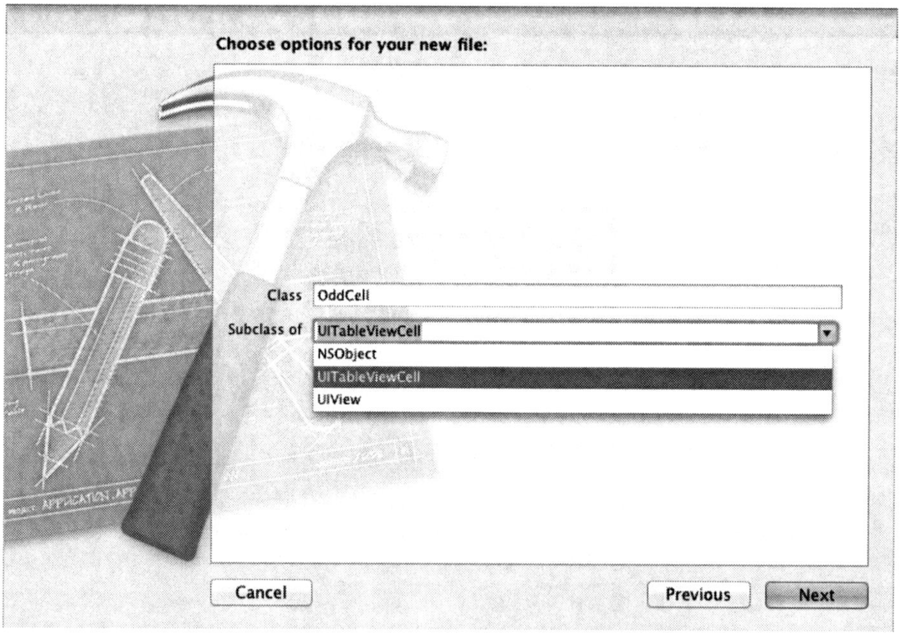

Figure 9–1. *Creating a new subclass*

The next screen allows you to choose which superclass your new class is going to belong to. You can either select `UITableViewCell` if it appears in the dropdown menu, or stick with the selected option of `NSObject` and click the Next button.

> **NOTE:** Apple frequently change the options presented in the screens you've just seen in different versions of Xcode, so it's possible that what you see during this process may differ. If that's the case, select `NSObject` as your superclass, and follow on to the next step.

Give your new class an appropriate name – I've called mine `OddCell` – and save it. You'll now see the implementation file for `OddCell` (or whatever name you've chosen).

Switch to the header file for a moment, either by selecting it in the left-hand pane, or hitting Ctrl + Command + Up Arrow.

You'll see a standard, empty header file. If you selected `NSObject` as your superclass a moment ago, you'll need to change this so that the class inherits instead from `UITableViewCell`. Tweak the code so it looks like Listing 9–1.

Listing 9–1. *`OddCell.h`*

```
#import <Foundation/Foundation.h>

@interface OddCell : UITableViewCell {

}

@end
```

Next, you will need to create properties for the custom controls within the cell. Firstly, add these to the header file (Listing 9–2):

Listing 9–2. *The revised `OddCell.h`*

```
@interface OddCell : UITableViewCell

@property (nonatomic, strong) IBOutlet UIImageView *backView;
@property (nonatomic, strong) IBOutlet UIImageView *iconView;
@property (nonatomic, strong) IBOutlet UILabel *cellTitle;
@property (nonatomic, strong) IBOutlet UILabel *cellContent;

@end
```

Then synthesize them in the class's implementation (Listing 9–3):

Listing 9–3. *The revised `OddCell.m`*

```
#import "OddCell.h"

@implementation OddCell

@synthesize backView = _backView;
@synthesize iconView = _iconView;
@synthesize cellTitle = _cellTitle;
@synthesize cellContent = _cellContent;

- (id)initWithStyle:(UITableViewCellStyle)style ↩
reuseIdentifier:(NSString *)reuseIdentifier
{
    self = [super initWithStyle:style reuseIdentifier:reuseIdentifier];
```

```
    if (self) {
        // Initialization code
    }
    return self;
}

- (void)setSelected:(BOOL)selected animated:(BOOL)animated
{
    [super setSelected:selected animated:animated];

    // Configure the view for the selected state
}

@end
```

> **NOTE:** If you initially created a subclass of `NSObject` and then converted this to a subclass of `UITableViewCell`, you'll have the "generic" init method rather than the `UITableViewCell`-specific version. Just replace the `NSObject` code with the version above.

Having got this far,you are now ready to build `OddCell`'s nib and wire up the class's properties with the outlets in the nib file.

Building the Cell in Interface Builder

Creating the cell itself is a four-stage process, which you will complete inside Interface Builder:

1. Create the nib file
2. Lay the custom controls out inside the nib
3. Conform the nib to your custom class
4. Link up the custom controls with the properties of the custom class

Creating the nib File

In Xcode, ctrl-click the group in which you want to create the new nib and select "New File" from the pop-up window.

Then, select the `User Interface` section in the iOS group, and select the `View` icon from the list of templates (Figure 9–2).

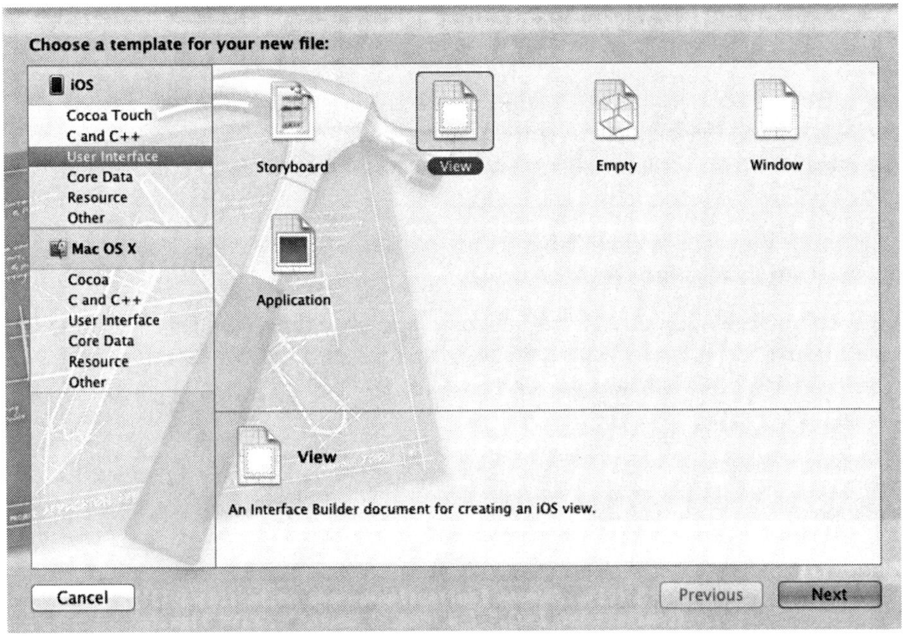

Figure 9–2. *Choosing a template*

In the next screen, you'll need to select the iPhone device family (Figure 9–3).

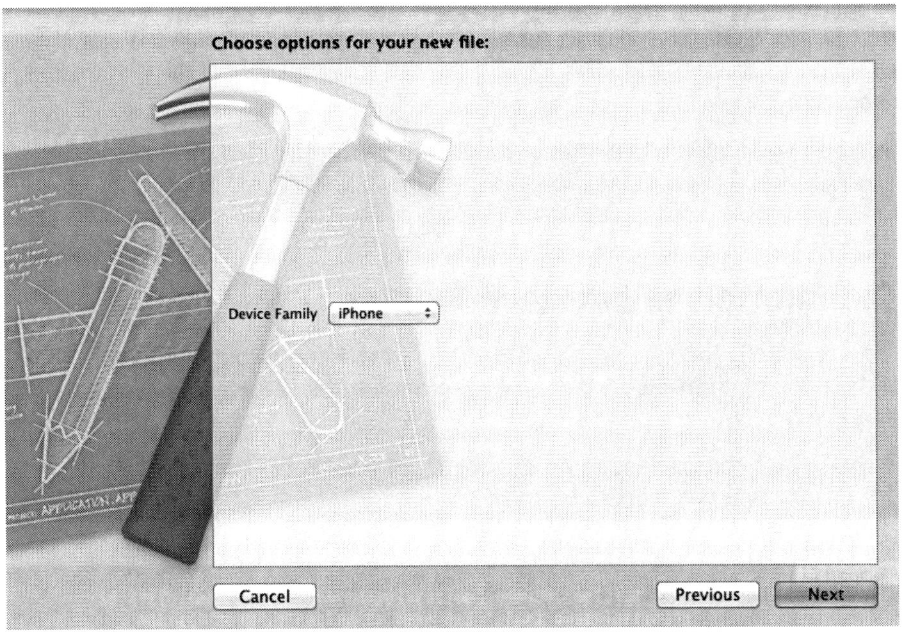

Figure 9–3. *Selecting the device family*

Then you'll need to provide a name for the cell (I'm calling it `OddCell` for consistency) and click `Create` to save it.

The new view will open up in Interface Builder, with a blank view. Xcode has assumed that this view needs to fill the full device screen, which is not what you are after. So somewhat counter-intuitively, the first thing you need to do after creating the new view is to delete it.

Highlight the icon for the view in the left-hand Objects list, and hit delete. You'll now have a completely empty Interface Builder pane.

This is now the point where you create the new cell. Mid-way down the list of objects in the Utilities area you'll find a Table View Cell. Drag this out into the center pane, and you'll have replaced the full-window view with a table view cell.

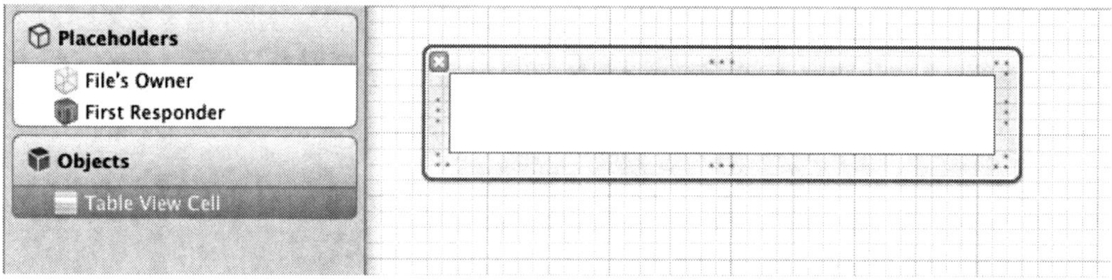

Placeholders
File's Owner
First Responder
Objects
Table View Cell

Figure 9–4. *The new empty cell*

The new cell will automatically have the full 320-pixel width, and be the 44-pixel height of a standard `UITableViewCell`. You can resize it in the same way as other `UIView` controls – either grab the sizing handles around the cell's border, or set the dimensions in the Size inspector.

Whichever method you use, make a note of the height – you will need this later to return from the `tableView:heightForCellAtIndexPath:` method. My `OddCell` is going to be 70 pixels high.

Laying Out Controls in Interface Builder

In essence, this is exactly the same process that you have been through before – drag instances of the controls from the Object Library into the `UITableViewCell`, then size and lay them out appropriately.

How you do this will obviously depend on the design of your cells – this is my work-in-progress `OddCell` nib, which has four controls:

- Two `UIImageViews`, one for the background, and one for the icon.
- Two `UILabels`, one for the cell's title and one for the cell's content.

Figure 9–5. *The* `OddCell` *nib in progress*

When fully instantiated, instances of `OddCell` will look like Figure 9–6.

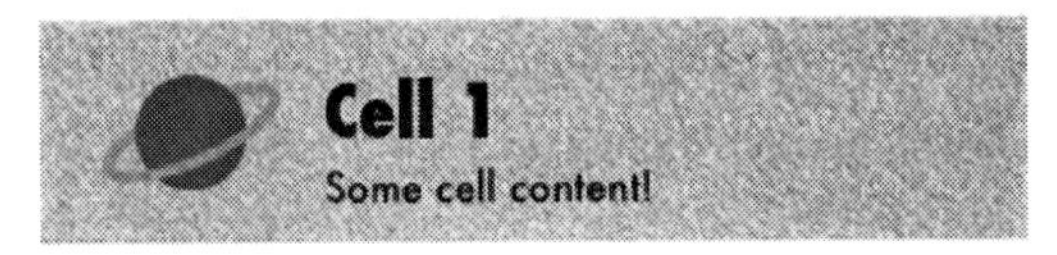

Figure 9–6. *The* `OddCell`

Conforming the Cell to the Custom Class

At the moment, the cell is an instance of `UITableViewCell`, as you would expect. In your custom class – which itself is a subclass of `UITableViewCell`, you have created a raft of outlets for custom controls.

The problem is that because your custom class is a *subclass* of `UITableViewCell`, the parent class neither knows nor cares about the outlets and properties that we created. In order to connect the controls inside the cell up to the outlets in the custom subclass, you are going to have to conform the cell to the subclass.

Fortunately, this is probably the simplest part of the whole process. In the Objects section, highlight the Table View cell icon (shown in Figure 9–7):

Figure 9–7. *The Objects section*

Then switch over to the Identity inspector, and expand the Custom Class section if it isn't visible. At the moment, it'll show that the cell is inheriting from `NSObject` – no great surprise there, as all Cocoa Touch objects ultimately inherit from `NSObject`.

What you need to do is to change this so that the cell's class is your custom subclass of `UITableViewCell`. Overtype the contents of the Custom Class section, and Xcode will autocomplete the field with the name of the `UITableViewCell` subclass.

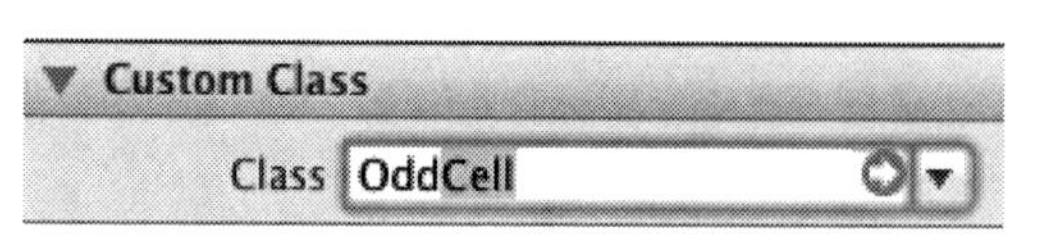

Figure 9–8. *Changing the cell's owner*

TIP: There will probably come a point in your table-building career when your app crashes as soon as your custom table is loaded with an error that looks something along the lines of this:

```
2011-11-05 19:58:13.263 myApp[6042:f803] *** Terminating app due to
uncaught exception 'NSUnknownKeyException', reason: '[<UITableViewCell
0x6895790> setValue:forUndefinedKey:]: this class is not key value
coding-compliant for the key cellSubtitle.'
```

Don't panic. This is almost certainly the result of something going wrong with the connections of the cell controls – check that you've made the connections from the custom cell, and not the file's owner.

Link Up Custom Controls

If you've created any controls in the cell through Interface Builder, as opposed to instantiating them in code, then these will currently be sitting in the cell as orphans. If they're not going to change in response to the cell's data – for example, if you've got a static background view – then that's fair enough. But if you *do* want the controls to reflect the data in the model, then they'll have to be connected to the outlets in the custom class.

This will be familiar by now. Ctrl-click on the Custom Cell in the Objects list to reveal the Outlets HUD, and drag from the circle out to the control in the cell itself:

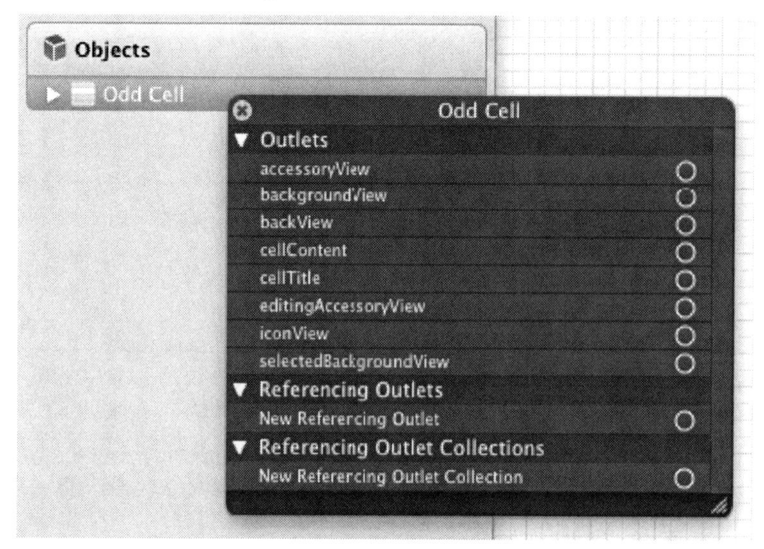

Figure 9–9. *The Outlets HUD*

Repeat this for all the dynamic controls that you've inserted into the cell.

> **NOTE:** Because this custom cell is a subclass of UITableViewCell, it inherits all UITableViewCell's properties such as accessoryView and backgroundView.

Creating the EvenCell

In this example, the EvenCell class is not too dissimilar to the OddCell class, but of course you've got free rein to create cells that are radically different if your app requires that.

Instances of EvenCell will look like Figure 9–10 :

Figure 9–10. *The EvenCell*

The EvenCell subclass is more-or-less identical to OddCell, save for an extra property:

Listing 9–4. *The EvenCell Class Header*

```
@interface EvenCell : UITableViewCell

@property (nonatomic, strong) IBOutlet UIImageView *backView;
@property (nonatomic, strong) IBOutlet UIImageView *iconView;
@property (nonatomic, strong) IBOutlet UILabel *cellTitle;
@property (nonatomic, strong) IBOutlet UILabel *cellMainContent;
@property (nonatomic, strong) IBOutlet UILabel *cellOtherContent;

@end
```

Setting the Cell Heights

Unless you tell it otherwise, the tableView assumes that it will be dealing with cells that have a standard height of 44 pixels. Because the custom cell types you have just created don't have standard sizes, you will need to implement the tableView:heightForRowAtIndexPath: method in order to get cells of the correct size.

If you miss this method, your table will still work – but it will attempt to cram the cells into a height of 44 pixels, and their contents will be cropped.

The tableView:heightForRowAtIndexPath: methodis shown in Listing 9–5 – it simply checks whether the indexPath is odd or even, and then returns the appropriate height measurement as a CGFloat.

Listing 9–5. *The* `tableView:heightForRowAtIndexPath:` *Method*

```
-(CGFloat)tableView:(UITableView *)tableView ➥
heightForRowAtIndexPath:(NSIndexPath *)indexPath {

    if (indexPath.row % 2 == 0) {
        // Even row
        return 50;
    }

    // Odd row
    return 70;
}
```

Creating Instances of the Custom Cells

Having gone to all the trouble of creating custom subclasses, and designing the layout of your custom cells, there comes a point where you will want to create actual instances of them.

It shouldn't come as a surprise to learn that this takes place in our old friend the `tableView:cellForRowAtIndexPath:` method. Whereas up until now you have been creating instances of standard `UITableViewCells`, now you are going to ring the changes slightly, and create instances of one of your custom classes.

This example is also slightly more sophisticated, in that there are two types of cell. The implication here is that there will be some kind of conditional code to choose which type of cell to create.

Before any cell types can be created, though, you will need to register their nib files with the `tableView` so that they can be created or dequeued as required. This only needs to take place once, so the obvious place to do this is in the `viewDidLoad` method of the table's controller:

```
    [self.tableView registerNib:[UINib nibWithNibName:@"OddCell" bundle:nil] ➥
forCellReuseIdentifier:kOddCellIdentifier];
    [self.tableView registerNib:[UINib nibWithNibName:@"EvenCell" bundle:nil] ➥
forCellReuseIdentifier:kEvenCellIdentifier];
```

Because the cell identifiers are a) absolutely critical for retrieving or creating the correct cell type and b) used in several places, I create constants for them at the top of the file. That way I'm less likely to mis-type the identifiers and waste hours tracking down bugs of my own creation!

```
#define kOddCellIdentifier @"OddCellIdentifier"
#define kEvenCellIdentifier @"EvenCellIdentifier"
```

Having registered the cell nibs, now they can be used in the `tableView:cellForRowAtIndexPath:` method.

Here's the first pass in Listing 9–6 – the `tableData` and `phraseData` properties are just `NSArrays` of Latin boilerplate phrases that I created earlier in the `viewDidLoad:` method:

Listing 9–6. *Returning Custom Cells from the `tableView:cellForRowAtIndexPath:` Method*

```
- (UITableViewCell *)tableView:(UITableView *)tableView ↵
cellForRowAtIndexPath:(NSIndexPath *)indexPath
{

    NSInteger rowMod = indexPath.row % 2;

    if (rowMod == 1) {
        // Odd row
        NSString *cellIdentifier = kOddCellIdentifier;

    OddCell *oddCell = (OddCell *)[tableView ↵
dequeueReusableCellWithIdentifier:cellIdentifier];

        oddCell.backView.image = [UIImage imageNamed:@"corkboard"];
        oddCell.iconView.image = [UIImage imageNamed:@"planet"];
        oddCell.cellTitle.text = [self.tableData objectAtIndex:indexPath.row];
        oddCell.cellContent.text = [self.phraseData objectAtIndex:indexPath.row];

        return oddCell;

    }

    // Even row
    NSString *CellIdentifier = kEvenCellIdentifier;

    EvenCell *evenCell = (EvenCell *)[tableView ↵
dequeueReusableCellWithIdentifier:cellIdentifier];

    evenCell.backView.image = [UIImage imageNamed:@"gingham"];
    evenCell.iconView.image = [UIImage imageNamed:@"star"];
    evenCell.cellTitle.text = [_tableData objectAtIndex:indexPath.row];
    evenCell.cellMainContent.text = [_phraseData objectAtIndex:indexPath.row];
    evenCell.cellOtherContent.text = @"Some other content!";

    return evenCell;

}
```

It's not too dissimilar to a standard `tableView:cellForRowAtIndexPath:` method, but there are some changes:

```
NSInteger rowMod = indexPath.row % 2;
```

`rowMod` is the remainder after dividing the row number by `2` – if it's `0`, the row is an even one, if `rowMod` is `1`, it's odd.

That allows you to create instances of the appropriate custom cell by attempting to dequeue an existing cached cell:

```
NSString *cellIdentifier = kOddCellIdentifier;

OddCell *oddCell = (OddCell *)[tableView ↵
dequeueReusableCellWithIdentifier:CellIdentifier];
```

If there isn't an instance of `OddCell` that can be recycled, the `tableView` will have created a new one behind the scenes, so it can be configured:

```
    oddCell.backView.image = [UIImage imageNamed:@"corkboard"];
    oddCell.iconView.image = [UIImage imageNamed:@"planet"];
    oddCell.cellTitle.text = [_tableData objectAtIndex:indexPath.row];
    oddCell.cellContent.text = @"Some cell content!";
```

And then returned to the `tableView`:

```
    return oddCell;
```

Creating instances of `EvenCell` is much the same process – which results in a `tableView` that looks like Figure 9–11:

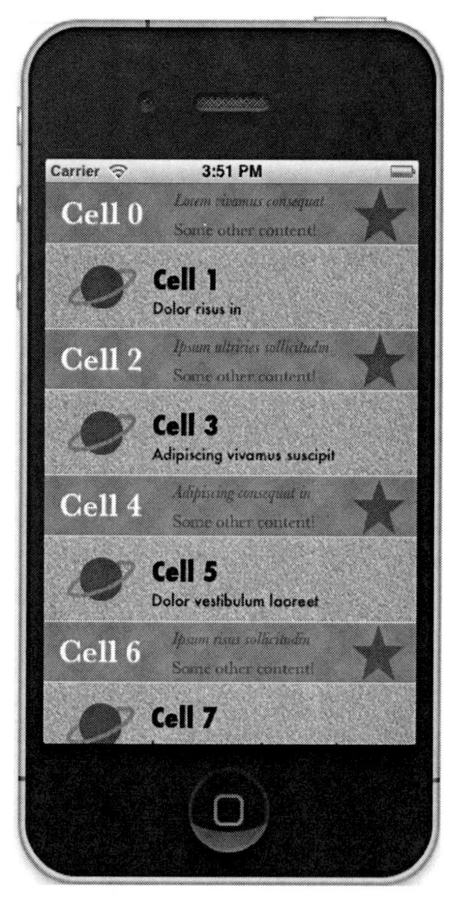

Figure 9–11. *Two different* `UITableViewCell` *subclasses in one table*

Some Refactoring

While this code works, there's some duplication that could be cleaned up a bit. In particular, there's two areas of practically identical code that dequeue or instantiate the cells that could be refactored out. Listing 9–7 shows a slightly more elegant method:

Listing 9–7. *A Refactored Version of* `tableView:cellForRowAtIndexPath:`

```
- (UITableViewCell *)tableView:(UITableView *)tableView ↩
cellForRowAtIndexPath:(NSIndexPath *)indexPath
{
    BOOL isEvenRow = (indexPath.row % 2 == 0);

    NSString *cellIdentifier = nil;
    NSString *nibName = nil;
    UIImage *backViewImage = nil;
    UIImage *iconViewImage = nil;

    NSString *cellTitle = [self.tableData objectAtIndex:indexPath.row];
    NSString *cellPhraseContent = [self.phraseData objectAtIndex:indexPath.row];

    if (isEvenRow) {
        // even row
        cellIdentifier = kEvenCellIdentifier;
        nibName = @"EvenCell";
        backViewImage = [UIImage imageNamed:@"gingham"];
        iconViewImage = [UIImage imageNamed:@"star"];

    } else {
        // odd row
        cellIdentifier = kOddCellIdentifier;
        nibName = @"OddCell";
        backViewImage = [UIImage imageNamed:@"corkboard"];
        iconViewImage = [UIImage imageNamed:@"planet"];

    }

    UITableViewCell *cell = [tableView ↩
dequeueReusableCellWithIdentifier:cellIdentifier];

    if (isEvenRow) {
        // Even row
        EvenCell *evenCell = (EvenCell *)cell;
        evenCell.backView.image = backViewImage;
        evenCell.iconView.image = iconViewImage;
        evenCell.cellTitle.text = cellTitle;
        evenCell.cellMainContent.text = cellPhraseContent;
        evenCell.cellOtherContent.text = @"Some other content!";

        return evenCell;

    }

    // Odd row
    OddCell *oddCell = (OddCell *)cell;

    oddCell.backView.image = backViewImage;
    oddCell.iconView.image = iconViewImage;
    oddCell.cellTitle.text = cellTitle;
    oddCell.cellContent.text = cellPhraseContent;

    return oddCell;

}
```

The main difference is that there's now a single, shared dequeuing process.

Handling Selection in Custom Cells

If you change the cell's backgroundView property, the chances are you'll also need to control the way the cell is highlighted when it's selected.

Cell selection is controlled by UITableViewCell's selectionStyle property – this can be in one of three states:

- UITableViewCellSelectionStyleNone
- UITableViewCellSelectionStyleBlue
- UITableViewCellSelectionStyleGray

When the selectionStyle value is set to None, there are no visible changes, but the other two causes the cell's background to appear to be filled with a solid color.

The cell also has two background views that sit behind the contentView – backgroundView, which is shown by default; and selectedBackgroundView, which sits between backgroundView and contentView (and isn't displayed by default).

This arrangement is shown in Figure 9–12:

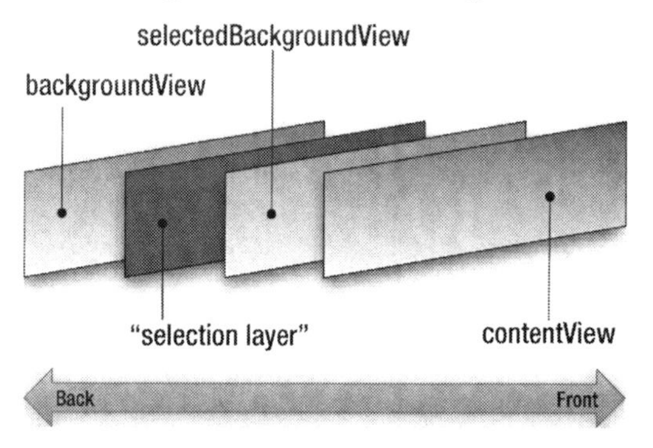

Figure 9–12. *The arrangement of views inside the cell*

The "selection layer" that's controlled by the selectionStyle property sits in front of the backgroundView – so if you've changed the backgroundView, it will be obscured by the default selection coloring when the cell is selected.

That might be OK, but if you want a background other than solid blue or gray, you'll need to change the selectedBackgroundView property. This sits behind contentView, but in front of the "selection layer" – so instead of seeing the solid colour, you'll see whatever is in the selectedBackgroundView.

This could be a solid colour – for example:

```
    UIView *redView = [[UIView alloc] ↵
initWithFrame:self.selectedBackgroundView.frame];
    [redView setBackgroundColor:[UIColor redColor]];
    cell.selectedBackgroundView = redView;
```

Or you could set it to an image:

```
    UIImageView *theSelectedView = [[UIImageView alloc] ↵
initWithImage:[UIImage imageNamed:@"bluePrint"]];
    cell.selectedBackgroundView = theSelectedView;
```

This will obscure the "selection layer", so you can control the background appearance of your custom cell.

Drawing Cells in Code with layoutSubviews

Laying out cells visually will take you so far, but if you prefer a code-based approach you can override the `layoutSubviews` *method* in the custom cell subclass, which allows you to tweak the standard `UITableViewCell` styles.

Overriding the layoutSubviews Method

The `layoutSubviews` method is called on the cell just before it's displayed – it's a last opportunity to tweak the layout and look of the cell before it's drawn.

If the contents of your cell can be fitted into one of the standard cell types, but you just want to move things around a bit, then overriding the `layoutSubviews` might be the quick fix you're after – the example below shows how you might move the `textLabel` and the `detailTextLabel` around to create a new cell style, but still exploit some of the standard elements.

You'll first need to create a custom `UITableViewCell` subclass – for the sake of argument, let's call that `CustomCell`.

Then in `CustomCell`'s implementation you'll override the `layoutSubviews` method – here's an example that takes `UITableViewCellStyleValue1`, swaps the `textLabel` and `detailTextLabel` around, and changes the fonts (the results of which will look like Figure 9–13):

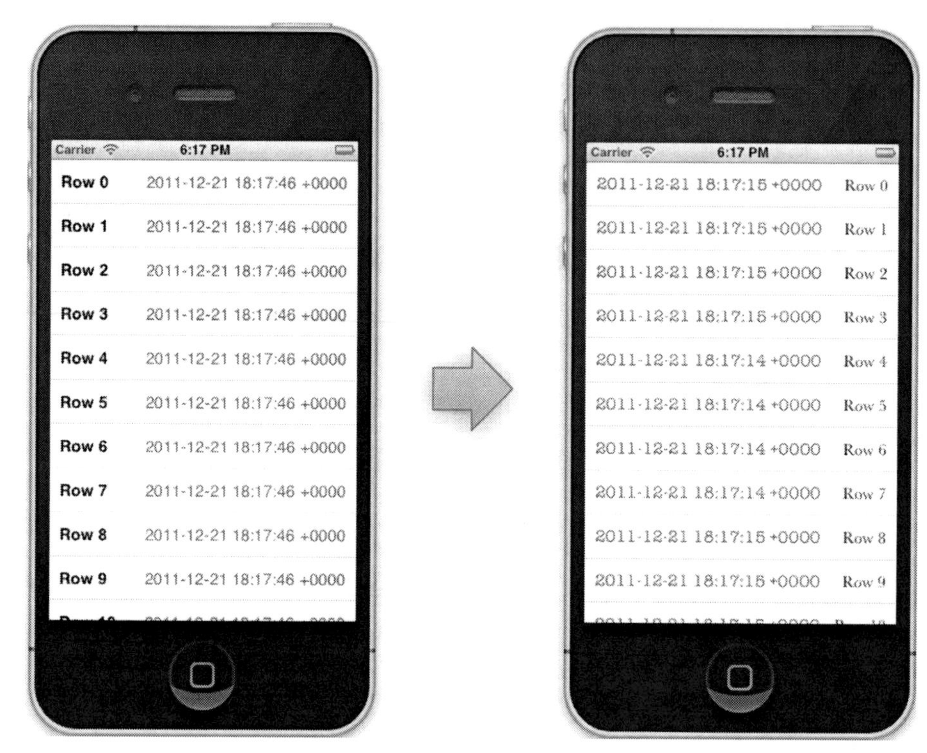

Figure 9–13. *Before and after*

The layoutSubviews method needed is shown in Listing 9–8:

Listing 9–8. *The* `layoutSubviews` *Method*

```
-(void)layoutSubviews {

    // Call superclass method
    [super layoutSubviews];

    // Calculate sizes
    CGFloat endOfTextLabel = CGRectGetMaxX(self.textLabel.frame);

    CGRect newDetailTextFrame = CGRectMake(self.textLabel.frame.origin.x, ➥
self.textLabel.frame.origin.y, self.detailTextLabel.frame.size.width, ➥
self.detailTextLabel.frame.size.height);

    CGFloat gapBetweenLabels = self.detailTextLabel.frame.origin.x - endOfTextLabel;

    CGFloat leftMargin = self.textLabel.frame.origin.x;

    CGFloat newTextLabelOriginX = leftMargin + self.detailTextLabel.frame.size.width;

    CGRect newTextLabelFrame = CGRectMake(newTextLabeloriginX + gapBetweenLabels, ➥
self.textLabel.frame.origin.y, self.textLabel.frame.size.width, ➥
self.textLabel.frame.size.height);

    // Change frames of default subviews
```

```
    self.textLabel.frame = newTextLabelFrame;
    self.detailTextLabel.frame = newDetailTextFrame;

    // Get current font sizes
    CGFloat currentTextLabelSize = self.textLabel.font.pointSize;

    CGFloat currentDetailTextLabelSize = self.detailTextLabel.font.pointSize;

    // Change fonts of default subviews
    self.textLabel.font = [UIFont fontWithName:@"Baskerville" ↵
size:currentTextLabelSize];

    self.detailTextLabel.font = [UIFont fontWithName:@"AmericanTypewriter" ↵
size:currentDetailTextLabelSize ];

}
```

Building the Cell in Code with the contentView

Although this app is creating two custom subclasses of `UITableViewCell`, up to this point you've used the tried and tested nib-based approach to building and laying out the cell's contents.

In this example, you will go a bit further than swapping things around – in fact, what you will do is to recreated the planets-and-stars cells in code rather than using Interface Builder.

At a high level, the process looks like this:

- Create a `UITableViewCell` subclass for each cell type (you will end up with one for `EvenCell` and one for `OddCell`)
- Set up the subclasses with properties for the controls that will be set externally as the cells are created and updated
- In the subclasses' `initWithStyle:reuseIdentifier:` method, create and add the various elements to the cell's `contentView`
- Optionally, update the `setSelected:animated:` method to create any custom cell selection traits
- Create instances of the custom cells in the `tableView` controller's `tableView:cellForRowAtIndexPath:` method as usual.

Creating the Cell Subclasses

You will need two subclasses – one for `EvenCell`, and one for `OddCell`. That's exactly the same process as previously – create a new file from the *Objective-C class* template, and create a subclass of `UITableViewCell` (shown in Figure 9–14).

Figure 9–14. *Creating a `UITableViewCell` subclass*

Setting Up the Subclass Properties

Our custom cell subclasses will need properties for the controls that will be affected as the cells are created and updated.

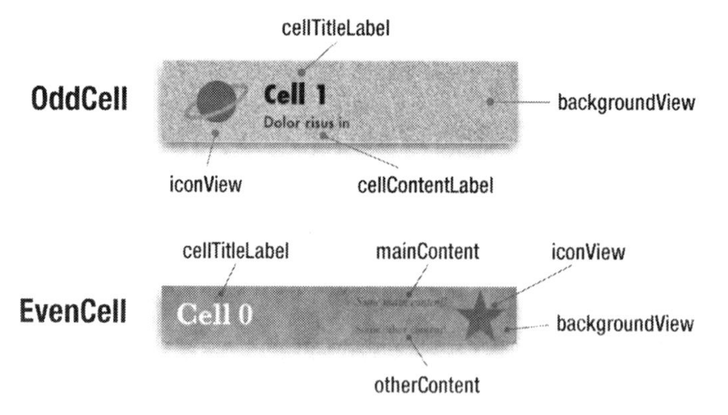

Figure 9–15. *The cell elements*

Figure 9–15 shows the elements of the cells – you will need properties for all of these bar the `backgroundView`, which is an in-built property of `UITableViewCell` that you will use inside the class to set the backgrounds of the cells.

The header file of the `OddCell` class is show in Listing 9–9, while the header file for `EvenCell` is shown in Listing 9–10:

Listing 9–9. *The* `OddCell.h` *File*

```
#import <UIKit/UIKit.h>

@interface OddCell : UITableViewCell

@property (nonatomic, strong) UILabel *cellTitleLabel;
@property (nonatomic, strong) UILabel *cellContentLabel;
@property (nonatomic, strong) UIImageView *iconView;

@end
```

Listing 9–10. *The* `EvenCell.h` *File*

```
#import <UIKit/UIKit.h>

@interface EvenCell : UITableViewCell

@property (nonatomic, strong) UIImageView *iconView;
@property (nonatomic, strong) UILabel *cellTitleLabel;
@property (nonatomic, strong) UILabel *mainContentLabel;
@property (nonatomic, strong) UILabel *otherContentLabel;

@end
```

Building the Cells

The heavy lifting of laying out the cells will take place in the `initWithStyle:reuseIdentifier:` method. You will create each cell element (all of which are subclasses of `UIView`), then add these to the cell's `contentView`.

Listing 9–11 is the `initWithStyle:reuseIdentifier:` method for `OddCell`:

Listing 9–11. `OddCell`*'s* `initWithStyle:reuseIdentifier:` *Method*

```
- (id)initWithStyle:(UITableViewCellStyle)style ↩
reuseIdentifier:(NSString *)reuseIdentifier
{
    self = [super initWithStyle:style reuseIdentifier:reuseIdentifier];
    if (self) {

        // background view
        UIImageView *theBackgroundView = [[UIImageView alloc] ↩
initWithImage:[UIImage imageNamed:@"corkboard"]];
        self.backgroundView = theBackgroundView;

        // cellTitle label
        _cellTitleLabel = [[UILabel alloc] init];
        _cellTitleLabel.frame = CGRectMake(92, 13, 208, 32);
        [_cellTitleLabel setBackgroundColor:[UIColor clearColor]];
        [_cellTitleLabel setFont:[UIFont ↩
fontWithName:@"Futura-CondensedExtraBold" size:23]];
        [_cellTitleLabel setTextColor:[UIColor blackColor]];

        // cellContent label
        _cellContentLabel = [[UILabel alloc] init];
        _cellContentLabel.frame = CGRectMake(92, 42, 208, 21);
```

```
        [_cellContentLabel setBackgroundColor:[UIColor clearColor]];
        [_cellContentLabel setFont:[UIFont fontWithName:@"Futura-Medium" size:13]];
        [_cellContentLabel setTextColor:[UIColor blackColor]];

        // iconView
        _iconView = [[UIImageView alloc] init];
        _iconView.frame = CGRectMake(20, 17, 58, 36);

        // Set up contentView
        [self.contentView addSubview:_cellTitleLabel];
        [self.contentView addSubview:_cellContentLabel];
        [self.contentView addSubview:_iconView];

    }

    return self;

}
```

The `initWithStyle:reuseIdentifier:` method for `EvenCell` is very similar, and is shown in Listing 9–12:

Listing 9–12. *EvenCell's* `initWithStyle:reuseIdentifier:` ***Method***

```
- (id)initWithStyle:(UITableViewCellStyle)style ↩
reuseIdentifier:(NSString *)reuseIdentifier
{
    self = [super initWithStyle:style reuseIdentifier:reuseIdentifier];
    if (self) {

        // background view
        UIImageView *theBackgroundView = [[UIImageView alloc] ↩
initWithImage:[UIImage imageNamed:@"gingham"]];
        self.backgroundView = theBackgroundView;

        // cellTitle label
        _cellTitleLabel = [[UILabel alloc] init];
        _cellTitleLabel.frame = CGRectMake(92, 13, 208, 32);
        [_cellTitleLabel setBackgroundColor:[UIColor clearColor]];
        [_cellTitleLabel setFont:[UIFont ↩
fontWithName:@"Futura-CondensedExtraBold" size:23]];
        [_cellTitleLabel setTextColor:[UIColor blackColor]];

        // mainContent label
        _mainContentLabel = [[UILabel alloc] init];
        _mainContentLabel.frame = CGRectMake(110, 2, 147, 21);
        [_mainContentLabel setBackgroundColor:[UIColor clearColor]];
        [_mainContentLabel setFont:[UIFont ↩
fontWithName:@"Baskerville-Italic" size:15]];
        [_mainContentLabel setTextColor:[UIColor blueColor]];

        // mainContent label
        _otherContentLabel = [[UILabel alloc] init];
        _otherContentLabel.frame = CGRectMake(110, 26, 147, 21);
        [_otherContentLabel setBackgroundColor:[UIColor clearColor]];
        [_otherContentLabel setFont:[UIFont fontWithName:@"Baskerville" size:15]];
        [_otherContentLabel setTextColor:[UIColor blueColor]];
```

```
        // iconView
        _iconView = [[UIImageView alloc] init];
        _iconView.frame = CGRectMake(265, 2, 45, 45);

        // Set up contentView
        [self.contentView addSubview:_cellTitleLabel];
        [self.contentView addSubview:_mainContentLabel];
        [self.contentView addSubview:_otherContentLabel];
        [self.contentView addSubview:_iconView];

    }

    return self;

}
```

Managing Selections

In your cells, you will want to display a different background image when the cell is selected, so you will need to override the default `setSelected:animated` method to managed the `selectedBackgroundView`. The changes for both subclasses are shown in Listing 9–13.

Listing 9–13. ***The*** `setSelected:animated:` ***Method***

```
- (void)setSelected:(BOOL)selected animated:(BOOL)animated
{
    [super setSelected:selected animated:animated];

    // Configure the view for the selected state
    if (selected) {

        UIImageView *theSelectedView = [[UIImageView alloc] initWithImage:[UIImage
imageNamed:@"bluePrint"]];
        self.selectedBackgroundView = theSelectedView;

        [_cellTitleLabel setTextColor:[UIColor redColor]];

    } else {

        self.selectedBackgroundView = nil;
        [_cellTitleLabel setTextColor:[UIColor blackColor]];

    }
}
```

The effect of this is shown in Figure 9–16:

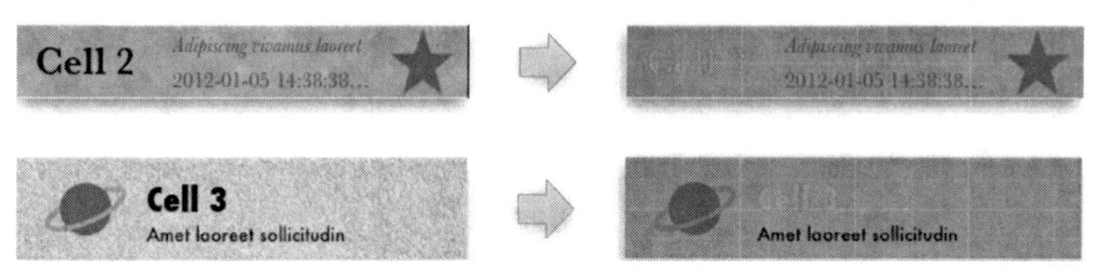

Figure 9–16. *The cells in normal and selected states*

Creating the Cells

The final stage in the process is to create instances of the custom cells in the `tableView:cellForIndexPath:` method:

Listing 9–14. *The `tableView:cellForRowAtIndexPath:`*

```
- (UITableViewCell *)tableView:(UITableView *)tableView ➥
cellForRowAtIndexPath:(NSIndexPath *)indexPath
{

    BOOL isEvenRow = (indexPath.row % 2 == 0);

    NSString *cellTitle = [self.tableData objectAtIndex:indexPath.row];
    NSString *cellPhraseContent = [self.phraseData objectAtIndex:indexPath.row];

    if (isEvenRow) {
        NSString *cellIdentifier = @"EvenCell";
        EvenCell *evenCell = (EvenCell *)[tableView ➥
dequeueReusableCellWithIdentifier:cellIdentifier];

        if (!evenCell) {
            evenCell = [[EvenCell alloc] initWithStyle:UITableViewCellStyleDefault ➥
reuseIdentifier:cellIdentifier];
        }

        evenCell.cellTitleLabel.text = cellTitle;
        evenCell.mainContentLabel.text = cellPhraseContent;
        evenCell.otherContentLabel.text = [NSString stringWithFormat:@"%@", ➥
[NSDate date]];
        evenCell.iconView.image = [UIImage imageNamed:@"star"];

        return evenCell;

    }

    NSString *cellIdentifier = @"OddCell";
    OddCell *oddCell = (OddCell *)[tableView ➥
dequeueReusableCellWithIdentifier:cellIdentifier];

    if (!oddCell) {
        oddCell = [[OddCell alloc] initWithStyle:UITableViewCellStyleDefault ➥
reuseIdentifier:cellIdentifier];
    }

    oddCell.cellTitleLabel.text = cellTitle;
```

```
    oddCell.cellContentLabel.text = cellPhraseContent;
    oddCell.iconView.image = [UIImage imageNamed:@"planet"];

    return oddCell;

}
```

The end results in Figure 9–17 are indistinguishable from the cells you created using nib files – but this time, the custom cells are constructed entirely in code with not a nib file to be seen.

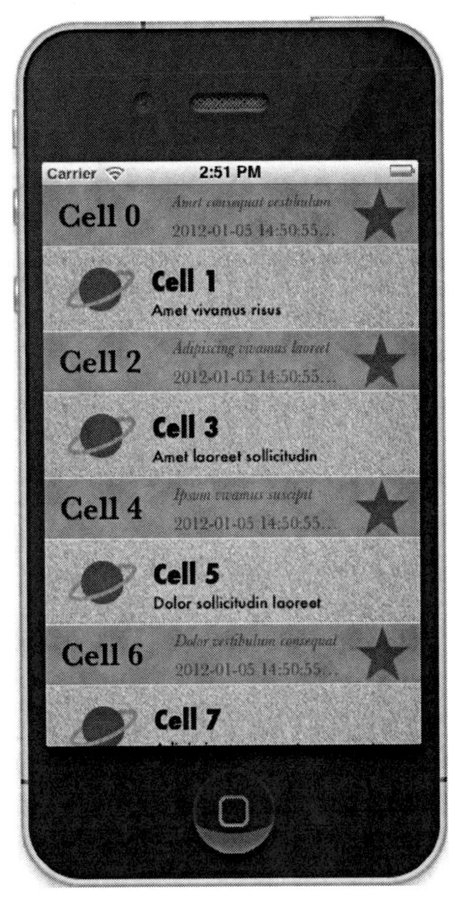

Figure 9–17. *The end results*

Debugging Layers

While the UIKit syntax makes working with `UIViews` reasonably easy, getting layouts right can be fiddly – particularly if you're trying to tweak layouts a few pixels at a time.

Changing the layout, rerunning the app in the Simulator, altering the layout again, re-running the app – that can quickly become a tedious process.

A very useful tool that can help make this less onerous is Introspect. It's a small set of tools that helps in debugging user interfaces – especially ones that are dynamically created.

Figure 9–18. *Introspect in action*

It provides a range of features such as highlighting of view frames, displaying their origins and sizes, and moving and resizing of view frames during runtime using shortcut keys. It will also log of properties of a view, including subclass properties, actions and targets, and print the view hierarchy to the console.

Installing the tools is as simple as including a library and adding a line of code to the application delegate – you can download it from the library's Github repo at `https://github.com/domesticcatsoftware/DCIntrospect`.

Summary

In this chapter, you've seen how to create your own custom subclass of `UITableViewCell` to give you the ultimate in control over the appearance and functions of your cells.

There's a range of approaches that you can use to tackle custom cells:

- Combining a custom subclass with a nib file
- Replacing the need for a nib file by building the cell entirely in code
- Modifying a standard cell type by overriding `layoutSubviews`

Choosing the approach to take is a case of trading off the level of control you need over the cell against the complexity and additional code overhead of each technique. Another factor is performance – custom subclasses allow you to take advantage of various techniques that can speed up the performance of your table views.

Chapter 10

Improving the Cell's Interaction

So far, the cells that you have been creating have been relatively static: the user's interaction with them has been limited to tapping for selection and editing.

That's not all you can do with cells, though, so this chapter looks at some of the tricks you can use to make the table view truly interactive:

- Embedding custom controls including buttons, switches, and sliders within the cell
- Implementing the widely used pull-to-refresh functionality
- Adding gesture recognizers to cells to support double taps and so on
- Adding swipe functionality to reveal hidden details
- Implementing search within the table's contents

No matter how interactive the table is, however, it's not going to deliver a good user experience if it's not responsive. Although we've been covering best-practice as we've gone along in earlier chapters, this chapter finishes up by looking at a checklist of ways to ensure that you squeeze maximum performance from your table views.

Embedding Custom Controls into Cells

Up to now, you've been mainly concerned with creating and presenting largely static tables. Although you've created cells that present dynamic data, the cells themselves have so far only responded to the basic taps and swipes associated with editing, deleting, and sorting.

Because `UITableViewCell` is a subclass of `UIView`, it allows you to do pretty much anything you can do with a "standard" `UIView`. This includes embedding custom controls such as buttons, sliders, and switches as subviews, and having those respond to user actions.

To begin with, here's a really trivial example. Each cell has a `UIButton` at the right-hand side, which pops up an alert view when it's tapped, as shown in Figure 10–1.

Figure 10–1. *Really simple buttons*

I don't go into detail about the main aspects of creating the table–that's pretty familiar by now–but there are two things you need to do in order to create the button and the alert view.

The first is to create a method to display the alert view when one of the buttons is tapped; this will need to be declared in the `tableView`'s controller's header file, and Listing 10–1 added to the implementation.

Listing 10–1. *The `didTapButtonInCell` Method*

```
-(void)didTapButtonInCell {

    UIAlertView *alert = [[UIAlertView alloc] initWithTitle:@"Something happened!" ➥
                                                     message:@"A button was tapped" ➥
                                                    delegate:nil ➥
                                           cancelButtonTitle:@"OK" ➥
                                           otherButtonTitles:nil];
    [alert show];

}
```

Now having created the `didTapButtonInCell` method, you need to add the buttons to the cells and connect them to this method. You do this in the `tableView:cellForRowAtIndexPath:` method (see Listing 10–2).

Listing 10–2. *The Revised `tableView:cellForRowAtIndexPath:` Method*

```
- (UITableViewCell *)tableView:(UITableView *)tableView ➥
cellForRowAtIndexPath:(NSIndexPath *)indexPath
{
    static NSString *CellIdentifier = @"Cell";

    UITableViewCell *cell = [tableView
dequeueReusableCellWithIdentifier:CellIdentifier];
    if (cell == nil) {
        cell = [[UITableViewCell alloc] initWithStyle:UITableViewCellStyleDefault ➥
reuseIdentifier:CellIdentifier];
    }

    cell.textLabel.text = [_tableData objectAtIndex:indexPath.row];

    // Create and add the button to the cell
    UIButton *theButton = [UIButton buttonWithType:UIButtonTypeRoundedRect];
    [theButton setFrame:CGRectMake(235, 7, 75, 30)];
    [theButton setTitle:@"Tap me!" forState:UIControlStateNormal];

    [theButton addTarget:self action:@selector(didTapButtonInCell) ➥
forControlEvents:UIControlEventTouchUpInside];

[cell.contentView addSubview:theButton];

    return cell;
}
```

This is pretty straightforward; in fact the first part is the boilerplate code that's provided with a subclass of `UITableViewController`. The button is created with

```
    UIButton *theButton = [UIButton buttonWithType:UIButtonTypeRoundedRect];
```

Then configured:

```
    [theButton setFrame:CGRectMake(235, 7, 75, 30)];
    [theButton setTitle:@"Tap me!" forState:UIControlStateNormal];
```

And the target method added:

```
    [theButton addTarget:self action:@selector(didTapButtonInCell) ➥
forControlEvents:UIControlEventTouchUpInside];
```

Finally, the newly created button is added to the cell's `contentView` so it's returned along with the cell. Tapping on any of the buttons will cause the alert view to pop up.

An alternative method is to add the button to the cell's `accessoryView`; as it's a subview of the `accessoryView`, you won't have to worry about hiding the custom button when the table is placed into editing mode.

```
    // Create and add the button to the accessory view
    UIButton *theButton = [UIButton buttonWithType:UIButtonTypeRoundedRect];

    // Set the X and Y coords of the button to 0
    [theButton setFrame:CGRectMake(0, 0, 75, 30)];

    [theButton setTitle:@"Tap me!" forState:UIControlStateNormal];
    [theButton addTarget:self action:@selector(didTapButtonCell) ➥
forControlEvents:UIControlEventTouchUpInside];

    // Add the button to the accessory view
    cell.accessoryView = theButton;
```

Reacting to Individual Controls

Impressive as this example might seem, there's one significant limitation. Each button is tied to the same method, so it isn't possible to do something that is related to a specific cell. A very simple example might be to pop up an alert view containing the `indexPath` of the button's cell.

The next example takes things a bit further to do exactly this. It uses a custom `UITableViewCell` subclass that has one property, the text to display in the cell, and a method that pops up an `alertView` containing the `indexPath` of the row.

The first step is to create the custom `UITableViewCell` subclass (I've called this `CustomCell`). It needs three custom methods:

- A customized `initWithStyle:reuseIdentifier:` method;
- A customized `setIndexPath:` method
- A `didTapButtonInCell` method to display the `alertView`.

It also needs an `NSIndexPath` property that will be set as the cell is created by the tableView controller's `tableView:cellForRowAtIndexPath:` method (see Listing 10–3).

Listing 10–3. ***The*** `CustomCell` ***Subclass's Header File***

```
#import <UIKit/UIKit.h>

@interface CustomCell : UITableViewCell

@property (nonatomic, strong) NSIndexPath *indexPath;

-(void)didTapButtonInCell;
```

```
@end
```

Listing 10–4 is UITableViewCell's designated initializer. It instantiates the custom cell with the required style and reuse identifier, and then creates a roundRect UIButton and adds this to the cell's contentView

> **NOTE:** The UIButton is created and added in the initWithStyle:reuseIdentifier: method because the drawRect method doesn't draw the text of a UIButton.

Listing 10–4. *The Custom initWithStyle:reuseIdentifier: Method*

```
- (id)initWithStyle:(UITableViewCellStyle)style ↩
reuseIdentifier:(NSString *)reuseIdentifier
{
    self = [super initWithStyle:style reuseIdentifier:reuseIdentifier];
    if (self) {
        // Initialization code
        UIButton *theButton = [UIButton buttonWithType:UIButtonTypeRoundedRect];
        [theButton setFrame:CGRectMake(0, 0, 75, 30)];
        [theButton addTarget:self action:@selector(didTapButtonInCell) ↩
forControlEvents:UIControlEventTouchUpInside];

        self.accessoryView = theButton;

    }
    return self;
}
```

Listing 10–5 overrides the default setIndexPath: method.

Listing 10–5. *The Custom setIndexPath: Method*

```
-(void)setIndexPath:(NSIndexPath *)theIndexPath {

    indexPath = theIndexPath;

    UILabel *theLabel = [[UILabel alloc] initWithFrame:CGRectMake(10, 7, 200, 25)];
    [theLabel setFont:[UIFont systemFontOfSize:18]];
    [theLabel setText:[NSString stringWithFormat:@"Row %d", self.indexPath.row]];

    [self.contentView addSubview:theLabel];

    UIButton *theButton = (UIButton *)self.accessoryView;
    [theButton setTitle:@"Tap me!" forState:UIControlStateNormal];

}
```

This method does three things: it sets the value of the indexPath property, then creates a UILabel containing the row number for that cell, adding this to the cell's contentView. It also sets the text of the button in the accessoryView.

Listing 10–6 shows the didTapButtonInCell method, which shouldn't contain any surprises.

Listing 10–6. *The* `didTapButtonInCell` *Method*

```
-(void)didTapButtonInCell {

    NSString *messageString = [NSString ➥
stringWithFormat:@"Button at section %d row %d was tapped.", ➥
_cellIndexPath.section, _cellIndexPath.row];

    UIAlertView *alert = [[UIAlertView alloc] initWithTitle:@"Button tapped!" ➥
 message:messageString delegate:nil cancelButtonTitle:@"OK" otherButtonTitles: nil];

    [alert show];

}
```

The `tableView:cellForRowAtIndexPath:` method in the `tableView`'s controller also needs to be altered, which is show in Listing 10–7.

Listing 10–7. *The Revised* `tableView:cellForRowAtIndexPath:` *Method*

```
- (UITableViewCell *)tableView:(UITableView *)tableView ➥
cellForRowAtIndexPath:(NSIndexPath *)indexPath
{
    static NSString *CellIdentifier = @"Cell";

    CustomCell *cell = (CustomCell *)[tableView ➥
dequeueReusableCellWithIdentifier:CellIdentifier];
    if (cell == nil) {
        cell = [[CustomCell alloc] initWithStyle:UITableViewCellStyleDefault ➥
reuseIdentifier:CellIdentifier];
    }

    cell.cellIndexPath = indexPath;

    return cell;
}
```

Putting this all together, you now have a set of cells with buttons that trigger row-specific actions, shown in Figure 10–2.

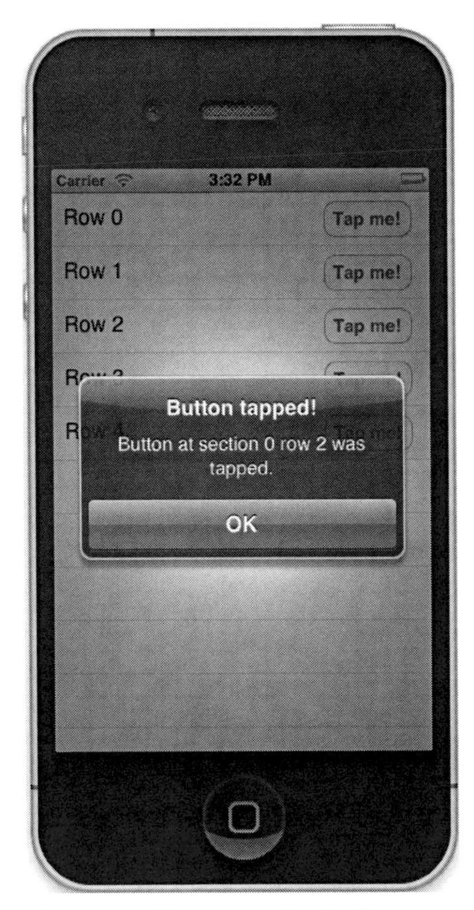

Figure 10–2. *The row-specific alertView*

A Practical Example of Controls in Cells

The previous example is deliberately simple. In practice, you're going to want something considerably more sophisticated.

Here's an example from one of my apps, which collects data for a series of clinical trials. After taking a blood pressure reading and entering the results, the users rate their mood using the 10 descriptors of the *Positive and Negative Affect Scale*, a widely used psychometric scoring tool. Each descriptor is rated on a 1 to 5 scale.

The `tableView`, shown in Figure 10–3, has two sections: section `zero` has one static cell with the text header, and section one has a custom cell for each of the sliders.

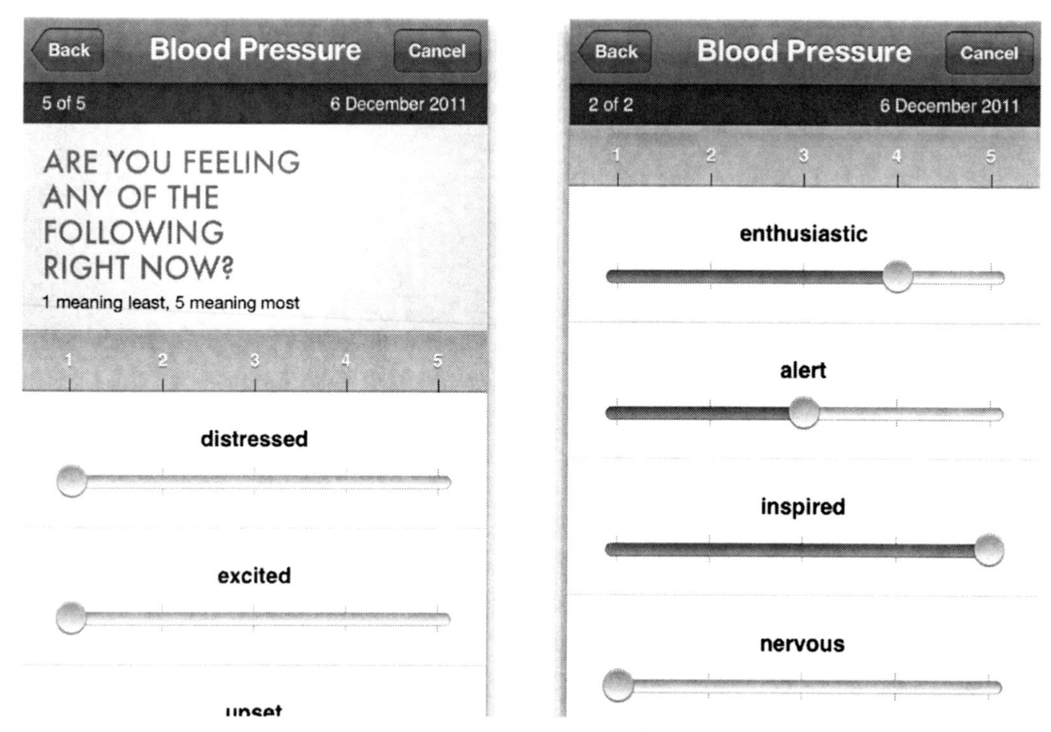

Figure 10–3. *The custom tableView*

The sliders themselves are `UISliders`, which sit on top of a `UIImageView` containing the tick marks, and "snap" to the marks.

The custom cell in its nib is shown in Figure 10–4 (the text in the nib is just a placeholder to help get the alignment right).

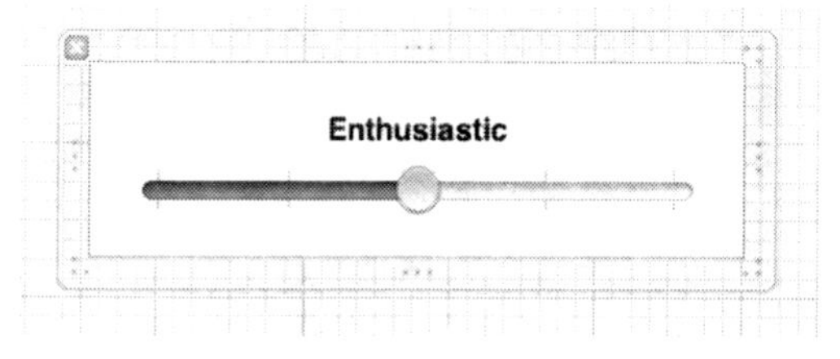

Figure 10–4. *The custom cell's nib*

The cell is subclassed from `UITableViewCell` as shown in Listing 10–8.

Listing 10–8. *The Custom Cell's Header File*

```
#import <UIKit/UIKit.h>

@interface PANASTableSliderCell : UITableViewCell

@property (nonatomic, strong) IBOutlet UILabel *sliderLabel;
@property (nonatomic, strong) IBOutlet UISlider *slider;
```

```
@end
```

The tableView:cellForRowAtIndexPath: deals with the creation of the ten slider cells. Listing 10–9 shows the section of the method that handles section one of the table.

Listing 10–9. *An Extract from the tableView Controller's tableView:cellForRowAtIndexPath: Method*

```
// ...

    if (indexPath.section == 1) {

        NSArray *topLevelObjects = [[NSBundle mainBundle] ↩
loadNibNamed:@"PANASTableSliderCell" owner:nil options:nil];

        PANASTableSliderCell *pCell = [topLevelObjects objectAtIndex:0];

        // Configure slider
        pCell.slider.tag = indexPath.row;
        pCell.slider.minimumValue = 0.0;
        pCell.slider.maximumValue = 4.0;
        pCell.slider.continuous = NO;
        [pCell.slider addTarget:self action:@selector(sliderDidChange:) ↩
forControlEvents:UIControlEventValueChanged];

        // Configure label
        pCell.sliderLabel.text = [sliderNames objectAtIndex:indexPath.row];
        [pCell setSelectionStyle:UITableViewCellSelectionStyleNone];

        // Set slider value
        pCell.slider.value = [[sliderValues objectAtIndex:indexPath.row] floatValue];

        // Return cell
        return pCell;
    }

// ...
```

The method starts by loading the nib file and extracting the PANASTableSliderCell object, which is a subclass of UITableViewCell:

```
    NSArray *topLevelObjects = [[NSBundle mainBundle] ↩
loadNibNamed:@"PANASTableSliderCell" owner:nil options:nil];

    PANASTableSliderCell *pCell = [topLevelObjects objectAtIndex:0];
```

Once the PANASTableSliderCell is extracted, the slider can then be configured to set the minimum and maximum values:

```
    pCell.slider.tag = indexPath.row;
    pCell.slider.minimumValue = 0.0;
    pCell.slider.maximumValue = 4.0;
    pCell.slider.continuous = NO;
```

UISliders have a UIControlEventValueChanged event that fires whenever the user changes the slider's value. It can be used to call a method; the sliderDidChange: method is added to the slider as a target:

```
    [pCell.slider addTarget:self action:@selector(sliderDidChange:) ➥
forControlEvents:UIControlEventValueChanged];
```

The slider's label is set, and selection of the cell is prevented:

```
    // Set slider value
    pCell.slider.value = [[sliderValues objectAtIndex:indexPath.row] floatValue];
```

And finally, the slider value is updated so that it displays the corresponding value from the sliderValues array. Initially, this will be zero, but if the value has been updated at any point, this ensures that the slider reflects the actual value so that it appears to "persist":

```
    pCell.slider.value = [[sliderValues objectAtIndex:indexPath.row] floatValue];
```

The sliderDidChange: method is responsible for updating the sliderValues array, and also implements the "snapping" of the slider to whole integer values. It's shown in Listing 10–10.

Listing 10–10. ***The sliderDidChange: Method***

```
-(IBAction)sliderDidChange:(id)sender {

    UISlider *slider = (UISlider *)sender;

    // Figure out what the intvalue of the slider is
    // and snap to nearest int
    int sliderIntValue = (int)slider.value;
    float sliderModValue = (float)sliderIntValue;

    if ( (slider.value - sliderModValue) >= 0.5 ) {
        sliderModValue ++;
    }

    slider.value = sliderModValue;

    [sliderValues replaceObjectAtIndex:slider.tag ➥
withObject:[NSNumber numberWithInt:sliderModValue]];


}
```

Adding Gestures to Cells

You're not limited to adding controls to cells: you can also enable additional functionality by attaching gesture recognizers. As you will see in the next section, that opens up the possibility of adding swipe gestures to expose additional information. A simpler interaction is to add the ability to double-tap on a cell in order to trigger some action or transformation.

Adding support for gestures is one area of the iOS SDK that's been radically simplified since version 3. Listing 10–11 shows how you would add a double-tap recognizer to each cell in the cellForRowAtIndexPath: method.

Listing 10–11. *Adding a `gestureRecognizer` to Each Cell*

```
-(UITableViewCell *)tableView:(UITableView *)theTableView ➥
cellForRowAtIndexPath:(NSIndexPath *)indexPath {

    static NSString *cellIdentifier = @"cellIdentifier";
    UITableViewCell *cell = [theTableView ➥
dequeueReusableCellWithIdentifier:cellIdentifier];

    if (!cell) {
        cell = [[UITableViewCell alloc] initWithStyle:UITableViewCellStyleDefault ➥
reuseIdentifier:cellIdentifier];
    }

    // ...
    // The usual cell configuration code goes here
    // ...

    // Create the UITapGestureRecognizer
    UITapGestureRecognizer *doubleTapRecognizer = [[UITapGestureRecognizer alloc] ➥
initWithTarget:self action:@selector(didDoubleTapCell:)];

    // Configure the number of taps
    doubleTapRecognizer.numberOfTapsRequired = 2;

    // Add the gestureRecognizer to the cell
    [cell addGestureRecognizer:doubleTapRecognizer];

    // Return the cell as usual
    return cell;

}
```

Having added the double-tap recognizer to the cell, you'll probably want to be able to distinguish which cell has been tapped – here's how you can access the cell in the example `didDoubleTapCell:` method:

```
-(IBAction)didDoubleTapCell:(UITapGestureRecognizer *)sender {

    UITableViewCell *cell = (UITableViewCell *)sender.view;

    // ...
    // Do something with the cell here...
    // ...

}
```

The `UIGestureRecognizer` instance that responded to the interaction is passed through to the method as `sender`. This has a `view` property that's a pointer to the `UIView` object to which the gesture recognizer was attached.

In this case, it's the `cell`, so the `sender.view` property can be cast to an instance of `UITableViewCell`, at which point you can treat it as the cell that it is.

Obviously you're not restricted to just tap gestures: pinches, pans, rotations, long presses, and swipes are all available. Some of these will work better in the limited size of a cell than others though, so some careful experimentation is called for in order to get the best overall user experience. You may find that some multi-touch gestures are only practical on the larger user interface of the iPad.

Swiping in Cells

Adding animation to an interface–if it's done sparingly and in the right places–can transform an app's user experience and bring the interface to life.

One of the most striking animation effects that has been applied to table views is the slide-the-cell-to-the-side-in-response-to-a-swipe effect. It's a great way of exposing additional functionality that relates to the contents of the cell without building a cluttered interface within the cell itself.

How Swiping Works

Although the effect is really impressive, implementing swipe-to-reveal in cells is actually quite simple. You need two views of the same size as the cell: one which is displayed when the cell is created (in Figure 10–5, that's `topView`), and the other which is the view that gets "revealed" as the `topView` swipes out (that's `swipeView` as displayed in Figure 10–5).

Initially, the two views start out "stacked" on top of each other. Strictly speaking, `UIViews` don't have layer behavior in the Photoshop sense, but stacking the cells mimics it.

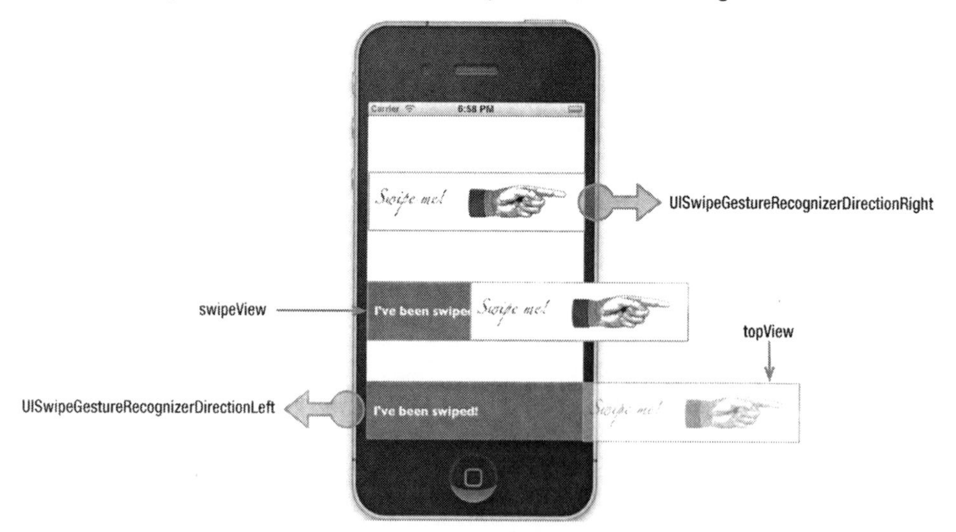

Figure 10–5. *Setting up the swipe-to-reveal interaction*

Then you'll need to add two `UIGestureRecognizers` to the cell: one to detect swiping left, and one to detect swiping right. (Up-and-down swipes aren't generally a good idea in table views, as they will interfere with the natural scrolling of the table.)

Each gesture recognizer has as its target a method that animates the movement of the views by changing their frame. topView starts with a frame origin of (0,0) and ends up with an origin of (320,0); in other words, it appears to slide off to the right. As it "slides," swipeView appears to be revealed from underneath.

By using UIView animation blocks, you can "chain" the animations together, as well as adding little visual tweaks that make the views appear to "bounce" as they move in and out of place. Adding some fake momentum to the animation can make it seem considerably more realistic.

Creating the Swipe-to-Reveal Table

Setting up the swipe-to-reveal table has three stages:

1. Create a UITableView, and wire up the delegate and data source.
2. Create a UITableViewCell subclass:
    - Implement the layout by overriding the initWithStyle: reuseIdentifier: method.
    - Implement the animation methods.
3. Create instances of the custom cell subclass to populate the table.

Creating the tableView

There's really not a lot to say about this, as it should be pretty routine by now. I've created a standard UITableViewController and implemented the usual methods.

Creating the UITableViewCell Subclass

You're going to need a custom cell. I've called mine SwipeCell, and I've implemented two UIView properties, and two swipe methods as shown in Listing 10–12.

Listing 10–12. *The SwipeCell Header File*

```
#import <UIKit/UIKit.h>

@interface SwipeCell : UITableViewCell

@property (nonatomic, strong) UIView *swipeView;
@property (nonatomic, strong) UIView *topView;

-(IBAction)didSwipeRightInCell:(id)sender;
-(IBAction)didSwipeLeftInCell:(id)sender;

@end
```

In the implementation file, the heavy lifting is done by the initWithStyle: reuseIdentifier: method shown in Listing 10–13.

Listing 10–13. *The* `SwipeCell's` *initWithStyle:reuseIdentifier: Method*

```
- (id)initWithStyle:(UITableViewCellStyle)style ➥
reuseIdentifier:(NSString *)reuseIdentifier
{
    self = [super initWithStyle:style reuseIdentifier:reuseIdentifier];
    if (self) {
        // Initialization code
        NSLog(@"self.contentView.width = %f", self.contentView.frame.size.width);

        // Create the top view
        _topView = [[UIView alloc] initWithFrame:CGRectMake(0, 0, ➥
self.contentView.frame.size.width, 80)];
        [_topView setBackgroundColor:[UIColor whiteColor]];

        // Create the top label
        UILabel *label = [[UILabel alloc] initWithFrame:CGRectMake(10, 20, 150, 40)];
        [label setFont:[UIFont fontWithName:@"Zapfino" size:18]];
        [label setTextColor:[UIColor blackColor]];
        [label setText:@"Swipe me!"];
        [_topView addSubview:label];

        // Create the top image
        UIImageView *pointImage = [[UIImageView alloc] ➥
initWithImage:[UIImage imageNamed:@"point"]];

        CGFloat pointImageXposition = self.contentView.frame.size.width - 160;
        [pointImage setFrame:CGRectMake(pointImageXposition, 18, 144, 44)];
        [_topView addSubview:pointImage];

        // Create the swipe view
        _swipeView = [[UIView alloc] initWithFrame:CGRectMake(0, 0, ➥
self.contentView.frame.size.width, 80)];
        [_swipeView setBackgroundColor:[UIColor darkGrayColor]];

        // Create the swipe label
        UILabel *haveSwipedlabel = [[UILabel alloc] ➥
initWithFrame:CGRectMake(10, 25, 200, 30)];
        [haveSwipedlabel setFont:[UIFont fontWithName:@"GillSans-Bold" size:18]];
        [haveSwipedlabel setTextColor:[UIColor whiteColor]];
        [haveSwipedlabel setBackgroundColor:[UIColor darkGrayColor]];
        [haveSwipedlabel setText:@"I've been swiped!"];
        [_swipeView addSubview:haveSwipedlabel];

        // Add views to contentView
        [self.contentView addSubview:_swipeView];
        [self.contentView addSubview:_topView];

        // Create the gesture recognizers
        UISwipeGestureRecognizer *swipeRight = [[UISwipeGestureRecognizer alloc] ➥
initWithTarget:self action:@selector(didSwipeRightInCell:)];
        [swipeRight setDirection:UISwipeGestureRecognizerDirectionRight];

        UISwipeGestureRecognizer *swipeLeft = [[UISwipeGestureRecognizer alloc] ➥
initWithTarget:self action:@selector(didSwipeLeftInCell:)];
        [swipeLeft setDirection:UISwipeGestureRecognizerDirectionLeft];
```

```
        [self addGestureRecognizer:swipeRight];
        [self addGestureRecognizer:swipeLeft];

        // Prevent selection highlighting
        [self setSelectionStyle:UITableViewCellSelectionStyleNone];

    }
    return self;
}
```

At first glance, there's quite a lot going on there, so let's step through it. The first task to create the topView:

```
    // Create the top view
    _topView = [[UIView alloc] initWithFrame:CGRectMake(0, 0, 320, 80)];
    [_topView setBackgroundColor:[UIColor whiteColor]];

    // Create the top label
    UILabel *label = [[UILabel alloc] initWithFrame:CGRectMake(10, 20, 150, 40)];
    [label setFont:[UIFont fontWithName:@"Zapfino" size:18]];
    [label setTextColor:[UIColor blackColor]];
    [label setText:@"Swipe me!"];
    [_topView addSubview:label];

    // Create the top image
    UIImageView *pointImage = [[UIImageView alloc] ➥
initWithImage:[UIImage imageNamed:@"point"]];
    [pointImage setFrame:CGRectMake(150, 18, 144, 44)];
    [_topView addSubview:pointImage];
```

This view fills the full width and height of the cell, and adds a label and an image.

Creating the bottom swipeView is virtually identical; it's got a different backgroundColor to provide a contrast with the topView:

```
    // Create the swipe view
    _swipeView = [[UIView alloc] initWithFrame:CGRectMake(0, 0, 320, 80)];
    [_swipeView setBackgroundColor:[UIColor darkGrayColor]];

    // Create the swipe label
    UILabel *haveSwipedlabel = [[UILabel alloc] ➥
initWithFrame:CGRectMake(10, 25, 200, 30)];
    [haveSwipedlabel setFont:[UIFont fontWithName:@"GillSans-Bold" size:18]];
    [haveSwipedlabel setTextColor:[UIColor whiteColor]];
    [haveSwipedlabel setBackgroundColor:[UIColor darkGrayColor]];
    [haveSwipedlabel setText:@"I've been swiped!"];
    [_swipeView addSubview:haveSwipedlabel];
```

Then having created the two views, we need to add them to the cell's contentView:

```
    [self.contentView addSubview:_swipeView];
    [self.contentView addSubview:_topView];
```

The order is important: remember that subviews are added to their superview from the "bottom" up. The last one to be added is the "front" view.

Having added the two views, the next job is to get the cell to respond to swipes. Prior to iOS4, this was painful to say the least; recognizing multitouch gestures is not a trivial task. Fortunately iOS4 introduced the UIGestureRecognizer class; by adding an instance of this class to a UIView, this provides the ability to capture a range of single and multitouch gestures.

The two gestures that are relevant here are swipes left and right. Adding these are a three-stage process:

1. Create an instance of the UIGestureRecognizer class and set its target method:

```
UISwipeGestureRecognizer *swipeRight = [[UISwipeGestureRecognizer alloc] ↵
initWithTarget:self action:@selector(didSwipeRightInCell:)];
```

2. Set the direction to which the gesture recognizer is to react:

```
[swipeRight setDirection:UISwipeGestureRecognizerDirectionRight];
```

3. Finally, add the gesture recognizer to the view that needs to handle the gestures (in this case, it's our instance of SwipeCell):

```
[self addGestureRecognizer:swipeRight];
```

Creating the gesture recognizer to handle leftward swipes is exactly the same process, but should set the gesture direction to UISwipeGestureRecognizerDirectionLeft.

Responding to the Gestures

Now that the gestures are recognized, it's time to create the animations. You are going to use UIView's fantastically-useful block-based animation methods to move things around.

OBJECTIVE-C BLOCKS

Blocks are a feature that was introduced to Objective-C in version 2.0. They're fairly common in other languages under names such as closures and lambas. Ruby and Lisp make extensive use of their implementations of blocks, but blocks were a relatively late addition to Objective-C.

Although blocks are an incredibly powerful feature of Objective-C, their syntax does leave something to be desired. Objective-C doesn't often get accused of being a graceful language, but blocks seem to be a throwback to a more obfuscated age; at first glance, you'd be forgiven for running away screaming.

However, they're being used more and more as new features are introduced into the iOS SDK, and there are a number of UIView methods due for deprecation that will been replaced by block-based methods. It's worth gritting your teeth and getting to grips with them. It'll pay off in the long run.

What Is a Block?

A block is a discrete chunk of code that can be passed around much like a variable. You can recognize them by the ^ operator. The basic syntax of a block looks like this:

```
BOOL (^myBlock)(int) = ^(int theVariable) {
   // Code goes here
```

```
}
```

This code can be unpacked a little:

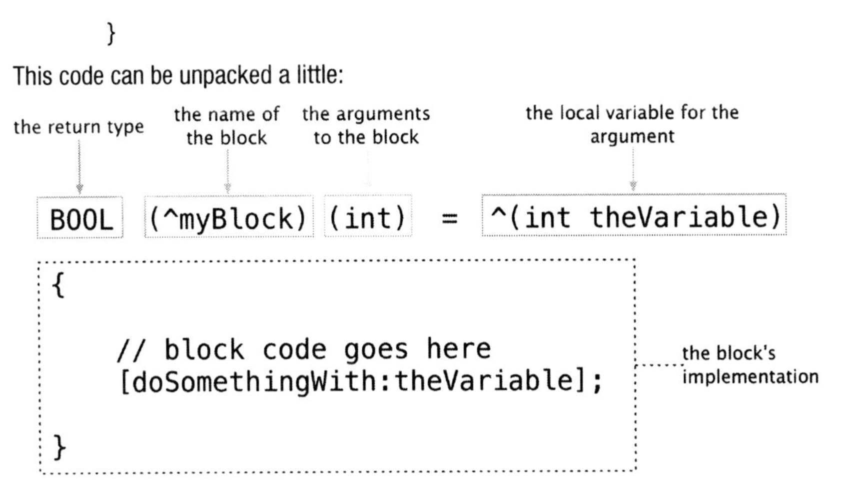

Blocks come into their own where you have chunks of code that need to be executed to perform tasks that are best run asynchronously. Animations are one example, but blocks are used extensively in other areas such as networking.

There isn't space here to go into much more detail, but there's a good explanation of blocks in Apple's Developer documentation, and, of course, a quick Google search will turn up any number of other guides and tutorials to suit various tastes.

The method to create the animation effect is `didSwipeRightInCell:`, shown in Listing 10–14.

Listing 10–14. *The `didSwipeRightInCell:` Method*

```
-(IBAction)didSwipeRightInCell:(id)sender {

    [UIView setAnimationCurve:UIViewAnimationCurveEaseIn];

    // Swipe top view left
    [UIView animateWithDuration:1.0 animations:^{

        [_topView setFrame:CGRectMake(320, 0, 320, 80)];

    } completion:^(BOOL finished) {

        // Bounce lower view
        [UIView animateWithDuration:0.15 animations:^{

            [_swipeView setFrame:CGRectMake(10, 0, 320, 80)];

        } completion:^(BOOL finished) {

            [UIView animateWithDuration:0.15 animations:^{
                [_swipeView setFrame:CGRectMake(0, 0, 320, 80)];
            }];
        }];
    }];

}
```

At first glance, this looks a bit gnarly, so let's step through the process stage-by-stage.

The animation starts by setting the animation's easing curve:

```
[UIView setAnimationCurve:UIViewAnimationCurveEaseIn];
```

to add the appearance of momentum and give the animation some "weight."

> **TIP:** `UIView` animations have an `animationCurve` property that allows you to fine-tune the appearance of the motion by controlling the speed of the animation over its course. There are four animation curve settings:
>
> **`UIViewAnimationCurveLinear`**—This is the default, and performs the animation at a constant speed from start to finish.
> **`UIViewAnimationCurveEaseOut`**—The animation starts quickly, and slows down as it reaches towards the end.
> **`UIViewAnimationCurveEaseIn`**—The animation starts slowly, and then speeds up as it gets towards the end.
> **`UIViewAnimationCurveEaseInOut`**—This combines `EaseIn` and `EaseOut`; the animation starts slowly, speeds up as it progresses, then slows down towards the end.
>
> Applying animation easing gives it the appearance of momentum. In the real world, an object has inertia so it takes a while to get moving, and then tends to slow down as it approaches its destination.
>
> Animation that's completely linear can seem to have a "mechanical" feel. That's fine if it's the effect you're after, but adding easing can give an interface a very subtle but effective polish.
>
> Apple uses easing extensively in the iOS interface; it's one of the reasons why iOS devices have such an impressively smooth user experience.

Then the animation starts. It needs to do three things, one after another:

1. Change the `topView` `origin`'s `X` position from `0` to `320`, to slide it from left to right. As it moves, it will appear to move off the right-hand edge of the screen.
2. As the `topView` reaches the right-hand edge of the screen, the `swipeView` `origin`'s `X` position increases slightly so it appears to "bounce."
3. After moving the `swipeView` slightly to the right, it moves back to the left to settle back into position.

TIP: Adding some "bounce" to your interface is a fun way to spice up the interaction. In this code, I've made the animation durations deliberately long so you can see what's going on. In a finished app, you'd probably want them to be a lot slower so that the effect is more subtle.

Tweaking animation timings can be a massive yak to shave, and it's one area where the Simulator simply doesn't cut it. The speed of the Simulator is directly dependent on the speed of your Mac. There's really no effective substitute for testing on different devices so that you can fine-tune the speed and duration of movements to get the best user experience.

This is where animation with blocks comes into its own, because you can "chain" animations together.

The basic block-based UIView animation syntax is

```
[UIView animateWithDuration:(NSTimeInterval)timeInterval animations:^{
    // animation code block
}];
```

timeInterval is a value in seconds; the code that's enclosed in the block will be executed over this period. Behind the scenes, iOS will figure out how this should be done to produce a smooth-looking result.

If you've got a number of individual animations that need to run in a sequence (which is what we're doing here) you can use another block-based UIView animation method:

```
[UIView animateWithDuration:(NSTimeInterval)timeInterval animations:^{

    // animation code block

} completion:^(BOOL finished) {

    // code to be executed
    // after first block finishes

}];
```

This method chains the two code blocks together; the second one is executed as soon as the first has finished.

The third method adds a delay to the execution of the first block:

```
[UIView animateWithDuration:timeInterval ➥
                      delay:timeDelay ➥
                    options:options ➥
                 animations:^{

    // animation code block

} completion:^(BOOL finished) {

    // completion block

}];
```

This allows you to start the execution of the first block after a delay (which is a value in seconds). There isn't a corresponding single-block method, but if there's nothing to be done after the first block is completed, you can simply leave the completion block empty.

Going back to the animation we need, you are going to build this up by embedding animation blocks inside animation blocks. This can get really complicated really quickly, so the practice I've gotten into is to "sketch out" the process in pseudo-code before I start to write the actual UIView animation code:

```
First animation - duration 1.0

        Main block:

                Move topView X to 320

        Completion block:

                  Second animation - duration 0.15

                        Main block:

                                Move swipeView X to 10

                        Completion block:

                                Third animation - duration 0.15

                                         Main block:

                                                Move swipeView X to 0
```

Once you've got everything blocked out in the right order (bad pun intended), it's relatively easy to turn that into actual UIView animation code.

Having built the animation to slide topView off and expose the swipeView, you will to need to reverse this. That's triggered by swiping left in the cell, which fires the didSwipeLeftInCell: method, shown in Listing 10–15.

Listing 10–15. *The didSwipeLeftInCell: Method*

```
-(IBAction)didSwipeLeftInCell:(id)sender {
    [UIView setAnimationCurve:UIViewAnimationCurveEaseIn];
    [UIView animateWithDuration:1.0 animations:^{
        [_topView setFrame:CGRectMake(-10, 0, 320, 80)];
    } completion:^(BOOL finished) {
        [UIView animateWithDuration:0.15 animations:^{
            [_topView setFrame:CGRectMake(0, 0, 320, 80)];
        }];
    }];
}
```

This is slightly less involved than swiping right; the method slides topView back to the left, and then beyond the left-hand edge of the screen by 10 pixels. The completion block moves topView back to the left-hand edge to produce the "bounce" effect.

> **TIP:** Another way of adding additional realism to your interface is the subtle use of gradients and fade effects in the graphics. If you were to add a gentle shadow effect to the top and bottom of the lower UIView in the example above, it would appear to sit "below" the surface of the table itself.
>
> There is a trade-off, however: gradients and shadows rely on image transparency. Transparency increases the processing required to composite the UI graphics, and can slow down performance (particularly table view scrolling).

Handling Rotation

Impressive though it is at the moment, the slide-to-reveal-enabled table does have a significant limitation: it looks awful if the device is rotated as shown in Figure 10–6.

Figure 10–6. *Oh noes!*

One way of dealing with this would simply be to not support rotation, but that's a bit of a cop-out. Let's tweak things so that the cells will slide nicely when in landscape.

The problem is being caused by the way that the width of the topView and swipeView are hard-coded:

```
// Create the top view
_topView = [[UIView alloc] initWithFrame:CGRectMake(0, 0, 320, 80)];

...

// Create the swipe view
_swipeView = [[UIView alloc] initWithFrame:CGRectMake(0, 0, 320, 80)];
```

The width of both views needs to match the width of the table in the current orientation.

Fortunately, that's pretty simple. The `autoresizingMask` of `UITableViewCell's` `contentView` is `UIViewAutoresizingFlexibleWidth`, which means that the `contentView` will stretch to fill the entire width of the `tableView` regardless of the device orientation.

You can exploit this by tweaking the dimensions of `topView` and `swipeView`:

```
    // Create the top view
    _topView = [[UIView alloc] initWithFrame:CGRectMake(0, 0, ↵
self.contentView.frame.size.width, 80)];
```

It would also be neater if you could get the image in the cell to remain a consistent distance from the edge of the cell so that it doesn't look like Figure 10–7.

Figure 10–7. *Eww!*

Currently the position of the image is hardcoded:

```
    [pointImage setFrame:150, 18, 144, 44)];
```

Let's tweak that so that it's relative to the edge of the cell:

```
    CGFloat pointImageXposition = self.contentView.frame.size.width - 160;
    [pointImage setFrame:CGRectMake(pointImageXposition, 18, 144, 44)];
```

Much better! (See Figure 10–8.)

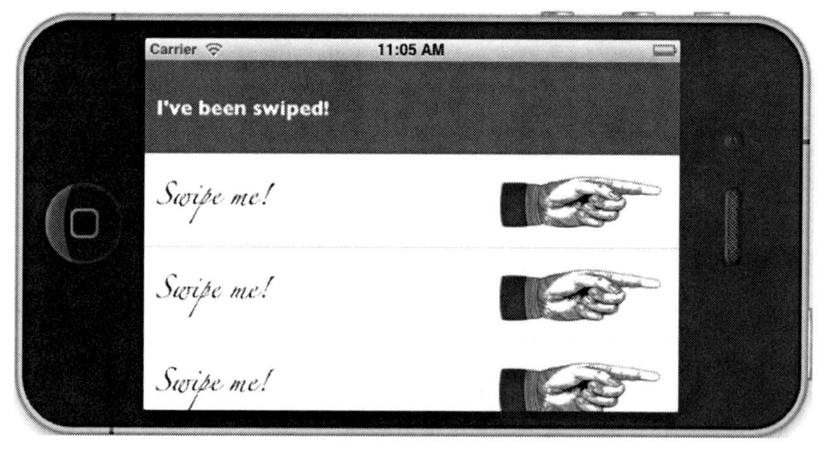

Figure 10–8. *The new, improved, resizable swipe-to-reveal table*

Tidying Up the Swipe Functionality

Although you can now feel rightly proud of your shiny swipe-to-reveal functionality, it does have some rough edges. As it stands, you can swipe more than one row at a time;

if the swipe was to reveal some functionality that acted on the cell, ideally you'd only want one row to be in the swiped state at any given moment.

The other problem is that the cell's swipe state is cached with the cell. As you scroll the table, cells will be recycled into the cache in whatever state they happen to be in. If they're subsequently dequeued, they'll reappear with whatever swipe state they had when they were cached, which won't necessarily be the state that they should be.

This problem will manifest itself as cells reappearing in the table in the "swiped" state, even though the user hasn't interacted with them in any way.

To get around this, you could tweak the cells so that they're "reset" if they get dequeued in the swiped state, but you can also solve the problem at source by "unswiping" any cells as soon as the table is scrolled.

This is going to involve amending both the cell subclass and the `tableView` controller:

- The `tableView` controller will keep track of which row is currently in the swiped state.
- When a cell is swiped or unswiped, it will call one of two delegate methods on the `tableView` controller to update the `tableView` about which row is now in the swiped state. Those methods will be declared in a custom protocol.
- If the `tableView` detects that a different row has been swiped, it will unswipe the row that was previously in the swiped state, if any.

Keeping Track of the Currently Swiped Row

This requires adding a property to the `SwipeTableController` to hold the `indexPath` of the currently-swiped row:

```
@property (nonatomic, strong) NSIndexPath *swipedCell;
```

Creating the Delegate Protocol

Protocols (such as `UITableViewDelegate`) are defined in a .h file. You will need a protocol called `SwipeCellProtocol`, so create a new file called `SwipeCellProtocol.h`, and declare the two methods that the protocol needs Listing 10–16.

Listing 10–16. *The `SwipeCellProtocol.h` File*

```
#import <Foundation/Foundation.h>

@protocol SwipeCellProtocol <NSObject>

-(void)didSwipeRightInCellWithIndexPath:(NSIndexPath *)indexPath;
-(void)didSwipeLeftInCellWithIndexPath:(NSIndexPath *)indexPath;

@end
```

Set Up the Delegate Protocol

First, declare that the `SwipeCellTableController` conforms to the `SwipeCellProtocol` by adding it to the header, and declare the two protocol methods shown in Listing 10–17.

Listing 10–17. *The Updated `SwipeCellTableController.h` File*

```
#import <UIKit/UIKit.h>
#import "SwipeCellProtocol.h"

@interface SwipeTableController : UITableViewController <SwipeCellProtocol>

@property (nonatomic, strong) NSIndexPath *swipedCell;

-(void)didSwipeRightInCellWithIndexPath:(NSIndexPath *)indexPath;
-(void)didSwipeLeftInCellWithIndexPath:(NSIndexPath *)indexPath;

@end
```

Next, define those two methods to the bottom of the implementation as shown in Listing 10–18 (you will come back to flesh them out shortly).

Listing 10–18. *Adding the Declarations*

```
-(void)didSwipeRightInCellWithIndexPath:(NSIndexPath *)indexPath{

}

-(void)didSwipeLeftInCellWithIndexPath:(NSIndexPath *)indexPath {
}
```

Updating the SwipeCell Class

Now you need to add the `delegate` property to the `SwipeCell` class, as well as a property to allow the `SwipeCell` instances to keep track of the row in which they're currently sitting (see Listing 10–19).

Listing 10–19. *The Updated `SwipeCell.h` File*

```
#import <UIKit/UIKit.h>
#import "SwipeCellProtocol.h"

@interface SwipeCell : UITableViewCell

@property (nonatomic, strong) UIView *swipeView;
@property (nonatomic, strong) UIView *topView;

@property (nonatomic, retain) NSIndexPath *indexPath;
@property (nonatomic, assign) id <SwipeCellProtocol> delegate;

-(IBAction)didSwipeRightInCell:(id)sender;
-(IBAction)didSwipeLeftInCell:(id)sender;

@end
```

Both these properties will need synthesizing in the implementation.

When the cell is swiped left or right, it will need to inform its delegate (the SwipeTableController) that something has happened. This means updating the didSwipeRightInCell: and didSwipeLeftInCell: methods as shown in Listings 10–20 and 10–21.

Listing 10–20. *The Updated didSwipeRightInCell: Method*

```
-(IBAction)didSwipeRightInCell:(id)sender {

    // Inform the delegate of the right swipe
    [delegate didSwipeRightInCellWithIndexPath:_indexPath];

    [UIView setAnimationCurve:UIViewAnimationCurveEaseIn];

    // Swipe top view left
    [UIView animateWithDuration:1.0 animations:^{

        [_topView setFrame:CGRectMake(self.contentView.frame.size.width, ➥
0, self.contentView.frame.size.width, 80)];

    } completion:^(BOOL finished) {

        // Bounce lower view
        [UIView animateWithDuration:0.15 animations:^{

            [_swipeView setFrame:CGRectMake(10, 0, ➥
self.contentView.frame.size.width, 80)];

        } completion:^(BOOL finished) {

            [UIView animateWithDuration:0.15 animations:^{
                [_swipeView setFrame:CGRectMake(0, 0, self.contentView.frame.size.width,
80)];
            }];
        }];
    }];

}
```

Listing 10–21. *The Revised didSwipeLeftInCell: Method*

```
-(IBAction)didSwipeLeftInCell:(id)sender {

    // Inform the delegate of the left swipe
    [delegate didSwipeLeftInCellWithIndexPath:_indexPath];

    [UIView setAnimationCurve:UIViewAnimationCurveEaseIn];

    [UIView animateWithDuration:1.0 animations:^{
        [_topView setFrame:CGRectMake(-10, 0, ➥
self.contentView.frame.size.width, 80)];
    } completion:^(BOOL finished) {
        [UIView animateWithDuration:0.15 animations:^{
            [_topView setFrame:CGRectMake(0, 0, ➥
self.contentView.frame.size.width, 80)];
        }];
    }];
```

```
}
```

Updating the SwipeTableController

Now you need to update the SwipeTableController's tableView:cellForRowAtIndexPath: method so it sets itself as the delegate of the SwipeCell, and sets the cell's indexPath property (see Listing 10–22).

Listing 10–22. *The Updated tableView:cellForRowAtIndexPath: Method*

```
- (UITableViewCell *)tableView:(UITableView *)tableView
cellForRowAtIndexPath:(NSIndexPath *)indexPath
{
    static NSString *CellIdentifier = @"cellIdentifier";

    SwipeCell *cell = (SwipeCell *)[tableView
dequeueReusableCellWithIdentifier:CellIdentifier];
    if (cell == nil) {
        cell = [[SwipeCell alloc] initWithStyle:UITableViewCellStyleDefault ➥
reuseIdentifier:CellIdentifier];
    }

    // Update the cell's indexPath property
    cell.indexPath = indexPath;

    // Set self as the cell's delegate
    cell.delegate = self;

    return cell;
}
```

The final stage (Listings 10–23 and 10–24) is to actually implement the two delegate methods.

Listing 10–23. *The* `didSwipeRightInCellWithIndexPath:` *Method*

```
-(void)didSwipeRightInCellWithIndexPath:(NSIndexPath *)indexPath{

    // Check if the newly-swiped cell is different to the currently
    // swiped cell - if it is, 'unswipe' it
    if ([_swipedCell compare:indexPath] != NSOrderedSame) {

        // Unswipe the currently swiped cell
        SwipeCell *currentlySwipedCell = (SwipeCell *)[self.tableView ➥
cellForRowAtIndexPath:_swipedCell];
        [currentlySwipedCell didSwipeLeftInCell:self];

    }

    // Update the tableView controller's _swipedCell property
    _swipedCell = indexPath;

}
```

Listing 10–24. *The `didSwipeLeftInCellWithIndexPath:` Method*

```
-(void)didSwipeLeftInCellWithIndexPath:(NSIndexPath *)indexPath {

    // If the currently swiped cell has just been 'unswiped',
    // reset the _swipedCell property
    if ([_swipedCell compare:indexPath] == NSOrderedSame) {
        _swipedCell = nil;
    }

}
```

Rerun the project now, and you will see that swiping a cell toggles any previously swiped cell.

Resetting Swiped Cells When the Table Scrolls

You've not quite finished; the final piece of the jigsaw is to reset any swiped cells if the `tableView` scrolls.

To do this, you can exploit the fact that `UITableView` is a subclass of `UIScrollView`, which means that the `tableView` has a `scrollViewDidScroll:` method that fires whenever it scrolls.

Add the method in Listing 10–25 to the bottom of the `SwipeTableController.m` file (it doesn't need to be declared in the header, because it's a `UIScrollView` method).

Listing 10–25. *The `scrollViewDidScroll:` Method*

```
-(void)scrollViewDidScroll:(UIScrollView *)scrollView {

    if (_swipedCell) {

        SwipeCell *currentlySwipedCell = (SwipeCell *)[self.tableView ➥
cellForRowAtIndexPath:_swipedCell];
        [currentlySwipedCell didSwipeLeftInCell:self];

    }

}
```

This isn't too tricky. If there's currently a swiped cell when the `tableView` scrolls, the method grabs a reference to the cell and fires the `didSwipeLeftInCell:` method to "unswipe" it.

If you run the project now, you'll see the top view slide back into place as soon as the table moves.

Adding Pull-to-Refresh to Table Views

Every so often, a new piece of user interface functionality comes along that makes you think, "Why has no one ever done this before?" (In my case, often followed by "Why didn't I think of that?")

Pull-to-refresh is one of those things.

In hindsight, it's so wonderfully simple, it's surprising that it took so long to appear. I first noticed it in the late and much lamented Tweetie app, and it's subsequently appeared in all kinds of apps; maybe one day Apple might even get around to implementing it in Mail?

Pull-to-refresh is an action that triggers the refresh of a table's data in response to the user pulling the table *down past the top*, and then letting go. Instead of springing straight back, you usually see some kind of activity indicator. Once the data has been updated (or sometimes, if the network call times out) the table "springs" back up again, and the contents get refreshed.

It's a brilliant piece of interface design, devastatingly simple, and something that quickly becomes second nature to users.

There are various open-source libraries out there that you can plug into your apps to give your tables pull-to-refresh functionality, but the problem with using libraries to solve this kind of problem is that you won't necessarily get to understand how the underlying functionality works.

It's not difficult to do, though, so let's enhance the table that you've just added swipe-to-reveal to by adding a very basic pull-to-refresh function.

> **NOTE:** The various open-source libraries out there are considerably more sophisticated and polished than the code we're about to implement, but they're also more complex and difficult to figure out at first. By adding a very basic implementation, you will see how the underlying process works.

How Pull-to-Refresh Works

Pull-to-refresh works by exploiting a delegate method of `UIScrollView`. If you recall from earlier, `UITableView` is a subclass of `UIScrollView`, and so inherits all its methods and delegate protocols.

The `UIScrollViewDelegate` protocol has a number of methods that are triggered by scrolling stopping and starting, which allows the application to react to the user initiating a scrolling action.

Scrolling has two facets: the user dragging a finger up, down, or across the screen, and the `tableView`'s scrolling in response.

It's important to bear in mind that the dragging and scrolling can be separate. That's how `tableViews` continue to scroll under their own momentum after a "flick" gesture.

The delegate method of particularly interest is `scrollViewDidEndDragging:willDecelerate:`

```
    -(void)scrollViewDidEndDragging:(UIScrollView *)scrollView ↩
willDecelerate:(BOOL)decelerate;
```

This method is triggered by the user lifting a finger from the screen, after having dragged the table up or down. You can use this to figure out where the `tableView` has been scrolled to by checking the `tableView`'s `contentOffset` property.

`contentOffset` is measured in pixels from the top of the first row of the `tableView`. If the `tableView` had a `contentSize` of say, 1,000 pixels, and was scrolled so that the halfway point of the table was at the top of the `tableView`'s frame, then the `contentOffset` would be 500 pixels.

What's not immediately obvious is that the `tableView` can have a *negative* `contentOffset`. If you flick a table back to the top, it "bounces," appearing to scroll beyond the top of the first row, and then bouncing back again.

Figure 10–9 illustrates this: the table is in the process of being dragged down from the top, which creates a gap at the top. The height of this gap is the negative content offset. (The size of the content offset is exaggerated in the diagram for clarity.)

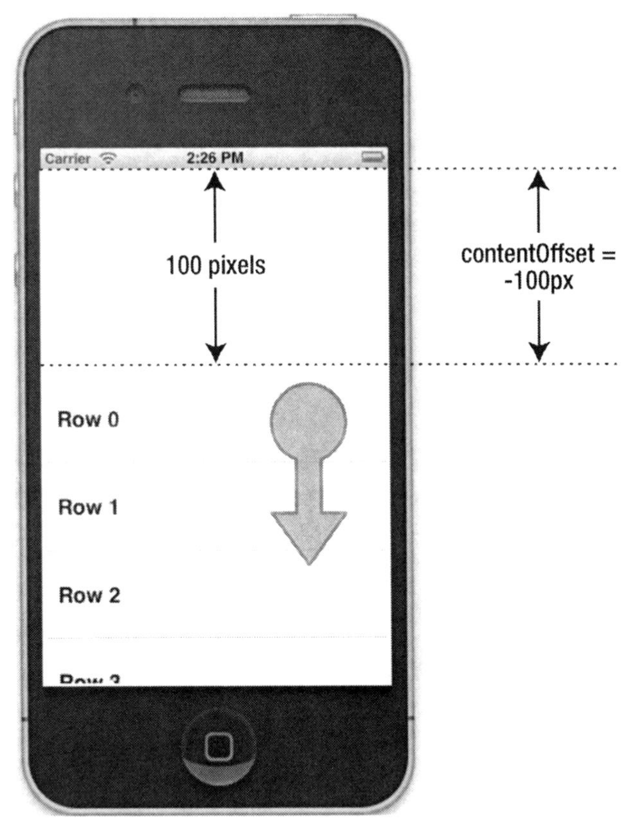

Figure 10–9. *A negative* `contentOffset`

At the instant that the user lifts their finger, the `scrollViewDidEndDragging:willDecelerate:` method will be called. If you check in that method whether the `contentOffset` is negative, you can find out if the table has been pulled down.

You need to be a little bit careful here, though: the table can go into negative offset when it bounces, so if you're going to use the presence of negative offset to trigger some action (such as a table refresh) then you will need to make sure that it's greater than would occur during a bounce. The exact value is something you'll want to play with, but I find somewhere around 60 pixels normally works quite well.

Implementing Pull-to-Refresh

Let's put this together: you will enhance the swipe-to-reveal table so that it triggers a simulated refresh action. Dragging the `tableView` down more than 60 pixels will display an activity spinner at the top, and then once the "update" has taken place the `tableView` will slide back up to the top, as shown in Figure 10–10.

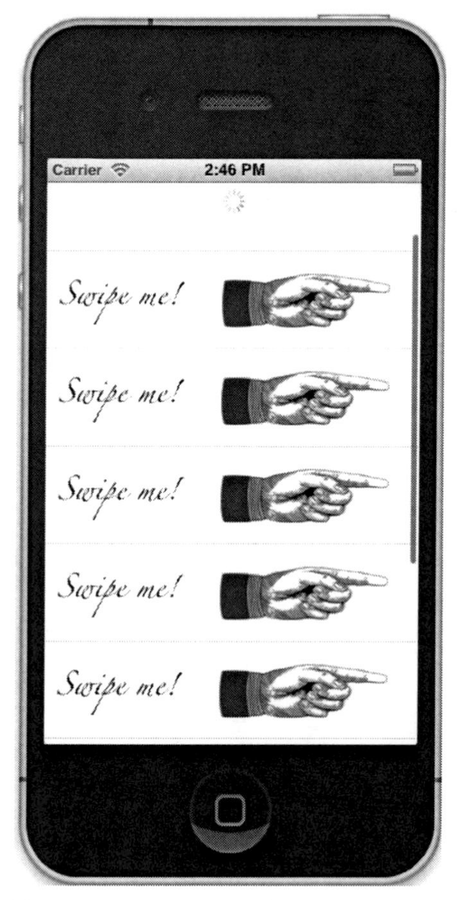

Figure 10–10. *The table with pull-to-refresh implemented*

The first thing you need to do is declare and synthesize some properties in the tableViewController:

```
@property (nonatomic, strong) UIWindow *mainWindow;
@property (nonatomic, strong) UIActivityIndicatorView *activityIndicator;
@property (nonatomic, strong) UIView *activityView;
```

You will also need a couple of methods to show and remove the activity spinner:

```
-(void)displayActivitySpinner;
-(void)removeActivitySpinner;
```

In a moment, you will need to add a view to the main window above the tableView, so you will need a reference to this. You will also need to set the background color of the main window to white so it matches the color of the tableView, shown in Listing 10–26.

Listing 10–26. *The viewDidAppear: Method*

```
- (void)viewDidAppear:(BOOL)animated
{
    [super viewDidAppear:animated];

    _mainWindow = [[UIApplication sharedApplication] keyWindow];
    [_mainWindow setBackgroundColor:[UIColor whiteColor]];

}
```

The next step is shown in Listing 10–27, which implements the UIScrollViewDelegate method that will capture the end of the drag.

Listing 10–27. *The scrollViewDidEndDragging:willDecelerate: Method*

```
-(void)scrollViewDidEndDragging:(UIScrollView *)scrollView ↩
willDecelerate:(BOOL)decelerate {

    CGFloat contentOffsetY = scrollView.contentOffset.y;

    if (contentOffsetY < -60.0) {
        [self displayActivitySpinner];
    }

}
```

This does two things: it captures the contentOffset of the tableView at the instant that the user's finger touches up, and checks whether it's less than minus 60 pixels (in other words, if the top of the table is pulled down less than 60 pixels, it won't trigger the "update").

Assuming that the tableView has moved more than 60 pixels, it fires the displayActivitySpinner method shown in Listing 10–28.

Listing 10–28. *The displayActivitySpinner Method*

```
-(void)displayActivitySpinner {

    _activityView = [[UIView alloc] initWithFrame:CGRectMake(0, 0, 320, 60)];
    [_activityView setBackgroundColor:[UIColor whiteColor]];
```

```
    _activityIndicator = [[UIActivityIndicatorView alloc] ➥
initWithActivityIndicatorStyle:UIActivityIndicatorViewStyleGray];
    [_activityIndicator setFrame:CGRectMake(145, 20, 30, 30)];
    [_activityIndicator startAnimating];
    [_activityView addSubview:_activityIndicator];

    [_mainWindow addSubview:_activityView];

    [UIView animateWithDuration:0.25 animations:^{
        [self.tableView setFrame:CGRectMake(0, 60, 320, 480)];
    } completion:^(BOOL finished) {
        [NSTimer scheduledTimerWithTimeInterval:2.0 target:self ➥
selector:@selector(removeActivitySpinner) userInfo:nil repeats:NO];
    }];
}
```

Let's step through this.

The first thing to do is to create a `UIView` that will be displayed above the top of the table and will contain the activity spinner:

```
    _activityView = [[UIView alloc] initWithFrame:CGRectMake(0, 0, 320, 60)];
    [_activityView setBackgroundColor:[UIColor whiteColor]];
```

It's good manners to show the user that something is happening in the background, so you can use a `UIActivityIndicator` for this, and add it to the middle of the `UIView` that you just created:

```
    _activityIndicator = [[UIActivityIndicatorView alloc] ➥
initWithActivityIndicatorStyle:UIActivityIndicatorViewStyleGray];
    [_activityIndicator setFrame:CGRectMake(145, 20, 30, 30)];
    [_activityIndicator startAnimating];
    [_activityView addSubview:_activityIndicator];
```

Then the `UIView` gets added to the `mainWindow`:

```
    [_mainWindow addSubview:_activityView];
```

Now it's time to move the `tableView` down to reveal the activity spinner. Once it's moved, in a "production" app you would call the method that refreshes the table's source data. This might involve downloading data from an online API somewhere; once the data have been retrieved, the table would be updated and then the `removeActivitySpinner` method called.

To update the whole table, call

```
    [tableView reloadData];
```

which fires all the familiar `dataSource` methods.

An alternative, if you've only got a few rows to reload, is the `reloadRowsAtIndexPaths:withRowAnimation:` method. This takes an array of the `indexPaths` that need updating in the first parameter.

If you've only got a single value to update, you could get a reference to the specific cell using:

```
    UITableViewCell *cellToUpdate = [tableView cellForRowAtIndexPath:indexPath];
```

Update the cell's properties with whatever data has been retrieved, and then call setNeedsDisplay on the cell:

```
cellToUpdate.value = [sourceData objectAtIndex:indexPath.row];
[cellToUpdate setNeedsDisplay];
```

For the purposes of demonstration, though, I've cheated by simply setting a delay before calling the removeActivitySpinner method. In reality, you'd probably be calling an external class to retrieve network data, and so might end up implementing removeActivitySpinner as a delegate method for the data retrieval class.

To make the interface a bit slicker, the movement is animated with a UIView animation block. The tableView's frame is shifted down by 60 pixels to reveal the activity spinner; then the completion block calls removeActivitySpinner after a short delay:

```
[UIView animateWithDuration:0.25 animations:^{

    [self.tableView setFrame:CGRectMake(0, 60, 320, 480)];

} completion:^(BOOL finished) {

    [NSTimer scheduledTimerWithTimeInterval:2.0 target:self ↵
selector:@selector(removeActivitySpinner) userInfo:nil repeats:NO];

}];
```

After a two-second delay (the fake data items are being retrieved from a snappy API!) the removeActivitySpinner method stops the activity spinner and removes it, then moves the tableView back up to the top of the window, shown in Listing 10–29.

Listing 10–29. *The removeActivitySpinner Method*

```
-(void)removeActivitySpinner {

    [_activityIndicator stopAnimating];
    [_activityView removeFromSuperview];

    [UIView animateWithDuration:0.250 animations:^{

        CGRect currentTableRect = self.tableView.frame;
        [self.tableView setFrame:CGRectMake(currentTableRect.origin.x, ↵
currentTableRect.origin.y - 40, currentTableRect.size.width, ↵
currentTableRect.size.height)];

    }];

}
```

The animation durations are probably longer than you'd want in a production application, but this is another situation where testing on a physical device is critically important to fine-tune the user experience.

If the table's data items were being loaded from a networked data source (such as an API) it would also be important to implement a time-out function so that the app doesn't get stuck in pull-to-refresh mode if the remote server isn't responding.

Searching in Tables

If you've got a table view displaying any significant amount of data, you owe it to your users to give them the means to navigate around easily. There's nothing more frustrating than having to scroll through hundreds of entries in search of the one that you're after.

Previously you've looked at adding indexes to the `tableView`; that's a good way of enabling the user to jump between sections. But sometimes even that's not enough. Wouldn't it be much better if you could provide a means of searching the content of the table so the user could find the row for which they were looking?

Fortunately in iOS 3 Apple introduced the `UISearchDisplayController` class and its associated delegate protocols. This class makes implementing search in table views almost trivially easy; building the same functionality from scratch would be significantly more work.

How the UISearchDisplayController Works

The `UISearchDisplayController` adds two elements to the view: a Search Bar, which is displayed at the top of the `tableView` and a Search Display Controller object, shown in Figure 10–11.

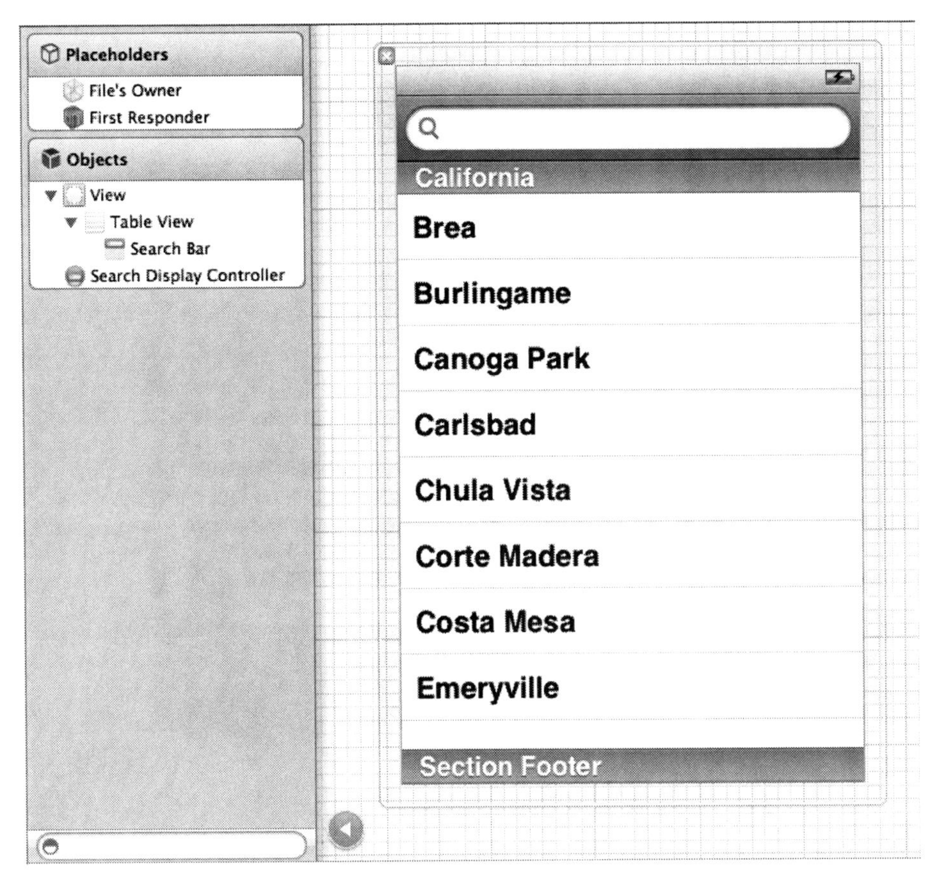

Figure 10–11. *Adding the Search Display Controller*

When the users tap in the search bar, a modal keyboard slides up from the bottom of the screen to allow them to enter the search text. All of the keyboard functionality is automated, so you don't need to worry about dealing with making it disappear when cancelled and so on.

As the user types in the search bar, typically the `searchDisplayController:shouldReloadTableForSearchString:` method is called, which in turn calls the `filterContentForSearchText:scope:` method to search through the table's source data and insert the results into a mutable array.

As soon as there are any results, the Search Display Controller displays a modal `tableView` and loads it with the contents of the filtered results array. The modal `tableView` uses the cell style from the main table, so to the user it appears as if the searching is taking place in the main table (see Figure 10–12).

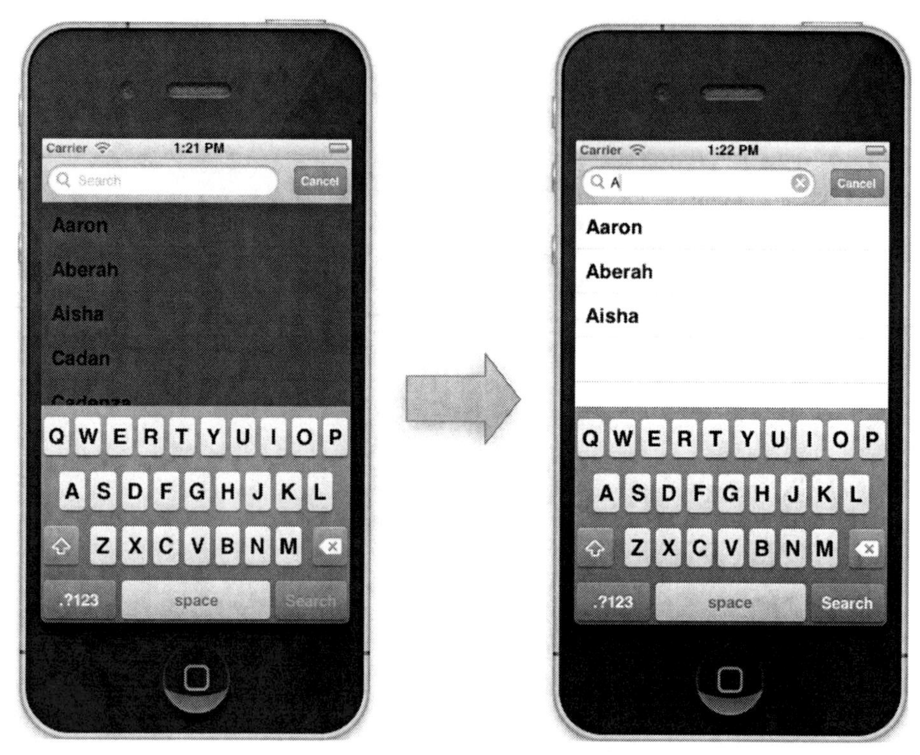

Figure 10–12. *Filtering the results as the user types*

Optionally, you can also add a button bar of "scopes"; these can be used to narrow down the search selection to a specific category of objects in your source data (e.g., you might want to add scopes to search within "Boys' names" or "Girls' names" and so on.)

Fortunately, the combination of Search Display Controller and protocols make the implementation a lot simpler than that description might lead you to think.

The process runs like this:

1. Conform the `tableView`'s controller to the `UISearchBarDelegate` and `UISearchDisplayDelegate` protocols.
2. Add a property to the `tableView`'s controller to hold the search results.
3. Add the Search Bar and Search Display Controller to the `tableView` in the nib file, and connect the various outlets.
4. Add the delegate methods, and the search method to the controller:
    - `searchDisplayController:shouldReloadTableForSearchString:`
    - `filterContentForSearchText:scope:`

5. Tweak the `numberOfRowsInSection:`, the `tableView:cellForRowAtIndexPath:` and `tableView:didSelectRowAtIndexPath:` methods to handle the newly installed search results table.

Adding the Search Bar Protocols

In order to add the search functionality, the `tableView`'s controller needs to adopt two protocols: `UISearchBarDelegate` and `UISearchDisplayDelegate`. That's just a case of adding these to the controller's header file. While you're there, it's also a good point to add a property for the mutable array that will (eventually) hold the results of the search, as in Listing 10–30.

Listing 10–30. *The Amended Header File*

```
#import <UIKit/UIKit.h>

@interface TableController : UITableViewController <UISearchBarDelegate, ↩
UISearchDisplayDelegate>

@property (nonatomic, strong) IBOutlet UITableView *tableView;

@property (nonatomic, strong) NSArray *tableData;
@property (nonatomic, strong) NSMutableArray *filteredTableData;

@end
```

Adding the Search Bar to the Table

The Search Bar and the Search Display Controller come as a pair, and can be found in the Objects browser, shown in Figure 10–13.

Figure 10–13. *The Search Bar and Search Display Controller*

When you drag this out from the Object browser into the view area, it will appear as a search bar. Hover over the top of the table, and it will drop into place when you release the mouse button (see Figure 10–14).

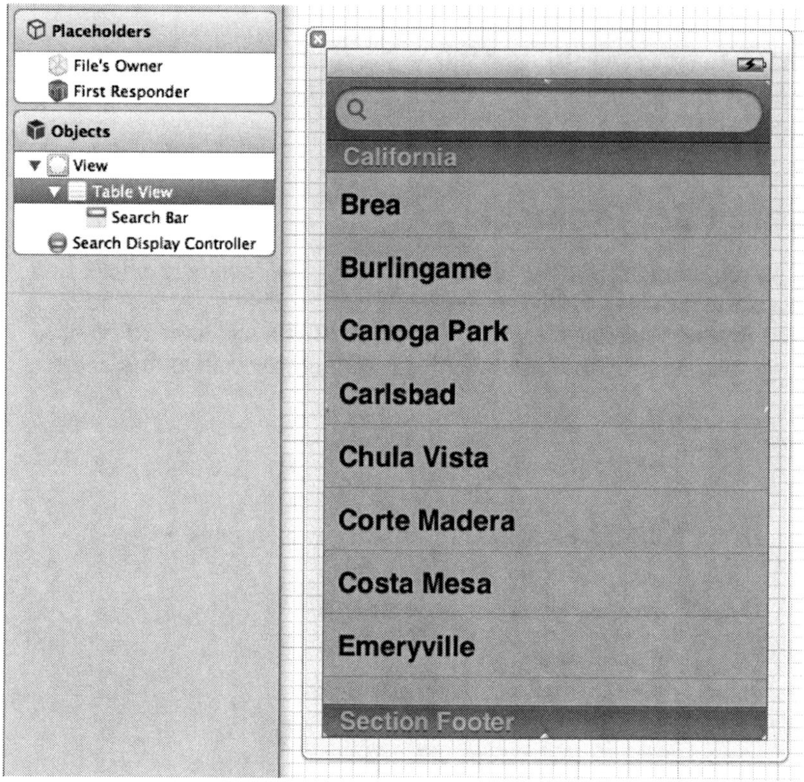

Figure 10–14. Adding the Search Bar

The Search Bar and the Search Display Controller *should* arrive in the nib file with the correct outlet connections, but Figure 10–15 displays what they are in case of problems.

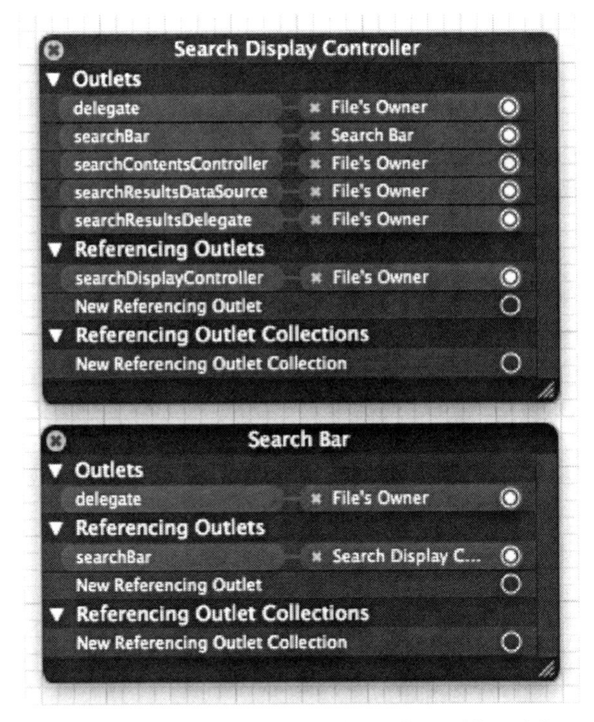

Figure 10–15. *The Search Display Controller and Search Bar outlet connections*

(Optionally) Setting Up the Scopes

The Scope Bar (Figure 10–16) optionally appears when the user clicks in the search bar; to enable this you need to:

- Select the 'Show Scope Bar" tick box in the Search Bar's options.
- Add text for the scope buttons in the Scope Titles section.

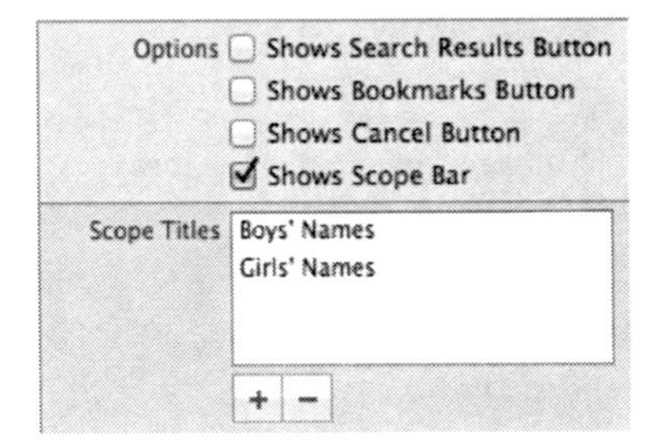

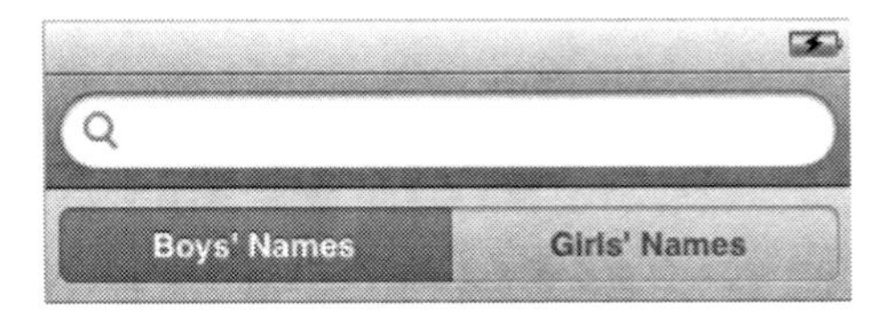

Figure 10–16. *Setting up the Scope Bar*

Adding the Delegate and Search Methods

Now it's the turn of the table view controller's implementation to be tweaked. It needs the `searchDisplayController:shouldReloadTableForSearchString:` and `filterContentForSearchText:scope:` methods shown in Listings 10–31 and 10–32.

Listing 10–31. *The `searchDisplayController:shouldReloadTableForSearchString:` Method*

```
- (BOOL)searchDisplayController:(UISearchDisplayController *)controller ➥
shouldReloadTableForSearchString:(NSString *)searchString
{

    [self filterContentForSeachText:searchString ➥
scope:[self.searchDisplayController.searchBar.scopeButtonTitles ➥
objectAtIndex:self.searchDisplayController.searchBar.selectedScopeButtonIndex]];

    // Return YES to cause the search result table view to be reloaded.
    return YES;
}
```

Listing 10–32. *The `searchDisplayController:shouldReloadTableForSearchScope:` Method*

```
- (BOOL)searchDisplayController:(UISearchDisplayController *)controller ➥
shouldReloadTableForSearchScope:(NSInteger)searchOption
{
    [self filterContentForSearchText:[self.searchDisplayController.searchBar text]  ➥
 scope: [[self.searchDisplayController.searchBar scopeButtonTitles] ➥
objectAtIndex:searchOption]];

    // Return YES to cause the search result table view to be reloaded.
    return YES;
}
```

These two methods take the search string and search scope, respectively, and call the `filterContentForSearchText:scope:` method shown in Listing 10–33.

Listing 10–33. *The `filterContentForSearchText:scope:` Method*

```
- (void)filterContentForSearchText:(NSString*)searchText scope:(NSString*)scope
{

        [self.filteredTableData removeAllObjects]; // First clear the filtered array.

        for (NameObject *name in tableData)
        {
                if ([scope isEqualToString:@"All"] || [name.gender ➥
isEqualToString:scope])
                {
                        NSComparisonResult result = [name compare:searchText ➥
options:(NSCaseInsensitiveSearch|NSDiacriticInsensitiveSearch) ➥
range:NSMakeRange(0, [searchText length])];
              if (result == NSOrderedSame)
                        {
                                [self.filteredTableData addObject:name];
              }
                }
```

```
        }
}
```

The details of this method obviously depend on the table's source data, but the basic principles are the same: first, the filteredTableData array is emptied to remove any existing search results. Then, the method iterates across the source data array and does a comparison between the contents of the search bar and the data object. If there's a match, then that object is added to the filteredTableData array that then acts as the data source for the Search Display Controller's table.

Updating Methods with tableView Parameters

Because there are now potentially two tableViews in action—your "original" one and the tableView displayed by the Search Display Controller that shows the results of the search. To cater for this, you will need to amend any method that takes a tableView as a parameter so that it can distinguish between the original table and the search version.

In this app, you'll need to amend the tableView:cellForRowAtIndexPath:, numberOfRowsInSection: and tableView:didSelectRowAtIndexPath: methods to handle the search results table.

```
if (tableView == self.searchDisplayController.searchResultsTableView) {

    // handle the search results table

} else {

    // handle the "normal" table

}
```

More Details on Search Display Controllers

At the time of writing, Apple provide a fully worked example of implementing a Search Display Controller bundled with the source code accompanying Xcode; search Xcode's documentation for the TableSearch project.

Happy, Healthy Tables

If the overall user experience of the iOS device family had to be boiled down to a single adjective, I'd go for "smooth." Everything about the interface of well-written apps moves without hesitation, stuttering, or jerkiness. Get it right, and the overall impression is that of a precision, well-oiled device.

Table views have a lot of moving parts, so if that level of smoothness is going to go wrong anywhere, it could be here. Although the UITableView and its supporting classes are designed and written for performance, it *is* possible to build table views that don't perform well, especially if you lose sight of some basic best practices.

In this section, we take a look at some things you can do—both quick fixes, and some more in-depth—to make sure that your tables perform as well as they possibly can.

Are the Cells Cached?

Building cells is expensive in processing terms, so the `UITableView` class provides caching and dequeuing functionality to allow constructed cells to be reused. This can make a dramatic difference if you've got more rows than can fit on the screen.

The place to check is the `tableView:cellForRowAtIndexPath:` method. For maximum efficiency, you should be doing one of two things:

- Attempting to dequeue an existing reusable cell before creating an new instance:

```
static NSString *CellIdentifier = @"CellIdentifier";

UITableViewCell *cell = [tableView ➥
dequeueReusableCellWithIdentifier:CellIdentifier];

    if (cell == nil) {
        cell = [[UITableViewCell alloc] ➥
initWithStyle:UITableViewCellStyleDefault reuseIdentifier:CellIdentifier];

    }
```

- Registering a nib file containing the cell layout:

```
static NSString *CellIdentifier = @"CellIdentifier";

[tableView registerNib:[UINib nibWithNibName:@"MyCell" bundle:nil] ➥
forCellReuseIdentifier:CellIdentifier];
```

The only exceptions to the first rule is if you are dealing with a static table; or if you'll never have more cells than will fit into the visible area. In that latter situation you can probably get away without cached cells, as they'll always remain visible.

Do Your Table Cells Have Varying Heights?

Behind the scenes, `UITableView` uses the cell height to build a number of elements relating to the "chrome" of the table. When all cells in the `tableView` are the same height, this can be done relatively cheaply, but if the cell height varies, these calculations get repeated every time a new cell is created.

To extract the last ounce of speed from a table view, it's more efficient to keep the cell heights identical. Whether this is possible is going to vary from project to project of course, but if your cell heights only vary within a limited range, you may find you're better off by designing them with a single consistent height and managing the differences within the internal cell layout.

Cut the Cost of Compositing

The iPhone and iPad have incredibly powerful GPUs considering the limitations of the form factor and battery constraints. Even so, they do have limits, and one thing that pushes at those limits is drawing views with transparency.

The reason is fairly apparent when you think about it. Put crudely, the device builds the view front-to-back and if a front layer is opaque, it doesn't need to bother with even considering what lies behind it when rendering the screen.

Create a layer with transparent pixels, though, and that calculation has to take place, and the more calculations that are needed, the slower the rendering process will become.

Life would be great if all elements of a view could be opaque, but of course it's never that simple. Gradients, drop shadows, and the like are all illusions that are only possible thanks to transparency, so a purely opaque interface would be a pretty dull one.

The key to maximum application performance is to use transparency only where it's needed. That then poses another dilemma: how can you tell what's transparent and what isn't? Fortunately, there's a tool that can help.

Checking Transparency with Instruments

Instruments is a powerful and often underutilized application that allows you to peer deep inside the workings of your apps. One of the features that it provides enables the visualization of the level of transparency in your views, which can then be used to fine-tune your interfaces.

The **Core Animation** instrument, as its name suggests, gives you a set of tools to examine what's going on with the interface drawing functions; this is what we use to check up on the transparency situation.

> **CAUTION:** Although many of Instruments' features will work with both devices and the Simulators, the feature of the Core Animation instrument that this technique uses currently only works on a physical device. You need to have an iPhone or iPad tethered to run these tools.

To start the analysis, connect your device and select it in the Scheme dropdown. Then select the **Product ➤ Profile** menu, which will build the project and fire up Instruments as shown in Figure 10–17.

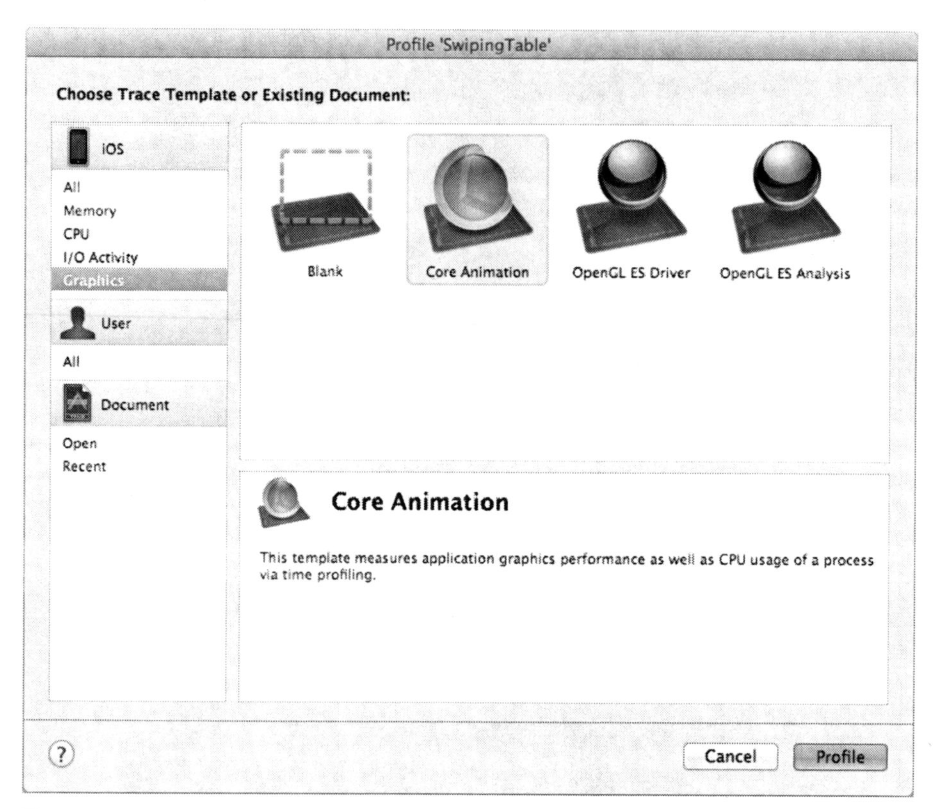

Figure 10–17. *Instruments' template window*

You'll be presented with the list of built-in templates; select the Graphics item from the left-hand menu, highlight **Core Animation**, then click the **Profile** button.

> **CAUTION:** Just as the default templates provided with Xcode change with each new release, so the templates that arrive with Instruments tend to alter. By the time you read this, things may well have changed again.

The Instruments window will appear after a few seconds, looking similar to Figure 10–18, and the app will be launched on the attached device.

Figure 10–18. *The Instruments app*

> **TIP:** If you don't see the list of options in the bottom-left quadrant of the window, click and drag the bottom bar up towards the middle of the window.

The magic occurs when you select the "**Color Blended Layers**" checkbox in the Debug Options area, shown in Figure 10–19.

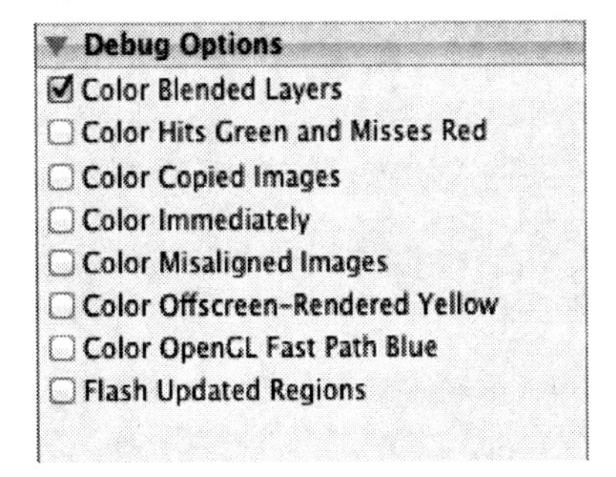

Figure 10–19. *The Debug options list*

This will apply a colored overlay to each view in the app window on the device. The overlay is colored from green (completely opaque) to red (completely transparent).

Figure 10–20 shows an example of a deliberately hideous interface with lots of varying degrees of transparency.

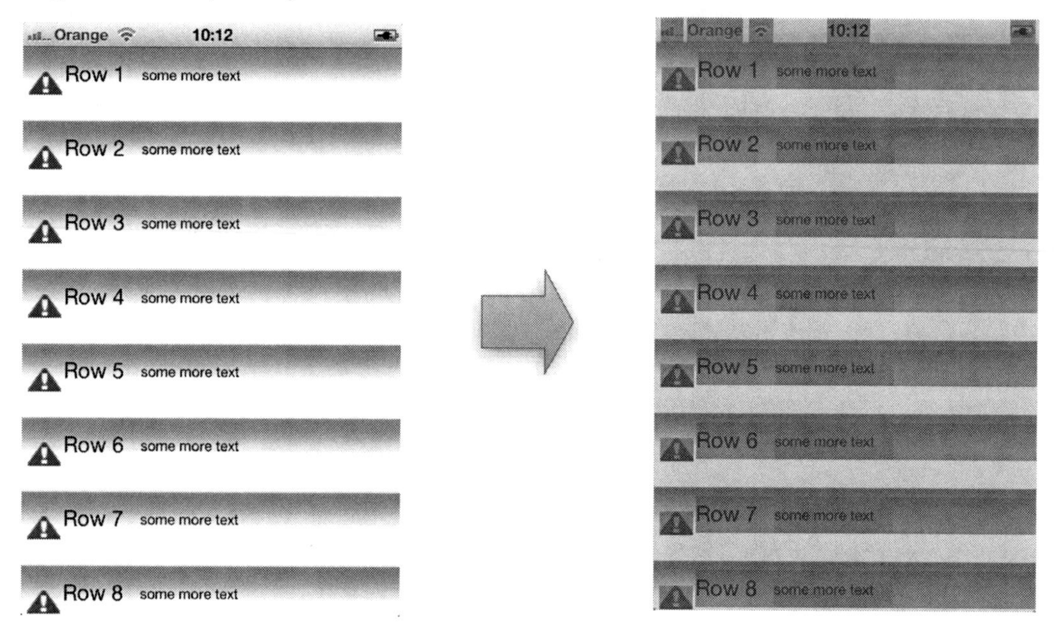

Figure 10–20. *The effect of turning on the Color Blended Layers option*

As you can see, there's a lot of transparency going on here, which is unsurprising when you look at the code (Listing 10–34) that builds the cell.

Listing 10–34. *Part of the `tableView:cellForRowAtIndexPath:` Method*

```
// Configure the cell...
    UIImageView *gradientImage = [[UIImageView alloc] ➥
initWithFrame:CGRectMake(0, 0, 320, 60)];
    [gradientImage setImage:[UIImage imageNamed:@"gradientBackground"]];

    UILabel *theLabel = [[UILabel alloc] initWithFrame:CGRectMake(35, 7, 300, 30)];
    [theLabel setText:[_tableData objectAtIndex:indexPath.row]];
    [theLabel setFont:[UIFont systemFontOfSize:18]];
    [theLabel setBackgroundColor:[UIColor clearColor]];

    UILabel *theSubtitle = [[UILabel alloc] initWithFrame:CGRectMake(100, 7, 100, 30)];
    [theSubtitle setText:@"some more text"];
    [theSubtitle setFont:[UIFont systemFontOfSize:12]];
    [theSubtitle setBackgroundColor:[UIColor clearColor]];

    UIImageView *iconView = [[UIImageView alloc] ➥
initWithFrame:CGRectMake(5, 20, 28, 19)];
    [iconView setImage:[UIImage imageNamed:@"warning"]];

    [cell.contentView addSubview:gradientImage];
    [cell.contentView addSubview:theLabel];
    [cell.contentView addSubview:theSubtitle];
    [cell.contentView addSubview:iconView];
```

Reducing the amount of transparency means rejigging the cell a bit. To start with, perhaps it's possible to reduce the size of the background gradient a bit, shown in Figure 10–21.

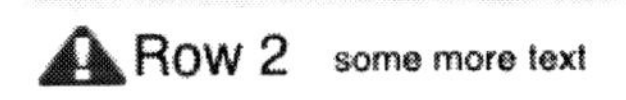

Figure 10–21. *Less gradient*

This now means that the cell's subheading sits over a completely white background so there's no need for that to have a transparent background color (shown in Figure 10–22.)

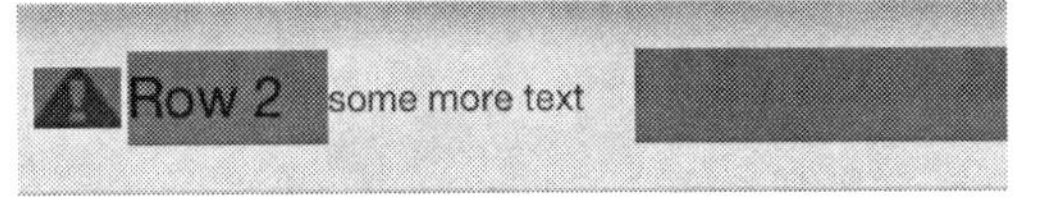

Figure 10–22. *A solid subtitle*

Good, but still room for improvement. Let's do the same with the main label, and see if still fits with the gradient background (Figure 10–23).

Figure 10–23. *Getting there*

Not too bad. The cell's icon is still a problem, though; this is a PNG image that has an alpha channel. If it had a solid white background instead, that would help (see Figure 10–24).

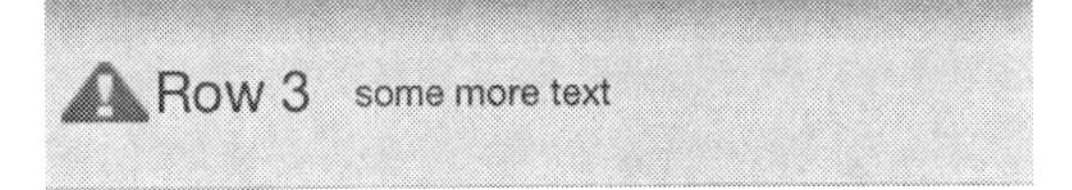

Figure 10–24. *Perfect!*

At this point you have got a green cell, indicating that all the transparency has been removed and greatly reducing the composition cost.

This is a deliberately simple example, and it's not always going to be possible to redesign the cell layouts to remove transparency completely. There's always a balancing act to be struck between optimization and staying faithful to the interface design. But if you are involved in the visual design process, transparency is always keeping in mind if you can influence the final design outcome.

Summary

In this chapter we've looked at bringing your table views to life by transforming cells from static displays of data through adding some interaction to the cells. There's a range of ways to do this:

- Embedding custom controls such as buttons, switches, and sliders within the cell
- Implementing pull-to-refresh functionality
- Adding gesture recognizers to cells to support double taps and so on
- Adding swipe functionality to reveal hidden details
- Implementing search within the table's contents

Finally, we've looked at some of the processes to ensure that the performance of your table views is as slick as possible.

Chapter 11

Table Views on iPad

Table views on the iPad work in exactly the same way as they do on the iPhone. That said, there are a few things to bear in mind when building interfaces for iPad apps.

- The larger screen means that you probably won't want the table to fill the full window; that means controlling the size when you lay out the view in Interface Builder, or setting the size programmatically.
- The greater screen real estate means that you can make cells a lot bigger (and their visual appearance correspondingly richer). Cells sized for the iPhone can seem very small and cramped on the bigger device.
- Having more space to play with makes it feasible to add a wider range of gestures to cells; the size of the iPad screen lends itself much more readily to exploiting multitouch gestures or rotations.

Having a larger user interface on the iPad also means that different kinds of controls become possible to implement. This chapter looks at the `UISplitViewController`, an iPad-specific view controller that provides a flexible two-pane interface familiar from apps such as Mail.

You'll see how the `UISplitViewController` is structured and configured, then build a skeleton app that updates a detail view in response to selections in a table view.

The UISplitViewController

The `UISplitViewController` is an iPad-specific controller that provides a way of controlling two side-by-side views: typically, the controller on the left-hand side shows a list of items in a `UITableView`, and the right-hand side shows a detail view relating to the selected item in the table.

Probably most familiar landscape split-view controller is to be found in the Mail app (Figure 11–1).

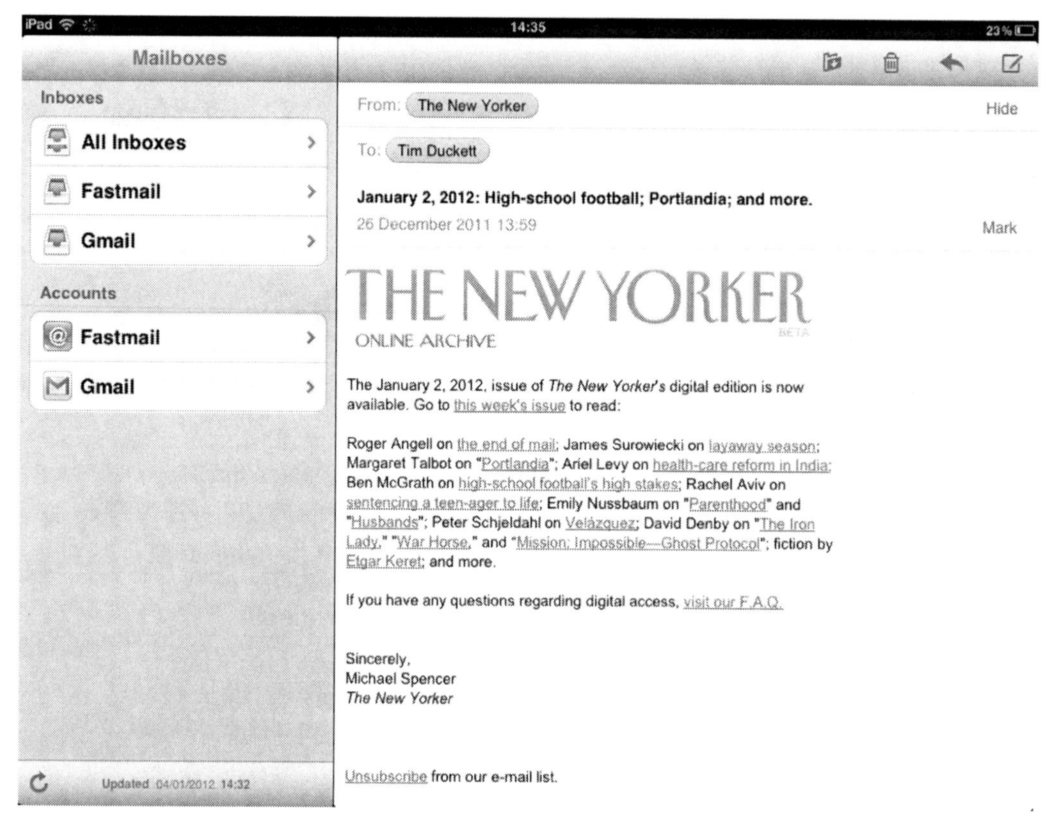

Figure 11–1. *The iPad's Mail app, an example of a landscape split-view controller*

In landscape orientation, the two views are shown side by side. When the iPad rotates into portrait orientation, the left-hand list view disappears, and the detail view fills the screen (Figure 11–2).

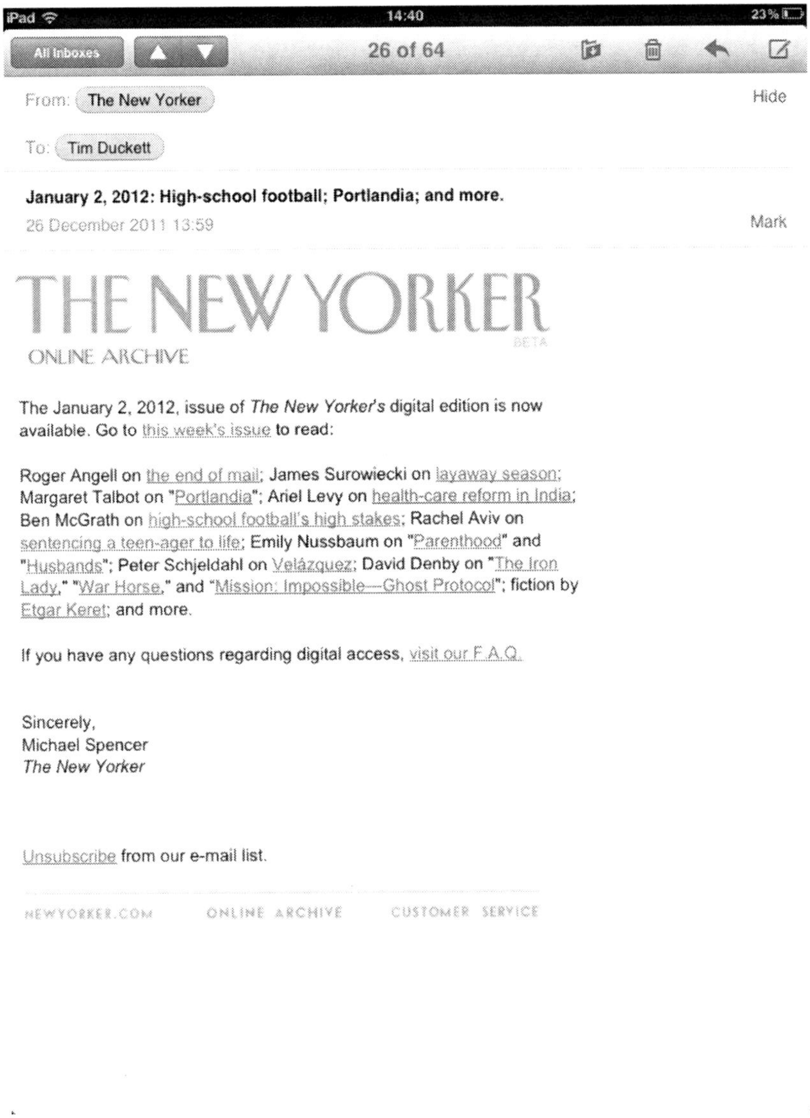

iPad 14:40 23%

All Inboxes 26 of 64

From: The New Yorker Hide

To: Tim Duckett

January 2, 2012: High-school football; Portlandia; and more.

26 December 2011 13:59 Mark

THE NEW YORKER

ONLINE ARCHIVE BETA

The January 2, 2012, issue of *The New Yorker's* digital edition is now available. Go to this week's issue to read:

Roger Angell on the end of mail; James Surowiecki on layaway season; Margaret Talbot on "Portlandia"; Ariel Levy on health-care reform in India; Ben McGrath on high-school football's high stakes; Rachel Aviv on sentencing a teen-ager to life; Emily Nussbaum on "Parenthood" and "Husbands"; Peter Schjeldahl on Velázquez; David Denby on "The Iron Lady," "War Horse," and "Mission: Impossible—Ghost Protocol"; fiction by Etgar Keret; and more.

If you have any questions regarding digital access, visit our F.A.Q.

Sincerely,
Michael Spencer
The New Yorker

Unsubscribe from our e-mail list.

NEWYORKER.COM ONLINE ARCHIVE CUSTOMER SERVICE

Figure 11–2. *The Mail app in portrait orientation; the message fills the full screen.*

Optionally, you can add a button to the navigation bar of the detail view that shows a popover controller containing the list view (in Figure 11–3, Mail's list view shows the mailboxes that this iPad is configured to use).

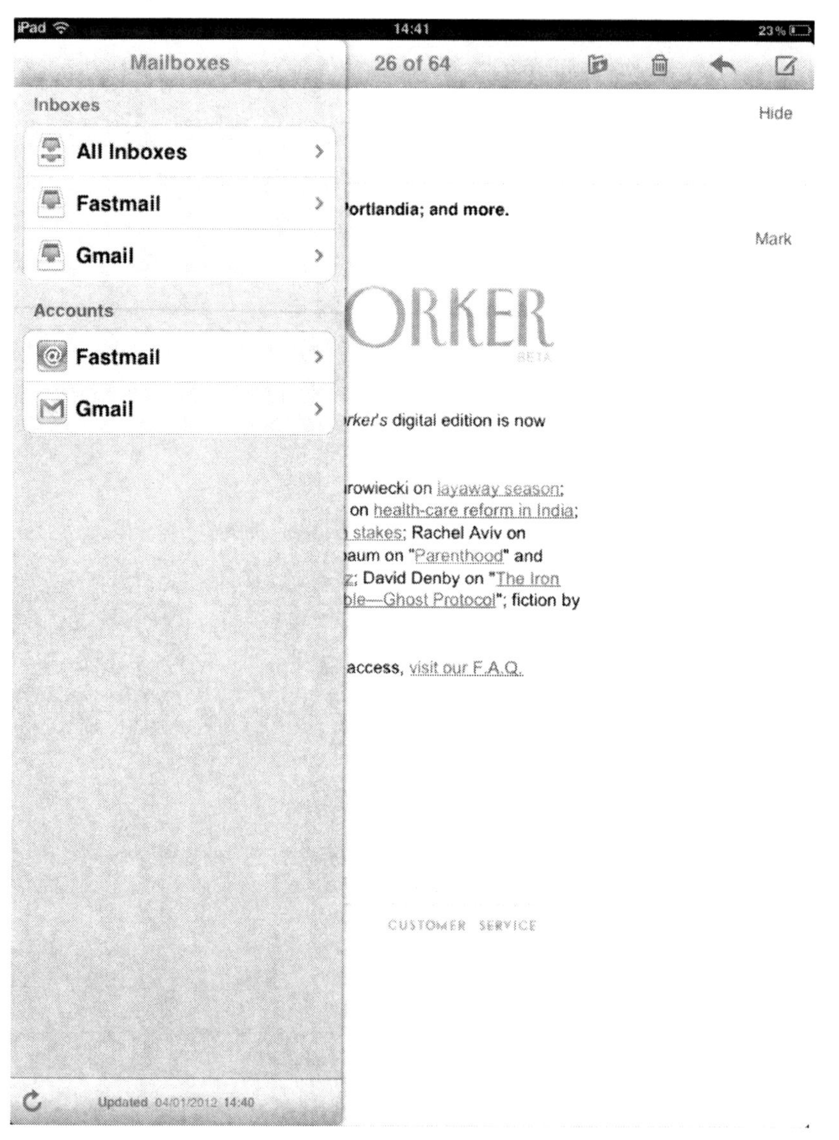

Figure 11–3. *The popover view, showing mailboxes*

The iPad's split-view controller is analogous to the way that the iPhone uses the combination of `UINavigationController` and `UITableViewController` to drill down into a detail view.

> **CAUTION:** The `UISplitViewController` is only available on the iPad. Trying to use it in an iPhone application will cause the app to crash.

Creating a UISplitViewController App

In this example, you will create a simple skeleton app that launches with a split-view controller, shows a list of items in the left-hand list view, and updates the detail view when an item is selected. It looks like Figure 11–4.

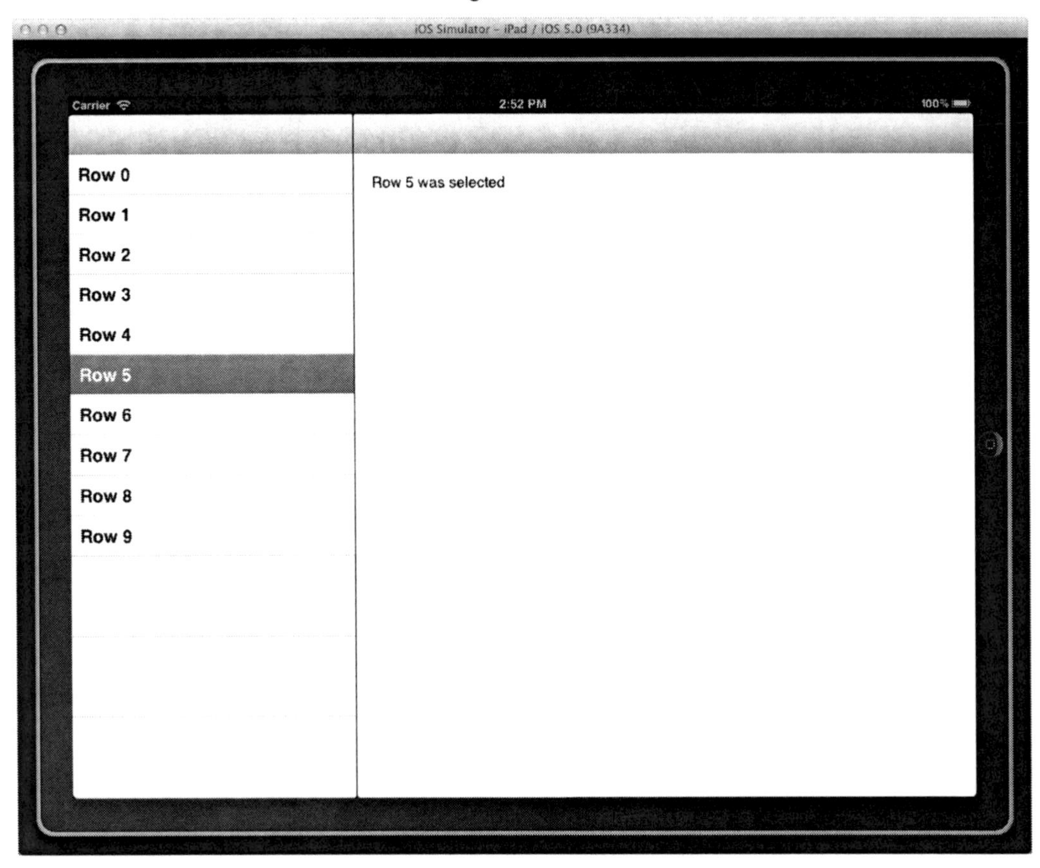

Figure 11–4. *The finished article*

Each side of the split-view controller holds a `UINavigationController`, which in turn holds a `UITableViewController` (on the left) and a `UIViewController` (on the right). A schematic view of how it fits together is shown in Figure 11–5.

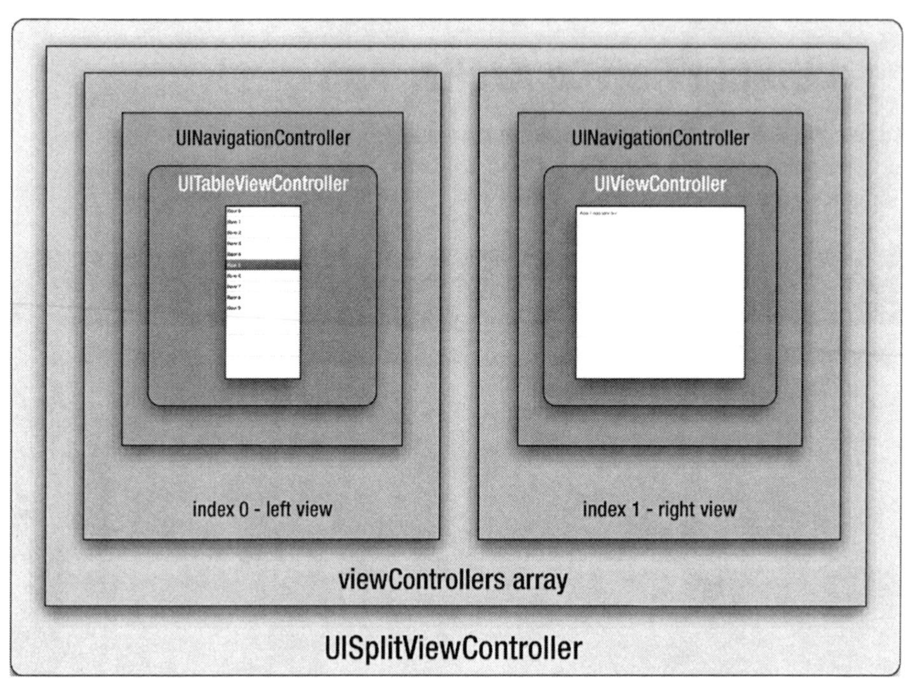

Figure 11–5. *The structure of the split-view controller*

Although it's not going to win any user interface design awards, it's functional and will give you a good skeleton for use in your (far more beautiful!) apps.

Building the app has seven stages:

1. Creating a new application from the *Single View* template, and discarding the parts you won't need
2. Creating a `UITableViewController` for the left-hand list view, and populating it with data
3. Creating a `UIViewController` for the right-hand detail view, and setting up the view's controls
4. In the `AppDelegate`, creating `UINavigationControllers` for each side, and adding the relevant controller as the root
5. Again in the `AppDelegate`, creating a `UISplitViewController` and adding the two `UINavigationControllers` to it
6. Implementing the `UISplitViewControllerDelegate` protocol methods to handle the showing and hiding of the list view after orientation changes
7. Implementing your own protocol to update the detail view in response to selections in the list view

On the face of it, that seems like quite a lot to do, but as with the UINavigationControllers that you have built in earlier chapters, in practice it's not nearly as complicated as it sounds.

> **NOTE:** Xcode ships with a *Master-Detail Application* template that provides a split-view controller for the iPad. I deliberately don't use that template in this example, not because there's anything wrong with it *per se*, but rather that by building a split-view application by hand, you get a better understanding of how the pieces fit together.
>
> In practice, there's no reason not to use the application templates if they fit your needs.

Creating a New Application

This is the simplest step of the process. Create a new project using the Single View Application template and give it a product name.

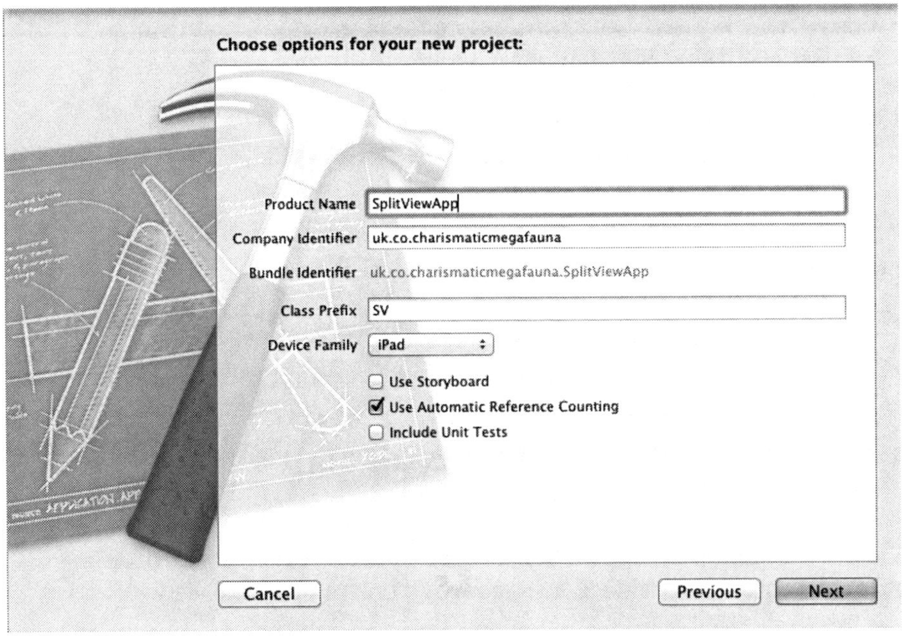

Figure 11–6. *Setting up the project options*

Make sure that the *Device Family* is set to iPad, and that the project does use Automatic Reference Counting, shown in Figure 11–6.

The Single View Application template creates a view controller that we don't need, so select these files (shown in Figure 11–7) and delete them (**Edit ➤ Delete**).

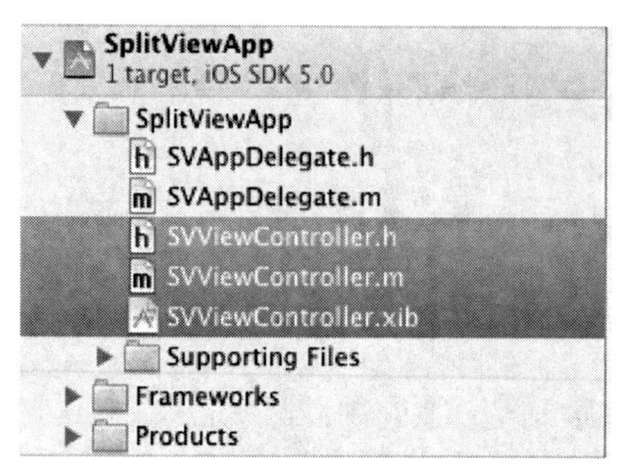

Figure 11–7. *The surplus-to-requirements files*

Make sure that you delete the files completely, not just the references. Click the Delete button as shown in Figure 11–8.

Do you want to permanently delete the 3 selected files from disk, or only remove the references to them?

This operation cannot be undone. Unsaved changes will be lost.

Cancel | Remove References Only | Delete

Figure 11–8. *Permanently delete the files*

> **CAUTION:** If you try to build the project at this point, the build will fail with missing file errors; you will fix that in a moment when we update the `AppDelegate`.

Creating the View Controllers for Each Side

Now you need to create the two view controllers that will sit in each side of the split view controller. On the left-hand side, there's the list view. A `UINavigationController` will hold a `UITableViewController` inside it, so we need to create this table view.

Add a new file to the project (**File ➤ New**) and select the `UIViewController` subclass from the templates shown in Figure 11–9.

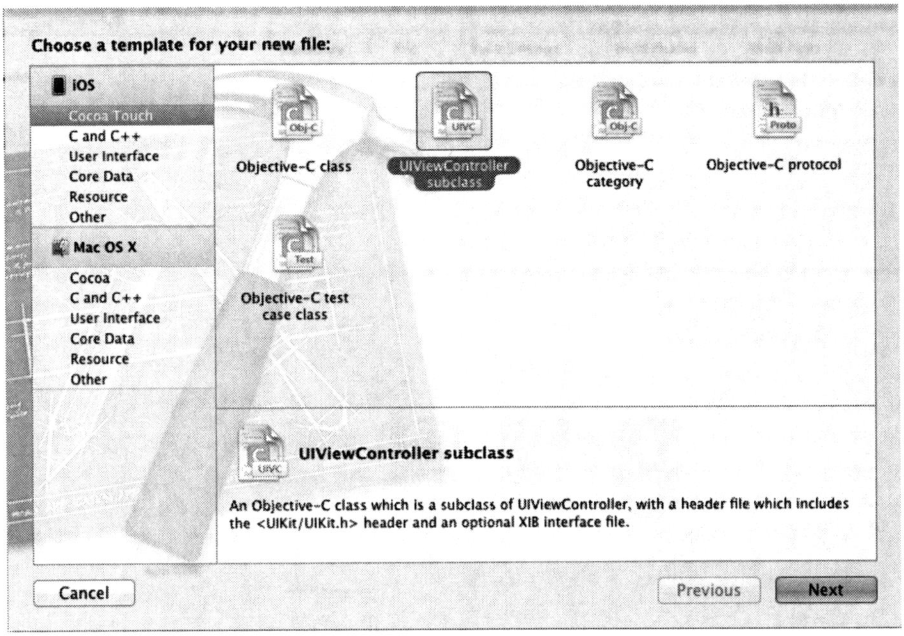

Figure 11–9. *Select the UIViewController template.*

Give this new file a name (I'm calling mine `LeftTableViewController`). Make sure :

- The new class is a subclass of `UITableViewController`
- It is targeting the iPad
- A xib file will be created

Figure 11–10 shows the options you need.

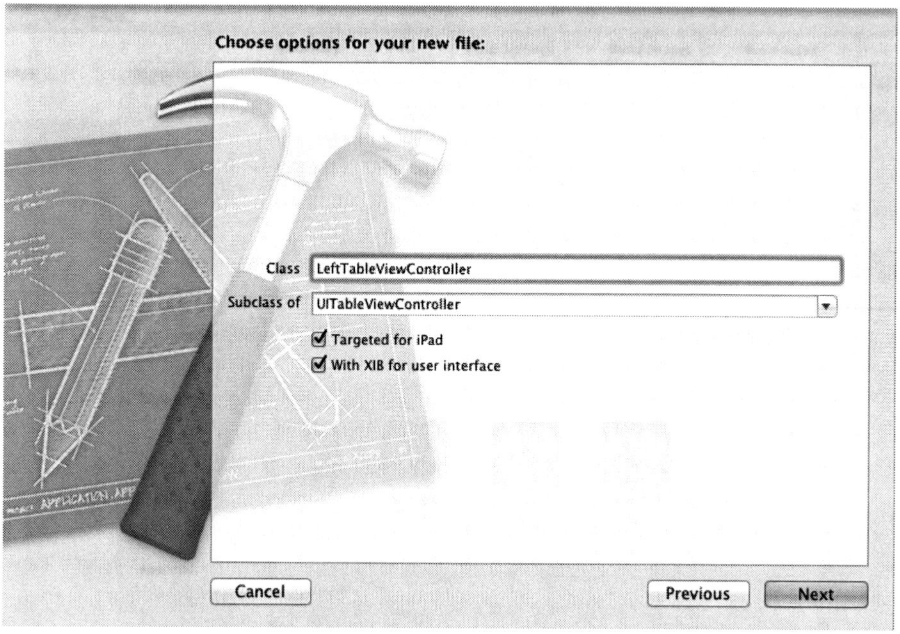

Figure 11–10. *The new view controller's options*

Next, you need to do the same for the detail view controller that will sit on the right. I'm calling mine `RightDetailViewController`.

Again, create a new file – make sure

- The new class is a subclass of `UIViewController`
- It is targeted for iPad
- A xib file will be created

The options shown in Figure 11–11.

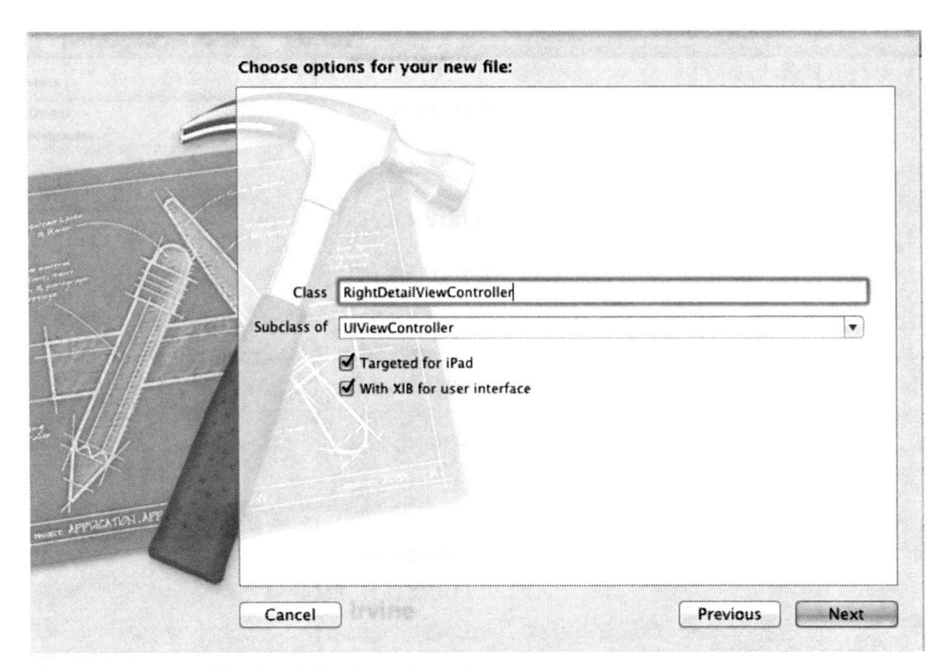

Figure 11–11. *The RightDetailViewController options*

With the two view controllers created, they need a bit of configuration so there's something to display. In the `LeftTableViewController`, update the `tableView` methods so that it displays 10 rows of some dummy content; the changes are shown in Listings 11–1 through 11–3.

Listing 11–1. *The Updated `numberOfSectionsInTableView:` Method*

```
- (NSInteger)numberOfSectionsInTableView:(UITableView *)tableView
{
    // Return the number of sections.
    return 1;
}
```

Listing 11–2. *The Updated `tableView:numberOfRowsInSection:` Method*

```
- (NSInteger)tableView:(UITableView *)tableView ➥
numberOfRowsInSection:(NSInteger)section
{
    // Return the number of rows in the section.
    return 10;
}
```

Listing 11–3. *The Updated `tableView:cellForRowAtIndexPath:` Method*

```
- (UITableViewCell *)tableView:(UITableView *)tableView ➥
cellForRowAtIndexPath:(NSIndexPath *)indexPath
{
    static NSString *CellIdentifier = @"Cell";

    UITableViewCell *cell = [tableView ➥
dequeueReusableCellWithIdentifier:CellIdentifier];
```

```
    if (cell == nil) {
        cell = [[UITableViewCell alloc] initWithStyle:UITableViewCellStyleDefault ➥
reuseIdentifier:CellIdentifier];
    }

    // Configure the cell...
    cell.textLabel.text = [NSString stringWithFormat:@"Row %d", indexPath.row];

    return cell;
}
```

You won't add anything dynamic to the detail view at this stage. Open the `RightDetailViewController`'s nib file and drop a `UILabel` into the view so there's something to display (along the lines of Figure 11–12).

Figure 11–12. *Add a `UILabel` to the `detailViewController`'s view.*

Setting up the Split-View Controller

Having created the two view controllers for each side of the split-view controller, you're now ready to start work on that.

Switch over the `AppDelegate` header file, and declare a property for the `UISplitViewController` shown in Listing 11–4.

Listing 11–4. *The `AppDelegate.h` File*

```
#import <UIKit/UIKit.h>

@interface SVAppDelegate : UIResponder <UIApplicationDelegate>

@property (strong, nonatomic) UIWindow *window;
@property (strong, nonatomic) UISplitViewController *splitViewController;

@end
```

Now switch to the implementation. At the moment it will have a reference to the view controller you deleted right at the start and a whole lot of code in the `application:didFinishLaunchingWithOptions:` method that needs to go. Clean things up so that the top of the file looks like Listing 11–5, and you will be ready to continue.

Listing 11–5. *The Top of the* `AppDelegate` *Implementation*

```
#import "SVAppDelegate.h"

@implementation SVAppDelegate

@synthesize window = _window;
@synthesize splitViewController = _splitViewController;

- (BOOL)application:(UIApplication *)application ↵
didFinishLaunchingWithOptions:(NSDictionary *)launchOptions
{
    self.window = [[UIWindow alloc] initWithFrame:[[UIScreen mainScreen] bounds]];
    // Override point for customization after application launch.


    [self.window makeKeyAndVisible];
    return YES;
}

... file continues ...

@end
```

Having cleared away the unneeded code, you need to import the two new view controllers:

```
#import "LeftTableViewController.h"
#import "RightDetailViewController.h"
```

Then it's time to set up the split-view controller in the `application:didFinishLaunchingWithOptions:` method (Listing 11–6).

Listing 11–6. *The Updated* `application:didFinishLaunchingWithOptions:` *Method*

```
- (BOOL)application:(UIApplication *)application ↵
didFinishLaunchingWithOptions:(NSDictionary *)launchOptions
{
    self.window = [[UIWindow alloc] initWithFrame:[[UIScreen mainScreen] bounds]];
    // Override point for customization after application launch.

    LeftTableViewController *leftTableVC = [[LeftTableViewController alloc] ↵
initWithNibName:@"LeftTableViewController" bundle:nil];
    UINavigationController *leftNavController = [[UINavigationController alloc] ↵
initWithRootViewController:leftTableVC];

    RightDetailViewController *rightDetailVC = [[RightDetailViewController alloc] ↵
initWithNibName:@"RightDetailViewController" bundle:nil];
    UINavigationController *rightNavController = [[UINavigationController alloc] ↵
initWithRootViewController:rightDetailVC];

    _splitViewController = [[UISplitViewController alloc] init];
    NSArray *viewControllers = [[NSArray alloc] ↵
initWithObjects:leftNavController, rightNavController, nil];

    _splitViewController.delegate = rightDetailVC;
    _splitViewController.viewControllers = viewControllers;
```

```
    [self.window addSubview:_splitViewController.view];

    [self.window makeKeyAndVisible];
    return YES;
}
```

Let's work through Listing 11–6 in detail. The first line allocates the application's window to fit the full screen of the device:

```
    self.window = [[UIWindow alloc] initWithFrame:[[UIScreen mainScreen] bounds]];
```

Next, you create an instance of the `LeftTableViewController`, and install that as the root controller of a `UINavigationController` called `leftNavController`:

```
    LeftTableViewController *leftTableVC = [[LeftTableViewController alloc] ➥
initWithNibName:@"LeftTableViewController" bundle:nil];

    UINavigationController *leftNavController = [[UINavigationController alloc] ➥
initWithRootViewController:leftTableVC];
```

The same process applies to an instance of `RightDetailViewController`:

```
    RightDetailViewController *rightDetailVC = [[RightDetailViewController alloc] ➥
initWithNibName:@"RightDetailViewController" bundle:nil];

    UINavigationController *rightNavController = [[UINavigationController alloc] ➥
initWithRootViewController:rightDetailVC];
```

You can then create the `splitViewController`:

```
    _splitViewController = [[UISplitViewController alloc] init];
```

A `UISplitViewController` has a property called `viewControllers`, which takes an `NSArray` of two objects that are instances or subclasses of `UIViewController`. The object at index `0` will be shown on the left-hand side, and the object at index `1` will be shown on the right.

You have got two `UINavigationControllers`: one for the left containing the tableView and one for the right containing the detail view. These are added to an `NSArray`:

```
    NSArray *viewControllers = [[NSArray alloc] ➥
initWithObjects:leftNavController, rightNavController, nil];
```

And the `splitViewController's viewControllers` property is set to the newly created `viewControllers NSArray`:

```
    _splitViewController.viewControllers = viewControllers;
```

`UISplitViewControllers` also need a delegate for some functionality that you will see in a moment. The object that will handle the delegate method will be your `RightDetailViewController`, so the `_splitViewController's delegate` property needs to be updated:

```
    _splitViewController.delegate = rightDetailVC;
```

That's got the `splitViewController` configured, so you can add its `view` to the `window`:

```
    [self.window addSubview:_splitViewController.view];
```

The final step is to set the window active, and return from the method:

```
[self.window makeKeyAndVisible];
return YES;
```

Just before running the app, you need to update the RightViewDetailController class so that it conforms to the UISplitViewControllerDelegate protocol. Switch to RightViewDetailController's header file, and add the protocol:

```
@interface RightDetailViewController : UIViewController ↵
<UISplitViewControllerDelegate>
```

At this point, you can run the app. Figure 11–13 shows the results in the Simulator. The table is shown on the left hand side and the detail view on the right.

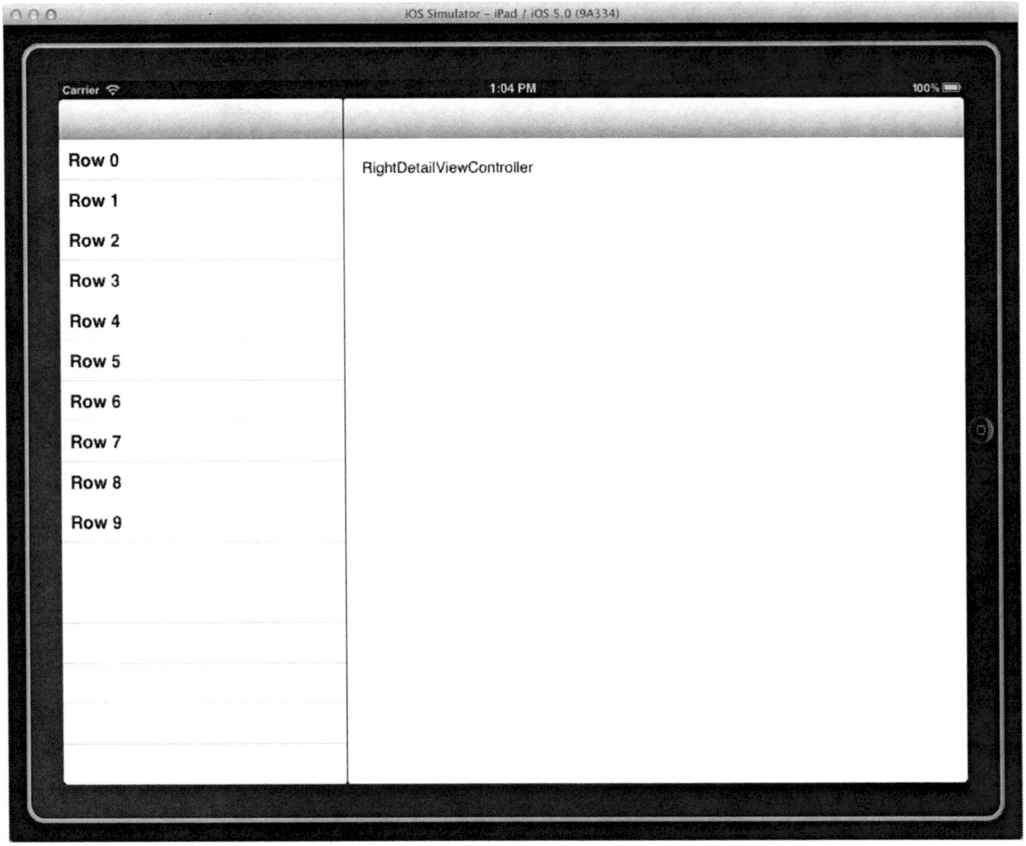

Figure 11–13. *The SplitViewApp running in the iPad simulator*

Handling Rotation

Impressive as this is, considering the amount of code you've written, there is a snag. If you rotate the Simulator (Command + Right Arrow or **Hardware ➤ Rotate Right**) the tableView disappears, as shown in Figure 11–14.

Figure 11–14. *The rotated Simulator*

Ideally, you would want to be able to get it back in a popover so that you could still select different items from the table while in Portrait orientation. Adding a title to the detail view's navigation bar wouldn't go amiss, either.

Fortunately for your carpal tunnels, `UISplitViewController` comes with a couple of delegate methods that will handle much of this for you. Whenever the device is rotated, the `splitViewController` will call one of two methods:

```
-(void)splitViewController:(UISplitViewController *)svc ➥
willHideViewController:(UIViewController *)aViewController ➥
```

```
withBarButtonItem:(UIBarButtonItem *)barButtonItem ↵
forPopoverController:(UIPopoverController *)pc;

-(void)splitViewController:(UISplitViewController *)svc ↵
willShowViewController:(UIViewController *)aViewController ↵
invalidatingBarButtonItem:(UIBarButtonItem *)barButtonItem;
```

(Your wrists will be pleased to know that Xcode will autocomplete these methods in a class that conforms to the `UISplitViewControllerDelegate` protocol!)

Earlier in the proceedings you set up the `RightDetailViewController` class to conform to the `UISplitViewControllerDelegate` protocol, and set `rightDetailVC` as the `splitViewController's delegate`.

Switch to `RightDetailViewController's` implementation file, and add the two methods in Listings 11–7 and 11–8.

Listing 11–7. *The* *`splitViewController:willHideViewController:withBarButtonItem:forPopoverController`* ***Method***

```
#pragma mark -
#pragma mark UISplitViewControllerDelegate

-(void)splitViewController:(UISplitViewController *)svc ↵
willHideViewController:(UIViewController *)aViewController ↵
withBarButtonItem:(UIBarButtonItem *)barButtonItem ↵
forPopoverController:(UIPopoverController *)pc {

    [barButtonItem setTitle:@"Show List"];
    self.navigationItem.leftBarButtonItem = barButtonItem;
}
```

Listing 11–8. *The* *`splitViewController: willShowViewController: invalidatingBarButtonItem:`* *method*

```
-(void)splitViewController:(UISplitViewController *)svc ↵
willShowViewController:(UIViewController *)aViewController ↵
invalidatingBarButtonItem:(UIBarButtonItem *)barButtonItem {

    self.navigationItem.leftBarButtonItem = nil;

}
```

Run the app again, and this time when you rotate the iPad (or Simulator) the results in Figure 11–15 appear.

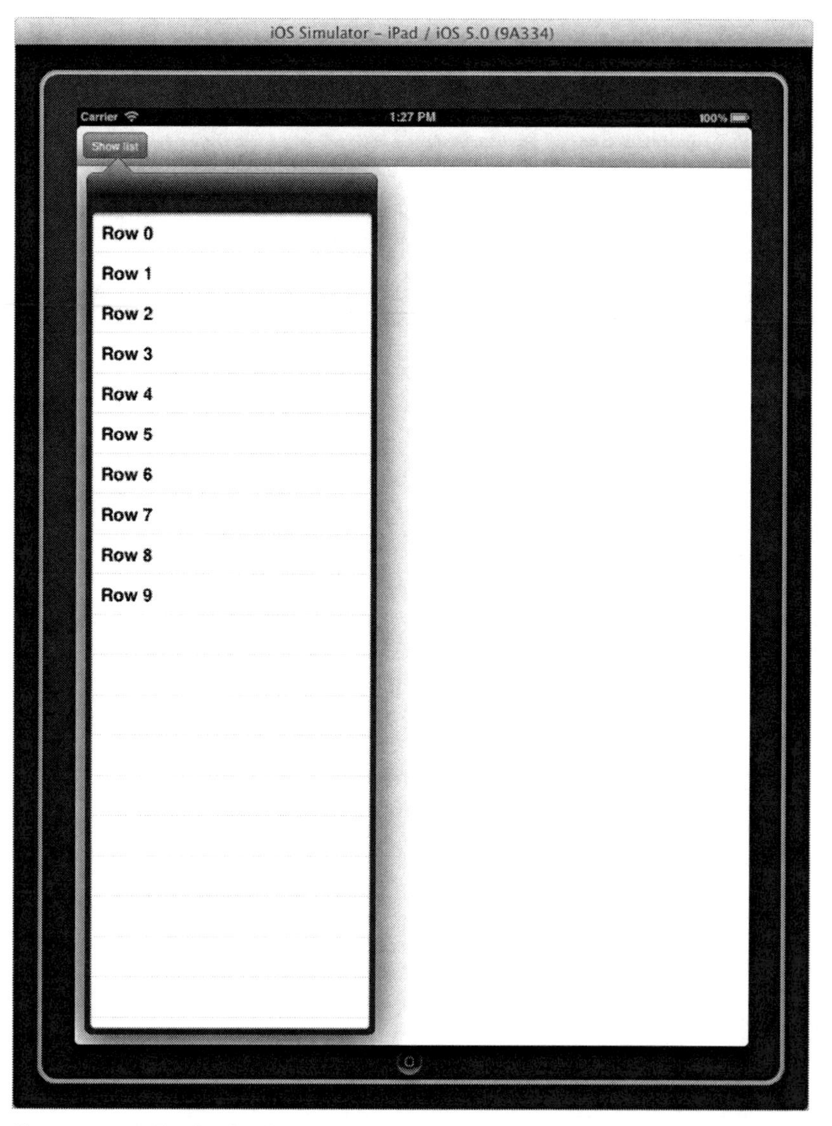

Figure 11–15. *The list view in a popover*

Much better! If you want to fine-tune things even further, you can control the size of the popover window by adding code such as

```
self.contentSizeForViewInPopover = CGSizeMake(320.0, 300.0);
```

to the `LeftTableViewController`'s `viewDidLoad` method.

Linking the List with the Detail

With the tableView behaving itself regardless of orientation, the time has come to link the two controllers together so the selection in the tableView is reflected in the detail view. There are various ways to do this, but the approach I use is to create a new protocol, then have the RightDetailViewController implement the updates as the delegate of LeftTableViewController.

This involves four steps:

1. Defining the protocol.
2. Setting up LeftTableViewController with a delegate property.
3. When the LeftTableViewController instance is created, setting the RightDetailViewController instance as its delegate.
4. Implementing the protocol methods in RightDetailViewController.

Defining the UpdateSplitDetailViewProtocol

You have a free rein on naming new protocols, but it's best to keep them at least somewhat descriptive. To define the protocol, we need a new file (**File ➤ New ➤ New File**). Select the **Objective-C Protocol** template from the Cocoa Touch list shown in Figure 11–16 and call it UpdateSplitDetailViewDelegate.

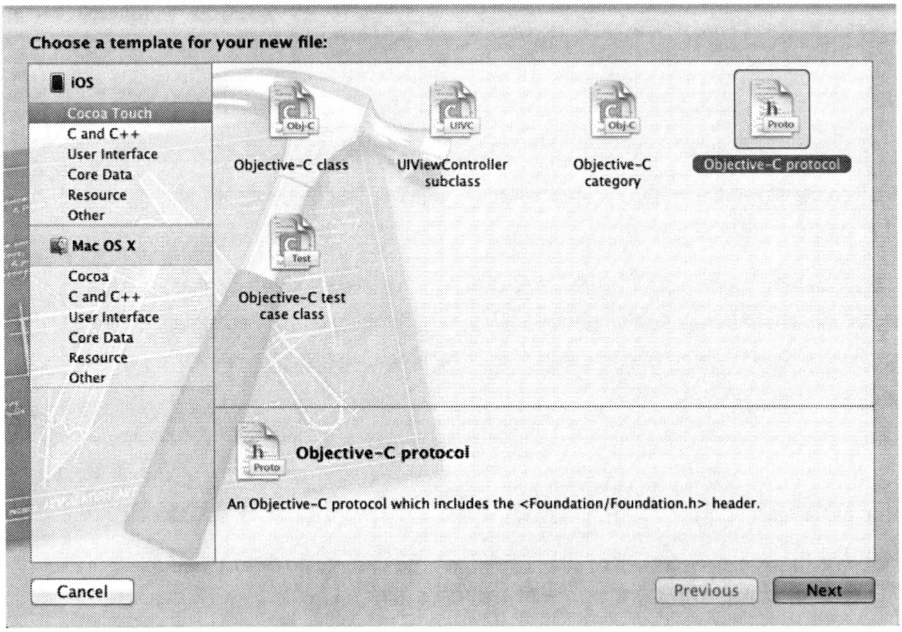

Figure 11–16. *Creating a new protocol*

As this is a simple example, it'll only need one method, so declare this as in Listing 11–9.

Listing 11–9. ***The* `UpdateSplitDetailViewDelegate` *Header***

```
#import <Foundation/Foundation.h>

@protocol UpdateSplitDetailViewDelegate <NSObject>

-(void)updateDetailViewWithDetail:(NSString *)detail;

@end
```

Save this file, then add the protocol to the `RightDetailViewController` (Listing 11–10).

Listing 11–10. ***The Updated* `RightDetailViewController.h` *File***

```
#import <UIKit/UIKit.h>

#import "UpdateSplitDetailViewProtocol.h"

@interface RightDetailViewController : UIViewController ➥
<UISplitViewControllerDelegate, UpdateSplitDetailViewDelegate>

@end
```

Now it's time to implement the protocol method temporarily: add the contents of Listing 11–11 to the `RightDetailViewController.m` file.

Listing 11–11. ***The* `updateDetailViewWithDetail:` *Method***

```
-(void)updateDetailViewWithDetail:(NSString *)detail {

    NSLog(@"updateDetailViewWithDetail:%@ called", detail);

}
```

> **TIP:** In case you're wondering why I've left the `updateDetailViewWithDetail:` method as a stub, I find it easier to get the various objects wired up together first before I start implementing the detail of the protocol methods.
>
> This way I can be sure that the objects are linked, the right methods are being called, and the right parameters passed before getting down to the details of method implementation. If you're sure that the right objects are talking to each other, it becomes a lot simpler to track down bugs in the code itself.

Setting Up LeftTableViewController with a Delegate Property

To add the delegate property to `LeftTableViewController`, you need to declare and synthesize it. That updates the header file to match Listing 11–12.

Listing 11–12. *LeftTableViewController.h*

```
#import <UIKit/UIKit.h>
#import "UpdateSplitDetailViewProtocol.h"

@interface LeftTableViewController : UITableViewController

@property (nonatomic, weak) id <UpdateSplitDetailViewProtocol> delegate;

@end
```

The corresponding synthesis is

```
@synthesize delegate;
```

> **CAUTION:** Make sure that you declare the `delegate` property as `weak`: objects should never retain their delegates with `strong` properties.

Connecting Up the Delegate

With the protocol defined, and the delegate property created, you can amend the `AppDelegate` so that the two controllers are wired together, as shown in Listing 11–13.

Listing 11–13. *The Updated `application:didFinishLaunchingWithOptions:` Method*

```
- (BOOL)application:(UIApplication *)application ➥
didFinishLaunchingWithOptions:(NSDictionary *)launchOptions
{
    self.window = [[UIWindow alloc] initWithFrame:[[UIScreen mainScreen] bounds]];
    // Override point for customization after application launch.

    LeftTableViewController *leftTableVC = [[LeftTableViewController alloc] ➥
initWithNibName:@"LeftTableViewController" bundle:nil];
    UINavigationController *leftNavController = [[UINavigationController alloc] ➥
initWithRootViewController:leftTableVC];

    RightDetailViewController *rightDetailVC = [[RightDetailViewController alloc] ➥
initWithNibName:@"RightDetailViewController" bundle:nil];
    UINavigationController *rightNavController = [[UINavigationController alloc] ➥
initWithRootViewController:rightDetailVC];

    leftTableVC.delegate = rightDetailVC;

    _splitViewController = [[UISplitViewController alloc] init];
    NSArray *viewControllers = [[NSArray alloc] ➥
initWithObjects:leftNavController, rightNavController, nil];

    _splitViewController.delegate = rightDetailVC;
    _splitViewController.viewControllers = viewControllers;

    [self.window addSubview:_splitViewController.view];

    [self.window makeKeyAndVisible];
    return YES;
}
```

Calling the Delegate Method

With the two controllers wired together, you can finally implement the code that causes the right-hand detail view to be updated in response to a selection in the left-hand table.

In the `LeftTableViewController.m` file, you need to update the `tableView:didSelectRowAtIndexPath:` method: remove the boilerplate template code, and replace it with Listing 11–14.

Listing 11–14. ***The Updated*** *`tableView:didSelectRowAtIndexPath:`* ***Method***

```
- (void)tableView:(UITableView *)tableView ↩
didSelectRowAtIndexPath:(NSIndexPath *)indexPath
{

    UITableViewCell *selectedCell = [tableView cellForRowAtIndexPath:indexPath];

    NSString *theDetail = selectedCell.textLabel.text;

    [delegate updateDetailViewWithDetail:theDetail];

}
```

Here you are getting a reference to the selected cell by asking the `tableView` for the cell with the `indexPath` passed into the method. Once the cell's been retrieved, it's possible to grab the contents of the `textLabel's text` property, and pass that over as a parameter to the `delegate's updateDetailViewWith:` method.

Relaunch the app, select a row in the table, and you should see the output of the `updateDetailWithDetail:` method in the console.

```
SplitViewApp[17422:f803] updateDetailViewWithDetail:Row 1 called
SplitViewApp[17422:f803] updateDetailViewWithDetail:Row 3 called
SplitViewApp[17422:f803] updateDetailViewWithDetail:Row 5 called
SplitViewApp[17422:f803] updateDetailViewWithDetail:Row 9 called
```

Completing the Protocol Method

Having wired everything together correctly, you are at the point where you can get the two controllers talking together usefully (well, as usefully as this sample application will get).

To keep this example simple, you will get the `detailView` to update with the contents of the row that's just been selected. Obviously in a real-world application, the update process would be significantly more sophisticated, but your example will get the principles established.

Start by declaring an outlet in `RightDetailViewController.h`, and synthesizing it:

```
@property (nonatomic, strong) IBOutlet UILabel *statusLabel;
```

And synthesize it in the implementation file with:

```
@synthesize statusLabel = _statusLabel;
```

Next, connect that outlet in `RightDetailViewController.xib` (Figure 11–17).

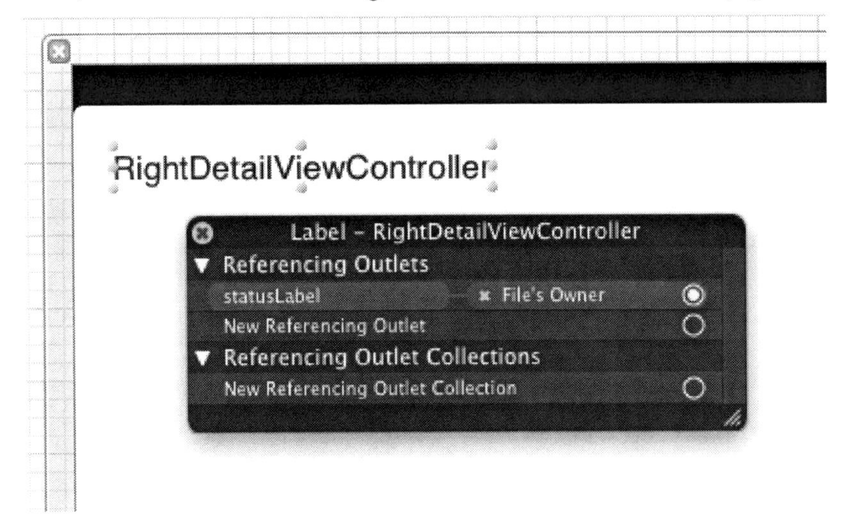

Figure 11–17. *The statusLabel connected*

And finally, alter the `updateDetailViewWithDetail:` method so that it updates the label's value, shown in Listing 11–15.

Listing 11–15. *The Updated `updateDetailViewWithDetail:` Method*

```
-(void)updateDetailViewWith:(NSString *)detail {

    NSLog(@"updateDetailViewWithDetail:%@ called", detail);

    _statusLabel.text = [NSString stringWithFormat:@"%@ was selected", detail];

}
```

Run the app once more, and as you select one of the rows, the text in the `detailView` is updated (shown in Figure 11–18).

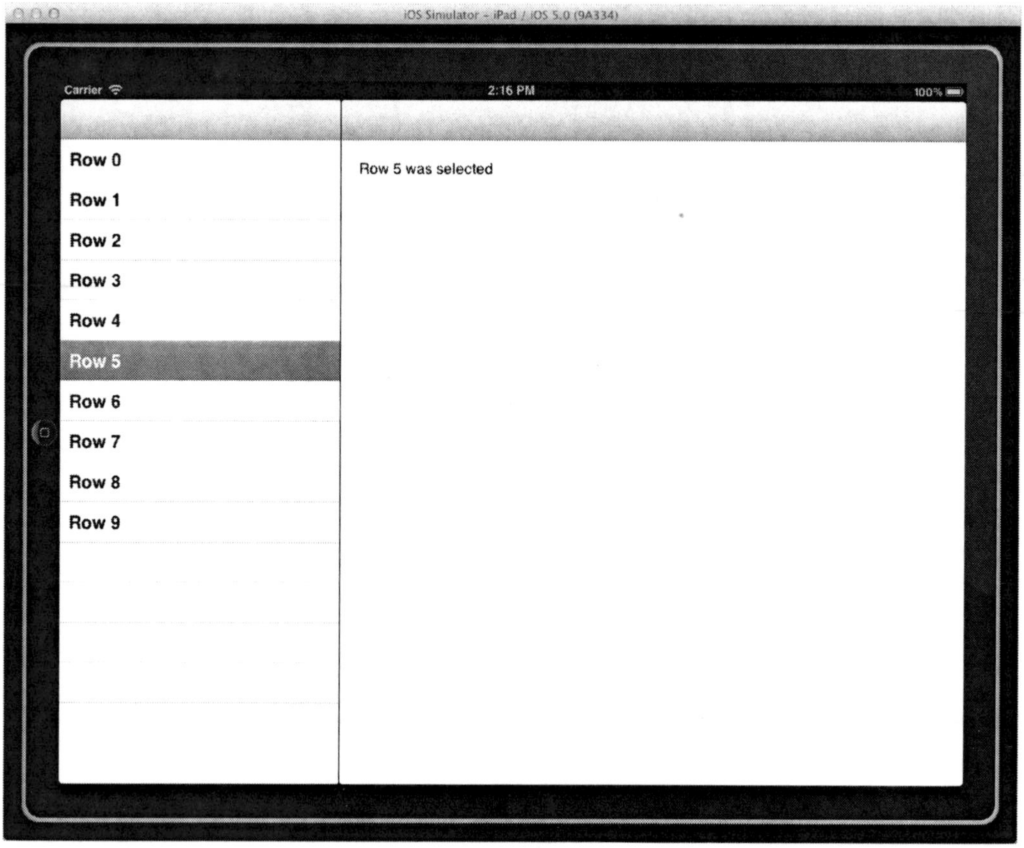

Figure 11–18. *The `tableView` and `detailView` working together*

One slight improvement remains to be made. Currently, if the left-hand view disappears, the selection will be lost. If you update `LeftTableViewController's` `viewDidLoad` method with

```
self.clearsSelectionOnViewWillAppear = NO;
```

then the selection will remain active across device rotations.

Summary

In this chapter you've looked at the structure of the `UISplitViewController`, and how it works with `UINavigationControllers`, `UITableViewControllers`, and `UIViewControllers` to present a two-panel interface. You've also seen how it handles device rotation, placing the left-hand table view into a popover view.

Then all of these elements came together into a skeleton `UISplitViewController` app, which tied together a table view with a detail view through the use of a custom protocol.

Index

D

E

F

G

H

I

J, K

L

M

N

O

P, Q

R

V, W, X, Y, Z

CPSIA information can be obtained at www.ICGtesting.com
Printed in the USA
LVOW110244150312